CONFESSIONS

AUGUSTINE was born in 354, the son of a Christian mother and a pagan father who farmed a few acres at Thagaste (now Souk-Ahras in eastern Algeria). Education at the hands of poor teachers could not hinder his acute mind from acquiring a mastery of classical Latin literature, especially Cicero and Virgil whose writings he knew almost by heart. He became a gifted teacher of literature and public speaking successively at Carthage, Rome, and Milan. At Carthage he met a woman by whom he had a son, and with whom he lived faithfully for fifteen years until at Milan she became a fatal block in the path of his secular career. A personal crisis followed. Already in Africa his religious quest took him to Manichee theosophy, then in Italy to scepticism and thence to the Neoplatonic mysticism of Plotinus. In July 386 in a Milan garden he resolved to abandon a secular career and the respectable marriage that would make this possible. Baptized by St Ambrose (387), he buried his widowed mother at Ostia and returned to North Africa (388). Against his will he was forced into ordination in 391 and five years later became bishop at Hippo (modern Annaba) for the remaining thirty-four years of his life. A fluent and voluminous writer on theology, philosophy, and sex, his writings made him influential and controversial both in his lifetime and in the subsequent history of Christendom. He died during the Vandal siege of his city (28 August 430).

HENRY CHADWICK is former Master of Peterhouse, Cambridge, and General Editor of the Oxford History of the Christian Church, and Oxford Early Christian Texts. His other publications include *Augustine* in the Past Masters Series (OUP, 1986), *Boethius: The Consolations of Music, Logic, Theology, and Philosophy* (Clarendon paperbacks, 1981), and *Early Christian Thought and the Classical Tradition* (OUP, 1984).

OXFORD WORLD'S CLASSICS

For over 100 years Oxford World's Classics have brought readers closer to the world's great literature. Now with over 700 titles—from the 4,000-year-old myths of Mesopotamia to the twentieth century's greatest novels—the series makes available lesser-known as well as celebrated writing.

The pocket-sized hardbacks of the early years contained introductions by Virginia Woolf, T. S. Eliot, Graham Greene, and other literary figures which enriched the experience of reading. Today the series is recognized for its fine scholarship and reliability in texts that span world literature, drama and poetry, religion, philosophy and politics. Each edition includes perceptive commentary and essential background information to meet the changing needs of readers.

OXFORD WORLD'S CLASSICS

SAINT AUGUSTINE

Confessions

Translated with an Introduction and Notes by
HENRY CHADWICK

OXFORD
UNIVERSITY PRESS

OXFORD
UNIVERSITY PRESS

Great Clarendon Street, Oxford OX2 6DP

Oxford University Press is a department of the University of Oxford.
It furthers the University's objective of excellence in research, scholarship,
and education by publishing worldwide in

Oxford New York

Athens Auckland Bangkok Bogotá Buenos Aires Calcutta
Cape Town Chennai Dar es Salaam Delhi Florence Hong Kong Istanbul
Karachi Kuala Lumpur Madrid Melbourne Mexico City Mumbai
Nairobi Paris São Paulo Singapore Taipei Tokyo Toronto Warsaw

with associated companies in Berlin Ibadan

Oxford is a registered trade mark of Oxford University Press
in the UK and in certain other countries

Published in the United States
by Oxford University Press Inc., New York

Translation, Introduction, and Notes © Henry Chadwick 1991

Database right Oxford University Press (maker)

First published as a World's Classics paperback 1992
Reissued as an Oxford World's Classics paperback 1998
Reissued 2008

British Library Cataloguing in Publication Data

Data available

Library of Congress Cataloging in Publication Data

Data available

ISBN 978-0-19-953782-2

19

Printed in Great Britain by
Clays Ltd, Elcograf S.p.A.

Contents

Introduction

AUGUSTINE'S *Confessions* will always rank among the greater master-pieces of western literature. Like Rousseau's book with the same title (but otherwise having little in common), the work has a perennial power to speak, even though written virtually sixteen centuries ago and certainly a book rooted in antiquity. The contemporary reader today may find much of it so 'modern' that at times it is a shock to discover how very ancient are the presuppositions and the particular context in which the author wrote. Because of this context and these presuppositions, a translation needs to be provided with some minimum of concise explanation if the reader is to grasp the point of Augustine's argument or the social context of his time (the work is a major source for social history as well as for religion). For this work is far from being a simple autobiography of a sensitive man, in youth captivated by aesthetic beauty and enthralled by the quest for a sexual fulfilment, but then dramatically converted to Christian faith through a grim period of distress and frustration, finally becoming a bishop known for holding pessimistic opinions about human nature and society. The *Confessions* is more than a narrative of conversion. It is a work of rare sophistication and intricacy, in which even the apparently simple autobiographical narrative often carries harmonics of deeper meaning. To understand the work one needs to comprehend a little about the author's mind, his loves and hates, his intellectual debts and principal targets for criticism. The *Confessions* is a polemical work, at least as much a self-vindication as an admission of mistakes. The very title carries a conscious double meaning, of confession as praise as well as of confession as acknowledgement of faults. And its form is extraordinary—a prose-poem addressed to God, intended to be overheard by anxious and critical fellow-Christians.

The emotional power and in places the rare beauty of the writing have not invariably captured readers. In ancient as in more recent times some have been unattracted by the sophistication of the style or by the conception and estimate of human capacity presupposed by the work. The earliest of surviving British writers, Pelagius (whose British origin is attested by Augustine himself), was seriously alarmed by the strong language about the nothingness of humanity and the totality of human dependence on God for the achievement of the good life. Pelagius feared the morally enervating effects of telling people to do nothing and to rely entirely on divine grace to impart the will to love the right and the good. Another contemporary critic wrote to Augustine to complain of the clever rhetoric; he felt that so brilliantly acute a mind could equally skilfully defend the opposite opinion with an equal éclat; like a high-powered lawyer, he would have been equally content whether prosecuting or defending. The elaborate manner of late Latin oratory, with its love of antitheses even if they were artificial (as some of Augustine's were), was a style that contemporaries admired but were accustomed to associate with insincerity. Augustine himself records that when he had to deliver a panegyric for the tenth anniversary of the accession of the emperor Valentinian II, he was not only filled with absurd nervousness about his public performance (some of which may have been due to Italian mockery of his African accent), but ashamed of the lies and bogus flattery that, as everyone knew, filled his discourse. He wrote for an age stamped with an elegant scepticism, for which a well-turned phrase gave more pleasure than a cogent argument for the truth. In several places in the *Confessions* and elsewhere Augustine's term for contemporary pagan culture was 'loquacity': it used fine words, even rococo elaboration, but had little or nothing to say. Nevertheless, Augustine's wish to distance himself from the secularity of contemporary oratory and the teaching of pagan literature never meant for him that, in setting forth the truth he had come to find in Christian faith, he felt bound to avoid the skills he had learnt in the rhetorical schools. He loved to use rhymes in his prose, and delighted in polished epigrammatic antitheses as much as any pagan writer. Only in his case the epigram almost always carries a sharp point directed to a religious target of extreme seriousness for him. His prose is more effective with short epigrams than with long periods. The presence of so much rhyming in the Latin diction presents an insoluble problem to the translator. It is impossible to reproduce in another language without resulting in absurdity.

Augustine shows an awareness that he will have Christian readers suspicious of his elaborate rhetorical style; at v. vi (10) their fears are expressly mentioned. These suspicious persons are no doubt identical with the puritan critics who felt that immediately upon his conversion he ought to have resigned his professorship of grammar and literature instead of waiting until the vacation to hand in his letter of formal resignation (IX. ii (4)). He felt bound to concede that his profession of 'selling words' in the 'bazaar of loquacity' was vulnerable to moral criticism. At the same time he expressed remarkable doubts and hesitations whether skill in public speaking can be acquired from a teacher (VIII. vi (13)). He was conscious that his own high ability in this respect was a natural endowment, a gift of God, not something he had learnt from any of the second-rate teachers whose instruction he had endured in youth.

The work was written at a considerable distance in time from the conversion at Milan, which lay in the past by thirteen or more years. The immediate stimulus to the writing seems to have come from the convergence of two factors. The first was an unfortunate and embarrassing row which had broken at the time when Augustine was made a bishop in 396. For a time after his return to North Africa from Italy in the late summer of 388 he had organized a lay community of his friends at Thagaste, quasi-monastic in character. But in 391 he had gone to Hippo Regius on the coast, and on attending the Church service on the Sunday morning he had been spotted by the old bishop, Valerius, a Greek-speaker from southern Italy. In his sermon the bishop pointed out his need for a presbyter, and suggested that Augustine would do well. It was far from uncommon at this period for ordination to be forced upon the candidate by the coercion of the congregation. Augustine was allowed no escape, and had to submit.

Four or five years later bishop Valerius was anxious to ensure that no other Church took Augustine away to be their bishop elsewhere, and persuaded the presiding bishop of Numidia (in North Africa, presidency went not with the see, except in the case of Carthage, but with seniority by date of consecration) that Augustine be ordained as assistant or coadjutor bishop with the right to succeed. Such an ordination was not in line with canon law, but that does not appear to have caused the difficulty. Augustine was clever, and therefore distrusted. Many recalled how combative he had once been against the Catholic Church before his conversion. Were the monasteries that he was attempting to found heretical nests of Manichee dualism? His lurid youth had not been forgotten. And then he had been baptized far away at Milan: were there reliable witnesses to attest to that? It was normal custom for a foreigner to be received to baptism only after good testimony to him had been received from his home land. It did not appear that Ambrose at Milan had asked for letters from Africa in support of this candidate.

The elderly presiding bishop wrote an irate letter to Valerius enumerating the complaints against Augustine. The letter was not kept confidential, and was exploited by unfriendly critics. The criticism was the more painful because of an inveterate schism, the Donatist schism in the African Churches since two rival bishops were ordained at Carthage in 311 in the aftermath of the Great Persecution. In Numidia the Donatists were in a majority in both town and countryside, and notably in Hippo itself. The Donatists got hold of the presiding bishop's letter and used it as a rod to beat Augustine.

Accordingly, the *Confessions* took some of its impetus from a wish to answer critics both inside and outside the Catholic community. The exploitation of the case against Augustine by the Donatists helps to explain the fact, at first sight surprising, that the work makes not even the most oblique reference to the existence of Donatists, though every day of Augustine's life as a bishop was certainly beset by problems arising out of the schism with all its rancour and periodic violence. No reader of the work would ever guess that Augustine was now presiding over a minority community in Hippo, under the necessity of fighting for its life against a militant majority.

The second stimulus to the composition of the work came from outside Africa. In the summer of 395 Augustine's friend Alypius, by then bishop of Thagaste, had written out of the blue to a notable convert to the ascetic life in Italy, Paulinus, a multi-millionaire aristocrat from Bordeaux (where he was a pupil of Ausonius); he owned land in Campania and became governor of that province. He suffered various family tragedies, was ordained priest in Barcelona, and finally settled at Nola in Campania as priest, later becoming bishop. He sold large parts of the estates belonging to himself and his wife, and his renunciation of the world and its gold caused a sensation. Alypius may have hoped to interest him in supporting ascetic foundations in his diocese. He sent him anti-Manichee works by Augustine. Paulinus' reply asked Alypius to send him an autobiography revealing how he had come to adopt the ascetic life, and by what way he had come to baptism and ordination. Alypius' answer does not survive. He shared the request with Augustine. The *Confessions* is not dedicated to Paulinus of Nola, but it can hardly be accidental that a substantial part of book VI consists of the biography of Alypius.

At the end of his life Augustine wrote a review and reappraisal of his output, the *Retractationes* (almost half of which consists in telling critics that he has nothing to withdraw so that one cannot translate the title 'Retractions'). When he came to the *Confessions* he observes that they serve to excite the human mind and affection towards God; the act of writing the book had done that for himself at the time, and 'that is the effect when it is read now'. Aware that not everyone has admired the work, he nevertheless adds 'However, they have given great pleasure to many brethren and still do so'.

The work was written during the last three years of the fourth century AD by a man in his mid-forties, recently made a bishop, needing to come to terms with a past in which numerous enemies and critics showed an unhealthy interest. Aurelius Augustinus had been born on 13 November 354 to parents of modest means, who owned a few acres of farmland at the small town of Thagaste, then in the Roman province of Numidia, now Souk-Ahras in the hills of eastern Algeria about 45 miles inland from the coast. His father Patrick was not a Christian until baptized on his deathbed in 372, but his mother Monica[1] was a devout believer coming from a Christian family. Her ambitions for her gifted son were divided between high and well-grounded hopes for his secular success and a yearning that, despite his wanderings from her own faith and moral standards, one day she would see him an orthodox Christian. He pained her at the age of 17 by taking to his bed a Carthage girl of low social standing, with whom he lived faithfully for fifteen years until his ambition for high office under the imperial government made her a disastrously unsuitable partner.

Aged 18 he was moved by his reading of a philosophical dialogue by Cicero, *Hortensius*, teaching that happiness is not found in

---

[1] Her name, spelt by Augustine Monnica, is probably Berber, and perhaps both parents were ethnically Berber. Their culture was Latin. Monnica had near relatives who were Donatists.

physical pleasures of luxurious food, drink, and sex, but in a dedication of the mind to the discovery of truth. Cicero's remarks on the way in which the majority of mankind look for happiness in the wrong place initially led him to pick up his Latin Bible. Its style, especially in the Old Testament, was often close to translationese, painful to an admirer of Cicero and Virgil. Before Jerome's revision of the Latin Bible, produced during the years from 383 to 405, the Old Latin Bible composed by second-century missionaries in Italy and Africa was colloquial and at times obscure to the point of being barbaric. Augustine found that once he had put it down, it was hard to pick it up again. Moreover, he was offended by the polygamy of Old Testament patriarchs and the different genealogies of Jesus in the Gospels of Matthew and Luke.

He was drawn to the theosophy of Mani, a Mesopotamian gnostic of the third century whose religion was zealously propagated by underground missionary work, despite fierce prohibitions from the imperial government. The religion of Mani's followers, called in Latin *Manichaei*, Manichees, expressed disgust at the physical world and especially at the human reproductive system. Procreation imprisoned divine souls in matter, which is inherently hostile to goodness and light. Manichees had a vegetarian diet, and forbade wine. There were two classes, Elect who were strictly obliged to be celibate, and Hearers allowed wives or concubines as long as they avoided procreating children, whether by contraceptives or by confining intercourse to the 'safe' period of the monthly cycle. Hearers prepared the correct food for the Elect. Manichee propaganda was combative against the orthodox Catholic Church, which granted married Christians to be in good standing, and admitted to the lectionary the Old Testament stories of Moses the murderer, David the adulterer, Joseph the state monopolist. Baptism and eucharist were held in contempt by Mani on the ground that Catholics ascribed to these sacraments a holiness which Manichees discerned in everything. Mani strongly denied the historical reality of the crucifixion of Jesus; for him the Cross was a symbol of the suffering of humanity. However, Manichees accepted the epistles of St Paul, appealing especially to Romans 7 to underpin their dualism of spirit and matter, light and darkness. Admittedly, they thought the New Testament writings had been interpolated.

Central to Manichee belief was their answer to the problem of evil, namely that God is good but not omnipotent, and though resistant to evil not strong enough to defeat it. What was abhorrent to Mani was to make the Creator supremely good and powerful, since that must end by making him responsible for the evil in his creation.

The evidence shows that Manichees were not recruited from the ignorant poor, and were in some cases reasonably educated people. Augustine specifically says that their books were not only finely bound but also written in 'a good Latin'. However, Mani's religion could be attractive only to those on the fringe of the Church. Those who joined them learnt a fantastic mythology designed to explain the eternal polarity of good and evil. Eclipses were explained by saying that the sun and moon were veiling their sight from the dreadful cosmic battles. The more Augustine learnt about astronomy, the greater the tension in his adherence to the Manichee faith. The *Confessions* shows that he continued in association with the Manichee community for a decade, even though towards the end of that time he was rapidly losing confidence in the system. In youth he had accepted Manicheism because he believed to be valid both its claim to be true Christianity and its grounds for rejecting Catholic orthodoxy. By the time he reached Milan he still regarded its negative criticisms of orthodoxy as valid, but had ceased to accept the Manichee mythology without which the system seemed to disintegrate.

Augustine was a born teacher. He began by opening his own school at Thagaste, but then moved to Carthage, second city of the western empire. There turbulent students impelled him to Rome, where fees were higher and pupils quieter. But the dishonesty of Roman students in swindling teachers (strikingly paralleled in Alexandria at this period) made him interested in a vacant post at Milan, which had the further attraction of being the seat of the court of Valentinian II, the western emperor. Manichee friends in Rome put his name to the strongly pagan prefect of Rome, Symmachus, who listened to a probationary discourse and no doubt ascertained that Augustine was no Catholic Christian and safe to send. Skilled orators and writers not infrequently found their way to high office. A striking parallel to Augustine's secular career is found in his elder contemporary Aurelius Victor, author of a surviving history of the empire, who was born in Africa of modest rural parents, but by his studies elevated himself; he became governor of Pannonia and later (389) prefect of Rome. At Milan Augustine gained entrance to the houses of powerful and rich senators, on whom ambitious young men would call during the afternoon. Augustine's secular ambitions, however, met with frustrating checks because he lacked money. If only he could acquire a rich wife, the dowry would provide the necessary premium for obtaining office. Almost all important appointments were for sale, a system that saved the fisc cash and simultaneously made room for some gifted candidates, like Augustine, without much class.

At Milan Augustine still had with him the Carthaginian mate, of low social status, whom he had picked up at the age of 17. She was no intellectual companion for him. Early in their liaison she produced a son, unwanted but then deeply loved. Named Adeodatus, he was clever and a source of pride to his father. (He died when only 17). If at Milan Augustine's ambitions were to be realized, his concubine was a liability. She would hardly do at government house, but in any event only a wife with a fat dowry could bring success. His mate's inferior social status made marriage out of the question in law and in social convention. So she returned to Carthage, and the parting was exquisitely painful on both sides. Meanwhile the strenuous efforts of Monica produced a fiancée; the marriage was deferred because the girl was still only 10 or 11 years old. In Roman law the minimum age was 12.

To modern readers nothing in Augustine's career seems more deplorable than his dismissal of his son's mother, the concubine of fifteen years. In the mentality of the fourth century no one would have been outraged unless the person concerned were a professing and baptized Christian, which at the time Augustine was not. Texts other than Augustine's disclose that for a young man it was regular custom to take a concubine until such time as he found a suitable fiancée, marriage being understood as a property deal between the two families. The bride's dowry was crucial. The modern criticism is not of Augustine so much as of the total society in which he was a member. His world was not very different from ours in this.

Augustine himself in episcopal retrospect came to judge his liaison with his partner as 'my sin'. As the couple were entirely faithful to one another and as, for the Church (as is shown by a canon of a Council at Toledo in 400), cohabitation by persons not legally married was no bar to communion provided they kept wholly to one another, this negative judgement may seem strong. The judgement hangs together with Augustine's mature doctrine of the proper nature of marriage. He describes his relationship to his concubine as a mere indulgence in physical satisfaction and 'habit'. (In Latin, 'habit', *consuetudo*, is an attested euphemism for marital intercourse.) What was absent was the intention to raise a family, the lifelong vow of fidelity, the sacramental bond. For the mature Augustine the indispensable and structural elements that constitute marriage are strikingly non-physical. Repeatedly in the *Confessions* he contrasts a marriage centred on companionship and responsible raising of a family with a merely physical relationship centred upon the satisfaction of appetite.

Augustine specifically mentions that he was talked out of marrying by his intimate friend and former pupil Alypius. A furtive sexual experience in early adolescence had left Alypius with a lasting sense of revulsion. He found Augustine's delight in his partner astonishing and unintelligible. It is perhaps necessary to be on one's guard against supposing that the young unconverted Augustine was an uninhibited Romantic. Although like Plotinus he can use erotic imagery for the beatific vision, he resembled most other ancient people in not finding sexual experience a source of profound psychological liberation. In the ancient world few people (not at least the writers of the erotica in the fifth book of the *Greek Anthology*) thought in anything like that kind of way. Everyone acknowledged that the mating impulse ensures the survival of the human race. But all philosophers with a serious claim to be respected as wise moralists—Plato, Aristotle, the Stoics, the Epicureans—were of one mind in being impressed by its risks and dangers and by the capacity of sexual desire to disrupt and even destroy the most rational of plans and intentions. None was more negative than the arch-hedonist Epicurus; and his follower, the Latin poet Lucretius, sharply formulated that general distaste for Venus and her works in the most impassioned section of his long poem 'On the nature of things'. If happiness is understood in terms of the reduction of emotional disturbance to the minimum, then the ancient attitude to sexuality is natural enough.

Augustine in his maturity accepted the consequence of his conversion. The negative Manichee attitude to sexuality was rejected, and replaced by many more positive statements than some writers have given Augustine the credit for. Against the Manichees he upheld the essential goodness of the procreative impulse. The Pelagian controversy, however, led him to see the process of reproduction as the transmitter of the irrationality and egotism that infects the sexual urge. By his stress on 'concupiscence' (uncontrolled desire) he set the West on the path to identifying sin with sex; that was not his intention.

Augustine came to think it an ingredient in the misery of the human condition that the sexual impulse is so frequently disobedient to the mind's higher intentions and instructions. Because it can tend to animality, it all too easily becomes destructive of both friendship and self-respect. After he had become a bishop, the counselling of married couples in trouble occupied much of his time and care, and he was well aware of the inconstancy of the human heart, of the tendency to have minor and trivial affairs which he once stigmatized as 'a male disease', and of the existence of husbands who knew their wives to be unfaithful to them but nevertheless found their embraces too enthralling to part with. Some men treated their wives as harlots.

His non-physical description of the essentials constituting marriage was in part influenced by his determination to affirm the bond between Joseph and Mary to be a genuine marriage. But the foundation for that affirmation was made possible by his belief that an ideal marriage is one of perfect mutual companionship. This portrait of an ideal marriage is painted in the fourteenth book of the *City of God*, where he sets out to describe the sexual bond between Adam and Eve before the Fall, a relationship controlled throughout by reason and will, never experiencing the frustration common to fallen mortals where the urge felt by one partner is not necessarily felt by the other at the same time; to both partners it was a source of the highest pleasure. The ideal language is rich in the sense of marriage as the supreme example of intimate friendship in mutual respect.

Adeodatus' mother was uneducated. Augustine came to find his own mother Monica possessed of great wisdom, but she spoke in a demotic syntax. In short, although he knew that well-educated and cultured women existed, yet they were the far side of the horizon. He himself never had one among his own circle of friends. So he felt sure that 'if God had wanted Adam to have a partner in scintillating conversation he would have created another man; the fact that God created a woman showed that he had in mind the survival of the human race'. The observation (from his *Literal Commentary on Genesis*, written not long after the *Confessions*) reflects Augustine's sense of antithesis and tension between a social estimate of marriage as a companionship with the meeting of minds and the business of reproduction. The society in which Augustine was raised took for granted the supportive and unpublic role of women. Yet near the end of the *Confessions* he would insist that men and women are entirely equal in mind and soul.

The personal crisis of his possible marriage, and the demeaning process of calling on powerful men of influence vainly hoping to enlist their support for his secular ambitions, coincided with an intellectual crisis. At Milan his lost belief in Mani was replaced by a scepticism about the possibility of any certainty. He devoured the writings of sceptical philosophers of the Academic school telling him that certainty is not available except in questions of pure mathematics. The psychological transition from radical scepticism to faith is sufficiently common to make it likely that his sceptical period on arrival at Milan prepared the ground for the coming conversion.

At Milan, however, there was a group of Platonists, some being Christians and others fellow-travellers, who used to read the treatises of Plotinus, who taught in Rome a century earlier, and of his biographer and editor Porphyry.[2] Some of their work had been translated from Greek into Latin by an eminent orator and teacher in Rome about 350, Marius Victorinus, who was himself impressed by the affinity between the Neoplatonists and the best Christian theology. In *Confessions* VIII Augustine recounts the narrative of Victorinus' final decision to offer himself for baptism, probably about 355, to the amazement of the pagan aristocracy of Rome. Plotinus, as his attack on the Gnostics shows (2. 9), cordially disliked theosophy, and Manicheism was uncongenial to the Neoplatonists generally. Sustained attacks survive from Alexander of Lycopolis in Egypt (about 300), and from Simplicius (about 530).

---

[2] In the *Confessions* Augustine does not specify the authors of 'the books of the Platonists' which influenced him. Scholars have disputed whether they were all tracts by Plotinus or all works by his pupil Porphyry. The probability is that Augustine read some by each of them. Since he also knew about the Neoplatonist Iamblichus (c.250–325) mentioned in *City of God* 8. 11, he is likely to have read other books from the Platonic school as well.

In particular the Platonic school offered a wholly different treatment of the problem of evil.

Three explanations were offered to mitigate the difficulty for affirming providence. First, the cosmos is a grand continuum, a great chain or hierarchy of being, descending by emanation from the highest to the lowest, from mind to matter, and in this graded series where existence is itself a good, the higher the level of being the higher the goodness. Therefore 'evil' is not Being but a lack of it, a deficiency inherent in having been placed on a lower step than higher entities. Since to exist is for a Platonist to be a 'substance', evil has no 'substance'. Secondly, matter is recalcitrant to beauty and form, and pulls the soul down to external things. Matter exploits a weakness in the will distorting it towards moral evil. Thirdly, evil results from the misuse of free choice by rational beings.

In Augustine's time there were a few educated people for whom all religion was superstition; but the dominant consensus held to belief in divine providence, visible in the mathematical order and coherence of the world, and given special manifestations to individuals by dreams and oracles. Design was evident to the eye. On the other hand the imperfection and contingency or indeterminacy of the world pointed to the existence of perfect and necessary Being, the ground of all existence. Nevertheless, twice in the *Confessions* (VI. v (7); VII. vii (11)) Augustine felt it necessary to affirm that, in all his wanderings, he never lost his belief in the being and the providence of God.

With a measured deliberation the *Confessions* records the absence of high motivations in the successive decisions which took him from a farm in the Numidian hills to the emperor's court at Milan. He left Thagaste for Carthage because his home town was painfully filled with associations with a dead friend; on to Rome because of student turbulence, and thence to Milan because of student dishonesty and because Manichees and a pagan city prefect used influence on his behalf. So it was that he 'came to Ambrose the bishop', and discovered how different Christian faith was from what he had supposed. Ambrose's sermons were certainly very different from the kind of thing he might have heard in some of the North African churches, where discourses lacked much rational structure. Through all his wanderings he discerned in retrospect the watchful hand of an unseen guardian, whose protection had been invoked upon him by Monica when as a baby he was made a catechumen. Decisions made with no element of Christian motive, without any questing for God or truth, brought him to where his Maker wanted him to be.

Ambrose's influence was not through any intimacy of personal contact, but through his discourses in the pulpit, which taught Augustine a very different way of interpreting the Bible. The sermons also presented a Christian theology that combined aversion from pagan religion with a large ingredient of Neoplatonism. Aversion from pagan religion is evident in Augustine's *Confessions*, which were written at a period when social tension between pagans and Christians in the empire was very high, in consequence of Theodosius' laws suppressing cult in the old temples.

Plotinus provided Augustine with a model and a vocabulary for a mystical quest directed to the union of the soul with God in a beatific vision. In book VII Augustine set out to describe his attempt to attain this union with the One, the supreme Good, by the methods he had learnt from the Neoplatonists. He was disappointed by the transience of the experience and by the fact that, when it had passed away, he found himself as fiercely consumed by pride and lust as ever. Yet he knew that in that 'flash of a trembling glance' he had had a dazzling glimpse of eternal Being, transcending his own all-too-changeable flux even when at his best.

Plotinus' mysticism was grounded in his belief that the purified soul, purged of all physical contact and all images of material things, is capable of achieving a union with God which is an experience of identity (Plotinus 4. 8. 1). Moreover, it is an experience in which the soul is lifted up beyond the successiveness of time to the simultaneity of eternity, and requires quiet and silence. For Plotinus too the experience came rarely and was frustratingly short-lived and transient (6. 9. 10. 1 ff.); and, like Augustine, Plotinus was fond of using erotic symbolism for the soul's union with the Good (e.g. 6. 7. 31; 6. 7. 33; 6. 9. 4. 18). Plotinus once affirms that a man should abandon high secular office if that enabled him to win the blessed vision of the One (1. 6. 7. 35). The method is that of introspection: 'Go into yourself' (1. 8. 9. 7–8). For the problem to be overcome is the drastic deterioration that has befallen the soul since it became implicated in and joined to matter (1. 8. 13. 20; 2. 3. 16. 26). In this world the soul is split into multiplicity and needs to return to unity; it experiences successiveness in the temporal process which distracts it from its ascent to eternity. Our use of words in which meaning is conveyed by one sound after another, never in a simultaneous present, is for Plotinus, as for Augustine, a symptom of the fallen condition of humanity (5. 3. 17. 24).

Nevertheless, 'all things are full of signs' (Plotinus 2. 3. 7. 12). Augustine's fascination with words and his awareness of the difficulty human beings have in communicating their meaning to one another, even when there is no linguistic barrier to cross, made him acutely conscious of the semantic problem. He affirmed the fact that we have to use words as signs to be a consequence of our fallen estate. All words are inadequate for the expression of divine mysteries.

The acute sense of the inadequacy of words explains why Augustine at the beginning of the *Confessions* experiences difficulty in finding any way of addressing God intelligibly, or speaking about God correctly. The answer to the question he finds in the reception of scripture in the Christian community. The Bible consists of words, human indeed but for the believing community a gift of God so that within the sign there is also a divine reality. The same principle holds good of the visible sacraments of baptism and eucharist, which in book XIII he will describe as necessary and indispensable and yet insufficient if they are not spiritually used and understood. The fact that in scripture God uses words to convey his gospel of love to humanity and his requirement of love to the neighbour carries the consequence that words are not excluded. So Augustine can address God in the way the psalmist did. He can use almost a cento of quotations from the Psalter, which was evidently in daily use in the quasi-monastic communities in which he lived from 388 onwards. Citations from the Psalms are even made integral to the literary structure of the work, so that in several cases a citation links the books together like a coupling. Particularly important for him are Psalms 4, 41 (42), and 138 (139). Because of this constant use of the Psalms, it is often the case that less than clear passages in the *Confessions* are explicable without difficulty when compared with the parallel expositions in his homilies on the psalter, which are also a primary source for the Latin Bible text used by him.

From the first paragraph of the *Confessions* onwards, Augustine can express Neoplatonic themes in language which sounds like a pastiche of the psalter. It is among the paradoxes of the work that the author wholly rejected pagan religious cult, but accepted a substantial proportion of Neoplatonic theology, so that the reader is surprised to discover how constantly echoes of Plotinus occur. A famous passage in book VII finds the essentials of Platonism in the prologue to St John's gospel, yet with the crucial exception of the incarnation. 'That the Word was made flesh I did not read there' (in the books of the Platonists). At the end of the same book he observes that those books had nothing to say about penitential confession or the eucharistic thanksgiving for our redemption. The Platonists saw far off the land of peace, but could not find the path to reach it. Yet when he describes the vision at Ostia shared by Monica and himself (perhaps a unique instance of a mystical experience for two simultaneously) the vocabulary is deeply indebted to Plotinus.

Plotinus and other literary echoes also enter the description in book VIII of his conversion at Milan in the summer of 386, so that it is a disputed question how much of the narrative is intended to be sober history and how much is a more poetic truth. There is an ambivalence to the writing. Did his friend Alypius, who was with him, also hear the voice as it were of a child, whether a boy or a girl, repeatedly saying *Tolle lege, tolle lege*—'Pick up and read'? The literary effect depends on the evident intention to describe a divine oracle uttered by a child (?) in whose mind nothing could have been more remote than the salvation of Augustine's soul. Utter randomness was of its essence. But, like Plotinus (3. 1. 1), Augustine did not believe in 'chance', which he thought merely a word for describing an event when we cannot discern the cause.

To the autobiography of the first nine books Augustine appended four further books. The tenth, on memory and the subconscious, is quite twice the length of most of the other books and has sometimes been thought to be an addition or afterthought. The subject-matter, however, is integrally linked with the rest of the work. The eleventh book discusses time and eternity, the twelfth the reconciliation of Platonic and Christian notions of Creation, while the thirteenth and last book astonishingly allegorizes the first chapter of Genesis to discover in it a most subtle piece of symbolic writing about the Church and sacraments. The last two books are commonly found to be exceptionally difficult for modern readers, because the context to which they are addressed is very distant.[3]

Much ink has been spilt on the endeavour to discover the overall plan, if any, which holds the different parts of the work together and imparts unity to it. At first sight the autobiographical books look scarcely connected with the last four books. There are, however, numerous subtle cross-references. The last four books make explicit what is only hinted at in the autobiographical parts, namely that the story of the soul wandering away from God and then in torment and tears finding its way home through conversion is also the story of the entire created order. It is a favourite Neoplatonic theme, but also, as Romans 8 shows, not absent from the New Testament.

The creation, made out of nothing, is involved in the perpetual change and flux of time. It falls into the abyss of formless chaos, but is brought to recognize in God the one source of order and rationality. Because it comes from God, it knows itself to be in need of returning to the source whence it came. So Augustine's personal quest and pilgrimage are the individual's experience in microcosm of what is true, on the grand scale, of the whole creation. Augustine found his story especially symbolized in St Luke's account of the parable of the prodigal son. But that parable also mirrors the evolutionary process of the world as understood by the Neoplatonic philosophers of the age. So the autobiographical books I–IX are more than a memoir: they illustrate a universal truth about human nature. They tell of a soul's wandering away into 'the region of destitution' (II. x (18))—a theme picked up at the start of book III in the description of his coming to Carthage where the place seethed with sexual provocations. But even in 'the region of death' (Ps. 138: 7–8) he found he could not escape God (IV. xii (18)). With book V begins the gradual ascent towards conversion, the disillusion born of the encounter with the Manichee leader Faustus of Mileu, so much dimmer than he had been led to expect, and he was on his way to meet Ambrose, unaware of the guiding divine hand but at last meeting a man of high culture as well as high class,

---

[3] Because of the Manichee controversy, Augustine in effect wrote five distinct expositions of Genesis 1: (*a*) *De Genesis contra Manichaeos*, of 388–9; (*b*) *De Genesi ad litteram imperfectus liber*, of 393, avoiding allegory; (*c*) *Confessions* XI–XII, to which XIII is a kind of revision, of 397–400; (*d*) *De Genesi ad litteram*, the literal commentary—more engaged in controversy with Porphyry and Neoplatonism than with Manichees; (*e*) *City of God* 11–12—again controversy with Neoplatonism.

who met him with affection and was everything a bishop ought to be (v. xiii (23)). So in book VI Augustine and his friends begin their quest. Book VII sees the exploration of the Platonist method and the profound impression made by reading Plotinus, with his exhortation to look within the soul and not at external things.

The first chapter of Genesis speaks of man being made in the image and likeness of God. The Platonic tradition (*Theaetetus* 176b) also spoke of the moral and religious ideal in terms of being as like God as possible, and of the inferior realm as 'the region of dissimilarity' (*Politicus* 273d). Augustine was seeking for certainty and stability. Book VIII speaks of the impact of three stories of conversion, of Marius Victorinus, of Antony, of the senior civil servants at Trier in the narrative of Ponticianus, until finally he comes to his own personal crisis in the Milan garden.

The vision of Ostia and the last hours of Monica form a climax in emotional intensity, and book IX is a turning point in the *Confessions*. With book X Augustine is no longer speaking about the past but explicitly about his state of mind in the present as a bishop ministering the word and sacraments to his people. But we are now paradoxically in an even more Neoplatonic world of thought than at any previous moment in the work, and remain so until the end of book XIII. Only from time to time the debate is interrupted by sudden passages of anti-Manichee polemic. It is a prime task for Augustine to show that the Manichee dismissal of the authority of the book of Genesis is utterly mistaken, since no book is richer in Christian mystery when properly interpreted. The narrative of the creation interpreted in books XII and XIII sets the context for the total account of the nature and destiny of the soul.

In regard to the principles for the right interpretation of scripture, Augustine is acutely aware that his exegesis has orthodox Catholic critics. He asks them to tolerate him, as he tolerates them, since both he and his critics accept the authority of the divinely given 'dominical books'. In scripture much may be obscure, so that many interpretations are possible; all may be valid provided that they do not depart from the apostolic rule of faith. Even through scripture, revelation is accommodated to human capacity. If there are absurdities or verbal superfluities, they are put there by providence to be signposts to a deeper meaning.

The Bible of Augustine

The Bible text used by Augustine was the Old Latin version made
from the Greek of both Old and New Testaments during the
second century. This version has the authority of being based on very
ancient Greek manuscripts, but its text occasionally produces forms
differing in some respects from those familiar to users of the English
translations. In the Psalter his numbering of the Psalms is that of the
Greek or Septuagint version, which is also the numbering of Jerome's
'Vulgate'. That is to say that from Psalm 10 to Psalm 148 the Latin
numbering is one less than that in the Hebrew text translated in the
majority of English versions. For Augustine, therefore, Psalms 9
and 10, and Psalms 114 and 115, are both run into a single psalm,
whereas 116 and 147 are divided into two. The references given
with the present translation are to Augustine's Latin Bible, so that
*from Psalm 10 to 148 the reader must add one to find the corresponding
passage in an English Bible*, whether King James or the Revised
English Bible or the New Jerusalem Bible.

Chapter and paragraph divisions

The medieval manuscripts have only the divisions into thirteen
books. The chapter numbers, given in small Roman numerals, go
back to the early printed editions of the late fifteenth and sixteenth
centuries. The paragraph numbers were first provided in the great
edition of all the works of Augustine (as far as then known) by the
French Benedictines of Saint-Maur, published at Paris in 1679.

Latin Text

M. Skutella produced for Teubner of Leipzig in 1934 a critical
edition on which all subsequent work has depended. A revision by
H. Juergens and W. Schaub was published at Stuttgart by Teubner
in 1981. In the same year the late Luc Verheijen also produced a
revision of Skutella for *Corpus Christianorum* 27. Skutella's text of
1934 is printed with French translation and distinguished notes by
A. Solignac in Bibliothèque Augustinienne, 13–14 (Paris, 1962).
Apart from excerpts made early in the sixth century by Eugippius,
and one manuscript of the sixth century in Rome, Skutella's edition
is based on ninth-century manuscripts, an age with a powerful
interest in Augustine's theology.

Bibliographical Note

A full list of significant books about the *Confessions* would be very long. In modern times a watershed was the revolutionary book by the French scholar Pierre Courcelle, *Recherches sur les Confessions de S. Augustin* (Paris, 1950; second edition, enlarged 1968). Post-Courcelle accounts may be found in the biography by Peter Brown, *Augustine of Hippo* (London, 1967 and later reprints), and in John O'Meara, *The Young Augustine* (London 1954, paperback 1980). On the Ostia vision, see Paul Henry, *The Path to Transcendence* (Pittsburgh, 1981); on Neoplatonism and the discussions of memory, time, and creation see R. Sorabji, *Time, Creation and the Continuum* (London, 1983). The greatest of intellectual biographies remains John Burnaby, *Amor Dei* (London, 1938 and later reprints). An outline in H. Chadwick, *Augustine*, Past Masters (Oxford, 1986 and later reprints).

Plotinus is translated by A. H. Armstrong in the Loeb Classical Library, including Porphyry's *Life* of Plotinus, 7 vols. (1966–88). Porphyry's writings are less accessible: English versions exist of his *Life of Pythagoras* in M. Hadas and M. Smith, *Heroes and Gods, Spiritual Biographies in Antiquity* (London, 1965); *The Nymph's Cave* in Arethusa Monographs 1 (Buffalo NY, 1969); *Abstinence from Animal Food* translated by Thomas Taylor (reprinted, London, 1965); *Letter to his wife Marcella*, translated by Alice Zimmern (London, 1896). A French version of *How the embryo is ensouled* (*Ad Gaurum*) in A. J. Festugière, *La Révélation d'Hermès Trismégiste* III (Paris, 1953). *Letter to Anebo*, translated into English by Thomas Taylor (2nd edn. London, 1895), with Iamblichus *On the Mysteries*. Of his immensely influential works on logic only the *Isagoge* is translated, by E. W. Warren (Pontifical Institute of Mediaeval Studies, Toronto, 1975). Important studies of Porphyry: J. J. O'Meara, *Porphyry's Philosophy from Oracles in Augustine* (Paris, 1959); P. Hadot, *Porphyre et Victorinus* (Paris, 1968); A. Smith, *Porphyry's place in the neoplatonic Tradition* (The Hague, 1974). There are Teubner texts of the *Life of Pythagoras, Abstinence, Letter to Marcella* (ed. A. Nauck, 2nd edn. 1886); of the *Sententiae* by E. Lamberz (1975).

Original Manichee texts survive mainly in Coptic and medieval Chinese. For a reliable guide, with bibliography, see S. N. C. Lieu, *Manicheism in the Later Roman Empire and in Medieval China* (Manchester, 1985).

Dates

Confessions

BOOK I

Early Years

i (1) 'You are great, Lord, and highly to be praised (Ps. 47: 2): great is your power and your wisdom is immeasurable' (Ps. 146:5). Man, a little piece of your creation, desires to praise you, a human being 'bearing his mortality with him' (2 Cor. 4: 10), carrying with him the witness of his sin and the witness that you 'resist the proud' (1 Pet. 5:5). Nevertheless, to praise you is the desire of man, a little piece of your creation. You stir man to take pleasure in praising you, because you have made us for yourself, and our heart is restless until it rests in you.[1]

'Grant me Lord to know and understand' (Ps. 118: 34, 73, 144) which comes first—to call upon you or to praise you, and whether knowing you precedes calling upon you. But who calls upon you when he does not know you? For an ignorant person might call upon someone else instead of the right one. But surely you may be called upon in prayer that you may be known. Yet 'how shall they call upon him in whom they have not believed? and how shall they believe without a preacher?' (Rom. 10: 14). 'They will praise the Lord who seek for him' (Ps. 21: 27).

In seeking him they find him, and in finding they will praise him. Lord, I would seek you, calling upon you—and calling upon you is an act of believing in you. You have been preached to us. My faith, Lord, calls upon you. It is your gift to me. You breathed it into me by the humanity of your Son, by the ministry of your preacher.[2]

ii (2) How shall I call upon my God, my God and Lord? Surely when I call on him, I am calling on him to come into me. But what place is there in me where my God can enter into me? 'God made heaven and earth' (Gen. 1: 1). Where may he come to me? Lord my God, is there any room in me which can contain you? Can heaven

---

[1] For Plotinus (6. 7. 23. 4) the soul finds rest only in the One. Augustine's sentence announces a major theme of his work.

[2] Probably Ambrose (as in Augustine's letter 147. 52) rather than Christ; i.e. the two phrases are contrasting, not parallel and equivalent. That the humanity of Christ is an example of faith is common in Augustine. See below, x. xliii (68).

and earth, which you have made and in which you have made me,
contain you? Without you, whatever exists would not exist. Then
can what exists contain you? I also have being. So why do I request
you to come to me when, unless you were within me, I would have
no being at all? I am not now possessed by Hades; yet even there are
you (Ps. 138: 8): for 'even if I were to go down to Hades, you would
be present'. Accordingly, my God, I would have no being,
I would not have any existence, unless you were in me. Or rather, I
would have no being if I were not in you 'of whom are all things,
through whom are all things, in whom are all things' (Rom. 11: 36).
Even so, Lord, even so. How can I call on you to come if I am
already in you? Or where can you come from so as to be in me? Can
I move outside heaven and earth so that my God may come to me
from there? For God has said 'I fill heaven and earth' (Jer. 23: 24).

iii (3)   Do heaven and earth contain you because you have filled
them? or do you fill them and overflow them because they do not
contain you? Where do you put the overflow of yourself after
heaven and earth are filled? Or have you, who contain all things, no
need to be contained by anything because what you will you fill by
containing it? We cannot think you are given coherence by vessels
full of you, because even if they were to be broken, you would not
be spilt. When you are 'poured out' (Joel 2: 28) upon us, you are
not wasted on the ground. You raise us upright. You are not
scattered but reassemble us. In filling all things, you fill them all
with the whole of yourself.

Is it that because all things cannot contain the whole of you, they
contain part of you, and that all things contain the same part of you
simultaneously? Or does each part contain a different part of you,
the larger containing the greater parts, the lesser parts the smaller?
Does that imply that there is some part of you which is greater,
another part smaller? Or is the whole of you everywhere, yet
without anything that contains you entire?[3]

iv (4)   Who then are you, my God? What, I ask, but God who is
Lord? For 'who is the Lord but the Lord', or 'who is God but our
God?' (Ps. 17: 32). Most high, utterly good, utterly powerful, most
omnipotent, most merciful and most just, deeply hidden yet most

---

[3] Plotinus (6. 4–5) devoted a treatise to the question of the omnipresence of being.
Closely parallel is Plotinus 5. 5. 9.

intimately present, perfection of both beauty and strength, stable and incomprehensible, immutable and yet changing all things, never new, never old, making everything new and 'leading' the proud 'to be old without their knowledge' (Job 9: 5, Old Latin version); always active, always in repose, gathering to yourself but not in need, supporting and filling and protecting, creating and nurturing and bringing to maturity, searching even though to you nothing is lacking: you love without burning, you are jealous in a way that is free of anxiety, you 'repent' (Gen. 6: 6) without the pain of regret, you are wrathful and remain tranquil. You will a change without any change in your design. You recover what you find, yet have never lost. Never in any need, you rejoice in your gains (Luke 15: 7); you are never avaricious, yet you require interest (Matt. 25: 27). We pay you more than you require so as to make you our debtor, yet who has anything which does not belong to you? (1 Cor. 4: 7). You pay off debts, though owing nothing to anyone; you cancel debts and incur no loss. But in these words what have I said, my God, my life, my holy sweetness? What has anyone achieved in words when he speaks about you? Yet woe to those who are silent about you because, though loquacious with verbosity,[4] they have nothing to say.

v (5) Who will enable me to find rest in you? Who will grant me that you come to my heart and intoxicate it, so that I forget my evils and embrace my one and only good, yourself? What are you to me? Have mercy so that I may find words. What am I to you that you command me to love you, and that, if I fail to love you, you are angry with me and threaten me with vast miseries? If I do not love you, is that but a little misery? What a wretch I am! In your mercies, Lord God, tell me what you are to me. 'Say to my soul, I am your salvation' (Ps. 34: 3). Speak to me so that I may hear. See the ears of my heart are before you, Lord. Open them and 'say to my soul, I am your salvation.' After that utterance I will run and lay hold on you. Do not hide your face from me (cf. Ps. 26: 9). Lest I die, let me die so that I may see it.[5]

---

[4] 'The loquacious' are regularly either pagan philosophical critics rejecting the Christian revelation or Manichees. The problematic nature of all human talk about God is stated by Plotinus 5. 3. 14 (we say what he is not, not what he is; if we can say what is true, that is by mantic inspiration).

[5] None can see God's face and live (Exod. 33: 20); yet the heavenly vision is life. For the epigram 'let me die lest I die' Augustine has a parallel in a sermon (231,3): 'Let me die (to sin) lest I die (in hell).' Cf. also below, II. ii (4).

(6)   The house of my soul is too small for you to come to it. May it be enlarged by you. It is in ruins: restore it. In your eyes it has offensive features. I admit it, I know it; but who will clean it up? Or to whom shall I cry other than you? 'Cleanse me from my secret faults, Lord, and spare your servant from sins to which I am tempted by others' (Ps. 31: 5). 'I believe and therefore I speak' (Ps. 115: 10). 'Lord, you know' (Ps. 68: 6). Have I not openly accused myself of 'my faults', my God, and 'you forgave me the iniquity of my heart' (Ps. 31: 5). I do not 'contend with you in a court of law' (Job 9: 3), for you are the truth. I do not deceive myself 'lest my iniquity lie to itself' (Ps. 26: 12). Therefore I do not contend with you like a litigant because, 'if you take note of iniquities, Lord, who shall stand?' (Ps. 129: 3).

vi (7)   Nevertheless allow me to speak before your mercy, though I am but dust and ashes (Gen. 18: 27). Allow me to speak: for I am addressing your mercy, not a man who would laugh at me. Perhaps even you deride me (cf. Ps. 2: 4), but you will turn and have mercy on me (Jer. 12: 15). What, Lord, do I wish to say except that I do not know whence I came to be in this mortal life or, as I may call it, this living death?[6] I do not know where I came from.[7] But the consolations of your mercies (cf. Ps. 50: 3; 93: 19) upheld me, as I have heard from the parents of my flesh, him from whom and her in whom you formed me in time. For I do not remember. So I was welcomed by the consolations of human milk; but it was not my mother or my nurses who made any decision to fill their breasts, but you who through them gave me infant food, in accordance with your ordinance and the riches which are distributed deep in the natural order. You also granted me not to wish for more than you were giving, and to my nurses the desire to give me what you gave them. For by an impulse which you control their instinctive wish was to give me the milk which they had in abundance from you. For the good which came to me from them was a good for them; yet it

---

[6] Echo of Lucretius 3. 869; Euripides quoted by Plato, *Gorgias* 492e: 'who knows if being alive is really being dead, and being dead is being alive?'

[7] On the origin of the soul's union with the body and on the possibility of pre-existence, Augustine is always unwilling to make any decision: see IX. xi (37). The Platonic doctrine of the soul's pre-existence and fall into the prison of the body is never affirmed. Nevertheless, the possibility of pre-existence is also not denied, and especially in *Confessions* XI–XII the language used of the soul's lapse from a divine eternity to the disruptive successiveness of temporal things is very close to Plotinus.

was not from them but through them. Indeed all good things come from you, O God, and 'from my God is all my salvation' (2 Sam. 23: 5). I became aware of this only later when you cried aloud to me through the gifts which you bestow both inwardly in mind and outwardly in body. For at that time I knew nothing more than how to suck and to be quietened by bodily delights, and to weep when I was physically uncomfortable.

(8)   Afterwards I began to smile, first in my sleep, then when awake. That at least is what I was told, and I believed it since that is what we see other infants doing. I do not actually remember what I then did.

   Little by little I began to be aware where I was and wanted to manifest my wishes to those who could fulfil them as I could not. For my desires were internal; adults were external to me and had no means of entering into my soul. So I threw my limbs about and uttered sounds, signs resembling my wishes, the small number of signs of which I was capable but such signs as lay in my power to use: for there was no real resemblance. When I did not get my way, either because I was not understood or lest it be harmful to me, I used to be indignant with my seniors for their disobedience, and with free people who were not slaves to my interests; and I would revenge myself upon them by weeping. That this is the way of infants I have learnt from those I have been able to watch. That is what I was like myself and, although they have not been aware of it, they have taught me more than my nurses with all their knowledge of how I behaved.

(9)   My infancy is long dead and I am alive. But you, Lord, live and in you nothing dies. You are before the beginning of the ages, and prior to everything that can be said to be 'before'. You are God and Lord of all you have created. In you are the constant causes of inconstant things. All mutable things have in you their immutable origins. In you all irrational and temporal things have the everlasting causes of their life. Tell me, God, tell your suppliant, in mercy to your poor wretch, tell me whether there was some period of my life, now dead and gone, which preceded my infancy? Or is this period that which I spent in my mother's womb? On that matter also I have learnt something, and I myself have seen pregnant women. What was going on before that, my sweetness, my God? Was I anywhere,

or any sort of person? I have no one able to tell me that—neither
my father nor my mother nor the experience of others nor my own
memory. But you may smile at me for putting these questions. Your
command that I praise you and confess you may be limited to that
which I know.

(10) So 'I acknowledge you, Lord of heaven and earth' (Matt. 11:
25), articulating my praise to you for my beginnings and my infancy
which I do not recall. You have also given mankind the capacity to
understand oneself by analogy with others, and to believe much
about oneself on the authority of weak women. Even at that time I
had existence and life, and already at the last stage of my infant
speechlessness I was searching out signs by which I made my
thoughts known to others. Where can a living being such as an
infant come from if not from you, God? Or can anyone become the
cause of his own making? Or is there any channel through which
being and life can be drawn into us other than what you make us,
Lord? In you it is not one thing to be and another to live: the
supreme degree of being and the supreme degree of life are one
and the same thing.[8] You are being in a supreme degree and are
immutable. In you the present day has no ending, and yet in you it
has its end: 'all these things have their being in you' (Rom. 11: 36).
They would have no way of passing away unless you set a limit to
them. Because 'your years do not fail' (Ps. 101: 28), your years are
one Today. How many of our days and days of our fathers have
passed during your Today, and have derived from it the measure
and condition of their existence? And others too will pass away and
from the same source derive the condition of their existence. 'But
you are the same'; and all tomorrow and hereafter, and indeed all
yesterday and further back, you will make a Today, you have made
a Today.[9]

If anyone finds your simultaneity beyond his understanding, it is
not for me to explain it. Let him be content to say 'What is this?'
(Exod. 16: 15). So too let him rejoice and delight in finding you
who are beyond discovery rather than fail to find you by supposing
you to be discoverable.

vii (11)   Hear me, God. (Ps. 54: 2). Alas for the sins of humanity!
(Isa. 1: 4) Man it is who says this, and you have pity on him,

[8] Plotinus (3. 6. 6. 15) says this also.
[9] This sketch on time and eternity anticipates book XI (esp. xiii (16)).

because you made him and did not make sin in him. Who reminds me of the sin of my infancy? for 'none is pure from sin before you, not even an infant of one day upon the earth' (Job 14: 4–5 LXX). Who reminds me? Any tiny child now, for I see in that child what I do not remember in myself.[10] What sin did I then have? Was it wrong that in tears I greedily opened my mouth wide to suck the breasts? If I were to do that now, gasping to eat food appropriate to my present age, I would be laughed at and very properly rebuked. At the time of my infancy I must have acted reprehensibly; but since I could not understand the person who admonished me, neither custom nor reason allowed me to be reprehended. As we grow up, we eliminate and set aside such ways. But I have never seen anyone knowingly setting aside what is good when purging something of faults.

Yet, for an infant of that age, could it be reckoned good to use tears in trying to obtain what it would have been harmful to get, to be vehemently indignant at the refusals of free and older people and of parents or many other people of good sense who would not yield to my whims, and to attempt to strike them and to do as much injury as possible?[11] There is never an obligation to be obedient to orders which it would be pernicious to obey. So the feebleness of infant limbs is innocent, not the infant's mind. I have personally watched and studied a jealous baby. He could not yet speak and, pale with jealousy and bitterness, glared at his brother sharing his mother's milk. Who is unaware of this fact of experience? Mothers and nurses claim to charm it away by their own private remedies. But it can hardly be innocence, when the source of milk is flowing richly and abundantly, not to endure a share going to one's blood-brother, who is in profound need, dependent for life exclusively on that one food.

But people smilingly tolerate this behaviour, not because it is nothing or only a trivial matter, but because with coming of age it will pass away. You can prove this to be the case from the fact that the same behaviour cannot be borne without irritation when encountered in someone of more mature years.

[10] Cicero (*De finibus* 5. 55) remarks on the value placed by philosophers on infant behaviour as a guide to the understanding of human nature.

[11] Seneca (*De Constantia Sapientis* 11. 2) observes how babies hit their mothers in anger.

(12) You, Lord my God, are the giver of life and a body to a baby. As we see, you have endowed it with senses. You have co-ordinated the limbs. You have adorned it with a beautiful form, and for the coherence and preservation of the whole you have implanted all the instincts of a living being. You therefore command me to praise you for that and to 'confess to you and to sing to your name, Most High' (Ps. 91: 2)—God, you are omnipotent and good—even if that were all that you had made. No one else could do that except you, the one from whom every kind of being is derived. The supreme beauty, you give distinct form to all things and by your law impose order on everything.[12] This period of my life, Lord, I do not remember having lived, but I have believed what others have told me and have assumed how I behaved from observing other infants. Despite the high probability of this assumption, I do not wish to reckon this as part of the life that I live in this world; for it is lost in the darkness of my forgetfulness, and is on the same level as the life I lived in my mother's womb. If 'I was conceived in iniquity and in sins my mother nourished me in her womb' (Ps. 50: 7), I ask you, my God, I ask, Lord, where and when your servant was innocent? But of that time I say nothing more. I feel no sense of responsibility now for a time of which I recall not a single trace.

viii (13) On my path to the present I emerged from infancy to boyhood,[13] or rather boyhood came upon me and succeeded infancy. Infancy did not 'depart', for it has nowhere to go. Yet I was no longer a baby incapable of speech but already a boy with power to talk. This I remember. But how I learnt to talk I discovered only later. It was not that grown-up people instructed me by presenting me with words in a certain order by formal teaching, as later I was to learn the letters of the alphabet. I myself acquired this power of speech with the intelligence which you gave me, my God. By groans and various sounds and various movements of parts of my body I would endeavour to express the intentions of my heart to persuade people to bow to my will. But I had not the power to express all that I wanted nor could I make my wishes understood by everybody. My grasp made use of memory: when people gave a name to an object and when, following the sound, they moved their body towards that

---

[12] Plotinus 1. 6. 6 says God is source of beauty.
[13] Books I–VII follow the six ages of man; cf. II. i (1); VII. i (1).

object, I would see and retain the fact that that object received from them this sound which they pronounced when they intended to draw attention to it. Moreover, their intention was evident from the gestures which are, as it were, the natural vocabulary of all races, and are made with the face and the inclination of the eyes and the movements of other parts of the body, and by the tone of voice which indicates whether the mind's inward sentiments are to seek and possess or to reject and avoid. Accordingly, I gradually gathered the meaning of words, occurring in their places in different sentences and frequently heard; and already I learnt to articulate my wishes by training my mouth to use these signs. In this way I communicated the signs of my wishes to those around me, and entered more deeply into the stormy society of human life. I was dependent on the authority of my parents and the direction of adult people.

ix (14)   O God, my God, 'what miseries I experienced'[14] at this stage of my life, and what delusions when in my boyhood it was set before me as my moral duty in life to obey those who admonished me with the purpose that I should succeed in this world, and should excel in the arts of using my tongue to gain access to human honours and to acquire deceitful riches. I was next sent to school to learn to read and write. Poor wretch, I did not understand for what such knowledge is useful. Yet if ever I was indolent in learning, I was beaten. This method was approved by adults, and many people living long before me had constructed the laborious courses which we were compelled to follow by an increase of the toil and sorrow (Gen. 3: 16) of Adam's children. We found however, Lord, people who prayed to you and from them we learnt to think of you, in our limited way, as some large being with the power, even when not present to our senses, of hearing us and helping us. As a boy I began to pray to you, 'my help and my refuge' (Ps. 93: 22), and for my prayer to you I broke the bonds of my tongue. Though I was only a small child, there was great feeling when I pleaded with you that I might not be caned at school. And when you did not hear me, which was so as 'not to give me to foolishness', (Ps. 21: 3), adult people, including even my parents, who wished no evil to come upon me, used to laugh at my stripes, which were at that time a great and painful evil to me.[15]

---

[14] Terence, *Adelphoe* 867.

[15] In spite of the criticism of Quintilian (1. 3. 13–17), corporal punishment was

(15)   Lord, is there anyone, any mind so great, united to you by a strong love—is there, I say, anyone (as with the character produced by a certain stolidity)—is there a man who is so devotedly united to you with mighty affection that he holds of small account racks and hooks and various torments of this brutal nature, which in all countries people with great terror pray you they may escape, and yet loves[16] those who are utterly terrified of them? Is this comparable to the way our parents laughed at the torments which our teachers inflicted on us as boys? We at least were no less scared and prayed no less passionately to escape them. Yet we were at fault in paying less attention than was required of us to writing or reading or using our minds about our books. Not, Lord, that there was a deficiency in memory or intelligence. It was your will to endow us sufficiently with the level appropriate to our age. But we loved to play, and punishments were imposed on us by those who were engaged in adult games. For 'the amusement of adults is called business'.[17] But when boys play such games they are punished by adults, and no one feels sorry either for the children or for the adults or indeed for both of them. Perhaps some refined arbiter of things might approve of my being beaten. As a boy I played ball-games, and that play slowed down the speed at which I learnt letters with which, as an adult, I might play a less creditable game. The schoolmaster who caned me was behaving no better than I when, after being refuted by a fellow-teacher in some pedantic question, he was more tormented by jealousy and envy than I when my opponent overcame me in a ball-game.

x (16)   Yet I was at fault, Lord God, orderer and creator of all things in nature, but of sinners only the orderer. Lord my God, I sinned by not doing as I was told by my parents and teachers. For later I was able to make good use of letters, whatever might be the intention of my adult guardians in wanting me to learn them. I was disobedient not because I had chosen higher things, but from love of sport. In competitive games I loved the pride of winning. I liked to tickle my ears with false stories which further titillated my desires

universal in schools of Augustine's time. Once (*City of God* 21. 14) he reflects on the paradox that sometimes a boy would prefer to be flogged than to learn his lesson.

[16] For 'loves' the emendation 'derides' is found in one manuscript (tenth century).

[17] Seneca cited by Lactantius (*Institutiones Divinae* 2. 4. 14). Plotinus 3. 2. 15. 36: 'All human concerns are children's games'.

(2 Tim. 4: 3–4). The same curiosity mountingly increased my appetite for public shows.[18] Public shows are the games of adults. Those who give them are persons held in such high dignity that almost everyone wishes this honour to come to their children. But they happily allow them to be flogged if such shows hinder the study which will bring them, they hope, to the position of giving such shows.

Look with mercy (Ps. 24: 16–18) on these follies, Lord, and deliver us (Ps. 78: 9) who now call upon you. Deliver also those who do not as yet pray, that they may call upon you and you may set them free.

xi (17) When I was still a boy, I had heard about eternal life promised to us through the humility of our Lord God, coming down to our pride, and I was already signed with the sign of the cross and seasoned with salt from the time I came from my mother's womb.[19] She greatly put her trust in you. You saw, Lord, how one day, when I was still a small boy, pressure on the chest suddenly made me hot with fever and almost at death's door. You saw, my God, because you were already my guardian, with what fervour of mind and with what faith I then begged for the baptism of your Christ, my God and Lord, urging it on the devotion of my mother and of the mother of us all, your Church. My physical mother was distraught. With a pure heart and faith in you she even more lovingly travailed in labour for my eternal salvation. She hastily made arrangements for me to be initiated and washed in the sacraments of salvation, confessing you, Lord Jesus, for the remission of sins. But suddenly I recovered. My cleansing was deferred on the assumption that, if I lived, I would be sure to soil myself; and

[18] i.e. circus (horse-racing), amphitheatre (gladiators and beast fights), theatre, and music hall. To pay the cost of such public entertainments brought high credit, and was expected of the rich. Villas and estates might be sold to pay the bill (thereby bringing land back into circulation in the economy).

[19] Catechumens were sanctified by the sign of the cross, prayer invoking the protection of God and the child's guardian angel, laying on of hands, and salt placed on the tongue as an act of exorcism. The Latin prayers accompanying these actions may be read in the eighth-century Gelasian Sacramentary. The salt survived in the Roman baptismal rite until 1969.

Before about 400, the intense significance attached to baptism as sacrament of the remission of sins, led many Christian parents to postpone baptism, often until the death-bed. Catechumens were entitled to bear the name 'Christian' but not that of the 'faithful' (fidelis).

after that solemn washing the guilt would be greater and more dangerous if I then defiled myself with sins.

So I was already a believer, as were my mother and the entire household except for my father alone. Though he had not yet come to faith, he did not obstruct my right to follow my mother's devotion, so as to prevent me believing in Christ. She anxiously laboured to convince me that you, my God, were my father rather than he, and in this endeavour you helped her to gain victory over her husband. His moral superior, she rendered obedient service to him, for in this matter she was being obedient to your authority.

(18)   I beg of you, my God, I long to know if it is your will, what was your purpose when at that time it was decided to defer my baptism? Was it for my good that the restraints on sinning were as it were relaxed? Or were they not in fact relaxed? Even now gossips speaking about one or another person can be heard on all sides saying in our ears: 'Let him be, let him do it; he is not yet baptized.' Yet in regard to bodily health we do not say: 'Let him inflict more wounds on himself, for he is not yet cured.' How much better for me if I had been quickly healed and if, thanks to the diligent care of my family and my own decisions, action had been taken by which I received the health of my soul and was kept safe under the protection which you would have given me (Ps. 34: 3). Certainly much better. But beyond boyhood many great waves of temptations were seen to be threatening. My mother was already well aware of that, and her plan was to commit to the waves the clay out of which I would later be shaped rather than the actual image itself.[20]

xii (19)   Nevertheless, even during boyhood when there was less reason to fear than during adolescence, I had no love for reading books and hated being forced to study them. Yet pressure was put on me and was good for me. It was not of my own inclination that I did well, for I learnt nothing unless compelled. No one is doing right if he is acting against his will, even when what he is doing is good. Those who put compulsion on me were not doing right either; the good was done to me by you, my God. They gave no consideration to the use that I might make of the things they forced me to learn. The objective they had in view was merely to satisfy the appetite for

---

[20]   The unstable, undrinkable sea is Augustine's standing image for humanity alienated from God. The 'clay' (Gen. 2: 6) is natural humanity, the 'image' humanity remade by grace. Cf. below, XIII. xii (13).

wealth and for glory, though the appetite is insatiable, the wealth is in reality destitution of spirit, and the glory something to be ashamed of. But you, by whom 'the hairs of our head are numbered' (Matt. 10: 30), used the error of all who pressed me to learn to turn out to my advantage. And my reluctance to learn you used for a punishment which I well deserved: so tiny a child, so great a sinner. So by making use of those who were failing to do anything morally right you did good to me, and from me in my sin you exacted a just retribution. For you have imposed order, and so it is that the punishment of every disordered mind is its own disorder.[21]

xiii (20)   Even now I have not yet discovered the reasons why I hated Greek literature when I was being taught it as a small boy.[22] Latin I deeply loved, not at the stage of my primary teachers but at the secondary level taught by the teachers of literature called 'grammarians' (*grammatici*). The initial elements, where one learns the three Rs of reading, writing, and arithmetic, I felt to be no less a burden and an infliction than the entire series of Greek classes. The root of this aversion must simply have been sin and the vanity of life, by which I was 'mere flesh and wind going on its way and not returning' (Ps. 77: 39). Of course, those first elements of the language were better, because more fundamental. On that foundation I came to acquire the faculty which I had and still possess of being able to read whatever I find written, and to write myself whatever I wish. This was better than the poetry I was later forced to learn about the wanderings of some legendary fellow named Aeneas (forgetful of my own wanderings) and to weep over the death of a Dido who took her own life from love. In reading this, O God my life, I myself was meanwhile dying by my alienation from you, and my miserable condition in that respect brought no tear to my eyes.[23]

(21)   What is more pitiable than a wretch without pity for himself who weeps over the death of Dido dying for love of Aeneas, but not weeping over himself dying for his lack of love for you, my God, light of my heart, bread of the inner mouth of my soul, the power

[21] The principle goes back to the *Gorgias* of Plato.

[22] Augustine was never fluent in Greek, but could make his own translations when needed. He knew more Greek than he sometimes admits.

[23] There is a reminiscence here of a story told by Plutarch and Aelian about Alexander tyrant of Pherae, who left a tragedy in a theatre because he did not wish to weep at fiction when unmoved by his own cruelty.

which begets life in my mind and in the innermost recesses of my
thinking. I had no love for you and 'committed fornication against
you' (Ps. 72: 27); and in my fornications I heard all round me the
cries 'Well done, well done' (Ps. 34: 21; 39: 16). 'For the friendship
of this world is fornication against you' (Jas. 4: 4), and 'Well done'
is what they say to shame a man who does not go along with them.
Over this I wept not a tear. I wept over Dido who 'died in pursuing
her ultimate end with a sword'.[24] I abandoned you to pursue the
lowest things of your creation. I was dust going to dust. Had I been
forbidden to read this story, I would have been sad that I could not
read what made me sad. Such madness is considered a higher and
more fruitful literary education than being taught to read and write.

(22)   But now may my God cry out in my soul and may your truth
tell me: 'It is not so, it is not so. The best education you received
was the primary.' Obviously I much prefer to forget the wanderings
of Aeneas and all that stuff than to write and read. It is true, veils
hang at the entrances to the schools of literature;[25] but they do not
signify the prestige of élite teaching so much as the covering up of
error.

Let no critics shout against me (I am not afraid of them now)
while I confess to you the longing of my soul, my God, and when I
accept rebuke for my evil ways and wish to love your good ways (Ps.
118: 101). Let there be no abuse of me from people who sell or buy
a literary education. If I put the question to them whether the poet's
story is true that Aeneas once came to Carthage, the uneducated
will reply that they do not know, while the educated will say it is
false. But if I ask with what letters Aeneas' name is spelled, all who
have learnt to read will reply correctly in accordance with the
agreement and convention by which human beings have determined
the value of these signs. Similarly, if I ask which would cause the
greater inconvenience to someone's life, to forget how to read and
write or to forget these fabulous poems, who does not see what
answer he would give, unless he has totally lost his senses? So it was

[24] Virgil, *Aeneid* 6. 457.
[25] In the Roman Empire veils before an entrance were a sign of the dignity of the person
beyond it; the higher the rank of a civil servant, the more veils were passed to gain access,
each being guarded. For his school at Milan Augustine employed a junior usher to control
the entrance veil.

The paragraph reflects the resentment against Augustine felt by secular professors of
literature because of his renunciation and conversion.

a sin in me as a boy when I gave pride of place in my affection to those empty fables rather than to more useful studies, or rather when I hated the one and loved the other. But to me it was a hateful chant to recite 'one and one is two', and 'two and two are four'; delightful was the vain spectacle of the wooden horse full of armed soldiers and the burning of Troy and the very ghost of Creusa.[26]

xiv (23)   Why then did I hate Greek which has similar songs to sing? Homer was skilled at weaving such stories, and with sheer delight mixed vanity. Yet to me as a boy he was repellent. I can well believe that Greek boys feel the same about Virgil when they are forced to learn him in the way that I learnt Homer. The difficulty lies there: the difficulty of learning a foreign language at all. It sprinkles gall, as it were, over all the charm of the stories the Greeks tell. I did not know any of the words, and violent pressure on me to learn them was imposed by means of fearful and cruel punishments. At one time in my infancy I also knew no Latin, and yet by listening I learnt it with no fear or pain at all, from my nurses caressing me, from people laughing over jokes, and from those who played games and were enjoying them. I learnt Latin without the threat of punishment from anyone forcing me to learn it. My own heart constrained me to bring its concepts to birth, which I could not have done unless I had learnt some words, not from formal teaching but by listening to people talking; and they in turn were the audience for my thoughts. This experience sufficiently illuminates the truth that free curiosity has greater power to stimulate learning than rigorous coercion. Nevertheless, the free-ranging flux of curiosity is channelled by discipline under your laws, God. By your laws we are disciplined, from the canes of schoolmasters to the ordeals of martyrs. Your laws have the power to temper bitter experiences in a constructive way, recalling us to yourself from the pestilential life of easy comforts which have taken us away from you.

xv (24)   'Lord hear my prayer' (Ps. 60: 2) that my soul may not collapse (Ps. 83: 3) under your discipline (Ps. 54: 2), and may not suffer exhaustion in confessing to you your mercies, by which you have delivered me from all my evil ways. Bring to me a sweetness surpassing all the seductive delights which I pursued. Enable me to love you with all my strength that I may clasp your hand with all my

[26] Virgil, *Aeneid* 2. 772.

heart. 'Deliver me from all temptation to the end' (Ps. 17: 30). You, Lord, are 'my king and my God' (Ps. 5: 3; 43: 5). Turn to your service whatever may be of use in what I learnt in boyhood. May I dedicate to your service my power to speak and write and read and count; for when I learnt vanities, you imposed discipline on me and have forgiven me the sin of desiring pleasure from those vanities. For in them I learnt many useful words, but these words can also be learnt through things that are not vain, and that is the safe way along which children should walk.

xvi (25)   Woe to you, torrent of human custom! 'Who can stand against you?' (Ps. 75: 8) When will you run dry? How long will your flowing current carry the sons of Eve into the great and fearful ocean which can be crossed, with difficulty, only by those who have embarked on the Wood of the cross (Wisd. 14: 7)? Have I not read in you of Jupiter, at once both thunderer and adulterer?[27] Of course the two activities cannot be combined, but he was so described as to give an example of real adultery defended by the authority of a fictitious thunderclap acting as a go-between. What master of oratory can hear with equanimity a person of his own profession saying out loud, 'Homer invented these fictions and attributed human powers to the gods; I wish he had attributed divine powers to us'?[28] It would be truer to say that Homer indeed invented these fictions, but he attributed divine sanction to vicious acts, which had the result that immorality was no longer counted immorality and anyone who so acted would seem to follow the example not of abandoned men but of the gods in heaven.

(26)   Yet, you infernal river, the sons of men are thrown into you, and fees are paid for them to learn these things. It is a matter of great public concern when a speech is made in the forum in full view of the laws decreeing that teachers' salaries be paid from public funds in addition to the fees paid by pupils.[29] The river of custom strikes the rocks and roars: 'This is why words are learnt; this is why one has to acquire the eloquence wholly necessary for

---

[27] Terence, *Eunuch* (cited in the next section which explains the allusions here).

[28] Cicero, *Tusculan Disputations* 1. 26. 65.

[29] Imperial legislation (e.g. a law of the emperor Gratian of 376) provided that municipal professors be paid a basic state salary; this would be supplemented by fees from pupils. The rates paid were publicly set up on inscriptions. A famous inscription in the North African town of Timgad of the year 362 lays down the salaries and fees chargeable by lawyers, paper and travel costs being extra.

carrying conviction in one's cause and for developing one's thoughts.'
It is as if we would not know words such as 'golden shower' and
'bosom' and 'deceit' and 'temples of heaven' and other phrases
occurring in the passage in question, had not Terence[30] brought on
to the stage a worthless young man citing Jupiter as a model for his
own fornication. He is looking up at a mural painting: 'there was
this picture representing how Jupiter, they say, sent a shower of
gold into Danae's lap and deceived a woman.' Notice how he
encourages himself to lust as if enjoying celestial authority:

But what a god (he says)! He strikes the temples of heaven with his
immense sound. And am I, poor little fellow, not to do the same as he? Yes
indeed, I have done it with pleasure.

There is no force, no force at all, in the argument that these
words are more easily learnt through this obscene text. The words
actually encourage the more confident committing of a disgraceful
action. I bring no charge against the words which are like exquisite
and precious vessels, but the wine of error is poured into them for
us by drunken teachers. If we failed to drink, we were caned and
could not appeal to any sober judge. Yet, my God, before whose
sight I now recall this without the memory disturbing me, I learnt
this text with pleasure and took delight in it, wretch that I was. For
this reason I was said to be a boy of high promise.

xvii (27) Let me, my God, say something also about the intelligence
which was your gift to me, and the ways in which I wasted it on
follies. A task was set me which caused me deep psychological
anxiety. The reward was praise but I feared shame and blows if I
did badly. I was to recite the speech of Juno in her anger and grief
that she 'could not keep the Trojan king out of Italy'.[31] I had
understood that Juno never said this. But we were compelled to
follow in our wanderings the paths set by poetic fictions, and to
express in plain prose the sense which the poet had put in verse.[32]
The speaker who received highest praise was the one who had
regard to the dignity of the imaginary characters, who most effectively
expressed feelings of anger and sorrow, and who clothed these
thoughts in appropriate language.

[30] *Eunuch* 585, 589 f.
[31] Virgil, *Aeneid* 1. 38.
[32] This educational method is recommended by Quintilian (10. 5. 2).

What could all this matter to me, true life, my God? What importance could it have for me that my recitation was acclaimed beyond many other readers of my age group? Was not the whole exercise mere smoke and wind? Was there no other subject on which my talent and tongue might be exercised? Your praises, Lord, your praises expressed through your scriptures would have upheld the tender vine of my heart, and it would not have been snatched away by empty trifles to become 'a shameful prey for the birds'. There is more than one way of offering sacrifice to the fallen angels.[33]

xviii (28)   When one considers the men proposed to me as models for my imitation, it is no wonder that in this way I was swept along by vanities and travelled right away from you, my God. They would be covered in embarrassment if, in describing their own actions in which they had not behaved badly, they were caught using a barbarism or a solecism in speech. But if they described their lusts in a rich vocabulary of well constructed prose with a copious and ornate style, they received praise and congratulated themselves. Lord you are 'long-suffering and very patient and true' (Ps. 102: 8; 85: 15; Isa. 42: 14 LXX); you see this and you keep silence. But will you always keep silence? Even at this moment you are delivering from this terrifying abyss the soul who seeks for you and thirsts for your delights (Ps. 41: 3), whose heart tells you 'I have sought your face; your face, Lord, I will seek' (Ps. 26: 8). To be far from your face is to be in the darkness of passion. One does not go far away from you or return to you by walking or by any movement through space. The younger son in your Gospel did not look for horses or carriages or ships;[34] he did not fly on any visible wing, nor did he travel along the way by moving his legs when he went to live in a far country and prodigally dissipated what you, his gentle father, had given him on setting out (Luke 15: 11–32), showing yourself even gentler on his return as a bankrupt. To live there in lustful passion is to live in darkness and to be far from your face.

[33] Though aware of Christian interpreters who dissented from this opinion, Augustine understood the fallen angels to be demonic powers and the gods of polytheism. The paganism pervading classical literature made many Christians reserved towards the study of the subject: cf. VIII. v (10) below. 'Prey': Virgil, *Georgic* II. 60.

[34] Verbal allusion to Plotinus 1. 6. 8. 29 (also a favourite passage for Ambrose); see also below VIII. xix (31). Augustine fuses images from Homer's *Odyssey* and the Parable of the Prodigal Son.

(29)   Look, Lord God, look with patience as you always do. See the exact care with which the sons of men observe the conventions of letters and syllables received from those who so talked before them. Yet they neglect the eternal contracts of lasting salvation received from you. This has gone to such lengths that if someone, who is educated in or is a teacher of the old conventional sounds, pronounces the word 'human' contrary to the school teaching, without pronouncing the initial aspirate, he is socially censured more than if, contrary to your precepts, he were to hate a human being, his fellow-man. It is as if he felt an enemy to be more destructive than his own hatred which has soured the relationship; or as if a man were thought to cause greater damage to someone else by persecuting him than he causes to himself by cherishing hostile attitudes.[35] Certainly the knowledge of letters is not as deepseated in the consciousness as the imprint of the moral conscience, that he is doing to another what he would not wish done to himself (Matt. 7: 12). How mysterious you are, God, dwelling on high in silence! (Isa. 33: 5). You alone are great. By your inexhaustible law you assign penal blindnesses to illicit desires. A man enjoying a reputation for eloquence takes his position before a human judge with a crowd of men standing round and attacks his opponent with ferocious animosity. He is extremely vigilant in precautions against some error in language, but is indifferent to the possibility that the emotional force of his mind may bring about a man's execution.[36]

xix (30)   These were the moral conventions of the world where I, as a wretched boy, lay on the threshold. This was the arena in which I was to wrestle. I was more afraid of committing a barbarism than, if I did commit one, on my guard against feeling envy towards those who did not. I declare and confess this to you, my God. These were the qualities for which I was praised by people whose approval was at that time my criterion of a good life. I did not see the whirlpool of shame into which 'I was cast out of your sight' (Ps. 30: 23). For in those endeavours I was the lowest of the low, shocking even the worldly set by the innumerable lies with which I deceived the slave who took me to school and my teachers and

---

[35] Augustine indirectly echoes Plato (*Gorgias* 469) that it is better to suffer than to do wrong.
[36] Like most of the Church Fathers, Augustine was against capital punishment.

parents because of my love of games, my passion for frivolous
spectacles, and my restless urge to imitate comic scenes.[37] I also
used to steal from my parents' cellar and to pocket food from their
table either to satisfy the demands of gluttony or to have something
to give to boys who, of course, loved playing a game as much as I,
and who would sell me their playthings in return. Even in this game
I was overcome by a vain desire to win and was often guilty of
cheating. Any breach of the rules I would not tolerate and, if I
detected it, would fiercely denounce it, though it was exactly what I
was doing to others. And if I was caught and denounced, I used to
prefer to let my rage have free rein rather than to give ground.

Is that childish innocence? It is not, Lord, is it? I pray you, my
God. Behaviour does not change when one leaves behind domestic
guardians and schoolmasters, nuts and balls and sparrows, to be
succeeded by prefects and kings, gold, estates, and slaves, as one
advances to later stages in life.[38] Likewise canes are replaced by
harsher punishments. So you, our king, have taken the small physical
size of a child as a symbol of humility; that was what you approved
when you said 'Of such is the kingdom of heaven' (Matt. 19: 14).

xx (31)   Yet, Lord, I must give thanks to you, the most excellent
and supremely good Creator and Governor of the universe, my
God, even though by your will I was merely a child. For at that time
I existed, I lived and thought and took care for my self-preservation
(a mark of your profound latent unity whence I derived my being).[39]
An inward instinct told me to take care of the integrity of my senses,
and even in my little thoughts about little matters I took delight in
the truth. I hated to be deceived, I developed a good memory, I
acquired the armoury of being skilled with words, friendship softened
me, I avoided pain, despondency, ignorance. In such a person what
was not worthy of admiration and praise? But every one of these
qualities are gifts of my God: I did not give them to myself. They
are good qualities, and their totality is my self. Therefore he who
made me is good, and he is my good, and I exult to him, (Ps. 2: 11)
for all the good things that I was even as a boy. My sin consisted in
this, that I sought pleasure, sublimity, and truth not in God but in

---

[37] The Latin is ambiguous and may mean 'restless urge for mimicry of comic scenes'.

[38] The theme here is found in Seneca, *De Constantia Sapientis* 12. 1.

[39] Augustine often states the Platonic axiom that existence is good and every being's
instinct for self-preservation reflects the mystery of divine Being and Unity.

his creatures, in myself and other created beings.[40] So it was that I plunged into miseries, confusions, and errors. My God, I give thanks to you, my source of sweet delight, and my glory and my confidence. I thank you for your gifts. Keep them for me, for in this way you will keep me. The talents you have given will increase and be perfected, and I will be with you since it was your gift to me that I exist.

[40] Augustine fuses St Paul (Romans 1) with Plotinus (1. 6. 8).

BOOK II

Adolescence

i (1) I intend to remind myself of my past foulnesses and carnal corruptions, not because I love them but so that I may love you, my God. It is from love of your love that I make the act of recollection. The recalling of my wicked ways is bitter in my memory, but I do it so that you may be sweet to me, a sweetness touched by no deception, a sweetness serene and content. You gathered me together from the state of disintegration in which I had been fruitlessly divided. I turned from unity in you to be lost in multiplicity.[1]

At one time in adolescence I was burning to find satisfaction in hellish pleasures. I ran wild in the shadowy jungle of erotic adventures. 'My beauty wasted away and in your sight I became putrid' (Dan. 10: 8), by pleasing myself and by being ambitious to win human approval.

ii (2) The single desire that dominated my search for delight was simply to love and to be loved. But no restraint was imposed by the exchange of mind with mind, which marks the brightly lit pathway of friendship. Clouds of muddy carnal concupiscence filled the air. The bubbling impulses of puberty befogged and obscured my heart so that it could not see the difference between love's serenity and lust's darkness. Confusion of the two things boiled within me. It seized hold of my youthful weakness sweeping me through the precipitous rocks of desire to submerge me in a whirlpool of vice.[2] Your wrath was heavy upon me and I was unaware of it. I had become deafened by the clanking chain[3] of my mortal condition, the penalty of my pride. I travelled very far from you, and you did not stop me. I was tossed about and spilt, scattered and boiled dry in my fornications. And you were silent. How slow I was to find my joy! At that time you said nothing, and I travelled much further away from

---

[1] The language here is characteristic of Porphyry (e.g. *ep. ad Marcellam* 10, p. 280, 25 Nauck) and Plotinus 6. 6. 1. 5. See below XI. xxix (39).

[2] Echo of Virgil, *Aeneid* 3. 422 (Scylla and Charybdis).

[3] Virgil, *Aeneid* 6. 558.

you into more and more sterile things productive of unhappiness, proud in my self-pity, incapable of rest in my exhaustion.

(3) If only someone could have imposed restraint on my disorder. That would have transformed to good purpose the fleeting experiences of beauty in these lowest of things, and fixed limits to indulgence in their charms. Then the stormy waves of my youth would have finally broken on the shore of marriage. Even so, I could not have been wholly content to confine sexual union to acts intended to procreate children, as your law prescribes, Lord. For you shape the propagation of our mortal race, imposing your gentle hand to soften the brambles which were excluded from your paradise.[4] Your omnipotence is never far from us, even when we are far from you.[5] Alternatively, I ought to have paid more vigilant heed to the voice from your clouds: 'Nevertheless those who are married shall have trouble in the flesh, and I would spare you' (Cor. 7: 28), and 'It is good for a man not to touch a woman' (1 Cor. 7: 1), and 'He who has no wife thinks on the things of God, how he can please God. But he who is joined in marriage thinks on the affairs of the world, how he can please his wife' (1 Cor. 7: 32–3). Had I paid careful attention to these sayings and 'become a eunuch for the sake of the kingdom of heaven' (Matt. 19: 12), I would have been happier finding fulfilment in your embraces.

(4) But I in my misery seethed and followed the driving force of my impulses, abandoning you. I exceeded all the bounds set by your law, and did not escape your chastisement—indeed no mortal can do so. For you were always with me, mercifully punishing me, touching with a bitter taste all my illicit pleasures. Your intention was that I should seek delights unspoilt by disgust and that, in my quest where I could achieve this, I should discover it to be in nothing except you Lord, nothing but you. You 'fashion pain to be a lesson' (Ps. 93: 20 LXX), you 'strike to heal', you bring death upon us so that we should not die apart from you (Deut. 32: 39).[6]

---

[4] Augustine's vision of the sex-life of Adam and Eve before the Fall passed from belief that their union was wholly spiritual (below XIII. xx (28)) to a conviction that it was both spiritual and physical, but controlled by reason and will, never by unreasoning passion, and wholly free of the thorny problems that beset sexuality in common experience.

[5] The Neoplatonist Porphyry wrote: 'He who knows God has God present to him, and he who does not know him is absent from him who is everywhere present.' (*Ad Gaurum* 12. 3). Cf. above, II. ii (3).

[6] Cf. above I. v. (6). The beneficence of punishment is affirmed in 2 Macc. 6: 12–16.

Where was I in the sixteenth year of the age of my flesh? 'Far away in exile from the pleasures of your house' (Mic. 2: 9). Sensual folly assumed domination over me, and I gave myself totally to it in acts allowed by shameful humanity but under your laws illicit. My family did not try to extricate me from my headlong course by means of marriage. The only concern was that I should learn to speak as effectively as possible and carry conviction by my oratory.

iii (5)   During my sixteenth year there was an interruption in my studies. I was recalled from Madauros, the nearby town where I had first lived away from home to learn literature and oratory. During that time funds were gathered in preparation for a more distant absence at Carthage, for which my father had more enthusiasm than cash, since he was a citizen of Thagaste with very modest resources.[7] To whom do I tell these things? Not to you, my God. But before you I declare this to my race, to the human race, though only a tiny part can light on this composition of mine. And why do I include this episode? It is that I and any of my readers may reflect on the great depth from which we have to cry to you (Ps. 129: 1). Nothing is nearer to your ears than a confessing heart and a life grounded in faith (cf. Rom. 10: 9). At that time everybody was full of praise for my father because he spent money on his son beyond the means of his estate, when that was necessary to finance an education entailing a long journey. Many citizens of far greater wealth did nothing of the kind for their children. But this same father did not care what character before you I was developing, or how chaste I was so long as I possessed a cultured tongue—though my culture really meant a desert uncultivated by you, God. You are the one true and good lord of your land, which is my heart.

(6)   In my sixteenth year idleness interposed because of my family's lack of funds. I was on holiday from all schooling and lived with my parents. The thorns of lust rose above my head, and there was no hand to root them out. Indeed, when at the bathhouse my father saw that I was showing signs of virility and the stirrings of adolescence,

---

[7] Augustine's biographer, Possidius, records that his father Patrick sat on the town council or *curia* of Thagaste, a position bringing social credit and financial burdens. The estate was not large, and in relative terms the family was reckoned 'poor', i.e. it possessed only a few slaves for the housework and the land, which in one letter Augustine describes as 'a few acres'. Naturally Augustine's family was not poor in an absolute sense; they were far from being destitute. But 'pauper' is once defined by Ovid as 'a man who knows how many sheep he has'. Patrick is likely to have known how many he had.

he was overjoyed to suppose that he would now be having grand-children, and told my mother so. His delight was that of the intoxication which makes the world oblivious of you, its Creator, and to love your creation instead of you. He was drunk with the invisible wine of his perverse will directed downwards to inferior things.[8] But in my mother's heart you had already begun your temple and the beginning of your holy habitation (Ecclus. 24: 14). My father was still a catechumen and had become that only recently. So she shook with a pious trepidation and a holy fear (2 Cor. 7: 15). For, although I had not yet become a baptized believer, she feared the twisted paths along which walk those who turn their backs and not their face towards you (Jer. 2: 27).

(7) Wretch that I am, do I dare to say that you, my God, were silent when in reality I was travelling farther from you? Was it in this sense that you kept silence to me? Then whose words were they but yours which you were chanting in my ears through my mother, your faithful servant? But nothing of that went down into my heart to issue in action. Her concern (and in the secret of my conscience I recall the memory of her admonition delivered with vehement anxiety) was that I should not fall into fornication, and above all that I should not commit adultery with someone else's wife. These warnings seemed to me womanish advice which I would have blushed to take the least notice of. But they were your warnings and I did not realize it. I believed you were silent, and that it was only she who was speaking, when you were speaking to me through her. In her you were scorned by me, by me her son, the son of your handmaid, your servant (Ps. 115: 16). But I did not realize this and went on my way headlong with such blindness that among my peer group I was ashamed not to be equally guilty of shameful behaviour when I heard them boasting of their sexual exploits. Their pride was the more aggressive, the more debauched their acts were; they derived pleasure not merely from the lust of the act but also from the admiration it evoked. What is more worthy of censure than vice? Yet I went deeper into vice to avoid being despised, and when there was no act by admitting to which I could rival my depraved companions, I used to pretend I had done things I had not done at

---

[8] Augustine's father celebrated the signs of his son's virility by becoming inebriated. The implications of this passage on Patrick's hopes for a grandchild appear the only evidence to suggest that Augustine was the eldest of the children.

all, so that my innocence should not lead my companions to scorn my lack of courage, and lest my chastity be taken as a mark of inferiority.[9]

(8)   Such were the companions with whom I made my way through the streets of Babylon.[10] With them I rolled in its dung as if rolling in spices and precious ointments (S. of S. 5. 4: 14). To tie me down the more tenaciously to Babylon's belly, the invisible enemy trampled on me (Ps. 55: 3) and seduced me because I was in the mood to be seduced. The mother of my flesh already had fled from the centre of Babylon (Jer. 51: 6), but still lingered in the outskirts of the city. Although she had warned me to guard my virginity, she did not seriously pay heed to what her husband had told her about me, and which she felt to hold danger for the future: for she did not seek to restrain my sexual drive within the limit of the marriage bond, if it could not be cut back to the quick. The reason why she showed no such concern was that she was afraid that the hope she placed in me could be impeded by a wife. This was not the hope which my mother placed in you for the life to come, but the hope which my parents entertained for my career that I might do well out of the study of literature. Both of them, as I realized, were very ambitious for me: my father because he hardly gave a thought to you at all, and his ambitions for me were concerned with mere vanities; my mother because she thought it would do no harm and would be a help to set me on the way towards you, if I studied the traditional pattern of a literary education. That at least is my conjecture as I try to recall the characters of my parents.

The reins were relaxed to allow me to amuse myself. There was no strict discipline to keep me in check, which led to an unbridled dissoluteness in many different directions. In all of this there was a thick mist shutting me off from the brightness of your face, my God, and my iniquity as it were 'burst out from my fatness' (Ps. 72: 7).

iv (9)   Theft receives certain punishment by your law (Exod. 20: 15), Lord, and by the law written in the hearts of men (Rom. 2: 14) which not even iniquity itself destroys. For what thief can with

---

[9] The theme of this paragraph is found in Ambrose, *Noah* 22, 81.

[10] Augustine's portrait of his wild years may be compared with the savage contemporary portrait of the riff-raff of Rome about 380 by the pagan historian Ammianus Marcellinus, who speaks of people spending their entire lives on alcohol, gambling, brothels, and public shows (28. 4. 28).

equanimity endure being robbed by another thief? He cannot tolerate it even if he is rich and the other is destitute. I wanted to carry out an act of theft and did so, driven by no kind of need other than my inner lack of any sense of, or feeling for, justice. Wickedness filled me. I stole something which I had in plenty and of much better quality. My desire was to enjoy not what I sought by stealing but merely the excitement of thieving and the doing of what was wrong. There was a pear tree near our vineyard laden with fruit, though attractive in neither colour nor taste. To shake the fruit off the tree and carry off the pears, I and a gang of naughty adolescents set off late at night after (in our usual pestilential way) we had continued our game in the streets. We carried off a huge load of pears. But they were not for our feasts but merely to throw to the pigs. Even if we ate a few, nevertheless our pleasure lay in doing what was not allowed.

Such was my heart, O God, such was my heart. You had pity on it when it was at the bottom of the abyss. Now let my heart tell you what it was seeking there in that I became evil for no reason.[11] I had no motive for my wickedness except wickedness itself. It was foul, and I loved it. I loved the self-destruction, I loved my fall, not the object for which I had fallen but my fall itself. My depraved soul leaped down from your firmament to ruin.[12] I was seeking not to gain anything by shameful means, but shame for its own sake.

v (10)   There is beauty in lovely physical objects, as in gold and silver and all other such things. When the body touches such things, much significance attaches to the rapport of the object with the touch. Each of the other senses has its own appropriate mode of response to physical things. Temporal honour and the power of giving orders and of being in command have their own kind of dignity, though this is also the origin of the urge to self-assertion. Yet in the acquisition of all these sources of social status, one must not depart from you, Lord, nor deviate from your law. The life which we live in this world has its attractiveness because of a certain measure in its beauty and its harmony with all these inferior objects that are beautiful. Human friendship is also a nest of love and gentleness because of the unity it brings about between

[11] Echo of Sallust's language about Catiline. Augustine presents himself as a new Catiline.

[12] Like Lucifer.

many souls. Yet sin is committed for the sake of all these things and others of this kind when, in consequence of an immoderate urge towards those things which are at the bottom end of the scale of good,[13] we abandon the higher and supreme goods, that is you, Lord God, and your truth and your law (Ps. 118: 142). These inferior goods have their delights, but not comparable to my God who has made them all. It is in him that the just person takes delight; he is the joy of those who are true of heart (Ps. 63: 11).

(11) When a crime is under investigation to discover the motive for which it was done, the accusation is not usually believed except in cases where the appetite to obtain (or the fear of losing) one of those goods which we have called inferior appears a plausible possibility. They are beautiful and attractive even if, in comparison with the higher goods which give true happiness, they are mean and base. A man committed murder. Why? Because he loved another's wife or his property; or he wanted to acquire money to live on by plundering his goods; or he was afraid of losing his own property by the action of his victim; or he had suffered injury and burned with desire for revenge. No one would commit murder without a motive, merely because he took pleasure in killing. Who would believe that? It was said of one brutal and cruel man [Catiline] that he was evil and savage without reason.[14] Yet the preceding passage gave the motive: 'lest disuse might make his hand or mind slow to react'. Why did he wish for that? Why so? His objective was to capture the city by violent crimes to obtain honours, government, and wealth; to live without fear of the laws and without the difficulty of attaining his ambitions because of the poverty of his family estate and his known criminal record. No, not even Catiline himself loved his crimes; something else motivated him to commit them.

vi (12) Wretch that I was, what did I love in you, my act of theft, that crime which I did at night in the sixteenth year of my life? There was nothing beautiful about you, my thieving. Indeed do you exist at all for me to be addressing you?

The fruit which we stole was beautiful because it was your creation, most beautiful of all Beings, maker of all things, the good

---

[13] Throughout his writings Augustine holds to a doctrine of gradations of goodness. The good of the body is inferior to that of the soul; the will, in itself midway, may turn to higher or to lower things, and may err by preferring inferior goods to superior.

[14] Sallust, *Catiline* 16 (also cited by Augustine, *Sermon on Ps. 108*, 3).

God, God the highest good and my true good. The fruit was beautiful, but was not that which my miserable soul coveted. I had a quantity of better pears. But those I picked solely with the motive of stealing. I threw away what I had picked. My feasting was only on the wickedness which I took pleasure in enjoying. If any of those pears entered my mouth, my criminality was the piquant sauce. And now, Lord my God, I inquire what was the nature of my pleasure in the theft. The act has nothing lovely about it, none of the loveliness found in equity and prudence, or in the human mind whether in the memory or in the senses or in physical vitality. Nor was it beautiful in the way the stars are, noble in their courses, or earth and sea full of newborn creatures which, as they are born, take the place of those which die;[15] not even in the way that specious vices have a flawed reflection of beauty.

(13) Pride imitates what is lofty; but you alone are God most high above all things. What does ambition seek but honour and glory? Yet you alone are worthy of honour and are glorious for eternity. The cruelty of powerful people aims to arouse fear. Who is to be feared but God alone? What can be seized or stolen from his power? When or where or how or by whom? Soft endearments are intended to arouse love. But there are no caresses tenderer than your charity, and no object of love is more healthy than your truth, beautiful and luminous beyond all things. Curiosity appears to be a zeal for knowledge; yet you supremely know all. Ignorance and stupidity are given the names of simplicity and innocence; but there is no greater simplicity than in you. And what greater innocence than yours, whereas to evil men their own works are damaging? Idleness appears as desire for a quiet life; yet can rest be assured apart from the Lord? Luxury wants to be called abundance and satiety; but you are fullness and the inexhaustible treasure of incorruptible pleasure. Prodigality presents itself under the shadow of generosity; but you are the rich bestower of all good things. Avarice wishes to have large possessions; you possess everything. Envy contends about excellence; but what is more excellent than you? Anger seeks revenge; who avenges with greater justice than you? Fear quails before sudden and unexpected events attacking things which are

---

[15] Augustine regarded the cycle of birth and death as 'beautiful'; i.e. death is evil to the individual, not to the race.

loved, and takes precautions for their safety; to you is anything unexpected or sudden? Or who can take away from you what you love? There is no reliable security except with you. Regret wastes away for the loss of things which cupidity delighted in. Its wish would be that nothing be taken away, just as nothing can be taken from you.

(14) So the soul fornicates (Ps. 72: 27) when it is turned away from you and seeks outside you the pure and clear intentions which are not to be found except by returning to you. In their perverted way all humanity imitates you. Yet they put themselves at a distance from you and exalt themselves against you. But even by thus imitating you they acknowledge that you are the creator of all nature and so concede that there is no place where one can entirely escape from you. Therefore in that act of theft what was the object of my love, and in what way did I viciously and perversely imitate my Lord? Was my pleasure to break your law, but by deceit since I had not the power to do that by force? Was I acting like a prisoner with restricted liberty who does without punishment what is not permitted, thereby making an assertion of possessing a dim resemblance to omnipotence? Here is a runaway slave fleeing his master and pursuing a shadow (Job 7: 2). What rottenness! What a monstrous life and what an abyss of death! Was it possible to take pleasure in what was illicit for no reason other than that it was not allowed?

vii (15) 'What shall I render to the Lord?' (Ps. 115: 2) who recalls these things to my memory, but my soul feels no fear from the recollection. I will love you, Lord, and I will give thanks and confession to your name because you have forgiven me such great evils and my nefarious deeds. I attribute to your grace and mercy that you have melted my sins away like ice (Ecclus. 3: 17). I also attribute to your grace whatever evil acts I have not done. What could I not have done when I loved gratuitous crime? I confess that everything has been forgiven, both the evil things I did of my own accord, and those which I did not do because of your guidance.

No one who considers his frailty would dare to attribute to his own strength his chastity and innocence, so that he has less cause to love you—as if he had less need of your mercy by which you forgive the sins of those converted to you. If man is called by you, follows your voice, and has avoided doing those acts which I am recalling and avowing in my own life, he should not mock the healing of a sick man by the Physician, whose help has kept him from falling sick, or at least enabled him to be less gravely ill. He should love you no less, indeed even more; for he sees that the one who delivered me from the great sicknesses of my sins is also he through whom he may see that he himself has not been a victim of the same great sicknesses.

viii (16) 'What fruit had I', wretched boy, in these things (Rom. 6: 21) which I now blush to recall, above all in that theft in which I loved nothing but the theft itself? The theft itself was a nothing, and for that reason I was the more miserable. Yet had I been alone I would not have done it—I remember my state of mind to be thus at the time—alone I would never have done it. Therefore my love in that act was to be associated with the gang in whose company I did it. Does it follow that I loved something other than the theft? No, nothing else in reality because association with the gang is also a nothing. What is it in reality? Who can teach me that, but he who 'illuminates my heart' (Ecclus. 2: 10) and disperses the shadows in it? What else has stirred my mind to ask and discuss and consider this question? If I had liked the pears which I stole and actually desired to enjoy them, I could by myself have committed that wicked act, had it been enough to attain the pleasure which I sought. I would not have needed to inflame the itch of my cupidity through the excitement generated by sharing the guilt with others. But my pleasure was not in the pears; it was in the crime itself, done in association with a sinful group.

ix (17) What was my state of mind? It is quite certain that it was utterly shameful and a disgrace to me that I had it. Yet what was it? 'Who understands his sins?' (Job 10: 15). It was all done for a giggle, as if our hearts were tickled to think we were deceiving those who would not think us capable of such behaviour and would have profoundly disapproved. Why then did I derive pleasure from an act I would not have done on my own? Is it that nobody can easily laugh when alone? Certainly no one readily laughs when alone; yet sometimes laughter overcomes individuals when no one else is present if their senses or their mind perceive something utterly absurd. But alone I would not have done it, could not conceivably have done it by myself. See, before you, my God, the living memory of my soul. Alone I would not have committed that crime, in which my pleasure lay not in what I was stealing but in the act of theft. But had I been alone, it would have given me absolutely no pleasure, nor would I have committed it. Friendship can be a dangerous enemy, a seduction of the mind lying beyond the reach of investigation.[16] Out of a game and a jest came an avid desire to do injury and an appetite to inflict loss on someone else without any motive on my part of personal gain, and no pleasure in settling a score. As soon as the words are spoken 'Let us go and do it', one is ashamed not to be shameless.

x (18)   Who can untie this extremely twisted and tangled knot? It is a foul affair, I have no wish to give attention to it; I have no desire to contemplate it. My desire is for you, justice and innocence, you are lovely and splendid to honest eyes; the satiety of your love is insatiable. With you is utter peace and a life immune from disturbance. The person who enters into you 'enters into the joy of the Lord' (Matt. 25: 21), and will not be afraid; he will find himself in the supreme Good where it is supremely good to be. As an adolescent I went astray from you (Ps. 118: 76), my God, far from your unmoved stability. I became to myself a region of destitution.[17]

---

[16] Similarly IX. ii. (2).

[17] The Prodigal Son is fused with a Neoplatonic theme of the soul's destitution without God, which is taken up at the beginning of book III and again in VII. x (16). Destitution in the soul distant from God is a theme in Porphyry (*De abstinentia* 3. 27 and *Sententiae* 40), based on Plato's *Symposium*.

BOOK III

Student at Carthage

i (1)   I came to Carthage and all around me hissed a cauldron of illicit loves. As yet I had never been in love and I longed to love; and from a subconscious poverty of mind I hated the thought of being less inwardly destitute. I sought an object for my love; I was in love with love, and I hated safety and a path free of snares (Wisd. 14: 11; Ps. 90: 3). My hunger was internal, deprived of inward food, that is of you yourself, my God. But that was not the kind of hunger I felt. I was without any desire for incorruptible nourishment, not because I was replete with it, but the emptier I was, the more unappetizing such food became. So my soul was in rotten health. In an ulcerous condition it thrust itself to outward things, miserably avid to be scratched by contact with the world of the senses. Yet physical things had no soul. Love lay outside their range. To me it was sweet to love and to be loved, the more so if I could also enjoy the body of the beloved. I therefore polluted the spring water of friendship with the filth of concupiscence. I muddied its clear stream by the hell of lust, and yet, though foul and immoral, in my excessive vanity, I used to carry on in the manner of an elegant man about town. I rushed headlong into love, by which I was longing to be captured. 'My God, my mercy' (Ps. 58: 18) in your goodness you mixed in much vinegar with that sweetness. My love was returned and in secret I attained the joy that enchains. I was glad to be in bondage, tied with troublesome chains, with the result that I was flogged with the red-hot iron rods of jealousy, suspicion, fear, anger, and contention.[1]

ii (2)   I was captivated by theatrical shows. They were full of representations of my own miseries and fuelled my fire. Why is it that a person should wish to experience suffering by watching grievous and tragic events which he himself would not wish to endure? Nevertheless he wants to suffer the pain given by being a spectator of these sufferings, and the pain itself is his pleasure.

---

[1] Beating with red-hot rods was part of the standard arsenal of the torturer, normally employed in Roman lawcourts on naked bodies in criminal cases to secure evidence, especially from slaves.

What is this but amazing folly? For the more anyone is moved by these scenes, the less free he is from similar passions. Only, when he himself suffers, it is called misery; when he feels compassion for others, it is called mercy.[2] But what quality of mercy is it in fictitious and theatrical inventions? A member of the audience is not excited to offer help, but invited only to grieve. The greater his pain, the greater his approval of the actor in these representations. If the human calamities, whether in ancient histories or fictitious myths, are so presented that the theatregoer is not caused pain, he walks out of the theatre disgusted and highly critical. But if he feels pain, he stays riveted in his seat enjoying himself.[3]

(3)   Tears and agonies, therefore, are objects of love. Certainly everyone wishes to enjoy himself. Is it that while no one wants to be miserable, yet it is agreeable to feel merciful? Mercy cannot exist apart from suffering. Is that the sole reason why agonies are an object of love? This feeling flows from the stream of friendship;[4] but where does it go? Where does it flow to? Why does it run down into the torrent of boiling pitch, the monstrous heats of black desires into which it is transformed? From a heavenly serenity it is altered by its own consent into something twisted and distorted. Does this mean mercy is to be rejected? Not in the least. At times, therefore, sufferings can be proper objects of love. But, my soul, be on your guard against uncleanness, under the protection of my God, 'the God of our fathers, to be praised and exalted above all for all ages' (Dan. 3: 52–5); be on your guard against uncleanness. Even today I am not unmoved to pity. But at that time at the theatres I shared the joy of lovers when they wickedly found delight in each other, even though their actions in the spectacle on the stage were imaginary; when, moreover, they lost each other, I shared their sadness by a feeling of compassion. Nevertheless, in both there was pleasure. Today I have more pity for a person who rejoices in wickedness than for a person who has the feeling of

---

[2] Echo of Cicero, *Pro Ligorio* 38.

[3] This passage is the most extended ancient discussion of tragic pity and catharsis, a theme famous since Aristotle, whose texts on this theme were not read by Augustine and his contemporaries. Augustine is closer to Plato, *Republic* 10. 606–7, and *Philebus* 48ab. As bishop, Augustine knew many of his people liked going to the theatre, and deplored it (*De catechizandis rudibus* 11 and 48) largely because of the frequently erotic content of the shows, but also because of the fictional character of the plays, fiction being, to his mind, a form of mendacity.   [4] On tension between sex and friendship cf. IV. ix (14).

having suffered hard knocks by being deprived of a pernicious pleasure or having lost a source of miserable felicity. This is surely a more authentic compassion; for the sorrow contains no element of pleasure.

Even if we approve of a person who, from a sense of duty in charity, is sorry for a wretch, yet he who manifests fraternal compassion would prefer that there be no cause for sorrow. It is only if there could be a malicious good will (which is impossible) that someone who truly and sincerely felt compassion would wish wretches to exist so as to be objects of compassion. Therefore some kind of suffering is commendable, but none is lovable. You, Lord God, lover of souls, show a compassion far purer and freer of mixed motives than ours; for no suffering injures you. 'And who is sufficient for these things?' (2 Cor. 2: 16).

(4) But at that time, poor thing that I was, I loved to suffer and sought out occasions for such suffering. So when an actor on stage gave a fictional imitation of someone else's misfortunes, I was the more pleased; and the more vehement the attraction for me, the more the actor compelled my tears to flow. There can be no surprise that an unhappy sheep wandering from your flock[5] and impatient of your protection was infected by a disgusting sore. Hence came my love for sufferings, but not of a kind that pierced me very deeply; for my longing was not to experience myself miseries such as I saw on stage. I wanted only to hear stories and imaginary legends of sufferings which, as it were, scratched me on the surface. Yet like the scratches of fingernails, they produced inflamed spots, pus, and repulsive sores. That was my kind of life. Surely, my God, it was no real life at all?

iii (5) Your mercy faithfully hovered over me from afar. In what iniquities was I wasting myself! I pursued a sacrilegious quest for knowledge, which led me, a deserter from you, down to faithless depths and the fraudulent service of devils. The sacrifices I offered them were my evil acts. And in all this I experienced your chastisement. During the celebration of your solemn rites within the walls of your Church, I even dared to lust after a girl and to start an affair that would procure the fruit of death.[6] So you beat me with heavy

---

[5] Reminiscence of Virgil, *Eclogue* 3. 3; cf. Luke 15: 4 ff.
[6] That is, sin: Rom. 7: 5.

punishments, but not the equivalent of my guilt; O my God, my great mercy, my refuge (Ps. 58: 18, 143: 2) from the terrible dangers in which I was wandering. My stiff neck took me further and further away from you. I loved my own ways, not yours. The liberty I loved was merely that of a runaway.[7]

(6)   My studies which were deemed respectable had the objective of leading me to distinction as an advocate in the lawcourts,[8] where one's reputation is high in proportion to one's success in deceiving people. The blindness of humanity is so great that people are actually proud of their blindness. I was already top of the class in the rhetor's school, and was pleased with myself for my success and was inflated with conceit. Yet I was far quieter than the other students[9] (as you know, Lord), and had nothing whatever to do with the vandalism which used to be carried out by the Wreckers. This sinister and diabolical self-designation was a kind of mark of their urbane sophistication. I lived among them shamelessly ashamed of not being one of the gang. I kept company with them and sometimes delighted in their friendship, though I always held their actions in abhorrence. The Wreckers used wantonly to persecute shy and unknown freshmen. Their aim was to persecute them by mockery and so to feed their own malevolent amusement. Nothing more resembles the behaviour of devils than their manner of carrying on. So no truer name could be given them than the Wreckers. Clearly they are themselves wrecked first of all and perverted by evil spirits, who are mocking them and seducing them in the very acts by which they love to mock and deceive others.

iv (7)   This was the society in which at a vulnerable age I was to study the textbooks on eloquence. I wanted to distinguish myself as an orator for a damnable and conceited purpose, namely delight in human vanity. Following the usual curriculum I had already come across a book by a certain Cicero,[10] whose language (but not his

---

[7] Runaway slaves in antiquity were rigorously pursued. Churches provided temporary asylum in cases where inhuman maltreatment was the cause of flight. But to take in a runaway was possible only for the rich and powerful. The liberty enjoyed, therefore, was that of an escaped prisoner, hunted by the authorities.   [8] Echo of Ovid, *Fasti* 4. 188.

[9] A contemporary student later recalled the young Augustine as being a quiet and bookish man (*ep.* 93. 51).

[10] 'A certain Cicero' might seem cold and distant were it not that the same idiom is used for the apostle Paul in XII. xv (20); i.e. it is a rhetorical convention of the time. The antithesis between Cicero's style and his heart (*pectus*) is genuinely negative: to a Christian, Cicero belonged to another culture.

heart) almost everyone admires. That book of his contains an exhortation to study philosophy and is entitled *Hortensius*.[11] The book changed my feelings. It altered my prayers, Lord, to be towards you yourself. It gave me different values and priorities. Suddenly every vain hope became empty to me, and I longed for the immortality of wisdom with an incredible ardour in my heart. I began to rise up to return to you. For I did not read the book for a sharpening of my style, which was what I was buying with my mother's financial support now that I was 18 years old and my father had been dead for two years. I was impressed not by the book's refining effect on my style and literary expression but by the content.[12]

(8) My God, how I burned, how I burned with longing to leave earthly things and fly back to you. I did not know what you were doing with me. For 'with you is wisdom' (Job 12: 13, 16). 'Love of wisdom' is the meaning of the Greek word *philosophia*.[13] This book kindled my love for it. There are some people who use philosophy to lead people astray. They lend colour to their errors and paint them over by using a great and acceptable and honourable name. Almost all those who in the author's times and earlier behaved in this way are noted in that book and refuted. That text is a clear demonstration of the salutary admonition given by your Spirit through your good and devoted servant (Paul): 'See that none deceives you by philosophy and vain seduction following human tradition; following the elements of this world and not following Christ; in him dwells all the fullness of divinity in bodily form' (Col. 2: 8–9). At that time, as you know, light of my heart, I did not yet know these words of the apostle. Nevertheless, the one thing that delighted me in Cicero's exhortation was the advice 'not to study one particular sect but to love and seek and pursue and hold fast and strongly embrace wisdom itself, wherever found'. One thing

[11] Cicero's *Hortensius*, composed in 45 BC near the end of his life, is lost except for quotations (many in Augustine). The work rebutted Hortensius' opinion that philosophical study has no social utility and does not contribute to human happiness. Cicero depended much on Aristotle's *Protreptikos* (also extant only in fragments), notably for the argument that only a philosopher can judge the truth of Hortensius' opinion, which is itself a philosophical statement. As book X of *Confessions* shows, Augustine was influenced by Cicero's analysis of the sources of happiness.

[12] Among Augustine's sharp criticisms of contemporary culture of his time is the proposition that it valued form far higher than content.

[13] This sentence comes from Cicero's *Hortensius*.

alone put a brake on my intense enthusiasm—that the name of Christ was not contained in the book. This name, by your mercy Lord (Ps. 24: 7), this name of my Saviour your Son, my infant heart had piously drunk in with my mother's milk, and at a deep level I retained the memory. Any book which lacked this name, however well written or polished or true, could not entirely grip me.

v (9) I therefore decided to give attention to the holy scriptures and to find out what they were like. And this is what met me: something neither open to the proud nor laid bare to mere children; a text lowly to the beginner but, on further reading, of mountainous difficulty and enveloped in mysteries. I was not in any state to be able to enter into that, or to bow my head to climb its steps. What I am now saying did not then enter my mind when I gave my attention to the scripture. It seemed to me unworthy in comparison with the dignity of Cicero.[14] My inflated conceit shunned the Bible's restraint, and my gaze never penetrated to its inwardness. Yet the Bible was composed in such a way that as beginners mature, its meaning grows with them. I disdained to be a little beginner. Puffed up with pride, I considered myself a mature adult.

vi (10) That explains why I fell in with men proud of their slick talk, very earthly-minded and loquacious. In their mouths were the devil's traps and a birdlime compounded of a mixture of the syllables of your name, and that of the Lord Jesus Christ, and that of the Paraclete, the Comforter, the Holy Spirit.[15] These names were never absent from their lips; but it was no more than sound and noise with their tongue. Otherwise their heart was empty of truth. They used to say 'Truth, truth', and they had a lot to tell me about it; but there was never any truth in them. They uttered false statements not only about you who really are the Truth, but also about the elements of the world, your creation. On that subject the

---

[14] The humble style of the Bible, together with a concern for maintaining the family property, is mentioned by Augustine as a major deterrent to conversion for the educated and well-to-do classes (*De catechizandis rudibus* 13). The second-century Old Latin (i.e. pre-Jerome) version was painfully close to translationese for large parts of the Old Testament. On the other hand, the sublimity of Genesis 1 and the prologue of St John's Gospel moved some non-Christian readers to deep admiration.

[15] The Manichees claimed to be authentic Christians, orthodox church members having in their view only half the truth, and taught a version of the doctrine of the Trinity, a Christology which excluded the reality of the humanity of Christ but spoke of Jesus as redeemer, and a doctrine that the Paraclete is the other self of Mani.

philosophers have said things which are true, but even them I would think to be no final authority for love of you, my supremely good Father, beauty of all things beautiful. Truth, truth: how in my inmost being the very marrow of my mind sighed for you! Those people used to sound off about you to me frequently and repeatedly with mere assertions and with the support of many huge tomes.[16] To meet my hunger, instead of you they brought me a diet of the sun and moon, your beautiful works—but they are your works, not you yourself, nor indeed the first of your works. For priority goes to your spiritual creation rather than the physical order, however heavenly and full of light.[17] But for myself, my hunger and thirst were not even for the spiritual creation but for you yourself, the truth 'in whom there is no changing nor shadow caused by any revolving' (Jas. 1: 17). The dishes they placed before me contained splendid hallucinations. Indeed one would do better to love this visible sun, which at least is truly evident to the eyes, than those false mythologies which use the eyes to deceive the mind. Nevertheless, because I took them to be you, I ate—not indeed with much of an appetite, for the taste in my mouth was not that of yourself. You were not those empty fictions, and I derived no nourishment from them but was left more exhausted than before.

Food pictured in dreams[18] is extremely like food received in the waking state; yet sleepers receive no nourishment, they are simply sleeping. But those fantasies had not the least resemblance to you as you have now told me, because they were physical images, fictional bodily shapes. But more certain objects of knowledge are the actually existing bodies which we see with our physical sight, whether they are celestial or earthly. We see them just as beasts and birds do, and they are more certain than the images we form of them. And yet again the pictures of these realities which our imagination forms are more reliable than the mythological pictures

[16] Manichees had exquisitely decorated liturgical books, finely bound, as orthodox Churches outside great cities, had not. Sun and moon they venerated as divine, or at least as residences for divine beings in transit in the celestial realm.

[17] That God first created a spiritual creation called 'heaven' in Gen. 1: 1, and unformed matter called 'earth' which was then given form, is a theme of book XII and of the contemporary *De Genesi contra Manichaeos* 1. 7. 11.

[18] Dreams were a lifelong interest for Augustine; see X. xxx (41) below. The vividness of dreams, indistinguishable from actuality, he regarded as deceptive. On the other hand, he knew of many converted to God through dreams, or guided in decisions. The subject was associated with the ancient discussions of the nature of inspiration.

of vast and unlimited entities whose being, by an extension of our image-making of real objects, we may postulate, but which do not exist at all. Such were the empty phantoms with which I was fed or rather was not fed.

But you, my love, for whom I faint that I may receive strength (2 Cor. 11: 10), you are not the bodies which we see, though they be up in heaven, nor even any object up there lying beyond our sight. For you have made these bodies, and you do not even hold them to be among the greatest of your creatures. How far removed you are from those fantasies of mine, fantasies of physical entities which have no existence! We have more reliable knowledge in our images of bodies which really exist, and the bodies are more certain than the images. But you are no body. Nor are you soul, which is the life of bodies; for the life of bodies is superior to bodies themselves, and a more certain object of knowledge.[19] But you are the life of souls, the life of lives. You live in dependence only on yourself, and you never change, life of my soul.

(11)   At that time where were you in relation to me? Far distant. Indeed I wandered far away, separated from you, not even granted to share in the husks of the pigs, whom I was feeding with husks.[20] How superior are the fables of the masters of literature and poets to these deceptive traps! For verses, poems, and 'the flight of Medea'[21] are certainly more useful than the Five Elements which take on different colours, each in accordance with one of the Five Caverns of Darkness[22]—things which have no reality whatever and kill anyone who believes they have. Verses and poetry I can transform into real nourishment. 'Medea flying through the air' I might recite, but would not assert to be fact. Even if I heard someone reciting the passage, I would not believe it. Yet the other [Manichee] myths I did believe. Wretched man that I was, by what steps was I brought

---

[19] It is axiomatic for Augustine that what the mind knows by discernment of eternal, metaphysical truth is more certain than its judgement of the perceptions of the five senses, which are unreliable.

[20] The husks of Luke 15: 16 are for Jerome (*ep.* 21. 13. 4) pagan literature. Apparently Augustine had become bored by the texts he had to teach his pupils (the pigs!).

[21] Medea's flight (cf. Ovid, *Metamorphoses* 7. 219–36), also mentioned elsewhere in Augustine's early writings (*Solil.* 2. 29; *ep.* 7. 4; *De moribus ecclesiae* 2. 14), was probably a standard subject for rhetorical exercises.

[22] In Manichee myth the Five Elements dwell in caverns of darkness, water, wind, fire, and smoke, productive respectively of reptiles, fish, birds, quadrupeds, and bipeds (Augustine, *De moribus* 2. 9. 14; Simplicius, *Commentary on Epictetus* 34).

down to the depths of hell, there to toil and sweat from lack of truth! For I sought for you, my God (I confess to you who took pity on me even when I did not yet confess). In seeking for you I followed not the intelligence of the mind, by which you willed that I should surpass the beasts, but the mind of the flesh. But you were more inward than my most inward part and higher than the highest element within me.

I had stumbled on that bold-faced woman, lacking in prudence, who in Solomon's allegory sits on a chair outside her door and says 'Enjoy a meal of secret bread and drink sweet stolen water' (Prov. 9: 17). She seduced me; for she found me living outside myself, seeing only with the eye of the flesh, and chewing over in myself such food as I had devoured by means of that eye.

vii (12) I was unaware of the existence of another reality, that which truly is,[23] and it was as if some sharp intelligence were persuading me to consent to the stupid deceivers when they asked me: 'Where does evil come from? and is God confined within a corporeal form? has he hair and nails? and can those be considered righteous who had several wives at the same time and killed people and offered animals in sacrifice?'[24] In my ignorance I was disturbed by these questions, and while travelling away from the truth I thought I was going towards it. I did not know that evil has no existence except as a privation of good, down to that level which is altogether without being. How could I see this when for me 'to see' meant a physical act of looking with the eyes and of forming an image in the mind? I had not realized God is a Spirit (John 4: 24), not a figure whose limbs have length and breadth and who has a mass. For mass is less in a part than in its whole, and if it is unlimited, it is less in a part defined within a given space than in its unlimited extension.[25] It is not everywhere entire as a Spirit and as

[23] The Platonic notion of degrees of being-and-goodness, a hierarchy in which every existent is good in its own order, made possible the relativization of evil central to Plato's vindication of divine power and goodness. Cf. II. v. (10) above.

[24] Manichees strongly attacked the book of Genesis (that 'man is made in God's image' assumes God to have human physical characteristics?), the polygamy of the patriarchs, and the character of Moses for his murder of the Egyptian (Exod. 2: 12). They thought the Old Testament animal sacrifices indistinguishable from paganism.

[25] Plotinus (6; 4–5) has two intricate tracts arguing (in commentary on Plato, *Parmenides* 131B) that omnipresence is a distinct concept from that of a universal physical diffusion of something with material magnitude. Augustine's language here (and in VII. i. (1)) is close to Plotinus 6. 5. 4. 5 ff.

God. Moreover, I was wholly ignorant of what it is in ourselves which gives us being, and how scripture is correct in saying that we are 'in God's image' (Gen. 1: 27).

(13)   I also did not know that true inward justice which judges not by custom but by the most righteous law of almighty God. By this law the moral customs of different regions and periods were adapted to their places and times, while that law itself remains unaltered everywhere and always.[26] It is not one thing at one place or time, another thing at another. Accordingly Abraham and Isaac and Jacob and Moses and David, and all those praised by the mouth of God were righteous. When untrained minds judge them wicked, they judge 'by man's day' (1 Cor. 4: 3) and assess the customs of the entire race by the criterion of their own moral code. It is as if a man, ignorant of which piece of armour is designed for which part of the body, should want to cover the head with a greave or put on his leg a helmet, and then complain that it is not a good fit. Or it is as if on a public holiday when trading is prohibited after noon, someone is furious not to be allowed to sell in the afternoon something which he was at liberty to sell in the morning. Or as if in a house one sees something being touched with the hands by a particular slave, which the waiter who serves the wine cups is not allowed to do; or as if something is allowed to happen behind the stables which is not permitted in the dining-room, and a man is indignant on the ground that, though it is one house and one family, the same liberties are not given to all members to do what they please anywhere they like.

This is the style of those who are irate when they hear that something was allowed to the just in that age which is not granted to the just now, and that God gave one command to the former and another to the latter for reasons of a change in historical circumstances, though both ancient and modern people are bound to submit to the same justice. Yet in one and the same person on a single day and in the same house they may see one action fitting for one member to perform, another action fitting for another. What has been allowed during a long period is not permitted one hour later. An act allowed or commanded in one corner is forbidden and

---

[26] The argument here about the relativity of positive laws is akin to that in Cicero's *Republic* III xi, 18–19; xxii, 33.

subject to punishment if done in an adjacent corner. Does that mean that justice is 'liable to variation and change'?[27] No. The times which it rules over are not identical, for the simple reason that they are times. But the grasp of human beings, 'whose life on earth is short' (Wisd. 15: 9), is not competent to harmonize cause and effect valid in earlier ages and among other nations of which they have no experience, in relation to the times and peoples of whom they have direct knowledge. Yet they can easily observe in a single body or at one time or in one house what is fitting for one member, at what moments, and for which parts or persons. By the one variation they are outraged, with the other they see no difficulty.

(14) At that time I did not know these things or give any thought to them. On all sides they hit me in the eye, and I failed to see them. When I wrote poetry,[28] I was not allowed to place a foot where I wished, but had to use different kinds of feet at different points in different metres. Even in the same verse one could not put the same foot in any and every place. The art of poetic composition did not have different rules in different places, but had all the same rules at all times. I had not the insight to see how the justice, to which good and holy people were obliged to submit, embraces within its principles all that it prescribes for all times in a far more excellent and sublime way, and, although it is in no respect subject to variation, yet it is not given all at once, but at various times it prescribed in differing contexts what is proper for the circumstances.[29] In my blindness I reprehended the holy fathers not only for acting at the time as God commanded and inspired them, but also for predicting the future as God revealed it to them.[30]

viii (15) Can it be wrong at any time or place to love God with all your heart and with all your soul and with all your mind and to love

---

[27] Echo of Virgil, *Aeneid* 4. 569 (of woman).

[28] Augustine was soon to win a public poetry competition (IV. iii (5)). The first five books of his work *On Music* are devoted to metre. The only surviving verse from his pen is three lines of an evening hymn sung at the lighting of the candle (*City of God* 15. 22).

[29] Augustine's ethic regards the Golden Rule as absolute, its application being relative to the situation and to the motive or intention of the doer. The criterion of every moral precept is love (*Enchiridion* 121). Nakedness is right in the baths, wrong at a dinner-party or lawcourt (*De natura boni* 23; *De doctrina christiana* 3. 12. 18). Nevertheless, no circumstances or intentions could make unnatural sexual acts acceptable. (Rom. 1: 24–8).

[30] The Manichees entirely rejected the orthodox belief that the Hebrew prophets predicted gospel events and the mission of the Church. Augustine answered at length in *Contra Faustum* 12–13, written at the same time as the *Confessions*.

your neighbour as yourself (Matt. 22: 37, 39)? Therefore shameful acts[31] which are contrary to nature, such as the acts of the Sodomites (Gen. 19: 5 ff.), are everywhere and always to be detested and punished. Even if all peoples should do them, they would be liable to the same condemnation by divine law; for it has not made men to use one another in this way. Indeed the social bond which should exist between God and us is violated when the nature of which he is the author is polluted by a perversion of sexual desire.

In saying that vicious acts contrary to human customs are to be avoided, we take account of variations in custom, so that the mutually agreed convention of a city or nation, confirmed by custom or law, is not to be violated by the lust of a citizen or foreigner. Any element that does not fit into the pattern of the whole is unacceptable to society.

But when God commands something contrary to the customs or laws of a people, even if that has never been previously done, it has to be done. If it has fallen into disuse, it must be restored. If it has not been established, it must be established. If it is lawful for a king in a city within his realm to give an order which none before him nor he himself had previously issued, and if it is not contrary to the social contract of his city to obey, or indeed if it would be contrary to the social agreement not to obey (for there is a general consent in human society that kings should be obeyed), then how much more must God, the governor of all his creation, be unhesitatingly obeyed in whatever he commands! Just as among the authorities in human society a superior authority has a greater power to command obedience than an inferior officer, so God is supreme over all.

(16)   We may next consider the case of injurious acts where there is a lust to do harm either by verbal insult or by physical violence. In either case the impulse may be caused by the motive of revenge, as in the case of enemy against enemy; or with that of gaining possession of someone else's property, as in the case of a bandit attacking a traveller;[32] or with the intention of averting evil, as when people

---

[31] Here and in the next section Augustine repeats a distinction made in his *De doctrina christiana* (3. 10. 14) between *flagitium*, a shameful act of transgression against God's law, and *facinus*, injury to a fellow human being. Cf. below IV. xv (25).

[32] In Augustine's time, while main highways were populated and safe, bandits (usually army deserters and runaway slaves) commonly mugged travellers on side-roads (*contra Academicos* 1. 5. 13; below, VII. xxi. (27)).

attack someone they fear; or out of envy, as when the less fortunate may attack someone better off, or when a man who has met with success in some undertaking turns against someone who, he fears, may become his equal or who he is pained to see is already his equal; or merely by the pleasure of watching other people's pain, like spectators of gladiators[33] or those who mock and ridicule others.

These are the chief kinds of wickedness. They spring from the lust for domination or from the lust of the eyes or from sensuality— either one or two of these, or all three at once (1 John 2: 16).[34] Thus an evil-living person transgresses your decalogue of three commands with our duty to you and seven with our duty to our fellow human beings, a psaltery of ten strings (Ps. 91: 2), God most high and most gentle. But what vicious acts can hurt you? You are not capable of being damaged. Or what injuries can be inflicted on you who cannot be harmed? Your punishment is that which human beings do to their own injury because, even when they are sinning against you, their wicked actions are against their own souls. 'Iniquity lies to itself' (Ps. 26: 9), when men either corrupt or pervert their own nature which you made and ordered, or when people immoderately use what is allowed, or when, turning to what is forbidden, they indulge a burning lust for 'that use which is contrary to nature' (Rom. 1: 26). Or they may be held guilty of bitter hostility against you in mind and words and in 'kicking against the goad' (Acts 9: 5; 26: 14). Or they brazenly delight in the collapse of the restraints of human society, and in private caucuses and splits, indulging their personal likes and dislikes.

That is the outcome when you are abandoned, fount of life and the one true Creator and Ruler of the entire universe, when from a self-concerned pride a false unity is loved in the part.[35] Return to you is along the path of devout humility. You purify us of evil habit, and you are merciful to the sins we confess. You hear the groans of prisoners (Ps. 101: 21) and release us from the chains we have made for ourselves, on condition that we do not erect against you the horns (Ps. 74: 5 f.) of a false liberty by avaricious desire to

[33] See below VI. viii (13).

[34] On this text Augustine based a developed, often repeated doctrine of three lusts of pleasure, pride, and 'curiosity'. Some Neoplatonic texts offer analogous ideas but no precise anticipation.

[35] The language is that of Plotinus on the One (6. 9).

possess more and, at the risk of losing everything, through loving our private interest more than you,[36] the good of all that is.

ix (17) Besides vicious and injurious acts and many iniquities there are also the sins of those who are making progress. By the criterion of perfection good judges have to condemn them, but they are to be encouraged with praise in hope of fruit, like the blade announcing the grain harvest. There are also acts which resemble a vicious or injurious act but are not sins, because they do not offend you, Lord our God, nor the consensus of the community. People accumulate resources for use as may be appropriate for the situation and the time; and it is uncertain whether or not the accumulating is done from mere lust for possession.[37] Or with a zealous intention for improvement, proper authority may inflict punishment, and it is uncertain whether the motive was a mere desire to hurt people. Accordingly, there are many actions which people do not approve but which are attested by you to be right; and there are many actions praised by mankind which on your testimony are to be censured. Frequently the overt act has one face, the intention of the person doing it has quite another, and the critical circumstances of the moment cannot be known to us. But when you suddenly issue a command which departs from customary expectation, even though at one time you forbade the doing of any such act, though for a time you conceal the reason for your authoritative verdict,[38] and though it may go against the agreed customs of a given human society, who would hesitate to say that your command is to be kept? A just human society is one which submits to you. But happy are those who know that you are the source of moral precepts. All the acts of your servants are done either to show what present need requires or to prefigure the future.[39]

x (18) I was ignorant of these principles and laughed at your holy servants and prophets. By my mockery I only achieved the result that I became ridiculous to you. Gradually and unconsciously I was

---

[36] Similar is x. xxix (40) below.

[37] Perhaps referring to Joseph's monopolistic dealings (Gen. 47: 13–20), to which Manichees may have taken exception.

[38] Characteristically Augustine regards divine authority as always capable of giving reasons, never merely arbitrary and inscrutable.

[39] Augustine's defence of (e.g.) Samson's suicide or the sacrifice of Isaac or the fate of Jephthah's daughter (all favourite targets for Manichee attacks on Old Testament morality) is that seemingly unethical acts contain prophecy; see, for example, *City of God* 1. 26.

led to the absurd trivialities of believing that a fig weeps when it is picked, and that the fig tree its mother sheds milky tears. Yet if some [Manichee] saint ate it, provided that the sin of picking it was done not by his own hand but by another's, then he would digest it in his stomach and as a result would breathe out angels, or rather as he groaned in prayer and retched he would bring up bits of God.[40] These bits of the most high and true God would have remained chained in that fruit, if they had not been liberated by the tooth and belly of that elect saint. And I in my pathetic state believed that more mercy should be shown to the fruits of the earth than to human beings for whose sake the fruits came to be. Indeed, if some hungry person, not being a Manichee, had asked for this food, and if one gave him a piece, that morsel would have been considered to be condemned to capital punishment.

xi (19) 'You put forth your hand from on high' (Ps. 143: 7), and from this deep darkness 'you delivered my soul' (Ps. 85: 13). For my mother, your faithful servant, wept for me before you more than mothers weep when lamenting their dead children. By the 'faith and spiritual discernment' (Gal. 5: 5) which she had from you, she perceived the death which held me, and you heard her, Lord. You heard her and did not despise her tears which poured forth to wet the ground under her eyes in every place where she prayed. You heard her. Hence she was granted the dream by which you encouraged her to allow me to live with her and to have me at the same table in the house. She had begun by refusing me, in her revulsion from and detestation of the blasphemies of my error.[41] Her vision was of herself standing on a rule made of wood. A young man came to her, handsome, cheerful, and smiling to her at a time when she was sad and 'crushed with grief' (Lam. 1: 13). He asked her the reasons why she was downcast and daily in floods of tears—the question being intended, as is usual in such visions, to teach her rather than to learn the answer. She had replied that she mourned my perdition. He then told her to have no anxiety and exhorted her to direct her

[40] The diet of the Manichee Elect, gathered and cooked for them by the Hearers (or catechumens), included certain fruits, the digestion of which was believed to assist in liberating from the body imprisoned particles of divinity. Permitted fruits did not include apples, because of Adam's Fall. Below IV. i (1).

[41] During the time when Augustine was dismissed as a heretic, he lived with his wealthy neighbour Romanianus, also a Manichee, who had helped with the cost of his education.

attention and to see that where she was, there was I also. When she looked, she saw me standing beside her on the same rule. How could this vision come to her unless 'your ears were close to her heart' (Ps. 9B: 38/10A: 17)? You are good and all-powerful, caring for each one of us as though the only one in your care, and yet for all as for each individual.

(20) Moreover, what was the source of the fact that when she had recounted the vision to me, I tried to twist its meaning to signify that she should not despair of becoming what I was? But she instantly replied without a moment's hesitation: 'The word spoken to me was not "Where he is, there will you be also", but "Where you are, there will he be also".'[42] I confess to you Lord that to the best of my memory (and it is a matter which I have frequently discussed) I was more moved by your answer through my vigilant mother than by the dream itself. My misinterpretation seemed very plausible. She was not disturbed and quickly saw what was there to be seen, and what I certainly had not seen before she spoke. By the dream the joy of this devout woman, to be fulfilled much later, was predicted many years in advance to give consolation at this time in her anxiety. For almost nine years then followed during which I was 'in the deep mire' (Ps. 68: 3) and darkness of falsehood. Despite my frequent efforts to climb out of it, I was the more heavily plunged back into the filth and wallowed in it. During this time this chaste, devout, and sober widow, one of the kind you love, already cheered by hope but no less constant in prayer and weeping, never ceased her hours of prayer to lament about me to you. Her 'prayer entered into your presence' (Ps. 87: 3). Nevertheless you still let me go on turning over and over again in that darkness.

xii (21) Meanwhile you gave her another answer that sticks in my memory. For I pass over much because I am hurrying on to those things which especially urge me to make confession to you, and there is much that I do not remember. You gave her another answer through one of your priests, a bishop brought up in the Church and well trained in your books. When that woman asked him to make time to talk to me and refute my errors and correct my evil doctrines and teach me good ones—for he used to do this for

---

[42] The ancient Roman marriage rite included the statement by the bride: 'Where you are, there will I be' (Quintilian I. 7. 28; Plutarch, *Roman Questions* 30).

those whom perhaps he found suitably disposed—he declined, wisely indeed as I later perceived. For he answered that I was still unready to learn, because I was conceited about the novel excitements of that heresy, and because, as she had informed him, I had already disturbed many untrained minds with many trivial questions. 'Let him be where he is', he said; 'only pray the Lord for him. By his reading he will discover what an error and how vast an impiety it all is.'

At the same time he told her how he himself as a small boy had been handed over to the Manichees by his mother, whom they had led astray. He had not only read nearly all their books but had even copied them. Although he had no one disputing with him and providing a refutation, it had become clear to him that that sect ought to be avoided, and therefore he had left it. When he had said this to her, she was still unwilling to take No for an answer. She pressed him with more begging and with floods of tears, asking him to see me and debate with me. He was now irritated and a little vexed and said: 'Go away from me: as you live, it cannot be that the son of these tears should perish.' In her conversations with me she often used to recall that she had taken these words as if they had sounded from heaven.

BOOK IV

Manichee and Astrologer

i (1)   During this same period of nine years, from my nineteenth to my twenty-eighth year, our life was one of being seduced and seducing, being deceived and deceiving (2 Tim. 3: 13), in a variety of desires. Publicly I was a teacher of the arts which they call liberal;[1] privately I professed a false religion—in the former role arrogant, in the latter superstitious, in everything vain. On the one side we pursued the empty glory of popularity, ambitious for the applause of the audience at the theatre when entering for verse competitions to win a garland of mere grass, concerned with the follies of public entertainments and unrestrained lusts. On the other side, we sought to purge ourselves of that filth by supplying food to those whose title was the Elect and Holy, so that in the workshop of their stomach they could manufacture for us angels and gods to bring us liberation.[2] This was how my life was spent, and these were the activities of myself and my friends who had been deceived through me and with me.

Proud people may laugh at me. As yet they have not themselves been prostrated and brought low for their soul's health by you, my God. But I shall nevertheless confess to you my shame, since it is for your praise (Ps. 105: 47). Allow me, I pray you, grant me leave to run through my memory, as it is in the present, of the past twistings of my mistaken life and to sacrifice to you 'a victim of jubilation' (Ps. 26: 6). Without you, what am I to myself but a guide to my own self-destruction? When all is well with me, what am I but an infant sucking your milk and feeding on you, 'the food that is incorruptible' (John 6: 27)? What is a human being (name anyone you may please) when he is merely a man? So let the mighty and powerful

---

[1] Literature, rhetoric and dialectic, leading on to the mathematical studies of arithmetic, geometry, music, and astronomy; called 'liberal' because they were the mark of a cultivated gentleman.

[2] In Manichee texts, every meal of the Elect is a holy feeding on particles of light concealed in fruits and plants, helping to gain remission of sins for those Hearers who prepare it. Above, III. x (18).

laugh at our expense. In our weakness and indigence (Ps. 73: 21), we may make our confession to you.

ii (2)   In those years I used to teach the art of rhetoric. Overcome by greed myself, I used to sell the eloquence that would overcome an opponent. Nevertheless, Lord, as you know (Ps. 68: 6), I preferred to have virtuous students (virtuous as they are commonly called). Without any resort to a trick I taught them the tricks of rhetoric, not that they should use them against the life of an innocent man, but that sometimes they might save the life of a guilty person.[3] God, from far off you saw me falling about on slippery ground and in the midst of much smoke (Isa. 42: 3) discerned the spark of my integrity which in my teaching office I manifested to people who 'loved vanity and sought after a lie' (Ps. 4: 3).

In those years I had a woman. She was not my partner in what is called lawful marriage. I had found her in my state of wandering desire and lack of prudence. Nevertheless, she was the only girl for me, and I was faithful to her. With her I learnt by direct experience how wide a difference there is between the partnership of marriage entered into for the sake of having a family and the mutual consent of those whose love is a matter of physical sex, and for whom the birth of a child is contrary to their intention—even though, if offspring arrive, they compel their parents to love them.

(3)   I also recall how, when I had decided to enter for a poetry competition at the theatre, a soothsayer of some sort sent to ask what fee I would give him to ensure victory. But I replied that I hated and abominated those vile mysteries, and that even if the crown were immortal and made of gold, I would not allow a fly to be killed to bring about my success.[4] For in his mysteries he would be going to kill animals, and by offering these creatures in honour of daemons, his intention was to gain their support for my winning. Yet my rejection of this evil proposition was not motivated by respect for the purity which you enjoin, 'God of my heart' (Ps. 72: 26). I knew nothing about love for you, of whom I had no conception other

---

[3] Augustine formulates the principle that an advocate should not throw dust in the eyes of the court, but is entitled to require that the prosecution prove their case, even when he may think his client guilty. He holds that it is worse for an innocent person to be condemned than for a guilty person to be acquitted. The theme is already in Cicero, *De officiis* 2. 51.

[4] Manichees wholly rejected animal sacrifices, and regarded the Old Testament requirement of such sacrifices as one of the stronger arguments against its authority.

than of physical objects luminous with light. In sighing after such fictions does not the soul 'commit fornication against you' (Ps. 72: 27) and 'trust in lies and feed the winds' (Prov. 10: 4)? I refused sacrifice to daemons on my behalf; yet by adherence to that superstition I sacrificed myself to them. What is it to 'feed the winds' if not to feed the spirits, that is, by one's errors to become an object of delight and derision to them?

iii (4) On the same ground I did not cease openly to consult those impostors called astrologers, because they offered, so to speak, no sacrifices, and no prayers were addressed to any spirit for the purpose of divining the future. Yet a true Christian piety consistently rejects and condemns this art. It is good to make confession to you, Lord, and to say 'Have mercy on me; heal my soul, for I have sinned against you' (Ps. 40: 5; 91: 2). I must not abuse your mercy so as to make it a licence for sin (Ecclus. 15: 21), but remember the Lord's saying 'Look, you are made whole, now do not sin, lest something worse happen to you' (John 5: 14). Astrologers try to destroy this entire saving doctrine when they say: 'The reason for your sinning is determined by the heaven', and 'Venus or Saturn or Mars was responsible for this act'.[5] They make a man not in the least responsible for his faults, but mere flesh and blood and putrid pride, so that the blame lies with the Creator and orderer of the heaven and stars. And who is this but our God, sweetness and source of justice, who 'will render to every man according to his works, and does not despise a contrite and humble heart'? (Rom. 2: 6; Ps. 50: 19).

(5) At that time there was a man of good judgement, very skilled in the art of medicine and in that respect of high reputation.[6] By virtue of his office as proconsul, not as a medical expert, he had with his own hand placed the crown in the poetry contest upon my sick head; for you alone are the healer of the disease that afflicted

---

[5] Plotinus (2. 3. 6) condemns the utter irrationality of supposing Mars or Venus responsible for adulteries.

[6] Helvius Vindicianus, named in VII. vi (8), was physician to the emperor Valentinian I, and a well-known medical authority of the time, author of textbooks. His rejection of astrology and divination was not characteristic of ancient physicians, who could normally consult almanacs or employ witch's spells before treating patients. Vindicianus held office as proconsul *c.*379–82; a change of career not unparalleled at this time; Symmachus (*ep.*1. 66) records an eminent physician Gelasius promoted to take charge of revenue for imperial estates in Africa in the year 380.

me, you who resist the proud but give grace to the humble (1 Pet. 5: 5;
Jas. 4: 6). Nevertheless even by means of that old man you did not
fail to help me or miss the opportunity of bringing healing to my
soul. I came to know him well and became an assiduous and regular
listener to his conversation; although his prose style was not highly
cultured, his opinions were lively and expressed in a delightful and
serious manner. From my remarks he discovered that I was addicted
to the books of those who cast horoscopes. In a kind and fatherly
way he advised me to throw them away and not to waste on that
nonsense the care and labour required for useful matters. He told
me that he had himself studied astrology so far that in his early
years he had intended to take it up formally as a way of earning his
living, saying that if he had the capacity to understand Hippocrates,
he would be able to understand these books also. Nevertheless he
had given up the subject and pursued medicine for the simple
reason that he discovered astrology to be utterly bogus. Being a
serious-minded person, he did not wish to make a living out of
deceiving people. 'But you', he said, 'have the profession of a
teacher of rhetoric, by which you earn your living in human society.
You are pursuing this delusory subject in your free time, not out of
any necessity to raise additional income. You should be the more
ready to believe my view of the matter, considering that I worked
hard to acquire so thorough a knowledge of astrology as to wish to
earn my living exclusively from this source.'

I asked him why it was that many of their forecasts turned out to
be correct. He replied that the best answer he could give was the
power apparent in lots, a power everywhere diffused in the nature
of things. So when someone happens to consult the pages of a poet
whose verses and intention are concerned with a quite different
subject, in a wonderful way a verse often emerges appropriate to
the decision under discussion. He used to say that it was no wonder
if from the human soul, by some higher instinct that does not know
what goes on within itself, some utterance emerges not by art but by
'chance' which is in sympathy with the affairs or actions of the
inquirer.[7]

---

[7] Vindicianus' arguments failed to dissuade Augustine (VII. vi (8)). His position was
not that a correct astrological prediction is the result of a purely random chance, but that
'chance' is our name for a cause we do not know, and in this instance the correctness of
prediction is the result of the internal sympathy of all parts of the cosmos. So also

(6)   This instruction, either by him or through him, you gave me. The doubt which you imprinted in my memory I was later to follow up with a personal investigation. But at that time neither he nor my dearest friend Nebridius (a thoroughly good and entirely chaste young man who thought all kinds of divination ridiculous)[8] was able to persuade me to abandon it. Their argument impressed me less than the authority of the writers on astrology. Moreover, I had not yet found the certain proof for which I was seeking, by which it would be clear beyond doubt that the true forecasts given by the astrologers when consulted were uttered by chance or by luck, not from the science of studying the stars.

iv (7)   During those years when first I began to teach in the town where I was born, I had come to have a friend who because of our shared interests was very close. He was my age, and we shared the flowering of youth. As a boy he had grown up with me, and we had gone to school together and played with one another. He was then not yet my friend, and when he did become so, it was less than a true friendship which is not possible unless you bond together those who cleave to one another by the love which 'is poured into our hearts by the Holy Spirit who is given to us' (Rom. 5: 5). Nevertheless, it was a very sweet experience, welded by the fervour of our identical interests. For I had turned him away from the true faith, to which, being only young, he had no strong or profound allegiance, towards those superstitions and pernicious mythologies which were the reason for my mother's tears over me. So under my influence this man's mind was wandering astray, and my soul could not endure to be without him. But you were present, immediately at the back of those who flee from you, at once both 'God of vengeances' (Ps. 93: 1) and fount of mercies: you turn us to yourself in wonderful ways. You took the man from this life when our friendship had

Plotinus 2. 3. The poetry of Virgil was often used for sortilege; Christians used the Bible, to the anxiety of bishops including Augustine, though it was crucial in the garden at Milan, below VIII. xii (29).

[8] Nebridius became Augustine's friend during his Manichee period at Carthage; his father owned a fine estate nearby. When Augustine moved to Milan, Nebridius followed as one of the group of friends seeking to share a common life devoted to 'the love of wisdom', and returned to North Africa in 388, regretting that Augustine went back to Thagaste instead of coming to him near Carthage. His premature death (IX. iii (6) below) came about 390. Augustine found his mind intensely stimulating, putting critical questions about divination or Manichee doctrine. He shared Augustine's Milanese enthusiasm for Neoplatonism, but 'hated a short answer to a large question'.

scarcely completed a year. It had been sweet to me beyond all the sweetnesses of life that I had experienced.

(8)   Who on his own can recount your praises for the experiences of his life alone (cf. Ps. 105: 2)? At that time what did you do, my God? 'How unsearchable is the abyss of your judgements' (Ps. 35: 7; Rom. 11: 33)! When he was sick with fever, for a long time he lay unconscious in a mortal sweat, and when his life was despaired of, he was baptized without his knowing it. To me this was a matter of no interest.[9] I assumed that his soul would retain what it had received from me, not what had happened to his body while he was unconscious. But it turned out quite differently. For he recovered and was restored to health, and at once, as soon as I could speak with him (and I was able to do so as soon as he could speak, since I never left his side, and we were deeply dependent on one another), I attempted to joke with him, imagining that he too would laugh with me about the baptism which he had received when far away in mind and sense. But he had already learnt that he had received the sacrament. He was horrified at me as if I were an enemy, and with amazing and immediate frankness advised me that, if I wished to be his friend, I must stop saying this kind of thing to him. I was dumbfounded and perturbed; but I deferred telling him of all my feelings until he should get better and recover his health and strength. Then I would be able to do what I wished with him. But he was snatched away from my lunacy, so that he might be preserved with you for my consolation. After a few days, while I was absent, the fever returned, and he died.

(9)   'Grief darkened my heart' (Lam. 5: 17). Everything on which I set my gaze was death. My home town became a torture to me; my father's house a strange world of unhappiness; all that I had shared with him was without him transformed into a cruel torment. My eyes looked for him everywhere, and he was not there. I hated everything because they did not have him, nor could they now tell me 'look, he is on the way', as used to be the case when he was alive and absent from me. I had become to myself a vast problem,[10] and I

---

[9] Augustine's unnamed friend came of a Catholic family, evidently responsible for his baptism. To baptize an unconscious sick person (if a catechumen) was accepted in the North African Churches. Manichees rejected baptism as a superfluous and useless external act.

[10] Repeated X. xxxiii (50).

questioned my soul 'Why are you sad, and why are you very distressed?' But my soul did not know what reply to give. If I had said to my soul 'Put your trust in God' (Ps. 41: 6, 12), it would have had good reason not to obey. For the very dear friend I had lost was a better and more real person than the [Manichee] phantom in which I would have been telling my soul to trust. Only tears were sweet to me, and in my 'soul's delights' (Ps. 138: 11) weeping had replaced my friend.

v (10) Now, Lord, all that belongs to the past, and with time my wound is less painful.[11] Can I hear from you who are the truth, and move the ear of my heart close to your mouth, so that you can explain to me why weeping is a relief to us when unhappy? Or, although present everywhere, have you thrust our misery far from you and remain in yourself (Wisd. 7: 27) while we are tossed about by successive trials? Yet if our tearful entreaties did not reach your ears, no remnant of hope would remain for us. How does it come about that out of the bitterness of life sweet fruit is picked by groaning and weeping and sighing and mourning? Does the sweetness lie in the hope that you hear us? That is certainly the case in our prayers which express the longing to reach their object. But surely that is not true of sadness and grief for what has been lost, such as overwhelmed me at that time. I had no hope that he would come back to life, and my tears did not petition for this. I merely grieved and wept. I was in misery and had lost the source of my joy. Or is weeping really a bitter thing which gives relief only when we cannot bear to think of the things which formerly we enjoyed, and which is pleasurable at the moments when we shrink from the memory of them?

vi (11) Why do I speak of these matters? Now is the time not to be putting questions but to be making confession to you. I was in misery, and misery is the state of every soul overcome by friendship with mortal things and lacerated when they are lost. Then the soul becomes aware of the misery which is its actual condition even before it loses them. At that time that was my state: I wept very bitterly and took my rest in bitterness. I was so wretched that I felt a greater attachment to my life of misery than to my dead friend. Although I wanted it to be otherwise, I was more unwilling to lose

---

[11] Echo of Ovid, *Remedium Amoris* 131.

my misery than him, and I do not know if I would have given up my life for him as the story reports of Orestes and Pylades:[12] if it is not fiction, they were willing to die for each other together, because it was worse than death to them not to be living together. But in me there had emerged a very strange feeling which was the opposite of theirs. I found myself heavily weighed down by a sense of being tired of living and scared of dying. I suppose that the more I loved him, the more hatred and fear I felt for the death which had taken him from me, as if it were my most ferocious enemy. I thought that since death had consumed him, it was suddenly going to engulf all humanity. That was, to the best of my memory, my state of mind.

Look into my heart, my God, look within. See this, as I remember it, my hope; for you cleanse me from these flawed emotions. You direct my eyes towards you and 'rescue my feet from the trap' (Ps. 24: 15). I was surprised that any other mortals were alive, since he whom I had loved as if he would never die was dead. I was even more surprised that when he was dead I was still alive, for he was my 'other self'. Someone has well said of his friend, 'He was half my soul'.[13] I had felt that my soul and his soul were 'one soul in two bodies'.[14] So my life was to me a horror. I did not wish to live with only half of myself, and perhaps the reason why I so feared death was that then the whole of my much loved friend would have died.[15]

vii (12) What madness not to understand how to love human beings with awareness of the human condition! How stupid man is to be unable to restrain feelings in suffering the human lot! That was my state at that time. So I boiled with anger, sighed, wept, and was at my wits' end. I found no calmness, no capacity for deliberation. I carried my lacerated and bloody soul when it was unwilling to be carried by me. I found no place where I could put it down. There was no rest in pleasant groves, nor in games or songs, nor in sweet-scented places, nor in exquisite feasts, nor in the pleasures of the bedroom and bed, nor, finally, in books and poetry. Everything was an object of horror, even light itself; all that was not he made me feel sick and was repulsive—except for groaning and tears. In them alone was there some slight relief. But when my weeping stopped,

[12] Echo of Cicero, *On Friendship* 7. 24.   [13] Horace, *Odes* 1, 3. 8.
[14] Ovid, *Tristia* 4. 4. 72; Aristotle in Diogenes Laertius 6. 1. 20.
[15] In his *Revisions* (*Retr.* 2. 6. 2) Augustine censured this last sentence as declamatory rhetoric, not serious confession.

my soul felt burdened by a vast load of misery. I should have lifted myself to you, Lord, to find a cure. I knew that, but did not wish it or have the strength for it. When I thought of you, my mental image was not of anything solid and firm; it was not you but a vain phantom. My error was my god. If I attempted to find rest there for my soul, it slipped through a void and again came falling back upon me. I had become to myself a place of unhappiness in which I could not bear to be; but I could not escape from myself. Where should my heart flee to in escaping from my heart? Where should I go to escape from myself? Where is there where I cannot pursue myself? And yet I fled from my home town, for my eyes sought for him less in a place where they were not accustomed to see him. And so from the town of Thagaste I came to Carthage.[16]

viii (13)   Time is not inert. It does not roll on through our senses without affecting us. Its passing has remarkable effects on the mind. See: it came and went 'from day to day' (Ps. 60: 9), and by its coming and going it implanted in me new hopes and other experiences to be remembering. Gradually it repaired me with delights such as I used to enjoy, and to them my grief yielded. But these delights were succeeded not by new sorrows but by the causes of new sorrows. The reason why that grief had penetrated me so easily and deeply was that I had poured out my soul on to the sand by loving a person sure to die as if he would never die. The greatest source of repair and restoration was the solace of other friends, with whom I loved what I loved as a substitute for you; and this was a vast myth and a long lie. By its adulterous caress, my mind which had 'itching ears' (2 Tim. 4: 3–4) was corrupted.

But this fable did not die for me when one of my friends died. There were other things which occupied my mind in the company of my friends: to make conversation, to share a joke, to perform mutual acts of kindness, to read together well-written books, to share in trifling and in serious matters, to disagree though without animosity—just as a person debates with himself—and in the very rarity of disagreement to find the salt of normal harmony, to teach each other something or to learn from one another, to long with impatience for those absent, to welcome them with gladness on

[16] Augustine left Thagaste without telling his mother, his travel costs being paid by the rich neighbour Romanianus. Probably there is a double allusion to the parable of the prodigal son and to Horace *Odes* II 16.19 ('what exile from home escapes himself?').

their arrival. These and other signs come from the heart of those who love and are loved and are expressed through the mouth, through the tongue, through the eyes, and a thousand gestures of delight, acting as fuel to set our minds on fire and out of many to forge unity.[17]

ix (14) This is what we love in friends. We love to the point that the human conscience feels guilty if we do not love the person who is loving us, and if that love is not returned—without demanding any physical response other than the marks of affectionate good will. Hence the mourning if a friend dies, the darkness of grief, and as the sweetness is turned into bitterness the heart is flooded with tears. The lost life of those who die becomes the death of those still living. 'Happy is the person who loves you' (Tobit 13: 18) and his friend in you, and his enemy because of you (Matt. 5: 44). Though left alone, he loses none dear to him; for all are dear in the one who cannot be lost. Who is that but our God, the God who made heaven and earth and filled them? By filling them he made them. (Jer. 23: 24).[18] None loses you unless he abandons you, and when he abandons you where can he go or fly for refuge (Ps. 138: 7) unless it be to move from your serenity to your anger? Where can he escape from finding that your law is in his penalty? And 'your law is truth' (Ps. 118: 142) and truth is you (John 14: 6).

x (15) 'O God of hosts, turn us and show us your face, and we shall be safe' (Ps. 79: 8). For wherever the human soul turns itself, other than to you, it is fixed in sorrows, even if it is fixed upon beautiful things external to you and external to itself, which would nevertheless be nothing if they did not have their being from you. Things rise and set: in their emerging they begin as it were to be, and grow to perfection; having reached perfection, they grow old and die.[19] Not everything grows old, but everything dies. So when things rise and emerge into existence, the faster they grow to be, the quicker they rush towards non-being. That is the law limiting their being. So much have you given them, namely to be parts of

---

[17] Cicero, *On Friendship* 98.

[18] Similarly 1. iii (3). The Platonic axiom is that in God's creation there can be no empty gaps; all is a full continuum of levels of being. Cf. *City of God* 11. 22; 12. 2; Plotinus 3. 3. 7; especially 6. 7. 16 'Filling brings into existence'.

[19] Echo of Sallust, *Jugurtha* 2. 3. Plotinus also thinks beauty can distract one from the Good (5. 5. 12).

things which do not all have their being at the same moment, but by passing away and by successiveness, they all form the whole of which they are parts. That is the way our speech is constructed by sounds which are significant. What we say would not be complete if one word did not cease to exist when it has sounded its constituent parts, so that it can be succeeded by another.

Let these transient things be the ground on which my soul praises you (Ps. 145: 2), 'God creator of all'.[20] But let it not become stuck in them and glued to them with love through the physical senses. For these things pass along the path of things that move towards non-existence. They rend the soul with pestilential desires; for the soul loves to be in them and take its repose among the objects of its love. But in these things there is no point of rest: they lack permanence. They flee away and cannot be followed with the bodily senses. No one can fully grasp them even while they are present. Physical perception is slow, because it is a bodily sense: its nature imposes limitations on it. It is sufficient for another purpose for which it was made. But it is not adequate to get a grip on things that are transient from the moment of the intended beginning to their intended end (cf. Ps. 138: 7). In your word, through which they are created, they hear: 'From here as far as there' (Job 38: 11).

xi (16)   Do not be vain, my soul. Do not deafen your heart's ear with the tumult of your vanity. Even you have to listen. The Word himself cries to you to return. There is the place of undisturbed quietness where love is not deserted if it does not itself depart. See how these things pass away to give place to others, and how the universe in this lower order is constituted out of all its parts. 'Surely I shall never go anywhere else', says the word of God. Fix your dwelling there. Put in trust there whatever you have from him, my soul, at least now that you are wearied of deceptions. Entrust to the truth whatever has come to you from the truth. You will lose nothing. The decayed parts of you will receive a new flowering, and all your sicknesses will be healed (Matt. 4: 23; Ps. 102: 3). All that is ebbing away from you will be given fresh form and renewed, bound tightly to you. They will not put you down in the place to which they descend, but still stand with you and will remain in the

---

[20] Ambrose's hymn, *Deus creator omnium*, from which Augustine quotes fairly frequently, e.g. below IX. xii (32); X. xxxv (52); XI. xxvii (35).

presence of the God who stands fast and abides (Ps. 101: 13, 27; 1 Pet. 1: 23).[21]

(17) Why then are you perversely following the leading of your flesh? If you turn away from it, it has to follow you. All that you experience through it is only partial; you are ignorant of the whole to which the parts belong. Yet they delight you. But if your physical perception were capable of comprehending the whole and had not, for your punishment, been justly restrained to a part of the universe, you would wish everything at present in being to pass away, so that the totality of things could provide you with greater pleasure. The words we speak you hear by the same physical perception, and you have no wish that the speaker stop at each syllable. You want him to hurry on so that other syllables may come, and you may hear the whole. That is always how it is with the sum of the elements out of which a unity is constituted, and the elements out of which it is constituted never exist all at the same moment. There would be more delight in all the elements than in individual pieces if only one had the capacity to perceive all of them. But far superior to these things is he who made all things, and he is our God. He does not pass away; nothing succeeds him.[22]

xii (18) If physical objects give you pleasure, praise God for them and return love to their Maker lest, in the things that please you, you displease him. If souls please you, they are being loved in God; for they also are mutable and acquire stability by being established in him. Otherwise they go their way and perish. In him therefore they are loved; so seize what souls you can to take with you to him, and say to them: 'Him we love; he made these things and is not far distant.' For he did not create and then depart; the things derived from him have their being in him. Look where he is—wherever there is a taste of truth. He is very close to the heart; but the heart has wandered from him. 'Return, sinners, to your heart' (Isa. 46: 8 LXX), and adhere to him who made you. Stand with him and you will stand fast. Rest in him and you will be at rest. Where are you going to along rough paths? What is the goal of your journey? The good which you love is from him. But it is only as it is related to him

[21] The homiletic tone of this piece has affinities with Ambrose's sermon *On Isaac* (which Augustine would have heard at Milan). 'You' is not God but man.

[22] The antithesis of parts and whole is paralleled in the Neoplatonist Porphyry, *Sententiae* 40.

that it is good and sweet. Otherwise it will justly become bitter; for all that comes from him is unjustly loved if he has been abandoned. With what end in view do you again and again walk along difficult and laborious paths (Wisd. 5: 7)? There is no rest where you seek for it. Seek for what you seek, but it is not where you are looking for it. You seek the happy life in the region of death; it is not there. How can there be a happy life where there is not even life?

(19) He who for us is life itself descended here and endured our death and slew it by the abundance of his life.[23] In a thunderous voice he called us to return to him, at that secret place where he came forth to us. First he came into the Virgin's womb where the human creation was married to him, so that mortal flesh should not for ever be mortal. Coming forth from thence 'as a bridegroom from his marriage bed, he bounded like a giant to run his course' (Ps. 18: 6). He did not delay, but ran crying out loud by his words, deeds, death, life, descent, and ascent—calling us to return to him. And he has gone from our sight that we should 'return to our heart' (Isa. 46: 8) and find him there. He went away and behold, here he is. He did not wish to remain long with us, yet he did not abandon us. He has gone to that place which he never left, 'for the world was made by him' (John 1: 10); and he was in this world, and 'came into this world to save sinners' (1 Tim. 1: 15). To him my soul is making confession, and 'he is healing it, because it was against him that it sinned' (Ps. 40: 5). 'Sons of men, how long will you be heavy at heart?' (Ps. 4: 3). Surely after the descent of life, you cannot fail to wish to ascend and live? But where will you ascend when you are 'set on high and have put your mouth in heaven'? (Ps. 72: 9). Come down so that you can ascend, and make your ascent to God. For it is by climbing up against God that you have fallen. Tell souls that they should 'weep in the valley of tears' (Ps. 83: 7). So take them with you to God, for by his Spirit you declare these things to them if you say it burning with the fire of love.

xiii (20)   At that time I did not know this. I loved beautiful things of a lower order, and I was going down to the depths. I used to say to my friends: 'Do we love anything except that which is beautiful? What then is a beautiful object? And what is beauty? What is it which charms and attracts us to the things we love? It must be the

---

[23] Death dies—a theme in a famous sonnet of John Donne: frequent in Augustine.

grace and loveliness inherent in them, or they would in no way move us.' I gave the subject careful attention, and saw that in bodies one should distinguish the beauty which is a kind of totality and for that reason beautiful, and another kind which is fitting because it is well adapted to some other thing, just as part of the body is adapted to the whole to which it belongs as a shoe to a foot and like instances. This thought bubbled up in my mind like a spring from the deepest level of my heart, and I wrote *On the Beautiful and the Fitting* in two or three books, I think—you know, God, for I have forgotten. I no longer have this work; I do not know how it went astray from me.

xiv (21)   What was it, Lord my God, which moved me to dedicate the work to Hierius,[24] the orator at Rome? I had never set eyes on him, but I loved the man for his renown as a person of high culture, and because I had heard some words of his quoted which gave me pleasure. But I loved him above all because others thought him delightful; they praised him to the skies, astonished that a Syrian previously educated in Greek eloquence could later become an admirable orator in Latin as well, and be extremely knowledgeable in the study of philosophical questions. A man can be praised and loved even though far distant from us. It would be absurd to suppose that this kind of love is transmitted from the mouth of the person praising him to the heart of the person hearing. But love in one person is infectious in kindling it in another. Hence it comes about that a person who is praised comes to be loved, when people believe that the praise comes from a sincere heart, that is, when the praise comes from one who loves him.

(22)   So at that period of my life I used to love people on the basis of human judgement, not your judgement, my God, in whom no one is deceived. Yet my sentiment was different from the kind of feeling one could have about a famous charioteer or a man who has a great popular following for his combats with wild beasts. It was an altogether distinct and serious feeling, being the kind of praise I would have liked to receive myself. I would not have wanted to be praised and loved like actors, though I myself used to praise and

[24] Hierius was a common name in the fourth century, some of that name being philosophers and orators (one corrected the manuscripts of Quintilian). The only certainty about the Roman orator is provided by Augustine.

love them. I would have preferred to live in obscurity than to be well known in that way, and would rather be hated than loved like them.[25] How does it come about that various kinds of love are felt in a single soul with different degrees of weight? How can it happen that a skill which I love in another I would hate in myself, since otherwise I would not detest and reject it: and yet both of us are human. For he is not like a good horse, an object of love to someone who does not wish to be a horse, even if he could. The same may be said of an actor with whom we share the same nature. How is it that I love in a human being what I would hate to be, when I also am human? Man is a vast deep, whose hairs you, Lord, have numbered, and in you none can be lost (Matt. 10: 30). Yet it is easier to count his hairs than the passions and emotions of his heart.

(23)   But that orator was of the type which I so loved that I wanted to be like him. And I wandered away in conceit and was carried about by every wind (Eph. 4: 14). Yet very secretly you were putting a check on me. How do I know and how can I be sure in making confession before you that my love for him was aroused by the regard of those praising him rather than by the actual achievements which evoked their praise? If, far from praising him, they had vilified him, and had given a critical and scornful account of his work, my interest would not have been kindled and aroused. Certainly the actual facts would have been no different, nor the man himself. The only alteration would have been in the feeling conveyed by the speakers. See how the human soul lies weak and prostrate when it is not yet attached to the solid rock of truth. The winds of gossip blow from the chests of people ventilating their opinions; so the soul is carried about and turned, twisted and twisted back again. The light is obscured from it by a cloud, the truth is not perceived. Yet look, it lies before us.

It was important to me whether my discourse and my studies were becoming known to the man. If they met with his approbation, I would have been vastly excited. But if he disapproved, my heart, being vain and void of the solidity you impart, would have been hurt. And yet this topic of the beautiful and the fitting, about which

---

[25] Actors, charioteers, combatants in the amphitheatre, enjoyed only low social status in antiquity, and were commonly thought morally disreputable.

I had written to him, was a theme which my mind enjoyed turning over and reflecting upon.[26] Although no one else admired the book, I thought very well of it myself.

xv (24)   I had not as yet come to see that the hinge of this great subject lies in your creative act, almighty one: you alone do marvellous things (Ps. 71: 8; 135: 4). My mind moved within the confines of corporeal forms. I proposed a definition and a distinction between the beautiful as that which is pleasing in itself, and the fitting as that which pleases because it fits well into something else. I supported this distinction by examples drawn from the body.[27] Moreover, I turned then to examine the nature of mind, but the false opinion which I held about spiritual entities did not allow me to perceive the truth. The truth with great force leapt to my eyes, but I used to turn away my agitated mind from incorporeal reality to lines and colours and physical magnitudes of vast size.[28] Because I could not see any such thing in the mind, I thought I could not see my mind. Furthermore, since in virtue I loved peace and in vice I hated discord, I noted that in virtue there is unity, in vice a kind of division. In the unity I thought I saw the rational mind and the nature of truth and of the highest good; whereas in the division there was some substance of irrational life and the nature of supreme evil. I attributed to this evil not only substance but life. Yet it could have no being without you, my God, from whom all things come (1 Cor. 8: 6). My opinion was miserable folly. In regard to virtue, I spoke of the Monad as sexless mind, whereas evil was the Dyad,[29] anger in injurious acts, lust in vicious acts. I did not know what I was talking about. I did not know nor had I learnt that evil is not a substance, nor is our mind the supreme and unchangeable good.

(25)   Just as crimes occur when the mind's motive force, which gives the impetus for action, is corrupt and asserts itself in an insolent and disturbed way, and as vicious acts occur if obsession has captured the mind's affective part which is at the root of the impulse to

---

[26] The Latin may imply that the work was cast in the form of a dialogue, like Augustine's *Soliloquies*, where he is in discussion with himself.

[27] This thesis recurs in several texts of the mature Augustine, e.g. *City of God* 22. 24. It is akin to his basic ethical distinction between what is enjoyed (ends) and what is used (means).

[28] The Manichee Light-deity is a huge physical entity. On colours see III. vi (11).

[29] The terminology is Pythagorean. The aesthetic theory of Augustine's book is linked to Stoic theories of symmetry as constitutive of beauty—ideas discussed by Plotinus 1. 6. 1.

carnal pleasures, so also errors and false opinions contaminate life if the reasoning mind is itself flawed. That was my condition at that time. For I did not know that the soul needs to be enlightened by light from outside itself, so that it can participate in truth, because it is not itself the nature of truth. You will light my lamp, O Lord. My God you will lighten my darknesses (Ps. 17: 29), and of your fullness we have all received (John 1: 16). You are the true light who illuminates every man coming into this world (John 1: 9), because in you there is no change nor shadow caused by turning (Jas. 1: 17).

(26) I tried to approach you, but you pushed me away so that I should taste of death (Matt. 16: 28); for you resist the proud (2 Peter 5: 5). What could be worse arrogance than the amazing madness with which I asserted myself to be by nature what you are?[30] I was changeable and this was evident to me from the fact that I wanted to be wise and to pass from worse to better. Yet I preferred to think you mutable rather than hold that I was not what you are. That is why I was pushed away, and why you resisted my inflated pride. I was imagining corporeal shapes. I being flesh accused flesh.[31] A 'wandering spirit' (Ps. 77: 39), I was not yet on my way back to you, but meandered on and on into things which have no being either in you or in me or in the body. They were not created for me on the ground of your truth, but were fictions invented by my vanity on the basis of the body. I used to talk to your little believers, fellow citizens of mine, from whom without knowing it I was in exile. Loquacious and inept, I used to say to them: 'Why then does the soul which God has made fall into error?' But I did not wish to hear someone saying: 'Why then does God err?' I used to argue that your unchangeable substance is forced into mistakes[32] rather than confess that my mutable nature deviated by its own choice and that error is its punishment.

(27) I was about 26 or 27 years old when I wrote that work, turning over in my mind fictitious physical images. These were a strident noise in the ears of my heart, with which I was straining, sweet truth, to hear your interior melody when I was meditating on

[30] Manichee doctrine held that a good human soul is the very substance of God.

[31] The alienation of all physical matter from God is central to Mani's belief.

[32] The Manichee Light-deity is of limited power, and does things under necessity, not by choice: cf. XIII. xxx (45) below.

the beautiful and the fitting. I wanted to stand still and hear you and rejoice with joy at the voice of the bridegroom (John 3: 29). But that was beyond my powers, for I was snatched away to external things by the voices of the error I espoused, and under the weight of my pride I plunged into the abyss. You did not grant joy and gladness to my hearing, nor did my bones exult, for they had not been brought to humility (Ps. 50: 10).

xvi (28) What good did it do me that at about the age of twenty there came into my hands a work of Aristotle which they call the *Ten Categories*?[33] My teacher in rhetoric at Carthage, and others too who were reputed to be learned men, used to speak of this work with their cheeks puffed out with conceit, and at the very name I gasped with suspense as if about to read something great and divine. Yet I read it without any expositor and understood it. I had discussions with people who said they had understood the *Categories* only with much difficulty after the most erudite teachers had not only given oral explanations but had drawn numerous diagrams in the dust. They could tell me nothing they had learnt from these teachers which I did not already know from reading the book on my own without having anyone to explain it. The book seemed to me an extremely clear statement about substances, such as man, and what are in them, such as a man's shape, what is his quality of stature, how many feet, and his relatedness, for example whose brother he is, or where he is placed, or when he was born, or whether he is standing or sitting, or is wearing shoes or armour, or whether he is active or passive, and the innumerable things which are classified by these nine genera of which I have given some instances, or by the genus of substance itself.

(29) What help was this to me when the book was also an obstacle? Thinking that absolutely everything that exists is comprehended under the ten categories, I tried to conceive you also, my God, wonderfully simple and immutable, as if you too were a subject of which magnitude and beauty are attributes.[34] I thought them to be

---

[33] A Latin translation of the *Categories* had been made not long before Augustine's time by Marius Victorinus, on whom see below VIII. ii (3).

[34] Plotinus (6. 2. 3) regarded the *Categories* as a classification system for this world, inapplicable to the divine realm. He opposed the opinion (held by Alexander of Aphrodisias, c.AD 200) that the *Categories* embrace all kinds of being, sensible and intelligible. Porphyry sought a middle way by interpreting the *Categories* to be concerned not with

in you as if in a subject, as in the case of a physical body, whereas you yourself are your own magnitude and your own beauty. By contrast a body is not great and beautiful by being body; if it were less great or less beautiful, it would nevertheless still be body. My conception of you was a lie, not truth, the figments of my misery, not the permanent solidity of your supreme bliss. You had commanded and it so came about in me, that the soil would bring forth thorns and brambles for me, and that with toil I should gain my bread (Gen. 3: 18).

(30)   Moreover, what advantage came to me from the fact that I had by myself read and understood all the books I could get hold of on the arts which they call liberal, at a time when I was the most wicked slave of evil lusts? I enjoyed reading them, though I did not know the source of what was true and certain in them. I had my back to the light and my face towards the things which are illuminated. So my face, by which I was enabled to see the things lit up, was not itself illuminated.[35] I learnt about the art of speaking and disputing, and about the dimensions of figures and music and numbers, with no great difficulty and without a teacher to instruct me. You know, Lord my God, that quick thinking and capacity for acute analysis are your gift. But that did not move me to offer them in sacrifice to you. And so these qualities were not helpful but pernicious, because I went to much pains to keep a good part of my talents under my own control. I did not dedicate my courage to you (Ps. 58: 10), but I travelled away from you into a far country to dissipate my substance on meretricious lusts (Luke 15: 13). What advantage did it bring me to have a good thing and not to use it well? I was not aware that these arts are very difficult to understand even for studious and intelligent people, until I tried to explain them to such people and found the student of outstanding quality was the one who did not lag behind me in my exposition.

(31)   But what good did this do for me? I thought that you, Lord God and Truth, were like a luminous body of immense size and myself a bit of that body. What extraordinary perversity! But that is

metaphysics, but with purely logical questions; this enabled Porphyry to mitigate the awkwardness of the *Categories* for the Platonic school, and to make the strange suggestion that Aristotle's book was intended for beginners in the study of philosophy.

[35] Echo of Plotinus 5. 5. 7. Cf. above II. iii (6).

how I was, and I do not blush, Lord God, to confess your mercies to me and to call upon you, for at that time I was not ashamed to profess before men my blasphemies and to 'bark against you' like a dog (Judith 11: 15). What profit, then, was it for me at that time that my agile mind found no difficulty in these subjects, and that without assistance from a human teacher I could elucidate extremely complicated books, when my comprehension of religion was erroneous, distorted, and shamefully sacrilegious? Or what serious harm did it cause to your little ones that their intelligence was much slower? They did not wander away far from you. In the nest of the Church they could grow like fledgelings in safety and nourish the wings of charity with the food of sound faith (Job 39: 26; Ps. 83: 4).

O Lord our God, under the covering of your wings (Exod. 19: 4) we set our hope. Protect us and bear us up. It is you who will carry us; you will bear us up from our infancy until old age (Isa. 46: 4). When you are our firm support, then it is firm indeed. But when our support rests on our own strength, it is infirmity. Our good is life with you for ever, and because we turned away from that, we became twisted. Let us now return to you that we may not be overturned. Our good is life with you and suffers no deficiency (Ps. 101: 28); for you yourself are that good. We have no fear that there is no home to which we may return because we fell from it. During our absence our house suffers no ruin; it is your eternity.[36]

---

[36] This passage is a mosaic of biblical allusions (Ps. 16: 8; 35: 8; 62: 8; Exod. 19: 4; Isa. 46: 4). The Latin has plays on words that cannot be reproduced in translation. On God's eternity as his 'house' see XII. xv (19).

BOOK V

Carthage, Rome, and Milan

i (1)   Accept the sacrifice of my confessions offered by 'the hand of my tongue' (Prov. 18: 21) which you have formed and stirred up to confess your name (Ps. 53: 8). 'Heal all my bones' (Ps. 6: 3) and let them say 'Lord who is like you?' (Ps. 34: 10). He who is making confession to you is not instructing you of that which is happening within him. The closed heart does not shut out your eye, and your hand is not kept away by the hardness of humanity, but you melt that when you wish, either in mercy or in punishment, and there is 'none who can hide from your heat' (Ps. 18: 7). Let my soul praise you that it may love you, and confess to you your mercies that it may praise you (Ps. 118: 175; 145: 2). Your entire creation never ceases to praise you and is never silent. Every spirit continually praises you with mouth turned towards you; animals and physical matter find a voice through those who contemplate them. So from weariness our soul rises towards you, first supporting itself on the created order and then passing on to you yourself who wonderfully made it (Ps. 71: 18; 135: 4). With you is restored strength and true courage.

ii (2)   Let the restless and wicked depart and flee from you (Ps. 138: 7). You see them and pierce their shadowy existence: even with them everything is beautiful, though they are vile.[1] What injury have they done you? Or in what respect have they diminished the honour of your rule, which from the heavens down to the uttermost limits remains just and intact? Where have those who fled from your face gone? Where can they get beyond the reach of your discovery? (Ps. 138). But they have fled that they should not see you, though you see them, and so in their blindness they stumble over you (Rom. 11: 7–11); for you do not desert anything you have made (Wisd. 11: 25). The unjust stumble over you and are justly chastised. Endeavouring to withdraw themselves from your gentleness, they stumble on your equity and fall into your anger. They evidently do

---

[1] In Augustine's Platonic and aesthetic interpretation of evil, the wicked are like the dark in the chiaroscuro of a beautiful picture: *City of God* 11. 23. The idea is already in Plotinus 3. 2. 11. 10 ff.

not know that you are everywhere. No space circumscribes you. You alone are always present even to those who have taken themselves far from you.[2] Let them turn and seek you, for you have not abandoned your creation as they have deserted their Creator (Wisd. 5: 7). Let them turn, and at once you are there in their heart—in the heart of those who make confession to you and throw themselves upon you and weep on your breast after travelling many rough paths. And you gently wipe away their tears (Rev. 7: 17; 21: 4), and they weep yet more and rejoice through their tears. For it is you, Lord, not some man of flesh and blood, but you who have made them and now remake and strengthen them. Where was I when I was seeking for you? You were there before me, but I had departed from myself. I could not even find myself, much less you.

iii (3)   In the presence of my God I speak openly of the twenty-ninth year of my life. There had arrived in Carthage a Manichee bishop named Faustus,[3] a great trap of the devil (1 Tim. 3: 7) by which many were captured as a result of his smooth talk. Although I admired his soft eloquence, nevertheless I came to discern his doctrines to diverge from the truth of matters about which I was keen to learn. I was interested not in the decoration of the vessel in which his discourse was served up but in the knowledge put before me to eat by this Faustus held in high respect among the Manichees. The repute which had preceded his encounter with me was that he was highly trained in all the disciplines of an educated gentleman, and especially learned in the liberal arts. Since I had done much reading in the philosophers and retained this in my memory, I compared some of their teachings with the lengthy fables of the Manichees. The philosophers' teachings seemed to be more probable than what the Manichees said. The philosophers 'were able to judge the world with understanding' even though 'they did not find its Lord' (Wisd. 13: 9). 'For you are great, Lord, you regard the

---

[2] Plotinus 6. 9. 7: 'God is outside none, is present unperceived to all; men flee to get away from him, but really flee from themselves.'

[3] At the same time as the *Confessions*, Augustine was writing a long refutation of Faustus of Mileu in Numidia, who had composed a strong attack on the Old Testament's authority for real Christians, i.e. Manichees, because of its animal sacrifices, womanizers like Solomon, murderers like Moses. The New Testament Faustus treated as interpolated, the Paraclete being the Manichee's guide to distinguish authentic parts. His arrival at Carthage falls *c.*382; he was exiled by the proconsul in 385, and died before Augustine wrote.

humble things, the exalted you know from far off' (Ps. 137: 6). By
the proud you are not found, not even if their curiosity and skill
number the stars and the sand, measure the constellations, and
trace the paths of the stars.

(4)   With the mind and intellect which you have given them, they
investigate these matters. They have found out much. Many years
beforehand they have predicted eclipses of sun and moon, foretelling
the day, the hour, and whether total or partial. And their calculation
has not been wrong. It has turned out just as they predicted. They
have put the rules which they discovered into books which are read
to this day. On this basis prediction can be made of the year, the
month of the year, the day of the month, the hour of the day, and
what proportion of light will be eclipsed in the case of either sun or
moon; and it happens exactly as predicted. People who have no
understanding of these things are amazed and stupefied. Those
who know are exultant and are admired. Their irreligious pride
makes them withdraw from you and eclipse your great light from
reaching themselves. They can foresee a future eclipse of the sun,
but do not perceive their own eclipse in the present. For they do not
in a religious spirit investigate the source of the intelligence with
which they research into these matters. Moreover, when they do
discover that you are their Maker, they do not give themselves to
you so that you may preserve what you have made. They do not slay
in sacrifice to you what they have made themselves to be. They do
not kill their own pride like high-flying birds, their curiosity like
'fishes of the sea', and their sexual indulgence like 'the beasts of the
field',[4] so that you, God, who are a devouring fire,[5] may consume
their mortal concerns and recreate them for immortality.

(5)   They have not known the Way, your Word through whom you
made the things that they count and also those who do the counting,
and the senses thanks to which they observe what they count, and
the mind they employ to calculate. Of your wisdom there is no
numbering (Ps. 146: 5). The Only-begotten himself was made for
us wisdom and righteousness and sanctification (1 Cor. 1: 30). He
was numbered among us (Isa. 53: 12) and paid tribute to Caesar

---

[4] A fusion of 1 John 2: 16 with an allegory of Ps. 8.

[5] Heb. 12: 29 cf. Virgil, *Aeneid* 2.758. There is possibly an allusion to the phoenix
myth.

(Matt. 22: 21). They have not known this way by which they may descend from themselves to him and through him ascend to him. They have not known this way, and think of themselves as exalted and brilliant with the stars. But see, they are crushed to the ground (Isa. 14: 12–13) and 'their foolish heart is darkened' (Rom. 1: 21–5). About the creation they say many things that are true; but the truth, the artificer of creation, they do not seek in a devout spirit and so they fail to find him. Or if they do find him, although knowing God they do not honour him as God or give thanks. They become lost in their own ideas and claim to be wise, attributing to themselves things which belong to you. In an utterly perverse blindness they want to attribute to you qualities which are their own, ascribing mendacity to you who are the truth, and changing the glory of the incorrupt God into the likeness of the image of corruptible man and birds and animals and serpents. They change your truth into a lie and serve the creation rather than the Creator (Rom. 1: 21–5).

(6) Nevertheless I used to recall many true observations made by them about the creation itself. I particularly noted the rational, mathematical order of things, the order of seasons, the visible evidence of the stars. I compared these with the sayings of Mani who wrote much on these matters very copiously and foolishly. I did not notice any rational account of solstices and equinoxes or eclipses of luminaries nor anything resembling what I had learnt in the books of secular wisdom. Yet I was ordered to believe Mani. But he was not in agreement with the rational explanations which I had verified by calculation and had observed with my own eyes. His account was very different.[6]

iv (7) Lord God of truth, surely the person with a scientific knowledge of nature is not pleasing to you on that ground alone. The person who knows all those matters but is ignorant of you is unhappy. The person who knows you, even if ignorant of natural science, is happy. Indeed the one who knows both you and nature is not on that account happier. You alone are his source of happiness if knowing you he glorifies you for what you are and gives thanks and is not lost in his own imagined ideas (Rom. 1: 21). A man who

---

[6] The Manichees believed eclipses occurred when the sun or the moon wished to veil their eyes from the terrible cosmic battles between the light and the darkness (Simplicius, *Commentary on Epictetus* 34 p. 167 Salmasius = 27 p. 72 ed. Dübner).

knows that he owns a tree and gives thanks to you for the use of it, even though he does not know exactly how many cubits high it is or what is the width of its spread, is better than the man who measures it and counts all its branches but does not own it, nor knows and loves its Creator. In an analogous way the believer has the whole world of wealth (Prov. 17: 6 LXX) and 'possesses all things as if he had nothing' (2 Cor. 6: 10) by virtue of his attachment to you whom all things serve; yet he may know nothing about the circuits of the Great Bear. It is stupid to doubt that he is better than the person who measures the heaven and counts the stars and weighs the elements, but neglects you who have disposed everything 'by measure and number and weight' (Wisd. 11: 21).

v (8)   Who asked this obscure fellow Mani to write on these things, skill in which is not essential to learning piety? You have said to man: 'See, piety is wisdom' (Job 28: 28). Mani could be ignorant of religion even if he knew natural science perfectly. But his impudence in daring to teach a matter which he did not understand shows that he could know nothing whatever of piety. It is vanity to profess to know these scientific matters, even if one understands them; but it is piety to make confession to you. Mani departed from this principle. He had very much to say about the world, but was convicted of ignorance by those who really understand these things, and from this one can clearly know what understanding he had in other matters which are harder to grasp. He did not wish the opinion of his abilities to be low. He even tried to persuade people that the Holy Spirit, the comforter and enricher of your faithful people, was with plenary authority personally present in himself.[7] So when he was found out, saying quite mistaken things about the heaven and stars and the movements of sun and moon, though these matters have nothing to do with religion, it was very clear that his bold speculations were sacrilegious. He not only wrote on matters of which he was ignorant, but also uttered his falsehoods with so mad a vanity and pride that he attempted to attribute them to himself as though he were a divine person.

(9)   When I hear this or that brother Christian, who is ignorant of these matters and thinks one thing the case when another is correct, with patience I contemplate the man expressing his opinion. I do

---

[7] Several Manichee texts say that the Paraclete is Mani's other self.

not see it is any obstacle to him if perhaps he is ignorant of the position and nature of a physical creature, provided that he does not believe something unworthy of you, Lord, the Creator of all things (1 Macc. 1: 24). But it becomes an obstacle if he thinks his view of nature belongs to the very form of orthodox doctrine, and dares obstinately to affirm something he does not understand. But such an infirmity in the cradle of faith is sustained by mother charity, until the new man 'grows up into a mature man and is no longer carried about by any wind of doctrine' (Eph. 4: 13). But in the case of that man who dared to pose as a teacher, an authority, as a leader and prince of those he persuaded of his ideas, so that his followers thought themselves to be going after not a mere man but your Holy Spirit, who would not judge that, once he had been convicted of purveying falsehoods, such folly should be detested and put wholly aside?

But I had not yet clearly ascertained whether Mani's words offered a possible explanation consistent with the changes of longer and shorter days and nights, the alternation of night and day, the eclipses and other phenomena of this kind which I had read about in other books. If perhaps this view were possible, the matter would become an open question to me whether the truth were this way or that; then notwithstanding the uncertainty, I could still advance his authority, based on the belief in his sanctity, as a support to my faith.[8]

vi (10)   In the nine years or so during which my vagabond mind listened to the Manichees, I waited with intense yearning for the coming of this Faustus. Other Manichees, whom I had happened to meet, were unable to answer the questions which I put. But they promised me that once Faustus had come and had conversation with me, these questions and any yet greater problems I might have would be resolved very easily and clearly. When he came, I found him gracious and pleasant with words. He said the things they usually say, but put it much more agreeably. But what could the most presentable waiter do for my thirst by offering precious cups? My ears were already satiated with this kind of talk, which did

---

[8] Augustine's *Literal Commentary on Genesis* is severely critical of Christians who bring their faith into discredit by treating Genesis as creation-science. Nevertheless, he could also argue that the correct literal interpretation of Genesis is a matter of such uncertainty that none can assert it to be at variance with science anyway.

not seem better to me because more elegantly expressed. Fine style does not make something true, nor has a man a wise soul because he has a handsome face and well-chosen eloquence. They who had promised that he would be so good were not good judges. He seemed to them prudent and wise because he charmed them by the way he talked.

I have come to know people of another type, who are suspicious and refuse to accept the truth if it is presented in polished and rich language.[9] But I had already been taught by you, my God, through wonderful and hidden ways, and I believe what you have taught me because it is true, and none other than you is teacher of the truth, wherever and from whatever source it is manifest. Already I had learnt from you that nothing is true merely because it is eloquently said, nor false because the signs coming from the lips make sounds deficient in a sense of style. Again, a statement is not true because it is enunciated in an unpolished idiom, nor false because the words are splendid. Wisdom and foolishness are like food that is nourishing or useless. Whether the words are ornate or not does not decide the issue. Food of either kind can be served in either town or country ware.

(11) For a long time I had eagerly awaited Faustus. When he came, I was delighted by the force and feeling he brought to his discourse and by the fitting language which flowed with facility to clothe his ideas. I was pleased and, as much as many and even more than many, I praised and spoke highly of him. But I was disappointed that in the public assembly of his audience I was not allowed to put a question, and to share with him the perplexing questions disturbing me, by informal conference and by the give and take of argument. When this became possible, I together with my close friends began to engage his attention at a moment when it was not out of place to exchange question and answer in discussion. When I put forward some problems which troubled me, I quickly discovered him to be ignorant of the liberal arts other than grammar and literature; and his knowledge was of a conventional kind. He had read some orations of Cicero, a very few books by Seneca, some pieces of poetry, and some volumes of his own sect composed in a Latin of good style. Every day he practised delivery of a discourse, and so

---

[9] Augustine's book 'On Christian Doctrine' has a critique of this view.

acquired a verbal facility which was made more agreeable and attractive by the controlled use of his mind and by a certain natural grace.

Lord my God, judge of my conscience, is my memory correct? Before you I lay my heart and my memory. At that time you were dealing with me in your hidden secret providence, and you were putting my shameful errors before my face (Ps. 49: 21) so that I would see and hate them.

vii (12)   After he had clearly showed his lack of training in liberal arts in which I had supposed him to be highly qualified, I began to lose all hope that he would be able to analyse and resolve the difficulties which disturbed me. Ignorance of the liberal arts is compatible with holding authentic piety, but not if one is a Manichee. Their books are full of immensely lengthy fables about the heaven and stars and sun and moon. I wanted Faustus to tell me, after comparing the mathematical calculations which I had read in other books, whether the story contained in the Manichee books was correct, or at least whether it had an equal chance of being so. I now did not think him clever enough to explain the matter. Nevertheless I put forward my problems for consideration and discussion. He modestly did not even venture to take up the burden. He knew himself to be uninformed on these matters and was not ashamed to confess it. He was not one of the many loquacious people, whom I have had to endure, who attempted to instruct me and had nothing to say. He had a heart which, if not right towards you, was at least very cautious with himself. He was not utterly unskilled in handling his own lack of training, and he refused to be rashly drawn into a controversy about those matters from which there would be no exit nor easy way of retreat. This was an additional ground for my pleasure. For the controlled modesty of a mind that admits limitations is more beautiful than the things I was anxious to know about. And in all the most difficult and subtle questions this was how I found him.

(13)   In consequence the enthusiasm I had for the writings of Mani was diminished, and I felt even greater despair of learning from their other teachers after having consulted on the many points which disturbed me the man who was particularly distinguished. However, I began to spend time with him because of his warm love

for literature, the subject which at that time I was teaching young
men as a professor of rhetoric at Carthage. I used to read with him
either books which he expressed a desire to hear or which I thought
appropriate for a mind of his ability. But my entire effort, on which
I had resolved, to advance higher in that sect was totally abandoned,
once I had come to know that man. My position was that I had not
found anything more satisfactory than that into which I had somehow
fallen. I decided to be content for the time being unless perhaps
something preferable should come to light. So the renowned Faustus,
who had been for many 'a snare of death' (Ps. 17: 6), without his
will or knowledge had begun to loosen the bond by which I had
been captured. For in your hidden providence your hands, my
God, did not forsake my soul. By my mother's tears night and day
sacrifice was being offered to you from the blood of her heart, and
you dealt with me in wonderful ways.

You, my God, brought that about. 'For the steps of man are
directed by the Lord, and he chooses his way' (Ps. 36: 23). How
can salvation be obtained except through your hand remaking what
you once made?

viii (14)   You were at work in persuading me to go to Rome and to
do my teaching there rather than at Carthage. The consideration
which persuaded me I will not omit to confess to you because in this
also your profoundly mysterious providence and your mercy very
present to us are proper matters for reflection and proclamation.
My motive in going to Rome was not that the friends who urged it
on me promised higher fees and a greater position of dignity,
though at that time these considerations had an influence on my
mind. The principal and almost sole reason was that I had heard
how at Rome the young men went quietly about their studies and
were kept in order by a stricter imposition of discipline. They did
not rush all at once and in a mob into the class of a teacher with
whom they were not enrolled, nor were pupils admitted at all unless
the teacher gave them leave. By contrast at Carthage the licence of
the students is foul and uncontrolled. They impudently break in
and with almost mad behaviour disrupt the order which each
teacher has established for his pupils' benefit. They commit many
acts of vandalism with an astonishing mindlessness, which would
be punished under the law were it not that custom protects them.

Thereby their wretched self-delusion is shown up. They act as if they were allowed to do what would never be permitted by your eternal law. They think they are free to act with impunity when by the very blindness of their behaviour they are being punished, and inflict on themselves incomparably worse damage than on others.[10] When I was a student, I refused to have anything to do with these customs; as a professor I was forced to tolerate them in outsiders who were not my own pupils. So I decided to go where all informed people declared that such troubles did not occur. But it was you, 'my hope and my portion in the land of the living' (Ps. 141: 6) who wished me to change my earthly home for 'the salvation of my soul' (Ps. 34: 3). You applied the pricks which made me tear myself away from Carthage, and you put before me the attractions of Rome to draw me there, using people who love a life of death, committing insane actions in this world, promising vain rewards in the next.[11] To correct my 'steps' (Ps. 36: 23; Prov. 20: 20) you secretly made use of their and my perversity. For those who disturbed my serenity were blinded with a disgraceful frenzy. Those who invited me to go elsewhere had a taste only for this earth. I myself, while I hated a true misery here, pursued a false felicity there.

(15) But you knew, God, why I left Carthage and went to Rome, and of that you gave no hint either to me or to my mother, who was fearfully upset at my going and followed me down to the sea. But as she vehemently held on to me calling me back or saying she would come with me, I deceived her. I pretended I had a friend I did not want to leave until the wind was right for him to sail. I lied to my mother—to such a mother—and I gave her the slip. Even this you forgave me, mercifully saving me from the waters of the sea, when I was full of abominable filth, so as to bring me to the water of your grace [in baptism]. This water was to wash me clean, and to dry the rivers flowing from my mother's eyes which daily before you irrigated the soil beneath her face.

Nevertheless since she refused to return home without me, with difficulty I persuaded her to stay that night in a place close to our

---

[10] Plotinus (3. 2. 8. 26–31) similarly comments that ruffians and hoodlums do themselves much injury.

[11] Augustine's appointment to Rome was facilitated by his Manichee connections.

ship, the memorial shrine to blessed Cyprian.[12] But that night I secretly set out; she did not come, but remained praying and weeping. By her floods of tears what was she begging of you, my God, but that you would not allow me to sail? Yet in your deep counsel you heard the central point of her longing, though not granting her what she then asked, namely that you would make me what she continually prayed for. The wind blew and filled our sails and the shore was lost to our sight. There, when morning came, she was crazed with grief, and with recriminations and groans she filled your ears. But you paid no heed to her cries. You were using my ambitious desires as a means towards putting an end to those desires, and the longing she felt for her own flesh and blood was justly chastised by the whip of sorrows. As mothers do, she loved to have me with her, but much more than most mothers; and she did not understand that you were to use my absence as a means of bringing her joy. She did not know that. So she wept and lamented, and these agonies proved that there survived in her the remnants of Eve, seeking with groaning for the child she had brought forth in sorrow (Gen. 3: 16). And yet after accusing me of deception and cruelty, she turned again to pray for me and to go back to her usual home. Meanwhile I came to Rome.

ix (16)   At Rome my arrival was marked by the scourge of physical sickness, and I was on the way to the underworld, bearing all the evils I had committed against you, against myself, and against others—sins both numerous and serious, in addition to the chain of original sin[13] by which 'in Adam we die' (1 Cor. 15: 22). You had not yet forgiven me in Christ for any of them, nor had he by his cross delivered me from the hostile disposition towards you which I had contracted by my sins. How could he deliver me from them if his cross was, as I had believed, a phantom?[14] Insofar as the death of his flesh was in my opinion unreal, the death of my soul was real. And insofar as the death of his flesh was authentic, to that extent the life of my soul, which disbelieved that, was inauthentic. The

[12] Cyprian, bishop of Carthage martyred in 258, was for the African Churches their outstanding hero, the vigil of whose feast day (14 September) was marked by all-night dancing.

[13] This is the earliest occurrence of this phrase to describe inherent human egotism, the inner condition contrasted with overt actions.

[14] Manichees disbelieved the reality of the crucifixion, for them a symbol of universal human suffering.

fevers became worse, and I was on my way out and dying. If at that time I had died, where was I going but into the fire and to the torments which, by your true order of justice, my deeds deserved? My mother did not know I was ill, but she was praying for me, though not beside me. But you are present everywhere. Where she was, you heard her, and where I was, you had mercy on me so that I recovered the health of my body. I still remained sick in my sacrilegious heart, for though in such great danger, I had no desire for your baptism. I did better as a boy when I begged for it from my devout mother, as I have recalled and confessed.[15] But I had grown in shame and in my folly used to laugh at the counsels of your medicine. Yet you did not allow me to die in this sad condition of both body and soul. If my mother's heart had suffered that wound, she would never have recovered. I cannot speak enough of the love she had for me. She suffered greater pains in my spiritual pregnancy than when she bore me in the flesh.

(17) I do not see how she could have recovered if my death in those circumstances had like a scourge struck across the compassion of her love. Where would have been all her prayers, so frequent as to be ceaseless? Nowhere except with you. But, God of mercies, would you despise the contrite and humble heart of a chaste and sober widow (cf. 1 Tim. 5: 10), liberal in almsgiving, obedient and helpful in serving your saints, letting no day pass without making an oblation at your altar, twice a day at morning and at evening coming to your Church with unfailing regularity, taking no part in vain gossip and old wives' chatter, but wanting to hear you in your words[16] and to speak to you in her prayers? Could you, who gave her this character, despise and repel from your assistance tears by which she sought of you, not gold and silver nor any inconstant or transitory benefit, but the salvation of her son's soul? No indeed, Lord, of course you were there and were hearing her petition, and were following through the order of events that you had predestined. You could not have misled her in those visions and your responses, both those which I have already mentioned, and those which I have omitted. At her faithful breast she held on to them, and in her unceasing prayer she as it were presented to you your bond of promises. For your mercy is for ever (Ps. 117: 1; 137: 8), and you

---

[15] II. xi (17).   [16] i.e. through the Bible.

deign to make yourself a debtor obliged by your promises to those
to whom you forgive all debts.

x (18)   You healed my sickness, and at that time made 'the son of
your maidservant' (Ps. 115: 16) whole in body as an interim step
towards giving him a better and more certain health. Even during
this period at Rome I was associated with those false and deceiving
Saints—not only with their Hearers, one of whom was the man in
whose house I had lain sick and recovered health, but also with
those whom they call Elect. I still thought that it is not we who sin,
but some alien nature which sins in us. It flattered my pride to be
free of blame and, when I had done something wrong, not to make
myself confess to you that you might heal my soul; for it was sinning
against you (Ps. 40: 5). I liked to excuse myself and to accuse some
unidentifiable power which was with me and yet not I. But the
whole was myself and what divided me against myself was my
impiety. That was a sin the more incurable for the fact that I did not
think myself a sinner. My execrable wickedness preferred the
disastrous doctrine that in me you, almighty God, suffer defeat
rather than that, to be saved, I needed to surrender to you.

You had not yet 'put a guard on my mouth and a gate of
continence about my lips' (Ps. 140: 2) to prevent my heart slipping
into evil words to find excuses for sinning with 'people who do
iniquity' (Ps. 140: 3). That is why I was still in close association
'with their Elect' (Ps. 140: 4), even though I had already lost hope
of being able to advance higher in that false doctrine. I had decided
to be content to remain with them if I should find nothing better;
but my attitude was increasingly remiss and negligent.

(19)   The thought had come into my mind that the philosophers
whom they call Academics were shrewder than others. They taught
that everything is a matter of doubt, and that an understanding of
the truth lies beyond human capacity. For to me that seemed clearly
to be their view, and so they are popularly held to think. I did not
yet understand their intention.[17]

I did not neglect to tell my host that he should not put the
excessive trust, which I perceived him to have, in the fabulous

---

[17] Augustine (*Against the Academics* III) accepted from Porphyry the opinion that the
scepticism of the ancient Academy about the possibility of assured knowledge about
anything went with an esoteric positive doctrine. Their intention was to safeguard Plato's
spiritual metaphysic from the materialism of Stoics and Epicureans.

matters of which Manichee books are full. But I was in more intimate friendship with them than with others who were not in that heresy. I did not defend it with the zest that at one time I had. Nevertheless my close association with them (the number of them secretly living in Rome was large) made me reluctant to look elsewhere. In particular I had no hope that truth could be found in your Church, Lord of heaven and earth (Gen. 24: 3), maker of all things visible and invisible (Col. 1: 16). The Manichees had turned me away from that. I thought it shameful to believe you to have the shape of the human figure, and to be limited by the bodily lines of our limbs.[18] When I wanted to think of my God, I knew of no way of doing so except as a physical mass. Nor did I think anything existed which is not material. That was the principal and almost sole cause of my inevitable error.

(20) For the same reason I also believed that evil is a kind of material substance with its own foul and misshapen mass, either solid which they used to call earth, or thin and subtle, as is the body of air. They imagine it to be a malignant mind creeping through the earth. And since piety (however bizarre some of my beliefs were) forbade me to believe that the good God had created an evil nature, I concluded that there are two opposed masses, both infinite, but the evil rather smaller, the good larger;[19] and of this pestilential beginning other blasphemous notions were the corollary. When my mind attempted to return to the Catholic faith, it was rebuffed because the Catholic faith is not what I thought. My God, to whom your mercies make it possible for me to make confession, I felt it more reverent to believe you infinite in all respects but one, namely the mass of evil opposed to you, than to think you in all parts limited to the shape of the human body. I thought it better to believe that you had created no evil—which in my ignorance I thought not merely some sort of substance but even corporeal, since I did not know how to think of mind except as a subtle physical entity diffused through space—rather than to believe that the nature of evil, as I understood it, came from you. Our Saviour himself, your only Son, I imagined emerging from the mass of your dazzling body

[18] Manichee attacks on Genesis 1 especially scorned the notion that man is in God's image.

[19] Manichees did not hold the area of Darkness to be equal to that of Light, but to be a black 'wedge' cutting into the Light.

of light for our salvation. I could believe of him only what my vain imagination could picture. I thought a nature such as his could not be born of the Virgin Mary without being mingled with flesh. That he could be mixed with us and not polluted I did not see, because my mental picture was what it was. I was afraid to believe him incarnate lest I had to believe him to be defiled by the flesh. Today your spiritual believers will kindly and lovingly laugh at me when they read these my confessions. Nevertheless that was the state of my mind.

xi (21)   I did not think there was any defence against the Manichees' criticisms of your scriptures. Sometimes, however, I desired to debate particular points with someone very learned in those books, and to discover what he thought about these questions. At Carthage the lectures of a certain Elpidius, who publicly spoke and debated against the Manichees, began to disturb me, when he cited matter from the scriptures to which there was no easy reply. The Manichee answer seemed to me weak. They did not easily produce their response before the public but did so to us in private. They asserted that the scriptures of the New Testament had been tampered with by persons unknown, who wanted to insert the Jews' law into the Christian faith. They were incapable of producing any uncorrupted copies. But the principal things which held me captive and somehow suffocated me, as long as I thought only in physical terms, were those vast masses. Gasping under their weight I could not breathe the pure and simple breeze of your truth.

xii (22)   I began to be busy about the task of teaching the art of rhetoric for which I had come to Rome. I first gathered some pupils at my lodging, and with them and through them I began to be known. I quickly discovered that at Rome students behaved in a way which I would never have had to endure in Africa. Acts of vandalism, it was true, by young hooligans did not occur at Rome; that was made clear to me. But, people told me, to avoid paying the teacher his fee, numbers of young men would suddenly club together and transfer themselves to another tutor,[20] breaking their word and

---

[20] Augustine's contemporary, a pagan Alexandrian schoolmaster named Palladas, has the identical complaint about his pupils, who would leave him for another teacher just as they were due to pay the annual fee of one gold *solidus* (*The Greek Anthology* 9, 174). At Antioch Libanius circumvented pupils' dishonesty by making a contract with their parents (*oratio* 43). A teacher with 40 pupils would be doing reasonably well, but was not

out of love of money treating fairness as something to be flouted. I cordially detested them, but not 'with a perfect hatred' (Ps. 138: 22); for I probably felt more resentment for what I personally was to suffer from them than for the wrong they were doing to anyone and everyone. Certainly such people are a disgrace and 'commit fornication against you' (Ps. 72: 27). They love the passing, transient amusements and the filthy lucre which dirties the hand when it is touched. They embrace a world which is fleeing away. They despise you, though you abide and call the prodigal back and pardon the human soul for its harlotry when it returns to you. Today too I hate such wicked and perverted people, though I love them as people in need of correction, so that instead of money they may prefer the doctrine which they learn and, above the doctrine, may prefer you, God, the truth, the abundant source of assured goodness and most chaste peace. But at that time I was determined not to put up with badly behaved people more out of my own interest than because I wanted them to become good for your sake.

xiii (23)   So after a notification came from Milan to Rome to the city prefect saying that at Milan a teacher of rhetoric was to be appointed with his travel provided by the government service, I myself applied through the mediation of those intoxicated with Manichee follies. My move there was to end my association with them, but neither of us knew that. An oration I gave on a prescribed topic was approved by the then prefect Symmachus,[21] who sent me to Milan.

And so I came to Milan to Ambrose the bishop, known throughout the world as among the best of men, devout in your worship. At that time his eloquence valiantly ministered to your people 'the abundance of your sustenance' and 'the gladness of oil' (Ps. 44: 8; 80: 17; 147: 14), and the sober intoxication of your wine.[22] I was led to him by you, unaware that through him, in full awareness, I might be led to

wealthy; moreover, he had to pay something to an usher to guard the entrance veil. Salaries and fees would be higher in larger cities (see above, I. xvi (26)). Elsewhere Augustine says that in small towns there was only a single teacher; the market perhaps would not have supported a second.

[21] Symmachus, a prominent and opulent pagan, became prefect of Rome in September 384. Augustine's arrival at Milan was probably in October.

[22] 'Sober intoxication', describing the ecstasy of a knowledge of God lying beyond reason, occurs in Ambrose and, before him, in the Jewish theologian Philo of Alexandria. Also Plotinus 6. 7. 35. 27.

you. That 'man of God' (2 Kgs. 1: 9) received me like a father and
expressed pleasure at my coming with a kindness most fitting in a
bishop. I began to like him, at first indeed not as a teacher of the
truth, for I had absolutely no confidence in your Church, but as a
human being who was kind to me. I used enthusiastically to listen to
him preaching to the people, not with the intention which I ought to
have had, but as if testing out his oratorical skill to see whether it
merited the reputation it enjoyed or whether his fluency was better
or inferior than it was reported to be. I hung on his diction in rapt
attention, but remained bored and contemptuous of the subject-
matter. My pleasure was in the charm of his language. It was more
learned than that of Faustus, but less witty and entertaining, as far
as the manner of his speaking went. But in content there could be no
comparison. Through Manichee deceits Faustus wandered astray.
Ambrose taught the sound doctrine of salvation. From sinners such
as I was at that time, salvation is far distant. Nevertheless, gradually,
though I did not realize it, I was drawing closer.

xiv (24)   I was not interested in learning what he was talking about.
My ears were only for his rhetorical technique; this empty concern
was all that remained with me after I had lost any hope that a way to
you might lie open for man. Nevertheless together with the words
which I was enjoying, the subject matter, in which I was unconcerned,
came to make an entry into my mind. I could not separate them.
While I opened my heart in noting the eloquence with which he
spoke, there also entered no less the truth which he affirmed,
though only gradually. First what he said began to seem defensible,
and I did not now think it impudent to assert the Catholic faith, which
I had thought defenceless against Manichee critics. Above all, I heard
first one, then another, then many difficult passages in the Old
Testament scriptures figuratively interpreted, where I, by taking
them literally, had found them to kill (2 Cor. 3: 6). So after several
passages in the Old Testament had been expounded spiritually, I
now found fault with that despair of mine, caused by my belief that
the law and the prophets could not be defended at all against the
mockery of hostile critics. However, even so I did not think the
Catholic faith something I ought to accept. Granted it could have
educated people who asserted its claims and refuted objections
with abundant argument and without absurdity. But that was not

sufficient ground to condemn what I was holding. There could be an equally valid defence for both. So to me the Catholic faith appeared not to have been defeated but also not yet to be the conqueror.

(25)   I then energetically applied my critical faculty to see if there were decisive arguments by which I could somehow prove the Manichees wrong. If I had been able to conceive of spiritual substance, at once all their imagined inventions would have collapsed and my mind would have rejected them. But I could not. However, in regard to the physical world and all the natural order accessible to the bodily senses, consideration and comparison more and more convinced me that numerous philosophers held opinions much more probable than theirs. Accordingly, after the manner of the Academics, as popularly understood, I doubted everything, and in the fluctuating state of total suspense of judgement I decided I must leave the Manichees, thinking at that period of my scepticism that I should not remain a member of a sect to which I was now preferring certain philosophers. But to these philosophers, who were without Christ's saving name, I altogether refused to entrust the healing of my soul's sickness. I therefore decided for the time being to be a catechumen in the Catholic Church, which the precedent of my parents recommended to me, until some clear light should come by which I could direct my course.

BOOK VI

Secular Ambitions and Conflicts

i (1) 'My hope from my youth' (Ps. 70: 5), where were you, and where did you 'withdraw' from me (Ps. 10: 1)? Did you not make me, and 'make me superior to the animals, and make me wiser than the birds of heaven' (Job 35: 10–11)? I was walking through darkness and 'a slippery place' (Ps. 34: 6). I was seeking for you outside myself,[1] and I failed to find 'the God of my heart' (Ps. 72: 26). I had come into the depth of the sea (Ps. 67: 23). I had no confidence, and had lost hope that truth could be found.

My mother, strong in her devotion, had already come to join me, following me by land and sea, and in all dangers serenely confident in you. During a hazardous voyage she encouraged the crew themselves who are accustomed to offering consolation to frightened travellers with no experience of the deep sea. She promised them a safe arrival, for in a vision you had promised this to her. She found me in a dangerous state of depression. I had lost all hope of discovering the truth. Yet when I informed her that I was not now a Manichee, though neither was I a Catholic Christian, she did not leap for joy as if she had heard some unexpected news; she was already free from anxiety about that part of my wretched condition, for which she wept over me as a person dead but to be revived by you. In her mind she was offering me before you on a bier, so that you could say, as you said to the widow's son 'Young man, I say to you, arise' (Luke 7: 12); and then he would recover and begin to speak and you would restore him to his mother.

So no excited jubilation caused her heart to beat faster when she heard that so large a part of what she daily and tearfully prayed for had already come about. I had not yet attained the truth, but I was rescued from falsehood. Moreover, because she felt certain that you were going to grant what remained, when you had promised the whole, very calmly and with her heart full of confidence she replied to me that she had faith in Christ that before she departed this life, she

---

[1] Plotinus says God is not to be sought in external things (6. 5. 1. 21).

would see me a baptized Catholic believer. That indeed she said to me. To you, fount of mercies, she redoubled her petitions and tears, begging that you would hasten your help (Ps. 69: 1) and lighten my darknesses (Ps. 17: 29). She would zealously run to the Church to hang on Ambrose's lips, to 'the fount of water bubbling up to eternal life' (John 4: 14). She loved that man as an angel of God (Gal. 4: 14) when she knew that it was through him that I had been brought to that state of hesitancy and wavering. I was to pass through that from sickness to health, but with a more acute danger intervening, like that high fever preceding recovery which the physicians call 'the critical onset'.[2]

ii (2)   In accordance with my mother's custom in Africa, she had taken to the memorial shrines of the saints cakes and bread and wine, and was forbidden by the janitor. When she knew that the bishop was responsible for the prohibition, she accepted it in so devout and docile a manner that I myself was amazed how easy it was for her to find fault with her own custom rather than to dispute his ban. Her spirit was not obsessed by excessive drinking, and no love of wine stimulated her into opposing the truth, as is the case with many men and women who, when one sings them the song of sobriety, feel as nauseated as drunkards when offered a watery drink. After bringing her basket of ceremonial food which she would first taste and then share round the company, she used to present not more than one tiny glass of wine diluted to suit her very sober palate. She would take a sip as an act of respect. If there were many memorial shrines of the dead which were to be honoured in that way, it was one and the same cup which she carried about and presented at each place. The wine was not merely drenched with water but also quite tepid; the share she gave to those present was only small sips. Her quest was for devotion, not pleasure. When she learnt that the famous preacher and religious leader had ordered that no such offerings were to be made, even by those who acted soberly, to avert any pretext for intoxication being given to drinkers and because the ceremonies were like meals to propitiate the departed spirits and similar to heathen superstition,[3] she happily

[2] Augustine (*Sermon on Ps. 72*) says: The sick feel less ill when recovery is distant, but are in a higher fever when it is close; physicians call this the 'accessio critica'.

[3] Ambrose (*On Elias* 62) mentions his ban. Augustine vainly tried to stop the inebriation at martyrs' shrines in Africa, where (as one letter records) drink was a major social

abstained. Instead of a basket full of the fruits of the earth, she learned to bring a heart full of purer vows to the memorials of the martyrs. She would give what she could to the needy; and then the communion of the Lord's body was celebrated at the shrines of the martyrs who in imitation of the Lord's passion were sacrificed and crowned.

Yet it seems to me, Lord my God—and this is the conviction of my heart in your sight (Ps. 18: 15)—that she would not have yielded easily on the prohibition of this custom if the ban had come from another whom she did not love like Ambrose. For the sake of my salvation she was wholly devoted to him, and he loved her for her deeply religious pattern of life. In good works 'fervent in spirit' (Rom. 12: 11), she was habitually at the Church. When he saw me, he often broke out in praise of her, congratulating me on having such a mother, unaware of what kind of son she had in me—someone who doubted all these things and believed it impossible to find the way of life.

iii (3)   I had not yet come to groan in prayer that you might come to my aid. My mind was intent on inquiry and restless for debate. Ambrose himself I thought a happy man as the world judges things, for he was held in honour by the great and powerful. Only his celibacy seemed to me painful. But I had no notion nor any experience to know what were his hopes, what struggles he had against the temptations of his distinguished position, what consolations in adversities, and the hidden aspect of his life—what was in his heart, what delicious joys came as he fed on and digested your bread. He for his part did not know of my emotional crisis nor the abyss of danger threatening me. I could not put the questions I wanted to put to him as I wished to do. I was excluded from his ear and from his mouth by crowds of men with arbitrations to submit to him, to whose frailties he ministered.[4] When he was not with them, which was a very brief period of time, he restored either his body with necessary food or his mind by reading. When he was reading, his eyes ran over the page and his heart perceived the sense, but his voice and tongue were silent. He

---

problem. The defensive tone here and in IX. viii (18) suggests rumours that Monica was addicted to the bottle. Plotinus (5. 5. 11) is sharply critical of pagan festivals which people attend for the beano rather than to honour the god.

[4] In consequence of 1 Cor. 6: 1 ancient bishops expended vast time and energy on arbitrations between members of their flock. Cf. VI. ix (15) below.

did not restrict access to anyone coming in, nor was it customary even for a visitor to be announced. Very often when we were there, we saw him silently reading and never otherwise. After sitting for a long time in silence (for who would dare to burden him in such intent concentration?) we used to go away. We supposed that in the brief time he could find for his mind's refreshment, free from the hubbub of other people's troubles, he would not want to be invited to consider another problem. We wondered if he read silently perhaps to protect himself in case he had a hearer interested and intent on the matter, to whom he might have to expound the text being read if it contained difficulties, or who might wish to debate some difficult questions. If his time were used up in that way, he would get through fewer books than he wished. Besides, the need to preserve his voice, which used easily to become hoarse, could have been a very fair reason for silent reading. Whatever motive he had for his habit, this man had a good reason for what he did.[5]

(4) Certainly no opportunity came my way to put the questions I wished to put to your holy oracle, his heart, except when there was something requiring only a brief interview. My hot passions required a considerable period when he could be free for me to pour out my story to him, and that was never found. However, every Lord's day[6] I heard him 'rightly preaching the word of truth' (2 Tim. 2: 15) among the people. More and more my conviction grew that all the knotty problems and clever calumnies which those deceivers of ours had devised against the divine books could be dissolved. I also learnt that your sons, whom you have regenerated by grace through their mother the Catholic Church, understood the text concerning man being made by you in your image (Gen. 1: 26) not to mean that they believed and thought you to be bounded by the form of a human body. Although I had not the least notion or even an obscure suspicion how there could be spiritual substance, yet I was glad, if also ashamed, to discover that I had been barking for years not against the Catholic faith but against mental figments of physical images. My rashness and impiety lay in the fact that what I ought to have verified by investigation I had simply asserted as an accusation. You who are most high and most near, most secret and most

[5] In antiquity silent reading was uncommon, not unknown.

[6] Augustine disapproved of planetary names for days of the week: 'One should say Dominica for Sunday.'

present, have no bodily members, some larger, others smaller, but are everywhere a whole and never limited in space.[7] You are certainly not our physical shape. Yet you made humanity in your image, and man from head to foot is contained in space.

iv (5) Being ignorant what your image consisted in, I should have knocked (Matt. 7: 7) and inquired about the meaning of this belief, and not insulted and opposed it, as if the belief meant what I thought. My concern to discover what I could hold for certain gnawed at my vitals the more painfully as I felt shame to have been suffering so long from illusion. Deceived with promises of certainty, with childish error and rashness I had mindlessly repeated many uncertain things as if they were certain. That they were false became clear to me only later. But it was certain that they were uncertain and for a period had been treated by me as certain when I contended against your Catholic Church with blind accusations. Even if it was not yet evident that the Church taught the truth, yet she did not teach the things of which I harshly accused her. So I was confused with shame. I was being turned around. And I was glad, my God, that your one Church, the body of your only Son in which on me as an infant Christ's name was put, did not hold infantile follies nor in her sound doctrine maintain that you, the Creator of all things, occupy a vast and huge area of space and are nevertheless bounded on all sides and confined within the shape of the human body.

(6) I was also pleased that when the old writings of the Law and the Prophets came before me, they were no longer read with an eye to which they had previously looked absurd, when I used to attack your saints as if they thought what in fact they did not think at all. And I was delighted to hear Ambrose in his sermons to the people saying, as if he were most carefully enunciating a principle of exegesis: 'The letter kills, the spirit gives life' (2 Cor. 3: 6).[8] Those texts which, taken literally, seemed to contain perverse teaching he would expound spiritually, removing the mystical veil. He did not say anything that I felt to be a difficulty; but whether what he said was true I still did not know. Fearing a precipitate plunge, I kept my heart from giving any assent, and in that state of suspended judge-

---

[7] Plotinus 3. 9. 4; 5. 5. 8–9.
[8] Cited in this sense by Ambrose, *Sermon 19*.

ment I was suffering a worse death. I wanted to be as certain about things I could not see as I am certain that seven and three are ten. I was not so mad as to think that I could consider even that to be something unknowable. But I desired other things to be as certain as this truth, whether physical objects which were not immediately accessible to my senses, or spiritual matters which I knew no way of thinking about except in physical terms.

By believing I could have been healed. My mind's eye thus purified would have been directed in some degree towards your truth which abides for ever and is indefectible. But just as it commonly happens that a person who has experienced a bad physician is afraid of entrusting himself to a good one, so it was with the health of my soul. While it could not be healed except by believing, it was refusing to be healed for fear of believing what is false. It resisted your healing hands, though you have prepared the medicines of faith,[9] have applied them to the sicknesses of the world, and have given them such power.

v (7) From this time on, however, I now gave my preference to the Catholic faith. I thought it more modest and not in the least misleading to be told by the Church to believe what could not be demonstrated—whether that was because a demonstration existed but could not be understood by all or whether the matter was not one open to rational proof—rather than from the Manichees to have a rash promise of knowledge with mockery of mere belief, and then afterwards to be ordered to believe many fabulous and absurd myths impossible to prove true. Then little by little, Lord, with a most gentle and merciful hand you touched and calmed my heart. I considered the innumerable things I believed which I had not seen, events which occurred when I was not present, such as many incidents in the history of the nations, many facts concerning places and cities which I had never seen, many things accepted on the word of friends, many from physicians, many from other people. Unless we believed what we were told, we would do nothing at all in this life. Finally, I realized how unmoveably sure I was about the identity of my parents from whom I came, which I could not know unless I believed what I had heard.

You persuaded me that the defect lay not with those who believed

[9] i.e. the Bible and the sacraments in the life of the Church.

your books, which you have established with such great authority among almost all nations, but with those who did not believe them. Nor were they to be listened to who might say to me 'How do you know that these books were provided for the human race by the Spirit of the one true and utterly truthful God?' That very thing was a matter in which belief was of the greatest importance; for no attacks based on cavilling questions of the kind of which I had read so much in the mutually contradictory philosophers could ever force me not to believe that you are (though what you are I could not know) or that you exercise a providential care over human affairs.

(8) My belief in this was sometimes stronger, sometimes weaker. But at least I always retained belief both that you are and that you care for us, even if I did not know what to think about your substantial nature or what way would lead, or lead me back, to you. So since we were too weak to discover the truth by pure reasoning and therefore needed the authority of the sacred writings, I now began to believe that you would never have conferred such pre-eminent authority on the scripture, now diffused through all lands, unless you had willed that it would be a means of coming to faith in you and a means of seeking to know you. Already the absurdity which used to offend me in those books, after I had heard many passages being given persuasive expositions, I understood to be significant of the profundity of their mysteries. The authority of the Bible seemed the more to be venerated and more worthy of a holy faith on the ground that it was open to everyone to read, while keeping the dignity of its secret meaning for a profounder interpretation. The Bible offered itself to all in very accessible words and the most humble style of diction, while also exercising the concentration of those who are not 'light of heart' (Ecclus. 19: 4). It welcomes all people to its generous embrace, and also brings a few to you through narrow openings (cf. Matt. 7: 13–14). Though the latter are few, they are much more numerous than would be the case if the Bible did not stand out by its high authority and if it had not drawn crowds to the bosom of its holy humility. These were my reflections and you were present to me. I sighed and you heard me. I wavered and you steadied me. I travelled along the broad way of the world, but you did not desert me.

vi (9)   I aspired to honours, money, marriage, and you laughed at
me. In those ambitions I suffered the bitterest difficulties; that was
by your mercy—so much the greater in that you gave me the less
occasion to find sweet pleasure in what was not you. Look into my
heart, Lord. In obedience to your will I recall this and confess to
you. May my soul now adhere to you. You detached it from the
birdlime which held me fast in death. How unhappy it was! Your
scalpel cut to the quick of the wound, so that I should leave all
these ambitions and be converted to you, who are 'above all things'
(Rom. 9: 5) and without whom all things are nothing, and that by
conversion I should be healed. How unhappy I was, and how
conscious you made me of my misery, on that day when I was
preparing to deliver a panegyric on the emperor![10] In the course of
it I would tell numerous lies and for my mendacity would win the
good opinion of people who knew it to be untrue. The anxiety of
the occasion was making my heart palpitate and perspire with the
destructive fever of the worry, when I passed through a Milan street
and noticed a destitute beggar. Already drunk, I think, he was joking
and laughing. I groaned and spoke with the friends accompanying
me about the many sufferings that result from our follies. In all our
strivings such as those efforts that were then worrying me, the
goads of ambition impelled me to drag the burden of my unhappiness
with me, and in dragging it to make it even worse; yet we had no
goal other than to reach a carefree cheerfulness. That beggar was
already there before us, and perhaps we would never achieve it. For
what he had gained with a few coins, obtained by begging, that is
the cheerfulness of temporal felicity, I was going about to reach by
painfully twisted and roundabout ways. True joy he had not. But
my quest to fulfil my ambitions was much falser. There was no
question that he was happy and I racked with anxiety. He had no
worries; I was frenetic, and if anyone had asked me if I would
prefer to be merry or to be racked with fear, I would have answered
'to be merry'. Yet if he asked whether I would prefer to be a beggar
like that man or the kind of person I then was, I would have chosen
to be myself, a bundle of anxieties and fears. What an absurd

[10] Since Valentinian II became emperor on 22 Nov. 375, the most probable date for
this panegyric is 22 Nov. 384. Augustine elsewhere mentions that he delivered a
panegyric at Milan for the inauguration of the new consul Bauto (*contra litteras Petiliani*
3. 30), 1 Jan. 385. Everyone knew that such speeches were mendacious (Plotinus 5. 5.
13. 14).

choice! Surely it could not be the right one. For I ought not to have put myself above him on the ground of being better educated, a matter from which I was deriving no pleasure. My education enabled me to seek to please men, not to impart to them any instruction, but merely to purvey pleasure. For that reason you 'broke my bones' (Ps. 41: 11; 50: 10) with the rod of your discipline (Ps. 22: 4).

(10)   Let them depart from my soul who say to it: 'There is a different quality in the source of pleasure: the beggar found his pleasure in drink, you wanted to find yours in glory.' But Lord what glory is there which is not in you? Just as his glory was not the real thing, so neither was my glory real, and it turned my head still further. That night the beggar was going to sleep off his intoxication. I slept and rose with mine, and was to sleep and get up again with it for many days. Of course there is a difference in the source of a person's pleasure, I know it. And the joy of a believing hope is incomparably greater than that vanity. But at that time there was also this gulf between us: he was far happier, not merely because he was soaked in cheerfulness while I was eviscerated with anxieties, but also because he had acquired wine by wishing good luck to passers-by, whereas I sought an arrogant success by telling lies. This is the sense of much that I said to my friends at the time. I often observed their condition to be much the same as mine, and my state I found to be bad; this caused me further suffering and a redoubling of my sense of futility. If success ever smiled on me, I would feel that it was not worth the effort to take the opportunity, since, almost before I had grasped it, the chance flew away.

vii (11)   The group of us who lived together as friends used to deplore these things. I used especially to discuss them with Alypius and Nebridius. Among this group Alypius came from the same town as myself. His parents were leading citizens. He was younger than I and had attended my classes when I began to teach in our town and later at Carthage. He was much attached to me because I seemed to him good and cultured, and I was attached to him because of the solid virtue of his character, which was already apparent when he was of no great age. Nevertheless, the whirlpool of Carthaginian morals, with their passion for empty public shows, sucked him into the folly of the circus games. At the time when he was miserably involved in that, I was using a public lecture room as

professor of rhetoric there. He had not yet heard me lecturing
because of a certain estrangement which had arisen between me
and his father. I had discovered his fatal passion for the circus, and
was gravely concerned because he seemed to me about to throw
away or even already to have thrown away a career of high promise.
But there was no means of warning him and recalling him by
imposing some degree of pressure, either by the benevolence of
friendship or by exercising the authority of a teacher. Moreover, I
thought that his opinion of me coincided with his father's. In fact
he did not so think of me. So he put aside his father's wish in this
matter and began to greet me, coming into my lecture room to
listen for a while and then to leave.

(12) I had forgotten my intention to have a word with him to
dissuade him from ruining such good abilities by a blind and rash
enthusiasm for empty games. But Lord, you who preside over the
government of everything which you have created, had not forgotten
him who among your sons was to be a presiding minister of your
mystery.[11] His amendment of life should really be attributed to you,
even if you brought it about through my agency, although I did not
know it. One day I was sitting at the usual place and my pupils were
present before me. He came in, greeted me, sat down, and gave his
attention to the subject under discussion. I was expounding a text
which happened to be in my hands. While I was expounding it, it
seemed opportune to use an illustration from the circus games
which I used to make my point clear, and to make the matter
clearer and more agreeable I was bitingly sarcastic about those
captivated by this folly. 'You know, our God' (Ps. 68: 6) that at that
moment I had no thought of rescuing Alypius from the plague. But
he took it to heart, and believed that I had said it exclusively with
him in mind. An allusion which another person might have taken as
cause for being angry with me, the noble young man took as cause
for anger with himself, and for loving me the more ardently. You
said long ago and inserted in your scriptures: 'Rebuke a wise man
and he will love you' (Prov. 9: 8). I had not rebuked him. But you
use all, both those aware of it and those unaware of it, in the order
which you know—and that order is just. Out of my heart and

---

[11] Alypius became bishop of Thagaste while Augustine was still presbyter at Hippo.
He frequently appears in Augustine's letters, and probably died soon after Augustine.

tongue you made burning coals (Ezek. 1: 13) by which you cauterized
and cured a wasting mind of high promise. Let silence about your
praises be for the person who does not consider your mercies (Ps. 77:
4); your mercies make confession to you from the marrow of my
being (Ps. 106: 8). For on hearing those words he jumped out of
the deep pit in which he was sinking by his own choice and where
he was blinded by an astonishing pleasure. With strict self-control
he gave his mind a shaking, and all the filth of the circus games
dropped away from him, and he stopped going to them. Finally, he
persuaded his reluctant father to allow him to attend me as a
teacher. His father yielded and granted his request. He began again
to attend my classes, and became involved together with me in
Manichee superstition. He admired the show of continence among
them, which he thought authentic and genuine. But it was a mad
and seductive ploy which 'captured precious souls' (Prov. 6: 26)
that do not yet know how to touch virtue at its depth and are easily
deceived by surface appearances. It was only a shadow and simulation
of virtue.

viii (13) Alypius did not indeed abandon the earthly career of
whose prizes his parents had sung to him. He had arrived in Rome
before I did to study law. There he had been seized by an incredible
obsession for gladiatorial spectacles and to an unbelievable degree.
He held such spectacles in aversion and detestation; but some of
his friends and fellow-pupils on their way back from a dinner
happened to meet him in the street and, despite his energetic
refusal and resistance, used friendly violence to take him into the
amphitheatre during the days of the cruel and murderous games.
He said: 'If you drag my body to that place and sit me down there,
do not imagine you can turn my mind and my eyes to those
spectacles. I shall be as one not there, and so I shall overcome both
you and the games.' They heard him, but none the less took him
with them, wanting perhaps to discover whether he could actually
carry it off. When they arrived and had found seats where they
could, the entire place seethed with the most monstrous delight in
the cruelty. He kept his eyes shut and forbade his mind to think
about such fearful evils. Would that he had blocked his ears as well!
A man fell in combat. A great roar from the entire crowd struck him
with such vehemence that he was overcome by curiosity. Supposing

himself strong enough to despise whatever he saw and to conquer it, he opened his eyes. He was struck in the soul by a wound graver than the gladiator in his body, whose fall had caused the roar. The shouting entered by his ears and forced open his eyes. Thereby it was the means of wounding and striking to the ground a mind still more bold than strong, and the weaker for the reason that he presumed on himself when he ought to have relied on you. As soon as he saw the blood, he at once drank in savagery and did not turn away. His eyes were riveted. He imbibed madness. Without any awareness of what was happening to him, he found delight in the murderous contest and was inebriated by bloodthirsty pleasure. He was not now the person who had come in, but just one of the crowd which he had joined, and a true member of the group which had brought him. What should I add? He looked, he yelled, he was on fire, he took the madness home with him so that it urged him to return not only with those by whom he had originally been drawn there, but even more than them, taking others with him.

Nevertheless, from this you delivered him by your most strong and merciful hand, and you taught him to put his confidence not in himself but in you (Isa. 57: 13). But that was much later.

ix (14) This experience, however, rested in his memory to provide a remedy in the future. So too did the following incident which happened when he was still a student and already my pupil at Carthage. He was in the forum at midday thinking about a declamation he was to give after the usual manner of scholastic exercises. You allowed him to be arrested by the officers of the market as a thief. I think the reason why you, our God, allowed this was so that the man who was destined to have such weighty responsibilities should even then begin to learn that in court trials one should be on one's guard against hasty credulity in condemning a man. He was walking up and down alone in front of the lawcourt with his wax tablets and stylus. Suddenly a young man who was one of the students and the real thief, carrying a hidden hatchet, came to the leaden gratings which cover the shops of the silversmiths without Alypius noticing him, and began to hack at the lead. The silversmiths below heard the sound of the hatchet, conferred in whispers, and sent people to catch whoever they might happen to find. The thief heard their voices, dropped his tool, and ran off in fear to avoid being caught with it. Alypius, who had not seen him go in, perceived him as he came out and saw him running off at speed. Wanting to know the reason, he went into the place, found the hatchet, and was standing and reflecting in bemused astonishment when suddenly the party who had been sent found him alone with the iron in his hand, the sound of which had stirred them into coming. They arrested him, dragged him off, and before a crowd of the tenants of the forum they gloried in having apprehended a thief redhanded. From there he was taken to be brought before the judges.

(15) But this was as far as Alypius' lesson went. At once Lord, you came to help an innocence of which you were the sole witness. As he was being taken either to prison or to torture, they met on the road a certain architect who had principal responsibility for public buildings. They were extremely delighted to meet him, for the tenants were commonly suspected by him of removing items which had disappeared from the forum. Now at last he would know the person responsible for the losses. But the man had often seen Alypius in the house of a certain senator to whom he paid frequent visits. He recognized him at once, and taking him by the hand removed him from the crowd and asked him the cause of such an embarrassing situation. When he knew what had occurred, he ordered all the people there, who were in an uproar and making threatening shouts, to come along with him. They came by the house of the young man who had done the deed. In front of the entrance there was a slave boy, so young that he had no fear of compromising his master and could easily be made to tell all. In the forum he had been spotted accompanying him. Alypius recognized him and told the architect. Alypius showed the boy the hatchet and asked him whose it was. 'Ours' he promptly replied. Then he was subjected to interrogation and revealed the rest. So the court case was transferred to that house, and the crowds which had already begun to triumph over Alypius were confounded. The future dispenser of your word and examiner of many arbitrations in your Church went away with increased experience and wisdom.

x (16) So I found Alypius at Rome. He attached himself to me with the strongest bond and was to accompany me to Milan, so that he would not be parted from me and also in order to practise law of which he had been a student, thereby falling in with his parents' wish rather than his own inclination. Three times already he had sat as an assessor[12] and manifested a self-control astonishing to others, while he was much more astonished to find that they preferred gold to their integrity. His character was tested not only by the seductions of avarice but also by the prick of fear. At Rome he was assessor to the count of the Italian Treasury.[13] There was at that time an extremely powerful senator. Many people were kept under his power by bribes or subdued by terror. He wanted as usual to use his influence to obtain something which by the laws was unlawful. Alypius resisted. A bribe was promised. He scorned it resolutely. Threats were made. He kicked them away, and everyone was amazed at so exceptional a character who neither wished to have as a friend nor feared to have as his enemy a powerful person, celebrated for his immense reputation, who had innumerable methods of either benefiting or injuring people. The judge himself, to whom Alypius was adviser, also wished to refuse the application, but did not openly turn it down and threw the responsibility for the case on to Alypius. He asserted that Alypius would not allow him to grant it. The plain truth was that, if he made the grant, Alypius would have resigned.

One thing alone almost led him astray because of his passion for books. He could have manuscripts copied for his own use at special government rates. He deliberated on the justice of this, and decided on the better choice, judging it more expedient to keep integrity, which would forbid it, than to use the power by which it was an allowed perquisite.

This is a small matter. But 'he who is faithful in little is faithful also in much' (Luke 16: 10–22). The word which proceeds from the mouth of your truth will never be empty (cf. Isa. 55: 11): 'If you have not been faithful in the unrighteous mammon, who will give you the true? And if you have not been faithful with someone else's property, who will give you your own?' (Luke 16: 11–12).

That was the character of the man who then attached himself to me and used to debate with me, hesitant what manner of life ought to be adopted.

[12] In Roman courts of law untrained magistrates sat with trained lawyers as assessors.

[13] The 'count of Italian largesses' was in charge of all government finance in Italy, immediately answerable to the Count of the Sacred (i.e. Imperial) Largesses, the supreme Treasury officer of State.

(17) Nebridius also, after leaving his home near Carthage and
Carthage itself where he spent most of his time, abandoned his
father's fine country seat, left home and his mother, who was not to
follow him, and came to Milan. In his burning enthusiasm for the
truth and for wisdom, his single motive was to live with me. Like
me he sighed, and like me he vacillated, ardent in his quest for the
happy life and a most acute investigator of very difficult questions.
So there were the mouths of three hungry people, sharing with
each other the sighs of their own state of need, and looking to you
'to give them their food in due season' (Ps. 114: 15; 103: 27). By
your mercy our worldly activities always brought some bitterness in
their train, and we reflected on the reason why we endured this. We
met only darkness and turned away in disappointment to say 'How
long is this to go on?' We frequently used to speak in this way. But
although that is what we said, we did not give up those activities.
There was no certain source of light which we could grasp after we
had abandoned them.

xi (18) I myself was exceedingly astonished as I anxiously reflected
how long a time had elapsed since the nineteenth year of my life,
when I began to burn with a zeal for wisdom, planning that when I
had found it I would abandon all the empty hopes and lying follies
of hollow ambitions. And here I was already thirty, and still mucking
about in the same mire in a state of indecision, avid to enjoy present
fugitive delights which were dispersing my concentration, while I
was saying: 'Tomorrow I shall find it; see, it will become perfectly
clear, and I shall have no more doubts. Faustus will come and
explain everything. What great men the Academic philosophers
were! Nothing for the conduct of life can be a matter of assured
knowledge. Yet let us seek more diligently and not lose heart. The
books of the Church we now know not to contain absurdities. The
things which seemed absurd can also be understood in another way
which is edifying. Let me fix my feet on that step where as a boy I
was placed by my parents, until clear truth is found. But where may
it be sought?

'When can it be sought? Ambrose has no time. There is no time
for reading. Where should we look for the books we need? Where
and when can we obtain them? From whom can we borrow them?
Fixed times must be kept free, hours appointed, for the health of

the soul. Great hope has been aroused. The Catholic faith does not
teach what we thought and we were mistaken in criticizing it. The
Church's educated men think it wrong to believe that God is bounded
by the shape of a human body. Why do we hesitate to knock at the
door which opens the way to all the rest? Our pupils occupy our
mornings; what should we do with the remaining hours? Why do we
not investigate our problem? But then when should we go to pay
respects to our more influential friends, whose patronage we need?[14]
When are we to prepare what our students are paying for? When
are we to refresh ourselves by allowing the mind to relax from the
tension of anxieties?

(19) 'Let all that perish! Let us set aside these vain and empty
ambitions. Let us concentrate ourselves exclusively on the investigation of the truth. Life is a misery, death is uncertain. It may
suddenly carry us off. In what state shall we depart this life? Where
are we to learn the things we have neglected here? And must we not
rather pay for this negligence with punishments? What if death
itself will cut off and end all anxiety by annihilating the mind? This
too, then, is a question needing scrutiny.

'But put aside the idea that death can be like that. It is not for
nothing, not empty of significance, that the high authority of the
Christian faith is diffused throughout the world. The deity would
not have done all that for us, in quality and in quantity, if with the
body's death the soul's life were also destroyed. Why then do we
hesitate to abandon secular hopes and to dedicate ourselves wholly
to God and the happy life?

'But wait a moment. Secular successes are pleasant. They have
no small sweetness of their own. Our motivation is not to be
deflected from them by a superficial decision; for it would be a
disgrace to return to the secular again. It is a considerable thing to
set out to obtain preferment to high office. And what worldly prize
could be more desirable? We have plenty of influential friends.

[14] A vivid picture of the social system presupposed here is given by the pagan historian
Ammianus Marcellinus (14. 6. 12–13) in a jaundiced account of the Roman aristocracy.
In the later Roman Empire it was common for highly placed persons to feel an obligation
towards dependent clients from the same region. The concentration of people from
North Africa in and around the Milan court at this time, reflected in Augustine's circle
of friends, strongly suggests that there was at least one highly placed person from Africa
who had power. In the next paragraph Augustine remarks that he had 'plenty of
influential friends.'

Provided that we are single-minded and exert much pressure, it
should be possible to obtain at least the governorship of a minor
province. It would be necessary to marry a wife with some money to
avert the burden of heavy expenditure,[15] and that would be the limit
of our ambition. Many great men entirely worthy of imitation have
combined the married state with a dedication to the study of
wisdom.'

(20)   That was what I used to say, and these winds blew first one
way, then the other, pushing my heart to and fro. Time passed by. I
'delayed turning to the Lord' and postponed 'from day to day'
(Ecclus. 5: 8) finding life in you. I did not postpone the fact that
every day I was dying within myself. I longed for the happy life, but
was afraid of the place where it has its seat, and fled from it at the
same time as I was seeking for it. I thought I would become very
miserable if I were deprived of the embraces of a woman. I did not
think the medicine of your mercy could heal that infirmity because I
had not tried it. I believed continence to be achieved by personal
resources which I was not aware of possessing. I was so stupid as
not to know that, as it is written (Wisd. 8: 21), 'no one can be
continent unless you grant it'. You would surely have granted it if
my inward groaning had struck your ears and with firm faith I had
cast my care on you.

xii (21)   Alypius discouraged me from marrying a wife. His theme
was that, if I did that, there would be no way whereby we could live
together in carefree leisure for the love of wisdom, as we had long
desired. In this matter he was himself by that time a person of
complete chastity in a way that surprised me. In his early adolescence
he had had an initial experience of sexual intercourse, but he had
not continued with it. Rather had he felt revulsion for it and
despised it, and thereafter lived in total continence. I resisted him
by appealing to the examples of those who, though married, had
cultivated wisdom and pleased God and kept loyal and loving
friendships. I was much inferior to them in greatness of soul.

---

[15] Necessary for douceurs to influential court officials to fix the appointment, all
important public offices at this period being up for sale. Distinction in rhetoric was
generally regarded as a qualification for public office, and the axiom was seldom
disputed (an exception being Gregory of Nazianzus who thought it ludicrous, *Orat.* 4.
43). But money was also required.

Fettered by the flesh's morbid impulse and lethal sweetness, I dragged my chain, but was afraid to be free of it. Like a man whose wound has been hit, I pushed aside the words of good advice like the hand loosing the bond. Over and beyond this, my words to Alypius were the serpent's persuasions, using my tongue to weave and scatter sweet snares in his path to entrap his honest and unfettered feet.

(22) He was astonished that I, for whom he had so deep a regard, should be stuck fast in the glue of this pleasure. Whenever we argued on this subject among ourselves, I used to assert that it was out of my power to live a celibate life. I defended myself when I saw his amazement, and used to say that there was a vast difference between his hurried and furtive experience, which he could now hardly remember and so could easily despise without the least difficulty, and the delights of my own regular habit. If the honourable name of marriage had been added to my life, he would have had no reason to be surprised that I could not despise married life. So he himself began to desire marriage, overcome by curiosity, not in the least by lust for sexual pleasure. He used to say that he wanted to know what it was without which my life, which met with his approval, would have seemed to me not life but torture. His mind being free of that chain was astonished at my bondage, and from amazement he passed into desire to experience it. From there perhaps he would have lapsed into that bondage which surprised him, since he wanted to make 'a pact with death' (Isa. 28: 18) and 'he who loves danger' will fall into it (Ecclus. 3: 27).

Neither of us considered it more than a marginal issue how the beauty of having a wife lies in the obligation to respect the discipline of marriage and bring up children. To a large extent what held me captive and tortured me was the habit of satisfying with vehement intensity an insatiable sexual desire. In his case astonishment drew him towards captivity. That is how we were until you, most high, not deserting our clay, had mercy on us poor wretches, and by wonderful and secret ways came to our aid.

xiii (23) Pressure to have me married was not relaxed. Already I submitted my suit, and already a girl was promised to me principally through my mother's efforts. Her hope was that once married I would be washed in the saving water of baptism. Every day she rejoiced to find me more prepared to consider it, and she saw her vows and your promises fulfilled in my faith.

At my request and at her own desire she petitioned you every day with a strong cry from her heart, that by a vision you would show her what was to happen after my coming marriage. But you never willed to grant this. She saw certain illusory and fantastic images, the product of the human spirit's efforts in its urgent concern for an answer. The account which she gave me was not marked by the confidence she normally showed when you disclosed the future to her, but she spoke contemptuously of what she saw. She used to say that, by a certain smell indescribable in words,[16] she could tell the difference between your revelation and her own soul dreaming. Nevertheless, pressure for the marriage continued, and the girl who was asked for was almost two years under age for marriage.[17] But she pleased me, and I was prepared to wait.

xiv (24)   Among our group of friends we had had animated discussions of a project: talking with one another we expressed detestation for the storms and troubles of human life, and had almost decided on withdrawing from the crowds and living a life of contemplation. This contemplative leisure we proposed to organize in the following way: everything that we could raise we would put into a common treasury and from everyone's resources would create a single household chest. In sincere friendship nothing would be the private property of this or that individual, but out of the resources of all one treasury would be formed; the whole would belong to each, and everything would belong to everybody. We saw that we could have about ten people in the same community. Some among us were extremely rich, above all Romanianus from our home town, who at this time had had to come to the court because of serious problems connected with his property. From my earliest years he had been a most intimate friend. He gave important support to this proposal and had great persuasive influence because his financial resources were much greater than anyone else's.

We decided that two of us, appointed like magistrates to serve for

[16] In Augustine's age it was common belief that evil spirits caused an unpleasant odour (e.g. *City of God* 10. 19).

[17] Under Roman law the minimum age was 12. Augustine ascribes here to Monica moral and religious reasons for fostering the marriage rather than his need to marry money to achieve his secular ambitions, mentioned above VI. xi (19).

one year,[18] should be responsible for all the necessary business, leaving the others free of cares. But later the thought began to occur to us whether this would be acceptable to the wives whom others among us already had, and which we ourselves wanted to acquire. On this the entire project which we had so well planned collapsed in our hands; it was broken up and abandoned.[19] Thereupon we returned to sighs and groans and careers following the broad and well-trodden ways of the world. 'Many thoughts were in our heart, but your counsel abides for ever' (Prov. 19: 21; Ps. 32: 11). By that counsel you laughed at our proposals and prepared your own dispositions, to 'give us meat in due season', 'to open your hand and fill our souls with blessing' (Ps. 144: 15 f.).

xv (25) Meanwhile my sins multiplied. The woman with whom I habitually slept was torn away from my side because she was a hindrance to my marriage. My heart which was deeply attached was cut and wounded, and left a trail of blood. She had returned to Africa vowing that she would never go with another man. She left with me the natural son I had by her. But I was unhappy, incapable of following a woman's example, and impatient of delay. I was to get the girl I had proposed to only at the end of two years. As I was not a lover of marriage but a slave of lust, I procured another woman, not of course as wife. By this liaison the disease of my soul would be sustained and kept active, either in full vigour or even increased, so that the habit would be guarded and fostered until I came to the kingdom of marriage. But my wound, inflicted by the earlier parting, was not healed. After inflammation and sharp pain, it festered. The pain made me as it were frigid but desperate.

xvi (26) Praise to you, glory to you, fount of mercies! As I became unhappier, you came closer. Your right hand was by me, already prepared to snatch me out of the filth (Jer. 28: 13), and to clean me up. But I did not know it. Nothing kept me from an even deeper whirlpool of erotic indulgence except fear of death and of your coming judgement which, through the various opinions I had held, never left my breast. With my friends Alypius and Nebridius I discussed the ultimate nature of good and evil.[20] To my mind

[18] Quietist groups of Neopythagoreans had comparable arrangements.

[19] When Augustine was in association with the Manichees in Rome, one named Constantius formed an ascetic community in his house, but it split up.

[20] Evidently based on Cicero, *De finibus* (1. 12. 40) echoed in the following words.

Epicurus would have been awarded the palm of victory, had I not believed that after death the life of the soul remains with the consequences of our acts, a belief which Epicurus rejected; and I asked: If we were immortal and lived in unending bodily pleasure, with no fear of losing it, why should we not be happy? What else should we be seeking for? I did not realize that that is exactly what shows our great wretchedness. For I was so submerged and blinded that I could not think of the light of moral goodness and of a beauty to be embraced for its own sake—beauty seen not by the eye of the flesh, but only by inward discernment.

In my sombre state I did not consider from what fountain came the flow of delightful conversation with friends (though on such sordid subjects), nor the fact that without friends I could not be happy even when my mind was at the time a flood of indulgence in physical pleasures.[21] My friends I loved indeed for their own sake; and I felt that in return they loved me for my sake.

What tortuous paths! How fearful a fate for 'the rash soul' (Isa. 3: 9) which nursed the hope that after it had departed from you, it would find something better! Turned this way and that, on its back, on its side, on its stomach, all positions are uncomfortable. You alone are repose.

You are present, liberating us from miserable errors, and you put us on your way, bringing comfort and saying: 'Run, I will carry you, and I will see you through to the end, and there I will carry you' (Isa. 46: 4).

---

[21] The latent underlying contrast is between the treatment of human beings as means and as ends.

BOOK VII

A Neoplatonic Quest

i (1)   By now my evil and wicked youth was dead. I was becoming a
grown man. But the older I became, the more shameful it was that I
retained so much vanity as to be unable to think any substance
possible other than that which the eyes normally perceive. From the
time that I began to learn something of your wisdom, I did not
conceive of you, God, in the shape of the human body. I always
shunned this, and was glad when I found the same concept in the
faith of our spiritual mother, your Catholic Church. But how
otherwise to conceive of you I could not see. I a mere man, and a man
with profound defects, was trying to think of you the supreme, sole
and true God. With all my heart I believed you to be incorruptible,
immune from injury, and unchangeable. Although I did not know
why and how, it was clear to me and certain that what is corruptible
is inferior to that which cannot be corrupted; what is immune from
injury I unhesitatingly put above that which is not immune; what
suffers no change is better than that which can change. My heart
vehemently protested against all the physical images in my mind,
and by this single blow I attempted to expel from my mind's eye the
swarm of unpurified notions flying about there.[1] Hardly had they
been dispersed when in the flash of an eye (1 Cor. 15: 52) they had
regrouped and were back again. They attacked my power of vision
and clouded it. Although you were not in the shape of the human
body, I nevertheless felt forced to imagine something physical
occupying space diffused either in the world or even through
infinite space outside the world.[2] Admittedly I thought of this as
incorruptible and inviolable and unchangeable, which I set above
what is corruptible, violable, and changeable. But I thought that
anything from which space was abstracted was non-existent, indeed
absolutely nothing, not even a vacuum, as when a body is removed
from a place, and the space remains evacuated of anything physical,
whether earthly, watery, airy or heavenly, but is an empty space—
like a mathematical concept of space without content.

---

[1] Echo of Virgil, *Aeneid* 3. 233.   [2] Similarly Plotinus 6. 5. 2.

(2)   So my heart had become gross (Matt. 13: 15), and I had no clear vision even of my own self. I thought simply non-existent anything not extended in space or diffused or concentrated or expanding, which does not possess, or is incapable of possessing, such qualities. My eyes are accustomed to such images. My heart accepted the same structure. I did not see that the mental power by which I formed these images does not occupy any space, though it could not form them unless it were some great thing.[3] I conceived even you, life of my life, as a large being, permeating infinite space on every side, penetrating the entire mass of the world, and outside this extending in all directions for immense distances without end; so earth had you, heaven had you, everything had you, and in relation to you all was finite; but you not so. Just as the sunlight meets no obstacle in the body of the air (this air which is above the earth) to stop it from passing through and penetrating it without breaking it up or splitting it, but fills it entirely: so I thought that you permeate not only the body of heaven and air and sea but even earth, and that in everything, both the greatest and the smallest things, this physical frame is open to receive your presence, so that by a secret breath of life you govern all things which you created, both inwardly and outwardly. This was my conjecture, for I was incapable of thinking otherwise; but it was false. For on that hypothesis a larger part of the earth would possess more of you and a smaller part less, and all things would be full of you in the sense that more of you would be contained by an elephant's body than a sparrow's to the degree that it is larger and occupies more space; so, piece by piece, you would be making different parts of yourself present to parts of the world, much of you in large parts, little of you in small parts. And that is not the case. But you had not yet 'lightened my darkness' (Ps. 17: 29).

ii (3)   For me, Lord, there was a sufficient refutation of those deceived deceivers and those word-spinners with nothing to say (for it was not your word which sounded out from them). It was enough to state the argument which used to be put forward by Nebridius long before at Carthage, an argument which struck us dumb when we heard it: The Manichees postulate a race of darkness in opposition to you. What could that have done to you, if you had

---

[3] Similarly Plotinus 4. 2. 1.

refused to fight against it? If they were to reply that you would have suffered injury, that would make you open to violation and destruction. But if nothing could harm you, that removes any ground for combat, and indeed for combat under such conditions that some portion of you, one of your members, or an offspring of your very substance, is mingled with hostile powers and with natures not created by you, and is corrupted by them and so changed for the worse that it is altered from beatitude to misery and needs help to deliver and purify it. They say this is the soul, enslaved, contaminated and corrupt, to which aid is brought by your word, free, pure, and intact; and yet your word is itself corruptible, because it is of one and the same substance as the soul. Thus if they say that you, whatever you are (that is your substance in virtue of which you have your being), are incorruptible, the entire story becomes false and execrable. But if corruptible, then without further discussion the very proposition is false and to be abominated.

This argument would have been enough to oppose those people whom I should have vomited forth from my overloaded stomach. For they had no escape from this dilemma without thinking and speaking about you with a horrible sacrilege of heart and tongue.

iii (4)   But a problem remained to trouble me. Although I affirmed and firmly held divine immunity from pollution and change and the complete immutability of our God, the true God who made not only our souls but also our bodies, and not only our souls and bodies, but all rational beings and everything, yet I had no clear and explicit grasp of the cause of evil. Whatever it might be, I saw it had to be investigated, if I were to avoid being forced by this problem to believe the immutable God to be mutable. Otherwise I might myself become the evil I was investigating. Accordingly, I made my investigation without anxiety, certain that what the Manichees said was untrue. With all my mind I fled from them, because in my inquiry into the origin of evil I saw them to be full of malice, in that they thought it more acceptable to say your substance suffers evil than that their own substance actively does evil.

(5)   I directed my mind to understand what I was being told, namely that the free choice of the will is the reason why we do wrong and suffer your just judgement;[4] but I could not get a clear

[4] Augustine could hear this theme (from Plato) in Ambrose's sermons, or read it in Plotinus 5. 1. 1.

grasp of it. I made an effort to lift my mind's eye out of the abyss, but again plunged back. I tried several times, but again and again sank back. I was brought up into your light by the fact that I knew myself both to have a will and to be alive. Therefore when I willed or did not will something, I was utterly certain that none other than myself was willing or not willing. That there lay the cause of my sin I was now coming to recognize. I saw that when I acted against my wishes, I was passive rather than active; and this condition I judged to be not guilt but a punishment.[5] It was an effortless step to grant that, since I conceived you to be just, it was not unjust that I was chastised. But again I said: 'Who made me? Is not my God not only good but the supreme Good? Why then have I the power to will evil and to reject good? Is it to provide a reason why it is just for me to undergo punishments? Who put this power in me and implanted in me this seed of bitterness (Heb. 12: 15), when all of me was created by my very kind God? If the devil was responsible, where did the devil himself come from? And if even he began as a good angel and became devil by a perversion of the will, how does the evil will by which he became devil originate in him, when an angel is wholly made by a Creator who is pure goodness?' These reflections depressed me once more and suffocated me. But I was not brought down to that hell of error where no one confesses to you (Ps. 6: 6), because people suppose that evil is something that you suffer rather than an act by humanity.

iv (6)   In this way I made an effort to discover other principles. I had already established that the incorruptible is better than the corruptible, and so I confessed that whatever you are, you are incorruptible. Nor could there have been or be any soul capable of conceiving that which is better than you, who are the supreme and highest good. Since it is most true and certain that the incorruptible is superior to the corruptible, as I had already concluded, had it been the case that you are not incorruptible I could in thought have attained something better than my God. Therefore, when I saw that the incorruptible is superior to the corruptible, I ought to have looked for you there and to have deduced from that principle the locus of evil, that is, the source of the corruption by which it is impossible for your being to be injured. There is absolutely no way

---

[5] On sin and suffering as divine justice see Plotinus 4. 3. 16.

corruption can injure our God—no act of will, no necessity, no unforeseen chance—since he is God and what he wills for himself is good, and he is that same good. Whereas to be corrupted is not good.

Moreover, you cannot be unwillingly compelled to anything; for your will is not greater than your power. It would be greater only if you were greater than yourself. For the will and power of God is God's very self.[6] And what can be unforeseen by you who know all things? No nature exists but you know it. Indeed, why need we say repeatedly 'Why is the being of God not a corruptible substance?' If it were so, that would not be God.

v (7)   I searched for the origin of evil, but I searched in a flawed way and did not see the flaw in my very search. I placed before my spirit a conspectus of the entire creation—all that we can perceive in it, earth, sea, air, stars, trees and mortal animals, and all that we cannot perceive, the firmament of heaven above, all the angels, and all the spiritual beings.[7] But I imagined these beings to be like bodies which are allocated to particular places. I conceived your creation as a single vast mass differentiated by various types of bodies, whether they were real bodies or whether the bodies with which my imagination invested the spirits. I did not make its size precisely what it is, for that I could not know, but I made it as great as seemed appropriate, but on every side finite. I visualized you, Lord, surrounding it on all sides and permeating it, but infinite in all directions, as if there were a sea everywhere and stretching through immense distances, a single sea which had within it a large but finite sponge;[8] and the sponge was in every part filled from the immense sea. This is the kind of way in which I supposed your finite creation to be full of you, infinite as you are, and said: 'Here is God and see what God has created. God is good and is most mightily and incomparably superior to these things. But being God, God created good creatures. See how God surrounds and fills them. Then where and whence is evil? How did it creep in? What is its root and what is its seed? Or does it not have any being? Why should we fear and avoid what has no being? If our fear is vain, it is certain that fear itself is evil, and that the heart is groundlessly

---

[6] Plotinus 6. 8. 13 is close.   [7] Verbal echo of Plotinus 5. 1. 4. 2 f.
[8] Plotinus (4. 3. 9. 38) uses the illustration of a net.

disturbed and tortured. And this evil is the worse for the fact that it has no being to be afraid of. Yet we still fear. Thus either it is evil which we fear or our fear which is evil. Where then does it come from since the good God made everything good? Certainly the greatest and supreme Good made lesser goods; yet the Creator and all that he created are good. What then is the origin of evil? Is it that the matter from which he made things was somehow evil? He gave it form and order, but did he leave in it an element which he could not transform into good?[9] If so, why? Was he powerless to turn and transform all matter so that no evil remained, even though God is omnipotent? Finally, why did God want to make anything out of such stuff and not rather use his omnipotence to ensure that there was no matter at all? Could it exist contrary to God's will? Or indeed, if matter was eternal, why did God allow it to exist for an infinite period of past time in its unordered state and only much later decided to do something with it? Or if now God willed suddenly to do something, would not the Almighty have preferred to cause it not to exist and to be himself alone the totality of the true, supreme, and infinite good? Or if, because he is good, it would not be well that he should not be making and creating something good, could he not abolish evil matter and reduce it to nothing, and himself make good matter out of which he would create everything? He would be less than omnipotent if he could not create something good unless assisted by a matter which he had not himself created.'

Such questions revolved in my unhappy breast, weighed down by nagging anxieties about the fear of dying before I had found the truth. But there was a firm place in my heart for the faith, within the Catholic Church, in your Christ, 'our Lord and Saviour' (2 Pet. 2: 20). In many respects this faith was still unformed and hesitant about the norm of doctrine. Yet my mind did not abandon it, but daily drank in more and more.

vi (8)   I had already rejected the fraudulent divinations and impious fantasies of the astrologers. May your mercies, my God, make grateful confession of that to you from the innermost parts of my soul! (Ps. 106: 8).

It was you, entirely you, who brought this about. For no other

---

[9] Plotinus 3. 2. 5. 23 'The supreme power can use evil for a noble end, and is capable of transforming formless things to give them a new form.'

could recall us from all deadly error than the life that knows no death, and the wisdom which itself needs no light, illuminating needy minds, the wisdom which governs the world down to the leaves that tremble on the trees. You healed the obstinacy with which I withstood the acute old man Vindicianus and Nebridius the young man with a mind of marvellous quality. The one vehemently, the other with some hesitancy but great frequency, declared that the art of forecasting the future is non-existent, but that human conjectures often have the power of chance. The fortune-tellers say so much that some of their predictions are fulfilled, not because the forecasters know but because merely by not keeping silent they hit on the truth.

Your providence brought me a friend. He was not a very frequent consulter of astrologers, and he was not well up in the literature of the subject, but, as I have said, consulted them out of curiosity. Yet he had some knowledge which he said he had learnt from his father. He did not know how much validity that might have for overthrowing confidence in the art.

He was a man named Firminus, liberally educated and well trained in rhetoric.[10] He consulted me as a close friend about some of his affairs, where his secular hope had been rising. He wanted to know what I thought about his 'constellations' as they call them. I, however, had already begun to be influenced by Nebridius' opinion of astrology. I did not refuse to offer a guess and to say what occurred to my hesitant mind. Nevertheless, I added that I was almost persuaded it was a ridiculous and vain practice. He then told me how his father had been extremely curious about astrological books, and had had a friend who was given to such studies as much as he and at the same time. An equal enthusiasm and close collaboration kindled the fire of their passion for these trivialities, to such a point that if dumb animals gave birth at their house, they recorded the moments of birth and made a note of the position of the heaven, as a basis for a collection of experiments in this pseudo-science.

Firminus said he had learnt from his father that at the time when his mother was expectant with him, a slave-girl of this friend of his father was likewise big with child. This could not pass unobserved

---

[10] For Firminus and his ambitions at Milan nothing is known beyond the information here. A letter to him, known to Augustine's ancient biographer Possidius, has not survived.

by the slave-girl's owner, who took pains to know the most precise details when his bitches were producing puppies. The two men made exact observations, the one of his wife, the other of his maidservant, for the days and hours and minutes, and it so came about that the women both had their infants at the identical time. So they had to make the same horoscopes for each newborn child identical to the minute, one for his son, the other for the little slave. For when the women began to be in labour, the two men informed each other what was going on in his own house, and they prepared messengers to send to one another, so that the news of the birth was given to each as soon as it had taken place. Each on his own estate easily arranged for the news to be carried instantly. The messengers sent by each man, he said, met at the halfway point between their houses, thereby excluding the possibility that either of them could make a different observation of the stars' position and of the precise time. Nevertheless, Firminus who was born into a well-to-do family had a career along the world's main roads.[11] His wealth increased; he was elevated to high honours. But that slave served his owners and experienced no relaxation of the yoke of his condition, as Firminus, who had known him, informed me.

(9) After I had heard this story, which I believed because of the character of the narrator, all my reluctance to abandon astrology dissolved and collapsed. First I tried to dissuade Firminus himself from this curious occultism. I told him that after inspecting his constellation had I been able to make a true forecast, I should have been able to see that his parents were distinguished citizens at their home-town, a noble family in their own city, born free, given a gentleman's education and liberal culture. And if the slave had consulted me, then on the basis of his stars which were identical with those of Firminus, were I able to offer him also a true forecast, I ought again to have seen there a family of the most abject status, with servile condition and other disadvantages utterly different and remote from Firminus' destiny.

Therefore it followed that after inspecting identical horoscopes I should give different forecasts in order to get it right, and that to offer identical forecasts would be to get it wrong. From this I drew

---

[11] Literally: the whitened roads. On main roads the Romans used chalk on the top layer. Even today a Roman road in Tunisia or Algeria looks white against the surrounding land.

the certain inference that true predictions on the basis of horoscopes are given not by skill but by chance, while false forecasts are due not to lack of skill in the art but to chance error.

(10) Starting from the approach to the subject which this story gave me, I ruminated further on these phenomena. For one of those charlatans who make money out of astrology, and whom I now wished to attack and with ridicule to refute, might resist me by arguing that false information was given either by Firminus to me or by his father to him. I therefore gave attention to those who are born twins. Most of them emerge from the womb in succession at a brief interval of time. They may contend that in the realm of nature this interval has considerable consequences. But it cannot be recorded by human observation and noted in the tables that the astrologer will inspect to give a true forecast. Moreover, the forecasts will not be true. Someone inspecting the identical tables ought to have been able to say that Esau and Jacob would have the same destiny. Yet things turned out differently in each case. Therefore he would be giving an incorrect prediction. If his forecast were correct, he would not predict the same destiny; yet the stars he studied were identical. Therefore a true forecast is based not on art but on chance.

You Lord, most just controller of the universe by your hidden discernment, act on those who consult fortune-tellers and those who are consulted, though they are unaware of it. So when someone consults a futurologist and he hears what he should hear, that is dependent on the hidden merits of souls and the profundity of your just judgement. Let not man say 'What is this? Why is that?' Let him not say it, let him not say it; for he is man.

vii (11) You, my helper, delivered me in this way from those chains. I was seeking the origin of evil and here was no solution. But you did not allow fluctuations in my thinking to carry me away from the faith which I held, that you exist and are immutable substance and care for humanity and judge us; moreover, that in Christ your Son our Lord, and by your scriptures commended by the authority of your Catholic Church, you have provided a way of salvation whereby humanity can come to the future life after death. These matters, therefore, were secure and firmly fortified in my mind while I was seeking feverishly for the origin of evil. What torments my heart suffered in mental pregnancy, what groans, my God! And though I did not know it, your ears were there.

As in silence I vigorously pursued my quest, inarticulate sufferings of my heart were loudly pleading for your mercy. You knew what I endured; no human being knew. How little of it my tongue could put into words for the ears of my closest friends! Neither the time nor my powers of speech were sufficient to tell them of the full tumult of my soul. But all of it came to your hearing, how 'I roared from the groaning of my heart, and my desire was before you, and the light of my eyes was not with me' (Ps. 37: 9–11). That was inward, while I was still in externals.[12] It was not in a place; but I was fixing my attention on things contained in space, and there I found no place to rest in, nor did those external things receive me so that I could say 'It is enough and it is well'. Nor did they allow me to return where it was enough and well for me. I was superior to these external objects but inferior to you, and you are my true joy if I submit to you, and you have made subject to me what you created to be lower than me. This was the correct mean, the middle ground in which I would find health, that I should remain 'in your image', and in serving you be master of my body.

But when in my arrogance I rose against you and ran up against the Lord 'under the thick boss of my shield' (Job 15: 26), even those inferior things came on top of me and pressed me down, and there was never any relaxation or breathing space. As I gazed at them, they attacked me on all sides in massive heaps. As I thought about them, the very images of physical objects formed an obstacle to my return, as if saying 'Where are you going to, unworthy, soiled man?' This grew out of my wound, for 'you have humbled the proud like a wounded man' (Ps. 88: 11). My swelling conceit separated me from you, and the gross swelling on my face closed my eyes.

viii (12)   But you, Lord 'abide for eternity and you will not be angry with us for ever' (Ecclus. 18: 1; Ps. 84: 6). You have mercy on dust and ashes, and it has pleased you to restore my deformities in your sight (Ps. 18: 15). By inward goads you stirred me to make me find it unendurable until, through my inward perception, you were

---

[12] The language here is full of reminiscences of Porphyry, with his Neoplatonic thesis that the knowledge of God is knowledge of nothing other than oneself, all physical and external things being abstracted. Cf. Plotinus 6. 5. 12.

a certainty to me. My swelling was reduced by your hidden healing hand, and my mind's troubled and darkened eye, under the hot dressing of salutary sorrows, was from 'day to day' (Ps. 60: 9) brought back to health.

ix (13)   First you wanted to show me how you 'resist the proud and give grace to the humble' (1 Pet. 5: 5), and with what mercy you have shown humanity the way of humility in that your 'Word was made flesh and dwelt among' men (John 1: 14). Through a man puffed up with monstrous pride,[13] you brought under my eye some books of the Platonists, translated from Greek into Latin.[14] There I read, not of course in these words, but with entirely the same sense and supported by numerous and varied reasons, 'In the beginning was the Word and the Word was with God and the Word was God. He was in the beginning with God. All things were made by him, and without him nothing was made. What was made is life in him; and the life was the light of men. And the light shone in the darkness, and the darkness did not comprehend it.' Moreover, the soul of man, although it bears witness of the light, is 'not that light', but God the Word is himself 'the true light which illuminates every man coming into the world'. Further, 'he was in this world, and the world was made by him, and the world did not know him'. But that 'he came to his own and his own did not receive him; but as many as received him, to them he gave the power to become sons of God by believing in his name', that I did not read there (John 1: 1–12).

(14)   Again, I read there that the Word, God, is 'born not of the flesh, nor of blood, nor of the will of man nor of the will of the flesh, but of God'. But that 'the word was made flesh and dwelt among us' (John 1: 13–14), I did not read there.

In reading the Platonic books I found expressed in different words, and in a variety of ways, that the Son, 'being in the form of the Father did not think it theft to be equal with God', because by nature he is that very thing. But that 'he took on himself the form of

---

[13] The man was evidently a pagan Neoplatonist, perhaps Manlius Theodorus, a powerful figure at Milan whose patronage was important to Augustine at the time of his conversion in 386 and who was a known enthusiast for Neoplatonic ideas. Theodorus' sympathy for Christianity, however, cooled, which would explain the icy reference in the *Confessions* here. He became consul in 399, and the poet Claudian celebrated this in verse. (If pagan 'pride' marked the man in 385, he was not Theodorus.)

[14] Translated by Marius Victorinus, the texts were of Plotinus and his disciple Porphyry.

a servant and emptied himself, was made in the likeness of men and found to behave as a man, and humbled himself being made obedient to death, even the death of the Cross so that God exalted him' from the dead 'and gave him a name which is above every name, that at the name of Jesus every knee should bow, of celestial, terrestrial, and infernal beings, and every tongue should confess that Jesus is Lord in the glory of God the Father' (Phil. 2: 6–11)—that these books do not have.

The books say that before all times and above all times your only-begotten Son immutably abides eternal with you, and that souls 'receive his fullness' (John 1: 16) to be blessed, and that they are renewed to be wise by participation in wisdom abiding in them. But they do not contain that 'at the right time he died for the impious' (Rom. 5: 6), and that you 'did not spare your only Son but gave him up for us all' (Rom. 8: 32). For you have hidden these things from the wise and revealed them to babes, that toiling and burdened they should come to him to be restored. For he is meek and humble of heart (Matt. 11: 25–9), and he directs the meek in judgement and teaches the docile his ways (Ps. 24: 9), seeing our humble condition and toil, and forgiving all our sins (Ps. 24: 18). But those who, like actors, wear the high boots of a supposedly more sublime teaching do not hear him who says 'Learn of me, that I am meek and humble in heart, and you shall find rest for your souls' (Matt. 11: 29). Even if they know 'God, they do not glorify him as God or give thanks, but are lost in their own thoughts and their foolish heart is obscured; professing themselves wise, they have become fools' (Rom. 1: 21–3).

(15)   So also I read of 'the glory of your incorruption' changed into idols and various images 'in the likeness of corruptible man and birds and beasts and serpents', that is the Egyptian food (lentils) for which Esau lost his birthright (Gen. 25: 33 f.). Your firstborn people honoured an animal's head instead of you, 'being turned in heart towards Egypt' (Acts 7: 39) and making your image, their own soul, bow down before a calf that eats hay (Ps. 105: 20). I found this in those books and did not feed on it.[15] It pleased you, Lord, to 'remove from Jacob the opprobrium of being junior' (Ps. 118: 22), and that the 'elder should serve the younger' (Rom. 9: 13); and you

---

[15] The Platonist books offered good philosophy, marred by bad polytheism.

called the Gentiles into your inheritance. And I had come to you from the Gentiles and fixed my attention on the gold which you willed your people to take from Egypt, since the gold was yours, wherever it was.[16] And through your apostle you said to the Athenians, 'In you we live and move and are' (Acts 17: 28), as also some of the pagans have said. And Athens is where these books [of the Platonists] came from.[17] I did not give attention to the idols of the Egyptians which they served with your gold and 'changed the truth of God into a lie and worshipped and served the creature more than the Creator' (Rom. 1: 25).

x (16)   By the Platonic books I was admonished to return into myself.[18] With you as my guide I entered into my innermost citadel, and was given power to do so because you had become my helper (Ps. 29: 11). I entered and with my soul's eye, such as it was, saw above that same eye of my soul the immutable light higher than my mind—not the light of every day, obvious to anyone, nor a larger version of the same kind which would, as it were, have given out a much brighter light and filled everything with its magnitude.[19] It was not that light, but a different thing, utterly different from all our kinds of light. It transcended my mind, not in the way that oil floats on water, nor as heaven is above earth. It was superior because it made me, and I was inferior because I was made by it. The person who knows the truth knows it, and he who knows it knows eternity. Love knows it.[20] Eternal truth and true love and beloved eternity: you are my God. To you I sigh 'day and night' (Ps. 42: 2). When I first came to know you, you raised me up to make me see that what I saw is Being, and that I who saw am not yet Being. And you gave a shock to the weakness of my sight by the strong radiance of your rays, and I trembled with love and awe.[21] And I found myself far from you 'in the region of dissimilarity',[22]

---

[16] The spoiling of the Egyptians by the Hebrews (Exod. 3: 22; 11:2) was for Irenaeus and Augustine (here and elsewhere) an allegory of the Christian right to select truth from pagan texts without accepting polytheism. The Exodus passage was ridiculed by the Manichees.

[17] In fact Plotinus taught in Rome, Porphyry lived in Sicily; but Athens was the symbolic home of classical Greek philosophy (e.g. *City of God* 18. 9).

[18] Plotinus 5. 1. 1.   [19] Ibid. 5. 3. 9. 10 f; 5. 3. 12. 40 f.

[20] Ibid. 1. 6. 7. 2 'one who has seen the good, the desire of every soul, knows what I mean when I say it is beautiful'; Plotinus continues that it is known with the passion of love. Similarly 6. 9. 9. 46.

[21] Ibid. 1. 6. 7. 12–19.   [22] Ibid. 1. 8. 13. 15 f. (from Plato, *Statesman* 273d).

and heard as it were your voice from on high: 'I am the food of the fully grown; grow and you will feed on me. And you will not change me into you like the food your flesh eats, but you will be changed into me.'

And I recognized that 'because of iniquity you discipline man' and 'cause my soul to waste away like a spider's web' (Ps. 38: 14), and I said: 'Surely truth cannot be nothing, when it is not diffused through space, either finite or infinite?' And you cried from far away: 'Now, I am who I am' (Exod. 3: 14). I heard in the way one hears within the heart, and all doubt left me.[23] I would have found it easier to doubt whether I was myself alive than that there is no truth 'understood from the things that are made' (Rom. 1: 20).

xi (17)   And I considered the other things below you, and I saw that neither can they be said absolutely to be or absolutely not to be. They are because they come from you. But they are not because they are not what you are. That which truly is is that which unchangeably abides. But 'it is good for me to stick fast to God' (Ps. 72: 28); for if I do not abide in him, I can do nothing (John 15: 5). But he 'abiding in himself makes all things new' (Wisd. 7: 27). 'You are my Lord because you have no need of my goodness' (Ps. 15: 2).

xii (18)   It was obvious to me that things which are liable to corruption are good. If they were the supreme goods, or if they were not good at all, they could not be corrupted. For if they were supreme goods, they would be incorruptible. If there were no good in them, there would be nothing capable of being corrupted. Corruption does harm and unless it diminishes the good, no harm would be done. Therefore either corruption does not harm, which cannot be the case, or (which is wholly certain) all things that are corrupted suffer privation of some good. If they were to be deprived of all good, they would not exist at all. If they were to exist and to be immune from corruption, they would be superior because they would be permanently incorruptible. What could be more absurd than to say that by losing all good, things are made better? So then, if they are deprived of all good, they will be nothing at all. Therefore as long as they exist, they are good.[24] Accordingly, whatever things

---

[23] On the total assurance given by the vision of the Good, see Plotinus 5. 5. 2.

[24] Augustine frequently states the Platonic axiom that existence is a good: cf. below, XIII. xxxi (46); Plotinus 1. 7. 2.

exist are good, and the evil into whose origins I was inquiring is not a substance, for if it were a substance, it would be good. Either it would be an incorruptible substance, a great good indeed, or a corruptible substance, which could be corrupted only if it were good. Hence I saw and it was made clear to me that you made all things good, and there are absolutely no substances which you did not make. As you did not make all things equal, all things are good in the sense that taken individually they are good, and all things taken together are very good. For our God has made 'all things very good' (Gen. 1: 31).

xiii (19)   For you evil does not exist at all, and not only for you but for your created universe, because there is nothing outside it which could break in and destroy the order which you have imposed upon it. But in the parts of the universe, there are certain elements which are thought evil because of a conflict of interest. These elements are congruous with other elements and as such are good, and are also good in themselves. All these elements which have some mutual conflict of interest are congruous with the inferior part of the universe which we call earth. Its heaven is cloudy and windy, which is fitting for it.

It is far from my mind now to say, 'Would that those things did not exist!' If I were to regard them in isolation, I would indeed wish for something better; but now even when they are taken alone, my duty is to praise you for them. That you are to be praised is shown by dragons on earth, and all deeps, fire, hail, snow, ice, the hurricane and tempest, which perform your word—mountains and all hills, fruitful trees and all cedars, beasts and all cattle, reptiles and winged birds; kings of the earth and all peoples, princes and all judges of the earth, young men and maidens, old men with younger: let them praise your name (Ps. 148: 7–12). Moreover, let these from the heavens praise you: let all your angels praise you in the height, our God all your powers, sun and moon, all stars and light, the heaven of heavens and the waters that are above the heavens: let them praise your name (Ps. 148: 1–5).

I no longer wished individual things to be better, because I considered the totality. Superior things are self-evidently better than inferior. Yet with a sounder judgement I held that all things taken together are better than superior things by themselves.

xiv (20)   'There is no health' (Ps. 37: 4, 8) in those who are displeased by an element in your creation, just as there was none in me when I was displeased by many things you had made. Because my soul did not dare to say that my God displeased me, it refused to attribute to you whatever was displeasing. Hence it came to adopt the opinion that there are two substances. But it found no rest and spoke a strange language. Returning from this deviation, it created for itself a god pervading all places in infinite space. It imagined this god to be you and installed him at its heart. It again became the temple of its own idol, an abomination to you. But afterwards you calmed my head without my realizing it, and 'shut my eyes that they should not see vanity' (Ps. 118: 37). I relaxed a little and my mad folly was put to sleep. I woke up in you and saw you to be infinite in another sense, and this way of seeing you did not come from the flesh.

xv (21)   I turned my gaze on other things. I saw that to you they owe their existence, and that in you all things are finite, not in the sense that the space they occupy is bounded but in the sense that you hold all things in your hand by your truth. So all things are real insofar as they have being, and the term 'falsehood' applies only when something is thought to have being which does not. And I saw that each thing is harmonious not only with its place but with its time, and that you alone are eternal and did not first begin to work after innumerable periods of time. For all periods of time both past and future neither pass away nor come except because you bring that about, and you yourself permanently abide.

xvi (22)   I learnt by experience that it is no cause for surprise when bread which is pleasant to a healthy palate is misery to an unhealthy one; and to sick eyes light which is desirable to the healthy is hateful. The wicked are displeased by your justice, even more by vipers and the worm which you created good, being well fitted for the lower parts of your creation. To these lower parts the wicked themselves are well fitted, to the extent that they are dissimilar to you, but they can become fitted for the higher parts insofar as they become more like you. I inquired what wickedness is; and I did not find a substance but a perversity of will twisted away from the highest substance, you O God, towards inferior things, rejecting its own inner life (Ecclus. 10: 10) and swelling with external matter.

xvii (23)   I was astonished to find that already I loved you, not a phantom surrogate for you. But I was not stable in the enjoyment of my God. I was caught up to you by your beauty and quickly torn away from you by my weight.[25] With a groan I crashed into inferior things. This weight was my sexual habit. But with me there remained a memory of you. I was in no kind of doubt to whom I should attach myself, but was not yet in a state to be able to do that. 'The body, which is corruptible, weighs down the soul, and our earthly habitation drags down the mind to think many things' (Wisd. 9: 15). Moreover, I was wholly certain that your invisible nature 'since the foundation of the world is understood from the things which are made, that is your eternal power and divinity' (Rom. 1: 20).

I asked myself why I approved of the beauty of bodies, whether celestial or terrestrial, and what justification I had for giving an unqualified judgement on mutable things, saying 'This ought to be thus, and that ought not to be thus'. In the course of this inquiry why I made such value judgements as I was making, I found the unchangeable and authentic eternity of truth to transcend my mutable mind. And so step by step I ascended from bodies to the soul which perceives through the body, and from there to its inward force, to which bodily senses report external sensations, this being as high as the beasts go. From there again I ascended to the power of reasoning to which is to be attributed the power of judging the deliverances of the bodily senses. This power, which in myself I found to be mutable, raised itself to the level of its own intelligence, and led my thinking out of the ruts of habit. It withdrew itself from the contradictory swarms of imaginative fantasies, so as to discover the light by which it was flooded. At that point it had no hesitation in declaring that the unchangeable is preferable to the changeable, and that on this ground it can know the unchangeable, since, unless it could somehow know this, there would be no certainty in preferring it to the mutable. So in the flash of a trembling glance it attained to that which is. At that moment I saw your 'invisible nature understood through the things which are made' (Rom. 1: 20). But I did not possess the strength to keep my vision fixed. My weakness reasserted itself, and I returned to my customary condition. I carried with me

---

[25] Closely similar language in Plotinus 6. 9. 4. 16–23. Plotinus also asks why the experience of mystical union with God is so transient (6. 9. 10). See also below x. xl (65).

only a loving memory and a desire for that of which I had the aroma but which I had not yet the capacity to eat.

xviii (24)   I sought a way to obtain strength enough to enjoy you; but I did not find it until I embraced 'the mediator between God and man, the man Christ Jesus' (1 Tim. 2: 5), 'who is above all things, God blessed for ever' (Rom. 9: 5). He called and said 'I am the way and the truth and the life' (John 14: 6). The food which I was too weak to accept he mingled with flesh, in that 'The Word was made flesh' (John 1: 14), so that our infant condition might come to suck milk from your wisdom by which you created all things. To possess my God, the humble Jesus, I was not yet humble enough. I did not know what his weakness was meant to teach.

Your Word, eternal truth, higher than the superior parts of your creation, raises those submissive to him to himself. In the inferior parts he built for himself a humble house of our clay. By this he detaches from themselves those who are willing to be made his subjects and carries them across to himself, healing their swelling and nourishing their love. They are no longer to place confidence in themselves, but rather to become weak. They see at their feet divinity become weak by his sharing in our 'coat of skin' (Gen. 3: 21).[26] In their weariness they fall prostrate before this divine weakness which rises and lifts them up.

xix (25)   I had a different notion, since I thought of Christ my Lord only as a man of excellent wisdom which none could equal.[27] I thought his wonderful birth from a virgin was an example of despising temporal things to gain immortality for us, and such divine care for us gave him great authority as teacher. But the mystery of the Word made flesh I had not begun to guess. I had only realized from the writings handed down concerning him that he ate and drank, slept, walked, was filled with joy, was sad, conversed. I knew that his flesh was not united to your Word without a soul and

[26] Augustine often allegorizes the 'coats of skin' of Adam and Eve to mean the mortality of the human condition.

[27] This was Porphyry's opinion, coupled with the rejection of the Church as mistakenly believing him to be divine: see *City of God* 10. 27–9. Porphyry, however, is not known to have accepted the Virgin Birth and to regard that as the ground of Jesus' special distinction as a wise man. Augustine associates this last opinion with Photinus who denied Christ's pre-existence before the incarnation, affirmed the Virgin Birth, and believed Christ wise through God's inspiration rather than to be the personal presence of God's wisdom. Condemned for heresy in 351, Photinus retained admirers.

a human mind. Everyone knows this if he knows the immutability of your Word. I knew it to the best of my understanding, nor had I the least doubt on the subject. To move the body's limbs at will at one moment, not another, to be affected by an emotion at one time, not another, to utter wise judgement by signs at one moment, at another to keep silence: these are characteristic marks of the soul and mind with their capacity to change. If the writings about him were wrong in so describing him, everything else would be suspected of being a lie, and there would remain no salvation for the human race based on faith in these books. So because the scriptures are true, I acknowledged the whole man to be in Christ, not only the body of a man or soul and body without a mind, but a fully human person. I thought that he excelled others not as the personal embodiment of the Truth, but because of the great excellence of his human character and more perfect participation in wisdom.

Alypius, on the other hand, thought Catholics believed him to be God clothed in flesh in the sense that in Christ there was only God and flesh. He did not think they held him to possess a human soul and mind. Because he was quite convinced that the actions recorded in the memorials of Christ could not have been done except by a created being endowed with life and reason, his move towards the Christian faith was slower. But later when he knew that this was the error of the Apollinarian heretics,[28] he was glad to conform to the Catholic faith. For my part I admit it was some time later that I learnt, in relation to the words 'The Word was made flesh', how Catholic truth is to be distinguished from the false opinion of Photinus.

The rejection of heretics brings into relief what your Church holds and what sound doctrine maintains. 'It was necessary for heresies to occur so that the approved may be made manifest' (1 Cor. 11: 19) among the weak.

xx (26) At that time, after reading the books of the Platonists and learning from them to seek for immaterial truth, I turned my attention to your 'invisible nature understood through the things

[28] Alypius was held back by his beliefs (a) that the gospels describe a real human being, (b) that the Church holds the incarnate Lord to be God veiled in flesh only, without a human mind. He was liberated when he found that the latter opinion had been censured as heresy when taught by Apollinaris of Laodicea in Syria during the 360s and 370s. Ambrose of Milan emphatically rejected Apollinaris' opinion.

which are made' (Rom. 1: 20). But from the disappointment I
suffered I perceived that the darknesses of my soul would not allow
me to contemplate these sublimities. Yet I was certain that you are
infinite without being infinitely diffused through finite space. I was
sure that you truly are, and are always the same; that you never
become other or different in any part or by any movement of
position, whereas all other things derive from you, as is proved by
the fact that they exist. Of these conceptions I was certain; but to
enjoy you I was too weak. I prattled on as if I were expert, but
unless I had sought your way in Christ our Saviour (Titus 1: 4), I
would have been not expert but expunged. I began to want to give
myself airs as a wise person. I was full of my punishment, but I shed
no tears of penitence. Worse still, I was puffed up with knowledge
(1 Cor. 8: 1). Where was the charity which builds on the foundation
of humility which is Christ Jesus? When would the Platonist books
have taught me that? I believe that you wanted me to encounter
them before I came to study your scriptures. Your intention was
that the manner in which I was affected by them should be imprinted
in my memory, so that when later I had been made docile by your
books and my wounds were healed by your gentle fingers, I would
learn to discern and distinguish the difference between presumption
and confession, between those who see what the goal is but not how
to get there and those who see the way which leads to the home of
bliss, not merely as an end to be perceived but as a realm to live in.
For if I had first been formed in mind by your holy books, and if
you had made me know your sweetness by familiarity with them,
and then I had thereafter met those volumes, perhaps they would
have snatched me away from the solid foundation of piety. Or if I
had remained firm in the conviction which I had imbibed to my
soul's health, I might have supposed that the same ideas could be
gained from those books by someone who had read only them.

xxi (27)   With avid intensity I seized the sacred writings of your
Spirit and especially the apostle Paul. Where at one time I used to
think he contradicted himself and the text of his words disagreed
with the testimonies of the law and the prophets, the problems
simply vanished. The holy oracles now presented to me a simple
face, and I learnt to 'rejoice with trembling' (Ps. 11: 7). I began
reading and found that all the truth I had read in the Platonists was

stated here together with the commendation of your grace, so that he who sees should 'not boast as if he had not received' both what he sees and also the power to see. 'For what has he which he has not received?' (1 Cor. 4: 7). Moreover, he is not only admonished to see you, who remain ever the same, but also healed to make it possible for him to hold on to you. So also the person who from a distance cannot yet see, nevertheless walks along the path by which he may come and see and hold you.

Even if a man 'delights in God's law in the inner man', what will he do with 'the other law in his members fighting against the law of his mind and bringing him into captivity under the law of sin, which is in his members?' (Rom. 7: 22–3). For you, Lord, are just. But 'we have sinned, we have done wickedly' (Dan. 3: 27, 29), we have behaved impiously (1 Kgs. 8: 47), and 'your hand has been heavy upon us' (Ps. 31: 4). We have been justly handed over to the ancient sinner, the president of death, who has persuaded us to conform our will to his will which 'did not remain in your truth' (John 8: 44).

What will wretched man do? 'Who will deliver him from this body of death' except your grace through Jesus Christ our Lord (Rom. 7: 24), who is your coeternal Son, whom you 'created in the beginning of your ways' (Prov. 8: 22). In him 'the prince of this world' (John 14: 30) found nothing worthy of death and killed him, and 'the decree which was against us was cancelled' (Col. 2: 14).

None of this is in the Platonist books. Those pages do not contain the face of this devotion, tears of confession, your sacrifice, a troubled spirit, a contrite and humble spirit (Ps. 50: 19), the salvation of your people, the espoused city (Rev. 21: 5), the guarantee of your Holy Spirit (2 Cor. 5: 5), the cup of our redemption. In the Platonic books no one sings: 'Surely my soul will be submissive to God? From him is my salvation; he is also my God and my saviour who upholds me; I shall not be moved any more' (Ps. 61: 2–3).

No one there hears him who calls 'Come to me, you who labour' (Matt. 11: 28). They disdain to learn from him, for 'he is meek and humble of heart'. 'For you have concealed these things from the wise and prudent and have revealed them to babes' (Matt. 11: 25).

It is one thing from a wooded summit to catch a glimpse of the homeland of peace and not to find the way to it, but vainly to attempt the journey along an impracticable route surrounded by the ambushes and assaults of fugitive deserters with their chief, 'the lion and the dragon' (Ps. 90: 13). It is another thing to hold on to the way that leads there, defended by the protection of the heavenly emperor. There no deserters from the heavenly army lie waiting to attack. For this way they hate like a torture.

In surprising ways these thoughts had a visceral effect on me as I read 'the least' of your apostles (1 Cor. 15: 9). I meditated upon your works and trembled (Hab. 3: 2).

BOOK VIII

The Birthpangs of Conversion

i (1) My God, in my thanksgiving I want to recall and confess your mercies over me. Let my bones be penetrated by your love (Ps. 85: 13) and say, 'Lord who is like you?' (Ps. 34: 10). 'You have broken my chains, I will sacrifice to you the sacrifice of praise' (Ps. 115: 16–17). I will tell how you broke them. Let all who adore you say when they hear these things: 'Blessed is the Lord in heaven and in earth; great and wonderful is his name' (Ps. 71: 18–19; 134: 6).

Your words stuck fast in my heart and on all sides I was defended by you. Of your eternal life I was certain, though I saw it 'in an enigma and as if in a mirror' (1 Cor. 13: 12). All doubt had been taken from me that there is indestructible substance from which comes all substance. My desire was not to be more certain of you but to be more stable in you. But in my temporal life everything was in a state of uncertainty, and my heart needed to be purified from the old leaven (1 Cor. 5: 7 f.). I was attracted to the way, the Saviour himself, but was still reluctant to go along its narrow paths. And you put into my heart, and it seemed good in my sight (Ps. 18: 15), that I should visit Simplicianus.¹ It was evident to me that he was a good servant of yours; your grace shone in him. I had also heard that from his youth he had lived a life dedicated to you. By this time he had become an old man, and after a long life of saintly zeal in pursuing your way he appeared to me a man of much experience and much learning. So indeed he was. Accordingly, I wanted to consult with him about my troubles, so that he could propose a method fitted for someone in my disturbed condition, whereby I could learn to walk in your way.

(2) I saw the Church full, with one going this way, another a different way.² My secular activity I held in disgust, and now that I was not burning with my old ambitions in hope of honour and

---

¹ Simplicianus succeeded Ambrose as bishop of Milan in 397 and died *c*.400; so he was still living when the *Confessions* were published.

² 1 Cor. 7: 7 (of married and unmarried). Augustine means that the Church included both married and unmarried believers (a marked difference from Manicheism).

money it was burdensome to me to tolerate so heavy a servitude. By now those prizes gave me no pleasure in comparison with your gentleness and 'the beauty of your house which I loved' (Ps. 25: 8). But I was still firmly tied by woman. The apostle did not forbid me to marry, though he exhorted me to something better and very much wished that all men were as unattached as he himself. But I being weaker chose a softer option, and because of this one factor I was inconstant in other respects and was wasting away with nagging anxieties. Moreover, there were other matters which were a tiresome distraction to me, but which I was compelled to put up with because they go with married life; once tied by that, I was restricted. From the mouth of truth I had heard that there are 'eunuchs who have castrated themselves for the kingdom of heaven's sake'. But, he says, 'let him who can accept this accept it' (Matt. 19: 12).

'Assuredly all men are vain in whom there is no knowledge of God; not even from the things which appear good can they find him who is' (Wisd. 13: 1). But now I was not in vanity of that kind. I had climbed beyond it, and by the witness of all creation I had found you our Creator and your Word who is God beside you and with you is one God, by whom you created all things (John 1: 1–3).

There are impious people of another sort who 'not knowing God, have not glorified him as God nor given thanks' (Rom. 1: 21). In this respect also I had fallen; but 'your right hand sustained me' (Ps. 17: 36). You took me thence and placed me where I could recover my strength. For you said to man 'Behold piety is wisdom', and 'Do not wish to appear wise' (Job 28: 28; Prov. 26: 5). 'Those who asserted themselves to be wise have been made foolish' (Rom. 1: 22).

And now I had discovered the good pearl. To buy it I had to sell all that I had; and I hesitated (Matt. 13: 46).

ii (3)   So I visited Simplicianus, father to the then bishop Ambrose in the receiving of grace.[3] Ambrose truly loved him as one loves a

[3] Simplicianus, at one time in Rome, moved to Milan and was the senior priest responsible for baptizing Ambrose when he, the provincial governor, in 374 was suddenly nominated to be bishop of Milan. In Rome Simplicianus knew Marius Victorinus, a rhetor of African origin, who embodied the ideal of high culture, writing (extant) books on grammar, rhetoric, and dialectic, translating some of Aristotle's logic, and presenting to Latin readers works by Porphyry and Plotinus. Victorinus read Neoplatonism into the prologue to St John's gospel, and could count himself a Christian fellow-traveller. After conversion in his seventies, his writings on Christian theology tend to present the faith as a kind of Platonism for the masses.

father. I told him the story of my wanderings in error. But when I mentioned that I had read some books of the Platonists, which had been translated into Latin by Victorinus, at one time rhetor in the city of Rome who had, I had heard, died a Christian, he congratulated me that I had not fallen in with the writings of other philosophers full of fallacies and deceptions 'according to the elements of this world' (Col. 2: 8), whereas in all the Platonic books God and his Word keep slipping in. Then, to exhort me to the humility of Christ hidden from the wise and revealed to babes (Matt. 11: 25) he recalled his memory of Victorinus himself, whom he had known intimately when he was at Rome. He told me a story about him which I will not pass over in silence. For the story gives occasion for me to confess to you in great praise for your grace.

Victorinus was extremely learned and most expert in all the liberal disciplines. He had read and assessed many philosophers' ideas, and was tutor to numerous noble senators. To mark the distinguished quality of his teaching he was offered and accepted a statue in the Roman forum, an honour which the citizens of this world think supreme.[4] Until he was of advanced years, he was a worshipper of idols and took part in sacrilegious rites. At that time almost all the Roman nobility was enthusiastic for the cult of Osiris[5] and 'Monstrous gods of every kind and Anubis the barking dog, Monsters who once bore arms against Neptune and Venus and against Minerva' (Virgil, *Aeneid* 8. 698 f.), gods that Rome once conquered but then implored for aid. The old Victorinus had defended these cults for many years with a voice terrifying to opponents. Yet he was not ashamed to become the servant of your Christ, and an infant born at your font, to bow his head to the yoke of humility and to submit his forehead to the reproach of the cross.[6]

(4) Lord God, 'you have inclined the heavens and come down, you have touched the mountains and they have smoked' (Ps. 143: 5).[7] By what ways did you make an opening into that heart? Simplicianus

---

[4] Jerome says the statue was in the Forum of Trajan.

[5] The Latin text has a corruption here; the translation above has a little manuscript support, but cannot claim to offer more than a guess at the general sense.

[6] The sign of the cross on the forehead in baptism.

[7] Augustine (*Sermon on Ps. 143*) interprets the 'inclined heavens' to mean the apostles who, when people wanted to honour them as gods, humbly pointed them to the true God; the 'mountains' are the proud, and 'smoke' when , at God's touch, they confess their sins (like Victorinus).

said Victorinus read holy scripture, and all the Christian books he investigated with special care. After examining them he said to Simplicianus, not openly but in the privacy of friendship, 'Did you know that I am already a Christian?' Simplicianus replied: 'I shall not believe that or count you among the Christians unless I see you in the Church of Christ.' Victorinus laughed and said: 'Then do walls make Christians?' He used frequently to say 'I am a Christian already', and Simplicianus would give the same answer, to which he equally often repeated his joke about walls. He was afraid to offend his friends, proud devil-worshippers. He thought that from the height of Babylonish dignity, as if from the cedars of Lebanon which the Lord had not yet broken (Ps. 28: 5), the full weight of their hostility would land on him. But after his reading, he began to feel a longing and drank in courage. He was afraid he would be 'denied' by Christ 'before the holy angels' (Luke 12: 9). He would have felt guilty of a grave crime if he were ashamed of the mysteries of the humility of your Word and were not ashamed of the sacrilegious rites of proud demons, whose pride he imitated when he accepted their ceremonies. He became ashamed of the emptiness of those rites and felt respect for the truth. Suddenly and unexpectedly he said to Simplicianus (as he told me): 'Let us go to the Church; I want to become a Christian.' Simplicianus was unable to contain himself for joy and went with him. Not long after he had received his instructions in the first mysteries, he gave in his name for baptism that he might be reborn, to the amazement of Rome and the joy of the Church. The proud 'saw and were angry. They gnashed with their teeth and were sick at heart' (Ps. 111: 10). But the Lord God was the hope of his servant; 'he paid no regard to vanities and lying follies' (Ps. 39. 5).

(5) Finally the hour came for him to make the profession of faith which is expressed in set form. At Rome these words are memorized and then by custom recited from an elevated place before the baptized believers by those who want to come to your grace. Simplicianus used to say that the presbyters offered him the opportunity of affirming the creed in private, as was their custom to offer to people who felt embarrassed and afraid. But he preferred to make profession of his salvation before the holy congregation. For there was no salvation in the rhetoric which he had taught; yet his profession of

that had been public. How much less should he be afraid in proclaiming your word, when he used to feel no fear in using his own words before crowds of frenzied pagans. When he mounted the steps to affirm the confession of faith, there was a murmur of delighted talk as all the people who knew him spoke his name to one another. And who there did not know him? A suppressed sound came from the lips of all as they rejoiced, 'Victorinus, Victorinus!' As soon as they saw him, they suddenly murmured in exaltation and equally suddenly were silent in concentration to hear him. He proclaimed his unfeigned faith with ringing assurance. All of them wanted to clasp him to their hearts, and the hands with which they embraced him were their love and their joy.

iii (6)   God of goodness, what causes man to be more delighted by the salvation of a soul who is despaired of but is then liberated from great danger than if there has always been hope or if the danger has only been minor? You also, merciful Father, rejoice 'more over one penitent than over ninety-nine just persons who need no penitence' (Luke 15: 4). We too experience great pleasure when we hear how the shepherd's shoulders exult when they carry the lost sheep, and as we listen to the story of the drachma restored to your treasuries while the neighbours rejoice with the woman who found it. Tears flow at the joy of the solemnities of your house (Ps. 25: 8) when in your house the story is read of your younger son 'who was dead and is alive again, was lost and has been found' (Luke 15: 32). You rejoice indeed in us and in your angels who are holy in holy love. You are always the same, and you always know unchangeably the things which are not always the same.[8]

(7)   What then is it in the soul which causes it to take more pleasure in things which it loves when they are found and recovered than if it has always had them? There are other examples which attest this fact, and everyday life is full of instances where the evidence cries out: 'That is the case.' A victorious emperor celebrates a triumph. He would not have conquered if he had not fought. The greater the danger in the battle, the greater the joy in the triumph. A storm throws people about on a voyage and threatens shipwreck. All grow pale at the imminence of death. Sky and sea become calm, and the relief is great because the fear has been great. A dear

---

[8] It is a Neoplatonic axiom that the immutable and eternal deity knows mutable and temporal things with a transcendent and immutable knowing.

person is sick, and his pulse reveals he is in a serious condition. All who wish him to recover his health feel sick in mind at the same time. He takes a turn for the better and, although he may not walk with his former strength, yet now there is joy as there was not before when he walked in good health and strength. Human beings obtain normal pleasures of human life not as they come on us unexpectedly and against our will, but after discomforts which are planned and accepted by deliberate choice. There is no pleasure in eating and drinking unless they are preceded by the unpleasant sensation of hunger and thirst. Drunkards eat salty things to make their desire uncomfortable. As drinking extinguishes the desire, there is delightful sensation. It is established custom that betrothed girls are not immediately handed over, lest the husband hold the bride being given to him to be cheaply gained if he has not sighed after her, impatient at the delay.

(8)   The same phenomenon appears in acts which are demeaning and execrable, in acts which are allowed and lawful, in the sincerest expressions of honourable friendship, and in the case of the one 'who was dead and is alive again, was lost and is found' (Luke 15: 32). In every case the joy is greater, the worse the pain which has preceded it. Why is this, Lord my God? You are eternal to yourself, you are your own joy; and beings round you continually rejoice in your society. Why is it that this part of the creation alternates between regress and progress, between hostilities and reconciliations? Or is that a restriction placed on them, a limit you have imposed, when 'from the highest heaven' (Ps. 112: 4) down to the lowest things on earth, from the beginning to the end of the ages, from an angel down to a worm, from the first movement down to the last, you have assigned to its proper place and time all kinds of good things and all your just works?

You are so high among the highest, and I am low among the lowest, a mean thing. You never go away from us. Yet we have difficulty in returning to you.

iv (9)   Come Lord, stir us up and call us back, kindle and seize us, be our fire and our sweetness. Let us love, let us run. Surely many return to you from a deeper hell of blindness than Victorinus. They approach and are illuminated as they receive light. Those who receive it obtain from you 'power to become your sons' (John 1: 9, 12). But if they are less well known to the people, there is less rejoicing over them even among those who know them. When many share in the joy, individuals also feel a richer delight. They kindle excitement among themselves and are inflamed by one another. Then those who are known to many are to many a personal influence towards salvation. Where they lead, many will follow. That is why on their account even those who have preceded them feel great joy; for their rejoicing is not only for them.

But God forbid that in your tabernacle the rich be preferred to the poor or the noble to those of low origin. You have chosen in preference the weak things of the world to confound the powerful, and you have chosen the low of this world and things that are despised and things which have no existence as if they had being, to bring to nothing things which have being. (1 Cor. 1: 27 f.). Yet the very same writer, the least of your apostles (1 Cor. 15: 9), by whose tongue you uttered those words, was the person who by combat humbled the pride of Paul the proconsul under the gentle yoke of your Christ, and commissioned him as a provincial governor of the great king (Acts 13: 7–12). Thereafter he himself, formerly named Saul, loved to be called Paul as a reminder of that great victory. The enemy suffers a severer defeat when he is overcome in a man upon whom he has a greater hold and by whose influence he dominates many. Pride in aristocratic nobility enables him to hold sway especially over the upper class, and by their title and authority he dominates many more. Special pleasure, therefore, was felt at the conversion of Victorinus' heart in which the devil had an impregnable fortress, and of Victorinus' tongue which he had used as a mighty and sharp dart to destroy many. Your children had good reason to rejoice the more jubilantly because our king had bound the strong man (Matt. 12: 29), and they saw his vessels being snatched away to be cleaned and made fit for your honour to be 'useful to the Lord for every good work' (2 Tim. 2: 21).

v (10)   As soon as your servant Simplicianus told me this story about Victorinus, I was ardent to follow his example. He had indeed told it to me with this object in view. Later on, he added, in the time of the emperor Julian when a law was promulgated forbidding Christians to teach literature and rhetoric,[9] Victorinus welcomed

---

[9] Julian's edict of 17 June 362 was based on the presupposition (shared by puritan Christians) that pagan literature and pagan religion are indissoluble. Christians such as

the law and preferred to abandon the school of loquacious chattering rather than your word, by which you make 'skilled the tongues of infants' (Wisd. 10: 21). I felt that he was not so much courageous as fortunate to find occasion for dedicating all his time to you. I sighed after such freedom, but was bound not by an iron imposed by anyone else but by the iron of my own choice. The enemy had a grip on my will and so made a chain for me to hold me a prisoner. The consequence of a distorted will is passion. By servitude to passion, habit is formed, and habit to which there is no resistance becomes necessity. By these links, as it were, connected one to another (hence my term a chain), a harsh bondage held me under restraint. The new will, which was beginning to be within me a will to serve you freely and to enjoy you, God, the only sure source of pleasure, was not yet strong enough to conquer my older will, which had the strength of old habit. So my two wills, one old, the other new, one carnal, the other spiritual, were in conflict with one another, and their discord robbed my soul of all concentration.

(11)   In this way I understood through my own experience what I had read, how 'the flesh lusts against the spirit and the spirit against the flesh' (Gal. 5: 17). I was split between them, but more of me was in that which I approved in myself than in that which I disapproved. In the latter case it was 'no more I' (Rom. 7: 17), since in large part I was passive and unwilling rather than active and willing. But I was responsible for the fact that habit had become so embattled against me; for it was with my consent that I came to the place in which I did not wish to be. Who has the right to object if a just penalty pursues a sinner? I no longer had my usual excuse to explain why I did not yet despise the world and serve you, namely, that my perception of the truth was uncertain. By now I was indeed quite sure about it. Yet I was still bound down to the earth. I was refusing to become your soldier,[10] and I was as afraid of being rid of all my burdens as I ought to have been at the prospect of carrying them.

Gregory of Nazianzus resented it. The admiring pagan Ammianus Marcellinus thought it should be condemned to everlasting silence as disgraceful. At Athens the famous sophist Prohaeresius declined to accept the special exemption granted him by Julian and, like Victorinus at Rome, resigned. Augustine himself (*City of God* 18. 52) thought the edict an act of persecuting intolerance.

[10] From Tertullian on (AD 200), Latin Christians spoke of baptism in military terms as enlistment in Christ's army by an oath (*sacramentum*), with the cross as the standard (*vexillum, signum*) and the sign of the cross over the forehead.

(12) The burden of the world weighed me down with a sweet drowsiness such as commonly occurs during sleep. The thoughts with which I meditated about you were like the efforts of those who would like to get up but are overcome by deep sleep and sink back again. No one wants to be asleep all the time, and the sane judgement of everyone judges it better to be awake. Yet often a man defers shaking off sleep when his limbs are heavy with slumber. Although displeased with himself he is glad to take a bit longer, even when the time to get up has arrived. In this kind of way I was sure it was better for me to render myself up to your love than to surrender to my own cupidity. But while the former course was pleasant to think about and had my notional assent, the latter was more pleasant and overcame me. I had no answer to make to you when you said to me 'Arise, you who are asleep, rise from the dead, and Christ shall give you light' (Eph. 5: 14). Though at every point you showed that what you were saying was true, yet I, convinced by that truth, had no answer to give you except merely slow and sleepy words: 'At once'—'But presently'—'Just a little longer, please'. But 'At once, at once' never came to the point of decision, and 'Just a little longer, please' went on and on for a long while. In vain I 'delighted in your law in respect of the inward man; but another law in my members fought against the law of my mind and led me captive in the law of sin which was in my members' (Rom. 7: 22). The law of sin is the violence of habit by which even the unwilling mind is dragged down and held, as it deserves to be, since by its own choice it slipped into the habit. 'Wretched man that I was, who would deliver me from this body of death other than your grace through Jesus Christ our Lord?' (Rom. 7: 24–5).

vi (13) Lord, my helper and redeemer, I will now tell the story, and confess to your name, of the way in which you delivered me from the chain of sexual desire, by which I was tightly bound, and from the slavery of worldly affairs. I went about my usual routine in a state of mental anxiety. Every day I sighed after you. I used to frequent your Church whenever I had time off from the affairs under whose weight I was groaning. With me was Alypius, unemployed in his work as a lawyer after a third period as assessor and waiting for someone else to whom he could again sell his advice, just as I was selling the art of public speaking—if oratory is something that can be conveyed by teaching. Nebridius, however, had yielded to the pressure of his friendship with us and was assistant teacher to Verecundus, a close friend to all of us, a citizen of Milan and instructor in literature there. Verecundus was in urgent need of reliable assistance, and by right of friendship claimed from our group the supply he badly wanted. So Nebridius was not attracted to this work by desire for the profits; for had he so wished, he could have made more money on his own as teacher of literature. He was a most gentle and kind friend, and recognizing the duty of generosity would not scorn our request. He performed his task most prudently, and took care not to become known to important people, as this world reckons them, so avoiding anything likely to distract his mind. He wanted to keep his mind free and to devote as many hours as possible to the pursuit of wisdom by investigating some problem or listening to conversation.

(14)   One day when Nebridius was absent for a reason I cannot recall, Alypius and I received a surprise visit at home from a man named Ponticianus, a compatriot in that he was an African, holding high office at the court. He wanted something or other from us. We sat down together to converse. By chance he noticed a book on top of a gaming table which lay before us. He picked it up, opened it, and discovered, much to his astonishment, that it was the apostle Paul. He had expected it to be one of the books used for the profession which was wearing me out. But then he smiled and looked at me in a spirit of congratulation. He was amazed that he had suddenly discovered this book and this book alone open before my eyes. He was a Christian and a baptized believer. He often prostrated himself before you, our God, at the Church with frequent and long times of prayer. When I had indicated to him that those scriptures were the subject of deep study for me, a conversation began in which he told the story of Antony the Egyptian monk, a name held in high honour among your servants, though up to that moment Alypius and I had never heard of him. When he discovered this, he dwelt on the story instilling in us who were ignorant an awareness of the man's greatness, and expressing astonishment that we did not know of him. We were amazed as we heard of your wonderful acts very well attested and occurring so recently, almost in our own time, done in orthodox faith and in the Catholic

Church. All of us were in a state of surprise, we because of the greatness of the story, he because we had not heard about it.

(15) From there his conversation moved on to speak of the flocks in the monasteries and their manner of life well pleasing to you and the fertile deserts of the wilderness. Of these we knew nothing. There was a monastery full of good brothers at Milan outside the city walls, fostered by Ambrose, and we had not known of it. He developed the theme and talked on while we listened with rapt silence. Then it occurred to him to mention how he and three of his colleagues (the date I do not know but it was at Trier), when the emperor was detained by a circus spectacle in the forenoon, went out for a walk in the gardens adjacent to the walls. There they strolled in couples, one as it turned out with Ponticianus, the other two separately wandering off on their own. In their wanderings they happened on a certain house where there lived some of your servants, poor in spirit: 'of such is the kingdom of heaven' (Matt. 5: 3). They found there a book in which was written the Life of Antony.[11] One of them began to read it. He was amazed and set on fire, and during his reading began to think of taking up this way of life and of leaving his secular post in the civil service to be your servant. For they were agents in the special branch.[12] Suddenly he was filled with holy love and sobering shame. Angry with himself, he turned his eyes on his friend and said to him: 'Tell me, I beg of you, what do we hope to achieve with all our labours? What is our aim in life? What is the motive of our service to the state? Can we hope for any higher office in the palace than to be Friends of the Emperor? And in that position what is not fragile and full of dangers? How many hazards must one risk to attain to a position of even greater danger? And when will we arrive there? Whereas, if I wish to become God's friend, in an instant I may become that now.' So he spoke, and in

[11] Antony's Life by Athanasius of Alexandria was translated into Latin by Evagrius of Antioch, a friend of Jerome, about 371; an earlier version was also in circulation.

[12] *Agentes in rebus* were an inspectorate of the imperial bureaucracy, sometimes used as intelligence gatherers and secret police, but mainly responsible to the Master of the Offices (who was among other things head of the intelligence service) for the operation of the *cursus publicus* or government communications system. Promotion in this department could lead as high as a provincial governorship, though this was rare. 'Friends of the Emperor' were not a branch of the civil service, but honoured individuals in high office; in the later Roman Empire all high office holders were vulnerable to palace revolutions and conspiracies.

pain at the coming to birth of new life, he returned his eyes to the book's pages. He read on and experienced a conversion inwardly where you alone could see and, as was soon evident, his mind rid itself of the world. Indeed, as he read and turned over and over in the turbulent hesitations of his heart, there were some moments when he was angry with himself. But then he perceived the choice to be made and took a decision to follow the better course. He was already yours, and said to his friend: 'As for myself, I have broken away from our ambition, and have decided to serve God, and I propose to start doing that from this hour in this place. If it costs you too much to follow my example, do not turn against me.' His friend replied that he would join him and be associated with him for such great reward and for so great a service. And both men, already yours, were building their tower at the right cost of forsaking all their property and following you (Luke 14: 28). Then Ponticianus and his companion who were walking through other parts of the garden in search of them, came to the same place and, on finding them, suggested returning home since the daylight had already begun to fade. But they told him of their decision and purpose, and how this intention had started and had become a firm resolve. They begged the others, if they did not wish to be associated with them, not to obstruct them. Ponticianus and his friend, however, did not change from their old career; nevertheless, as he told us, they wept for themselves. They offered their friends devout congratulations, and commended themselves to their prayers. Then, dragging their hearts along the ground, they went off into the palace. The others fixed their hearts on heaven and stayed at the house. Both had fiancées. When later their fiancées heard this, they also dedicated their virginity to you.

vii (16) This was the story Ponticianus told. But while he was speaking, Lord, you turned my attention back to myself. You took me up from behind my own back where I had placed myself because I did not wish to observe myself (Ps. 20: 13), and you set me before my face (Ps. 49: 21) so that I should see how vile I was, how twisted and filthy, covered in sores and ulcers.[13] And I looked and was appalled, but there was no way of escaping from myself. If I tried to avert my gaze from myself, his story continued relentlessly,

---

[13] Echo of Seneca, *De Ira* 2. 36. 1.

and you once again placed me in front of myself; you thrust me before my own eyes so that I should discover my iniquity and hate it. I had known it, but deceived myself, refused to admit it, and pushed it out of my mind.

(17) But at that moment the more ardent my affection for those young men of whom I was hearing, who for the soul's health had given themselves wholly to you for healing, the more was the detestation and hatred I felt for myself in comparison with them. Many years of my life had passed by—about twelve—since in my nineteenth year I had read Cicero's *Hortensius*, and had been stirred to a zeal for wisdom. But although I came to despise earthly success, I put off giving time to the quest for wisdom. For 'it is not the discovery but the mere search for wisdom which should be preferred even to the discovery of treasures and to ruling over nations and to the physical delights available to me at a nod.'[14] But I was an unhappy young man, wretched as at the beginning of my adolescence when I prayed you for chastity and said: 'Grant me chastity and continence, but not yet.' I was afraid you might hear my prayer quickly, and that you might too rapidly heal me of the disease of lust which I preferred to satisfy rather than suppress. I had gone along 'evil ways' (Ecclus. 2: 10) with a sacrilegious superstition, not indeed because I felt sure of its truth but because I preferred it to the alternatives, which I did not investigate in a devout spirit but opposed in an attitude of hostility.

(18) I supposed that the reason for my postponing 'from day to day' (Ecclus. 5: 8) the moment when I would despise worldly ambition and follow you was that I had not seen any certainty by which to direct my course. But the day had now come when I stood naked to myself, and my conscience complained against me: 'Where is your tongue? You were saying that, because the truth is uncertain, you do not want to abandon the burden of futility. But look, it is certain now, and the burden still presses on you. Yet wings are won by the freer shoulders of men who have not been exhausted by their searching and have not taken ten years or more to meditate on these matters.' This is how I was gnawing at my inner self. I was violently overcome by a fearful sense of shame during the time that

[14] A quotation or at least paraphrase of Cicero (*Hortensius*, fragment 106 Grilli). Cf. XII. i (1) below.

Ponticianus was telling his story. When he had ended his talk and
settled the matter for which he came, he went home and I was left
to myself. What accusations against myself did I not bring? With
what verbal rods did I not scourge my soul so that it would follow
me in my attempt to go after you! But my soul hung back. It
refused, and had no excuse to offer. The arguments were exhausted,
and all had been refuted. The only thing left to it was a mute
trembling, and as if it were facing death it was terrified of being
restrained from the treadmill of habit by which it suffered 'sickness
unto death' (John 11: 4).

viii (19)   Then in the middle of that grand struggle in my inner
house, which I had vehemently stirred up with my soul in the
intimate chamber of my heart, distressed not only in mind but in
appearance, I turned on Alypius and cried out: 'What is wrong with
us? What is this that you have heard? Uneducated people are rising
up and capturing heaven (Matt. 11: 12), and we with our high
culture without any heart—see where we roll in the mud of flesh
and blood. Is it because they are ahead of us that we are ashamed to
follow? Do we feel no shame at making not even an attempt to
follow?' That is the gist of what I said, and the heat of my passion
took my attention away from him as he contemplated my condition
in astonished silence. For I sounded very strange. My uttered
words said less about the state of my mind than my forehead,
cheeks, eyes, colour, and tone of voice.

Our lodging had a garden. We had the use of it as well as of the
entire house, for our host, the owner of the house, was not living
there. The tumult of my heart took me out into the garden where
no one could interfere with the burning struggle with myself in
which I was engaged, until the matter could be settled. You knew,
but I did not, what the outcome would be. But my madness with
myself was part of the process of recovering health, and in the
agony of death I was coming to life. I was aware how ill I was,
unaware how well I was soon to be. So I went out into the garden.
Alypius followed me step after step. Although he was present, I felt
no intrusion on my solitude. How could he abandon me in such a
state? We sat down as far as we could from the buildings. I was
deeply disturbed in spirit, angry with indignation and distress that I
was not entering into my pact and covenant with you, my God,
when all my bones (Ps. 34: 10) were crying out that I should enter

into it and were exalting it to heaven with praises. But to reach that destination one does not use ships or chariots or feet.[15] It was not even necessary to go the distance I had come from the house to where we were sitting. The one necessary condition, which meant not only going but at once arriving there, was to have the will to go—provided only that the will was strong and unqualified, not the turning and twisting first this way, then that, of a will half-wounded, struggling with one part rising up and the other part falling down.

(20) Finally in the agony of hesitation I made many physical gestures of the kind men make when they want to achieve something and lack the strength, either because they lack the actual limbs or because their limbs are fettered with chains or weak with sickness or in some way hindered. If I tore my hair, if I struck my forehead, if I intertwined my fingers and clasped my knee, I did that because to do so was my will. But I could have willed this and then not done it if my limbs had not possessed the power to obey. So I did many actions in which the will to act was not equalled by the power. Yet I was not doing what with an incomparably greater longing I yearned to do, and could have done the moment I so resolved. For as soon as I had the will, I would have had a wholehearted will. At this point the power to act is identical with the will. The willing itself was performative of the action. Nevertheless, it did not happen. The body obeyed the slightest inclination of the soul to move the limbs at its pleasure more easily than the soul obeyed itself, when its supreme desire could be achieved exclusively by the will alone.

ix (21) What is the cause of this monstrous situation? Why is it the case? May your mercy illuminate me as I ask if perhaps an answer can be found in the hidden punishments and secret tribulations that befall the sons of Adam? What causes this monstrous fact? and why is it so? The mind commands the body and is instantly obeyed. The mind commands itself and meets resistance. The mind commands the hand to move, and it is so easy that one hardly distinguishes the order from its execution. Yet mind is mind, and hand is body. The mind orders the mind to will. The recipient of the order is itself, yet it does not perform it. What causes this monstrosity and why does this happen? Mind commands, I say, that it should will, and would

[15] Echo of Plotinus 1. 6. 8. 21.

not give the command if it did not will, yet does not perform what it commands. The willing is not wholehearted, so the command is not wholehearted. The strength of the command lies in the strength of will, and the degree to which the command is not performed lies in the degree to which the will is not engaged. For it is the will that commands the will to exist, and it commands not another will but itself. So the will that commands is incomplete, and therefore what it commands does not happen. If it were complete, it would not need to command the will to exist, since it would exist already. Therefore there is no monstrous split between willing and not willing. We are dealing with a morbid condition of the mind which, when it is lifted up by the truth, does not unreservedly rise to it but is weighed down by habit. So there are two wills. Neither of them is complete, and what is present in the one is lacking to the other.

x (22)   'Let them perish from your presence' (Ps. 67: 3) O God, as do 'empty talkers and seducers' of the mind (Titus 1: 10)[16] who from the dividing of the will into two in the process of deliberation, deduce that there are two minds with two distinct natures, one good, the other bad. They really are evil themselves when they entertain these evil doctrines. Yet the very same people would be good if they held to the true doctrines and assented to the truth. As your apostle says to them 'You were at one time darkness, but now are light in the Lord' (Eph. 5: 8). But they wish to be light not in the Lord but in themselves because they hold that the nature of the soul is what God is. They have in fact become a thicker darkness in that by their horrendous arrogance they have withdrawn further away from you—from you who are 'the true light illuminating every man coming into this world' (John 1: 9). They should give heed to what you say and blush: 'Come to him and be illuminated, and your faces will not blush' (Ps. 33: 6).

In my own case, as I deliberated about serving my Lord God (Jer. 30: 9) which I had long been disposed to do, the self which willed to serve was identical with the self which was unwilling. It was I. I was neither wholly willing nor wholly unwilling. So I was in conflict with myself and was dissociated from myself. The dissociation came about against my will. Yet this was not a manifestation of the nature of an alien mind but the punishment suffered in my own

[16] Manichees.

mind. And so it was 'not I' that brought this about 'but sin which dwelt in me' (Rom. 7: 17, 20), sin resulting from the punishment of a more freely chosen sin, because I was a son of Adam.

(23) If there are as many contrary natures as there are wills in someone beset by indecision, there will be not two wills but many. If a person is deliberating whether to go to the Manichees' conventicle or to the theatre, they cry: 'Here are two natures, a good one leads one way, a bad one leads the other way. How otherwise explain the opposition of two wills to one another?' But I affirm that they are both evil, both the will to attend their meeting and the will to go to the theatre. They think that the intention to go along to them can only be good. What then? If one of us Catholic Christians were deliberating and, with two wills quarrelling with one another, fluctuated between going to the theatre or to our Church, surely the Manichees would be quite undecided what to say about that. Either they will have to concede that to go to our Church is an act of good will, as is the case with those worshippers who are initiated into its sacraments and feel the obligation thereby imposed, or they will have to think two evil natures and two evil minds are in conflict within a single person. This argument will prove untrue their usual assertion that one is good, the other bad. The alternative for them will be to be converted to the true view and not to deny that in the process of deliberation a single soul is wavering between different wills.

(24) Accordingly, when they note two wills in one person in conflict with each other, let them no more say that two conflicting minds are derived from two rival substances, and that two conflicting principles are in contention, one good, the other evil. God of truth, you condemn them and refute and confound them. For both wills are evil when someone is deliberating whether to kill a person by poison or by a dagger; whether to encroach on one estate belonging to someone else or a different one, when he cannot do both; whether to buy pleasure by lechery or avariciously to keep his money; whether to go to the circus or the theatre if both are putting on a performance on the same day, or (I add a third possibility) to steal from another person's house if occasion offers, or (I add a fourth option) to commit adultery if at the same time the chance is available. Suppose that all these choices are confronted at one moment of time, and all are equally desired, yet they cannot all be

done simultaneously. They tear the mind apart by the mutual incompatibility of the wills—four or more according to the number of objects desired. Yet they do not usually affirm that there is such a multiplicity of diverse substances.

The same argument holds for good wills. For I ask them whether it is good to delight in a reading from the apostle, or if it is good to take pleasure in a sober psalm, or if it is good to discourse upon the gospel. In each case they will reply 'good'. What then? If all these offer equal delight at one and the same time, surely the divergent wills pull apart the human heart while we are deliberating which is the most attractive option to take? All are good and yet are in contention with each other until the choice falls on one to which is then drawn the entire single will which was split into many. So also when the delight of eternity draws us upwards and the pleasure of temporal good holds us down, the identical soul is not wholehearted in its desire for one or the other. It is torn apart in a painful condition, as long as it prefers the eternal because of its truth but does not discard the temporal because of familiarity.

xi (25) Such was my sickness and my torture, as I accused myself even more bitterly than usual. I was twisting and turning in my chain until it would break completely: I was now only a little bit held by it, but I was still held. You, Lord, put pressure on me in my hidden depths with a severe mercy wielding the double whip[17] of fear and shame, lest I should again succumb, and lest that tiny and tenuous bond which still remained should not be broken, but once more regain strength and bind me even more firmly. Inwardly I said to myself: Let it be now, let it be now. And by this phrase I was already moving towards a decision; I had almost taken it, and then I did not do so.[18] Yet I did not relapse into my original condition, but stood my ground very close to the point of deciding and recovered my breath. Once more I made the attempt and came only a little short of my goal; only a little short of it—yet I did not touch it or hold on to it. I was hesitating whether to die to death and to live to life. Ingrained evil had more hold over me than unaccustomed

---

[17] Virgil, *Aeneid* 5. 547.

[18] Persius' fifth satire (quoted below VIII. xii (28)) portrays a lover who swears to give up his mistress but returns on her first appeal (5. 157). An epigram in the Greek Anthology (5. 24) concerns a lover whose conscience warns him to fly from his mistress but his will has not the strength.

good. The nearer approached the moment of time when I would become different, the greater the horror of it struck me. But it did not thrust me back nor turn me away, but left me in a state of suspense.

(26) Vain trifles and the triviality of the empty-headed, my old loves, held me back. They tugged at the garment of my flesh and whispered: 'Are you getting rid of us?' And 'from this moment we shall never be with you again, not for ever and ever'. And 'from this moment this and that are forbidden to you for ever and ever.' What they were suggesting in what I have called 'this and that'—what they were suggesting, my God, may your mercy avert from the soul of your servant! What filth, what disgraceful things they were suggesting! I was listening to them with much less than half my attention. They were not frankly confronting me face to face on the road, but as it were whispering behind my back, as if they were furtively tugging at me as I was going away, trying to persuade me to look back. Nevertheless they held me back. I hesitated to detach myself, to be rid of them, to make the leap to where I was being called. Meanwhile the overwhelming force of habit was saying to me: 'Do you think you can live without them?'

(27) Nevertheless it was now putting the question very half-heartedly. For from that direction where I had set my face and towards which I was afraid to move, there appeared the dignified and chaste Lady Continence, serene and cheerful without coquetry, enticing me in an honourable manner to come and not to hesitate. To receive and embrace me she stretched out pious hands, filled with numerous good examples for me to follow. There were large numbers of boys and girls, a multitude of all ages, young adults and grave widows and elderly virgins. In every one of them was Continence herself, in no sense barren but 'the fruitful mother of children' (Ps. 112: 9), the joys born of you, Lord, her husband. And she smiled on me with a smile of encouragement as if to say: 'Are you incapable of doing what these men and women have done? Do you think them capable of achieving this by their own resources and not by the Lord their God? Their Lord God gave me to them. Why are you relying on yourself, only to find yourself unreliable? Cast yourself upon him, do not be afraid. He will not withdraw himself so that you fall. Make the leap without anxiety; he will catch you and heal you.'

I blushed with embarrassment because I was still listening to the mutterings of those vanities, and racked by hesitations I remained undecided. But once more it was as if she said: '"Stop your ears to your impure members on earth and mortify them" (Col. 3: 5). They declare delights to you, but "not in accord with the law of the Lord your God"' (Ps. 118: 85). This debate in my heart was a struggle of myself against myself. Alypius stood quite still at my side, and waited in silence for the outcome of my unprecedented state of agitation.

xii (28)   From a hidden depth a profound self-examination had dredged up a heap of all my misery and set it 'in the sight of my heart' (Ps. 18: 15). That precipitated a vast storm bearing a massive downpour of tears. To pour it all out with the accompanying groans, I got up from beside Alypius (solitude seemed to me more appropriate for the business of weeping), and I moved further away to ensure that even his presence put no inhibition upon me. He sensed that this was my condition at that moment. I think I may have said something which made it clear that the sound of my voice was already choking with tears. So I stood up while in profound astonishment he remained where we were sitting. I threw myself down somehow under a certain figtree,[19] and let my tears flow freely. Rivers streamed from my eyes, a sacrifice acceptable to you (Ps. 50: 19), and (though not in these words, yet in this sense) I repeatedly said to you: 'How long, O Lord? How long, Lord, will you be angry to the uttermost? Do not be mindful of our old iniquities.' (Ps. 6: 4). For I felt my past to have a grip on me. It uttered wretched cries: 'How long, how long is it to be?' 'Tomorrow, tomorrow.'[20] 'Why not now? Why not an end to my impure life in this very hour?'

(29)   As I was saying this and weeping in the bitter agony of my heart, suddenly I heard a voice from the nearby house[21] chanting as if it might be a boy or a girl (I do not know which), saying and repeating over and over again 'Pick up and read, pick up and read.' At once my countenance changed, and I began to think intently whether there might be some sort of children's game in which such

---

[19] Perhaps a symbolic reference to the figtree of Adam (Gen. 3: 7; cf. John 1: 48).

[20] Persius, *Satires* 5. 66.

[21] The oldest manuscript reads here 'from the house of God'. The child's voice is in any event a divine oracle to Augustine. The variant may echo Ps. 41: 5.

a chant is used. But I could not remember having heard of one. I checked the flood of tears and stood up. I interpreted it solely as a divine command to me to open the book and read the first chapter I might find. For I had heard how Antony happened to be present at the gospel reading, and took it as an admonition addressed to himself when the words were read: 'Go, sell all you have, give to the poor, and you shall have treasure in heaven; and come, follow me' (Matt. 19: 21).[22] By such an inspired utterance he was immediately 'converted to you' (Ps. 50: 15). So I hurried back to the place where Alypius was sitting. There I had put down the book of the apostle when I got up. I seized it, opened it and in silence read the first passage on which my eyes lit: 'Not in riots and drunken parties, not in eroticism and indecencies, not in strife and rivalry, but put on the Lord Jesus Christ and make no provision for the flesh in its lusts' (Rom. 13: 13–14).

I neither wished nor needed to read further. At once, with the last words of this sentence, it was as if a light of relief from all anxiety flooded into my heart. All the shadows of doubt were dispelled.

(30) Then I inserted my finger or some other mark in the book and closed it. With a face now at peace I told everything to Alypius. What had been going on in his mind, which I did not know, he disclosed in this way. He asked to see the text I had been reading. I showed him, and he noticed a passage following that which I had read. I did not know how the text went on; but the continuation was 'Receive the person who is weak in faith' (Rom. 14: 1). Alypius applied this to himself, and he made that known to me. He was given confidence by this admonition. Without any agony of hesitation he joined me in making a good resolution and affirmation of intention, entirely congruent with his moral principles in which he had long been greatly superior to me. From there we went in to my mother, and told her. She was filled with joy. We told her how it had happened. She exulted, feeling it to be a triumph, and blessed you who 'are powerful to do more than we ask or think' (Eph. 3: 20). She saw that you had granted her far more than she had long been praying for in her unhappy and tearful groans.

The effect of your converting me to yourself was that I did not

---

[22] Athanasius, *Life of Antony* 2.

now seek a wife and had no ambition for success in this world. I stood firm upon that rule of faith on which many years before you had revealed me to her.[23] You 'changed her grief into joy' (Ps. 29: 12) far more abundantly than she desired, far dearer and more chaste than she expected when she looked for grandchildren begotten of my body.

[23] See above, III. xi (19–20).

BOOK IX

Cassiciacum: to Monica's death

i (1) 'O Lord, I am your servant, I am your servant and the son of your handmaid. You have snapped my chains. I will sacrifice to you the offering of praise' (Ps. 115: 16–17). Let my heart praise you and my tongue, and 'let all my bones say, Lord who is like you?' (Ps. 34: 10). Let them speak, answer me, and say to my soul 'I am your salvation' (Ps. 34: 3).

Who am I and what am I? What was not evil in my deeds or, if not deeds, in my words or, if not words, in my intention? But you, Lord, 'are good and merciful' (Ps. 102: 8). Your right hand had regard to the depth of my dead condition, and from the bottom of my heart had drawn out a trough of corruption. The nub of the problem was to reject my own will and to desire yours. But where through so many years was my freedom of will? From what deep and hidden recess was it called out in a moment? Thereby I submitted my neck to your easy yoke and my shoulders to your light burden (Matt. 11: 30), O Christ Jesus 'my helper and redeemer' (Ps. 18: 15). Suddenly it had become sweet to me to be without the sweets of folly. What I once feared to lose was now a delight to dismiss. You turned them out and entered to take their place, pleasanter than any pleasure but not to flesh and blood, brighter than all light yet more inward than any secret recess, higher than any honour but not to those who think themselves sublime. Already my mind was free of 'the biting cares'[1] of place-seeking, of desire for gain, of wallowing in self-indulgence, of scratching the itch of lust. And I was now talking with you, Lord my God, my radiance, my wealth, and my salvation.

ii (2) I made a decision 'in your sight' (Ps. 18: 15) not to break off teaching with an abrupt renunciation, but quietly to retire from my post as a salesman of words in the markets of rhetoric. I did not wish my pupils, who were giving their minds not to your law (Ps. 118: 70) nor to your peace, but to frenzied lies and lawcourt squabbles, to

---

[1] Horace, *Odes* 1. 18. 4.

buy from my mouth weapons for their madness. Fortunately there were only a few days left before the Vintage Vacation [22 August– 15 October]. I decided to put up with them so that I could resign with due formality. Redeemed by you, I was not now going to return to putting my skills up for sale. Our plan was formed with your knowledge but was not publicly known, except to our intimate circle. It was agreed among us that it was not to be published generally. Meanwhile, to us who were climbing out of the 'valley of tears' (Ps. 83: 6 f.) and singing a 'song of steps' (Ps. 119–33), you had given 'sharp arrows and destroying coals' to answer any deceitful tongues of criticism (Ps. 119: 3 f.). Tongues that appear to be offering helpful advice can actually be hostile opponents and, in offering love, may devour us in the way people consume food.[2]

(3)   You pierced my heart with the arrow of your love,[3] and we carried your words transfixing my innermost being (cf. Ps. 37: 3). The examples given by your servants whom you had transformed from black to shining white and from death to life, crowded in upon my thoughts. They burnt away and destroyed my heavy sluggishness, preventing me from being dragged down to low things. They set me on fire with such force that every breath of opposition from any 'deceitful tongue' (Ps. 119: 2 f.) had the power not to dampen my zeal but to inflame it the more. However, because of your name which you have sanctified throughout the earth (Ezek. 36: 23), my vow and profession would no doubt have some to approve it. So it would have seemed like ostentation if, rather than waiting for the imminent vacation period, I were prematurely to resign from a public position which had a high profile before everyone. The consequence would be that everyone would turn their scrutiny on what I had done in deliberately anticipating the coming day of the Vacation, and there would be much gossip that I was ambitious to appear important. What gain was it for me that people should be thinking and disputing about my state of mind and that a decision which was good to me should be evil spoken of? (Rom. 14: 16).[4]

---

[2] Cf. above II. ix (17).

[3] The symbol of Christ as heavenly Eros was familiar from the Latin version of Origen's commentary on the Song of Songs. Augustine's African critic, Arnobius the younger, could write of 'Christ our Cupid'. Cf. below X. vi (8).

[4] The argument answers the implied criticism of puritan Christians that if his conversion had been 100 per cent real, he would immediately and dramatically have

(4) Furthermore, during that summer in consequence of too heavy a teaching load in literary studies, my lungs had begun to weaken. Breathing became difficult. Pains on the chest were symptoms of the lesion, and deprived me of power to speak clearly or for any length of time. At first this worried me because it was virtually enforcing the necessity of resigning the burden of my teaching responsibility or, if I could be cured and recover strength, at least taking some time off. But now that a total intention to 'be at leisure and see that you are God' (Ps. 45: 11) was born in me and had become quite firm (that you knew, my God), I also began to be pleased that my indisposition was a genuine excuse which softened the irritation felt by people who, being concerned for the education of their sons, were unwilling that I should ever be free. Full of joy in this regard, therefore, I tolerated that interval of time until it was over—it may have been about twenty days. Yet it required courage to be tolerant, because I no longer had the interest in money which ordinarily enabled me to endure a heavy work-load. In continuing my work I would have felt quite crushed if the desire for profit had not been replaced by patience. One of your servants, my brothers, might say that I had sinned in this matter, in that with my heart already fully determined upon your service, I had allowed myself to sit for even one hour in the seat of mendacity (Ps. 1: 1). I would not contest that. But, most merciful God, did you not grant pardon and remission for this fault together with my other horrendous and mortal sins,[5] in the holy water of baptism?

iii (5) Verecundus was torn by anxiety at the happiness which had come to us because he was firmly tied by the chains of his obligations and saw himself losing our society. He was not yet a Christian, but his wife was a baptized believer. Fettered by her more than anything else, he was held back from the journey on which we had embarked. He used to say that he did not wish to be a Christian except in the

---

renounced so profane a profession. The criticism from other secular professors of literature he had already scorned: I. xiii (22).

[5] Augustine followed 1 John 5: 16–17 in the distinction between pardonable sins and 'sins unto death' and the early Christian interpretation of the latter to mean major sins (apostasy, murder, adultery) bringing shame on the community, not only the individual; the major sins required some formal act by the Church to give full restoration after penitential discipline had manifested serious sorrow. But Augustine also saw that no clear-cut line can be drawn between venial and mortal (*City of God* 21. 27).

way which was not open to him.[6] Most generously he offered us hospitality at his expense for as long as we were there. Repay him, Lord, at the rewarding of the just (Luke 14: 14). Indeed you have already rewarded him with their lot (Num. 23: 10). For when we were absent during our stay in Rome,[7] he was taken ill in body, and in his sickness departed this life a baptized Christian. So you had mercy not only on him but also on us. We would have felt tortured by unbearable pain if, in thinking of our friend's outstanding humanity to us, we could not have numbered him among your flock. Thanks be to you, our God: we are yours. Your encouragements and consolations so assure us. Faithful to your promises, in return for Verecundus' country estate at Cassiciacum[8] where we rested in you from the heat of the world, you rewarded him with the loveliness of your evergreen paradise. For you forgave his sins upon earth and translated him to the mountain flowing with milk,[9] your mountain, the mountain of abundance (Ps. 67: 16).

(6) Though at that time Verecundus was upset, Nebridius shared in our joy. He also was not yet a Christian. He had fallen into that ditch of pernicious [Manichee] error which taught him to believe that the flesh of your Son, the truth, was illusory. Nevertheless he had emerged from that to the attitude that, though not yet initiated into any of the sacraments of your Church, he was an ardent seeker after truth. Soon after my conversion and regeneration by your baptism, he too became a baptized Catholic believer. He was serving you in perfect chastity and continence among his own people in Africa, and through him his entire household became Christian, when you released him from bodily life. Now he lives in Abraham's bosom (Luke 16: 22). Whatever is symbolized by 'bosom', that is where my Nebridius lives, a sweet friend to me, but, Lord, your former freedman and now adopted son.[10] There he lives; for what other place could hold so remarkable a soul? There he lives,

---

[6] As an ascetic, since married Christians enjoyed second-class status.

[7] In summer 387 Augustine left Milan for Africa, but was delayed by civil war. He buried Monica at Ostia, 13 Nov. 387, but stayed in Rome till Aug. 388.

[8] Near Como.

[9] The Old Latin version of the Psalms (*in monte incaseato*, in the cheesy mountain) gave a rhetorical assonance with Cassiciacum.

[10] Cf. Gal. 4: 5–7. Nebridius—God's freedman by baptism, adopted son in paradise. If the text implies that Nebridius' social status was that of a freedman, which is possible, he was a well-to-do member of that class.

in that place concerning which he used to put many questions to me—a poor little man without expert knowledge. He no longer pricks up his ear when I speak, but puts his spiritual mouth to your fountain and avidly drinks as much as he can of wisdom, happy without end. I do not think him so intoxicated by that as to forget me, since you, Lord, whom he drinks, are mindful of us.

So that was our state. We comforted Verecundus in his sadness by the fact that my conversion did not put an end to our friendship, and we exhorted him to the faith appropriate to his rank, that is, to married life. But I waited for the time when Nebridius would follow my example. He was so close to doing so that he could have done it and was on the point of acting when at last those days ran their course. They seemed long and numerous because of my longing for freedom and leisure to sing with all my inmost being: 'My heart has said to you, I have sought your face: your face, Lord, will I seek' (Ps. 26: 8).

iv (7) The day came when I was actually liberated from the profession of rhetor, from which in thought I was already freed. But now it became reality. You delivered my tongue from a task from which you had already delivered my heart, and I blessed you with joy as I set out for the country villa with all my circle. The books that I wrote there were indeed now written in your service, and attest my discussions with those present and with myself alone before you.[11] But they still breathe the spirit of the school of pride, as if they were at the last gasp. The discussions with Nebridius, who was not there, are shown by my correspondence.

When can time suffice for me to recall all your great benefits towards us at that time, especially when I have to hurry on to other more important matters? My memory calls me back to that period, and it becomes sweet for me, Lord, to confess to you by what inward goads you tamed me; how you levelled me by 'bringing down the mountains and hills' of my thoughts and 'made straight my crooked ways and smoothed my roughnesses' (Isa. 40: 4); and how

[11] At Cassiciacum during the months between conversion (July 386) and baptism at Milan by Ambrose at Easter 387, Augustine used shorthand transcripts of the conversations with his circle as the basis for a set of philosophical dialogues: *Against the Academics, The Happy Life, Order* (of providence), *Soliloquies.* The dialogues and the correspondence with Nebridius, which Augustine published probably as a memorial to his dead friend, are deeply Neoplatonic, while explicitly Christian. They also have numerous literary echoes of Cicero, Terence, etc.

you subjected Alypius too, my heart's brother, to the name of your
only-begotten Son, our Lord and Saviour Jesus Christ (2 Pet. 3: 18).
For at first he was scornfully critical of inserting Christ's name in
my books. He wanted them to smell of the 'cedars' of the schools
'which the Lord had now felled' (Ps. 28: 5) rather than of the
healthgiving herbs of the Church which are a remedy against
serpents.

(8)   My God, how I cried to you when I read the Psalms of David,
songs of faith, utterances of devotion which allow no pride of spirit
to enter in! I was but a beginner in authentic love of you, a
catechumen resting at a country villa with another catechumen,
Alypius. My mother stayed close by us in the clothing of a woman
but with a virile faith, an older woman's serenity, a mother's love,
and a Christian devotion. How I cried out to you in those Psalms,
and how they kindled my love for you! I was fired by an enthusiasm
to recite them, were it possible, to the entire world in protest
against the pride of the human race. Yet they are being sung in all
the world and 'there is none who can hide himself from your heat'
(Ps. 18: 7). What vehement and bitter anger I felt against the
Manichees! But then my pity for them returned because they were
ignorant of your remedies, the sacraments. They were madly hostile
to the antidote which could have cured them.[12] As I read the fourth
Psalm during that period of contemplation, I would have liked them
to be somewhere nearby without me knowing they were there,
watching my face and hearing my cries, to see what that Psalm had
done to me: 'When I called upon you, you heard me, God of my
righteousness; in tribulation you gave me enlargement. Have mercy
on me, Lord, and hear my prayer' (Ps. 4: 2). Without me knowing
that they were listening, lest they should think I was saying things
just for their sake, I wish they could have heard what comments I
made on these words. But in truth I would not have said those
things, nor said them in that kind of way, if I had felt myself to be
heard or observed by them. Nor, had I said them, would they have
understood how I was expressing the most intimate feeling of my
mind with myself and to myself.

(9)   I trembled with fear and at the same time burned with hope
and exultation at your mercy, Father (Ps. 30: 7–8). All these

---

[12] Many Manichee texts express contempt for baptism and eucharist.

emotions exuded from my eyes and my voice when 'your good Spirit' (Ps. 142: 10) turned towards us to say: 'Sons of men, how long will you be dull at heart? And why do you love vanity and seek after a lie?' (Ps. 4: 3). For I had loved vanity and sought after a lie. And you Lord had already 'magnified your holy one' (Ps. 4: 4), raising him from the dead and setting him at your right hand (Eph. 1: 20), whence he sent from on high his promise, the Paraclete, the Spirit of truth (John 14: 16 f.). He had already sent him but I did not know it. He had sent him because he was already 'magnified' by rising from the dead and ascending to heaven. But before that 'the Spirit was not yet given because Jesus was not yet glorified' (John 7: 39). The prophecy proclaims: 'How long will you be dull at heart? Why do you love vanity and seek after a lie? Know that the Lord has magnified his holy one.' (Ps. 4: 3–4). The prophet cries 'How long?' and cries 'Know.' But I, so long in ignorance, loved vanity and sought after a lie. As I heard the Psalm, I trembled at words spoken to people such as I recalled myself to have been. For in the fantasies which I had taken for truth, there was vanity and deceit. In the pain felt at my memory of it, I often cried out loud and strong. I wish I could have been heard by those who even now still love vanity and seek after a lie. Perhaps they would have been disturbed and vomited it up; and you would have 'heard them when they cried to you'. For by a true physical death 'he who intercedes for us died for us' (Rom. 8: 34).

(10) I read 'Be angry and sin not' (Ps. 4: 5). How was I moved, my God! I had already learnt to be angry with myself for the past, that I should not sin in future. And I was right to be angry. For it was no race of darkness of another nature sinning through me, as the Manichees say, who feel no anger against themselves and yet 'treasure up for themselves anger in the day of wrath and of the revelation of your just judgement' (Rom. 2: 5). But now the goods I sought were no longer in the external realm, nor did I seek for them with bodily eyes in the light of this sun. In desiring to find their delight in externals, they easily become empty and expend their energies on 'the things which are seen and temporal' (2 Cor. 4: 18). With starving minds they can only lick the images of these things.[13] Would that they were wearied by hunger and would say 'Who will

[13] Plotinus 1. 6. 8. 8.

show us good?' (Ps. 4: 6 f.). So let us say, and let them hear: 'The
light of your countenance, Lord, is signed upon us.' (Ps. 4: 7). For
we are not 'the light that illuminates every man' (John 1: 9). We
derive our light from you, so that we 'who were once darkness are
light in you' (Eph. 5: 8). If only they could see the eternal to be
inward! I had tasted this, but was enraged that I was unable to show
it to them, even if they were to bring their heart to me, though their
eyes are turned away from you towards external things, and if they
were to say 'Who will show us good?' In the place where I had been
angry with myself, within my chamber where I felt the pang of
penitence, where I had made a sacrifice offering up my old life and
placing my hope in you as I first began to meditate on my renewal:
there you began to be my delight, and you gave 'gladness in my
heart' (Ps. 4: 7). And I cried out loud when I acknowledged
inwardly what I read in external words. I had no desire for earthly
goods to be multiplied, nor to devour time and to be devoured by
it.[14] For in the simplicity of eternity I had another kind of 'corn and
wine and oil' (Ps. 4: 9).

(11)   At the following verse I uttered a cry from the bottom of my
heart: 'in peace . . . the selfsame', and at the words 'I will go to sleep
and have my dream' (Ps. 4: 9). Who will bar our way when the word
is realized which is written 'Death is swallowed up in victory' (1 Cor.
15: 54)? For you are supremely 'the selfsame' in that you do not
change (Mal. 3: 6). In you is repose[15] which forgets all toil because
there is none beside you, nor are we to look for the multiplicity of
other things which are not what you are. For 'you Lord, have
established me in hope by means of unity' (Ps. 4: 10).

As I read, I was set on fire, but I did not discover what to do for
the deaf and dead of whom I had been one, when I was a plague, a
bitter and blind critic barking at the scriptures which drip with the
honey of heaven and blaze with your light. Because of the enemies
of these scriptures, I was 'sick with disgust' (Ps. 138: 21).

(12)   It is hard to recount all those days on vacation. But I have not
forgotten them, and I will not pass over in silence the acute pain of
your chastisement and the miraculous rapidity with which your

[14] Several texts in Augustine speak of the successiveness of time as that from which
the divine eternity saves us.
[15] The One is repose: Plotinus 6. 8. 16. 26; cf. 6. 9. 11 (the mystic experiences unity
with no multiplicity, is filled with God, and becomes repose).

mercy brought relief. At that time you tortured me with toothache, and when it became so bad that I lost the power to speak, it came into my heart to beg all my friends present to pray for me to you, God of health of both soul and body. I wrote this on a wax tablet and gave it to them to read. As soon as we fell on our knees in the spirit of supplication, the pain vanished. But what agony it was, and how instantly it disappeared! I admit I was terrified, 'my Lord my God' (Ps. 37: 23). I had experienced nothing like it in all my life. Your will was brought home to me in the depths of my being, and rejoicing in faith I praised your name. This faith did not allow me to be free of guilt over my past sins, which had not yet been forgiven through your baptism.

v (13) At the end of the Vintage Vacation my resignation took effect and I notified the people at Milan that they should provide another salesman of words for their pupils. The reasons were both that I had chosen to serve you, and that I had insufficient strength for that profession because of breathing difficulty and pain on the chest. By letter I informed your bishop, the holy man Ambrose, of my past errors and my present desire, asking what he would especially recommend me to read out of your books to make me readier and fitter to receive so great a grace. He told me to read the prophet Isaiah, I think because more clearly than others he foretold the gospel and the calling of the Gentiles. But I did not understand the first passage of the book, and thought the whole would be equally obscure. So I put it on one side to be resumed when I had had more practice in the Lord's style of language.

vi (14) When the time came for me to give in my name for baptism, we left the country and returned to Milan. Alypius also decided to join me in being reborn in you. He had already embraced the humility that befits your mysteries, and tamed his body to a tough discipline by asceticism of extraordinary boldness: he went barefoot on the icy soil of Italy.[16] We associated with us the boy Adeodatus, my natural son begotten of my sin. You had made him a

---

[16] Some Christians late in the fourth century, especially round Brescia, walked barefoot after the example of Moses at the burning bush or the prophet Isaiah who went barefoot for three years. Successive bishops deplored this, evidently in vain. Much ancient evidence records the axiom that for cultic acts bare feet are necessary; Augustine himself found it impossible to stop the practice when he became a bishop. Monks in ancient Egypt removed their shoes for communion. In Syria it was customary for candidates for baptism, in the West for Rogation processions.

fine person. He was about fifteen years old, and his intelligence surpassed that of many serious and well-educated men. I praise you for your gifts, my Lord God, Creator of all and with great power giving form to our deformities. For I contributed nothing to that boy other than sin. You and no one else inspired us to educate him in your teaching.[17] I gratefully acknowledge before you your gifts. One of my books is entitled *The Teacher*.[18] There Adeodatus is in dialogue with me. You know that he was responsible for all the ideas there attributed to him in the role of my partner in the conversation. He was 16 at the time. I learnt many other remarkable things about him. His intelligence left me awestruck. Who but you could be the Maker of such wonders? Early on you took him away from life on earth. I recall him with no anxiety; there was nothing to fear in his boyhood or adolescence or indeed his manhood. We associated him with us so as to be of the same age as ourselves in your grace. We were baptized,[19] and disquiet about our past life vanished from us. During those days I found an insatiable and amazing delight in considering the profundity of your purpose for the salvation of the human race. How I wept during your hymns and songs! I was deeply moved by the music of the sweet chants of your Church. The sounds flowed into my ears and the truth was distilled into my heart. This caused the feelings of devotion to overflow. Tears ran, and it was good for me to have that experience.

vii (15)   The Church at Milan had begun only a short time before to employ this method of mutual comfort and exhortation. The brothers used to sing together with both heart and voice in a state of high enthusiasm. Only a year or a little more had passed since Justina, mother of the young king Valentinian, was persecuting your servant Ambrose in the interest of her heresy.[20] She had been led

---

[17] The sentence is crucial evidence that Adeodatus was not brought up as a Manichee, and therefore that his mother was a Catholic girl.

[18] The book is an acute study of non-verbal communication.

[19] 24 April 387, at the baptistery of Milan cathedral by bishop Ambrose. Adeodatus' death, whether by illness or accident, occurred about two years later, not long after the discussions written up by Augustine in *The Teacher* (which show that the boy was educated both in scripture and in Virgil, and had some knowledge of Punic).

[20] Justina, the Arian wife of Valentinian I (who died in 375), came to Milan with her son Valentinian II (b.371), and engaged in a lengthy struggle against Ambrose, the anti-Arian bishop from 374, issuing an edict of toleration for Arianism in January 386 with a demand that Ambrose surrender basilicas for Arian worship. Ambrose arranged for his people to provide a permanent sit-in to prevent military force from confiscating any Churches for the Arian Goths to use at Easter 386.

into error by the Arians. The devout congregation kept continual guard in the Church, ready to die with their bishop, your servant. There my mother, your handmaid, was a leader in keeping anxious watch and lived in prayer. We were still cold, untouched by the warmth of your Spirit, but were excited by the tension and disturbed atmosphere in the city. That was the time when the decision was taken to introduce hymns and psalms sung after the custom of the eastern Churches, to prevent the people from succumbing to depression and exhaustion. From that time to this day the practice has been retained and many, indeed almost all your flocks, in other parts of the world have imitated it.

(16)   This was the time when through a vision you revealed to the bishop already mentioned the place where lay hidden the bodies of the martyrs Protasius and Gervasius. For many years you had kept them from corruption, hidden away in your secret treasury, out of which at the right moment you produced them to restrain the fury of a woman, indeed a lady of the royal family. When they had been produced and dug out, they were transferred with due honour to Ambrose's basilica,[21] and some people vexed by impure spirits were healed, the very demons themselves making public confession. Moreover, a citizen who had been blind many years and was well known in the city, heard the people in a state of tumultuous jubilation and asked the reason for it. On learning the answer, he leapt up and asked his guide to lead him there. When he arrived, he begged admission so that he might touch with his cloth the bier on which lay your saints whose 'death is precious in your sight' (Ps. 115: 15). When he did this and applied the cloth to his eyes, immediately they were opened. From that point the news spread fast, praises of you were fervent and radiant, and the mind of that hostile woman, though not converted to sound faith, was nevertheless checked in

---

[21] Today's Church of S. Ambrogio near the University. Augustine, followed by Ambrose's biographer Paulinus, gives the misleading impression that the discovery of the saints' relics was directly connected with Ambrose's struggle at Holy Week 386 against Justina and the Arians, as if they were miraculously produced from the arsenals of divine wrath to vindicate Catholicism and a very clever bishop Ambrose. In fact the evidence is clear that the two incidents were only marginally connected. Ambrose needed martyrs' relics for his new Basilica Ambrosiana (so called at the time). Augustine and Paulinus, but not Ambrose, say the discovery of relics came as a result of a revelation. The martyrs' graves were found in June 386, long after the Easter excitements had passed away. That they vindicated Catholic orthodoxy was secondary.

its anger. 'Thanks be to you, my God' (Luke 18: 11). From what starting-point and to what end have you led my memory to include even these events in my confession to you, when I have passed over much that I have forgotten? Yet at that time when 'the perfume of your unguents' (Cant. 1: 3) was so strong, I was not pursuing you. And so I wept much at the chants of your hymns. In the past I had sighed for you, and now at last was breathing your air to the extent that air is free to move in a house of straw.

viii (17) 'You make people to live in a house in unanimity' (Ps. 67: 7). So you made Evodius a member of our circle, a young man from my home town.[22] When he was a civil servant as an agent in the special branch, he was converted to you before we were. He was baptized and resigned his post on taking up your service. We were together and by a holy decision resolved to live together. We looked for a place where we could be of most use in your service; all of us agreed on a move back to Africa.

While we were at Ostia by the mouths of the Tiber,[23] my mother died. I pass over many events because I write in great haste. Accept my confessions and thanksgivings, my God, for innumerable things even though I do not specifically mention them. But I shall not pass over whatever my soul may bring to birth concerning your servant, who brought me to birth both in her body so that I was born into the light of time, and in her heart so that I was born into the light of eternity. I speak not of her gifts to me, but of your gifts to her. She had not made herself or brought herself up. You created her, and her father and mother did not know what kind of character their child would have. She was trained 'in your fear' (Ps. 5: 8) by the discipline of your Christ, by the government of your only Son in a believing household through a good member of your Church. She used to speak highly not so much of her mother's diligence in training her as of a decrepit maidservant who had carried her father when he was an infant, in the way that infants are often carried on the back of older girls. Because of this long service and for her seniority and high moral standards in a Christian house, she was

---

[22] Evodius travelled to Rome, Ostia, and on to Africa with Augustine. Augustine gave him a role as interlocutor in two dialogues. About 400 he became bishop of Uzali, about 414 exchanged letters on intricate theological matters with Augustine, and played an active role in controversy against Manichees and Pelagians.

[23] Echo of Virgil, *Aeneid* 1. 13.

held in great honour by her masters. So she was entrusted with responsibility for her master's daughters and discharged it with diligence and, when necessary, was vehement with a holy severity in administering correction. In training them she exercised a discreet prudence. Outside those times when they were nourished by a most modest meal at their parents' table, even if they were burning with thirst, she allowed them to drink not even water, wishing to avert the formation of a bad habit. She used to add the wise word: 'Now you drink water because it is not in your power to get wine. But when you come to have husbands and become mistresses of store-rooms and cellars, water will seem dull stuff but the drinking habit will be unbreakable.' By this method of laying down rules for behaviour and by her authoritative way of giving commands, she restrained the greedy appetite of a tender age, and brought the girls' thirst to respectable moderation, so that they should not later hanker after anything they ought not to touch.

(18) Nevertheless, as your servant told me her son, a weakness for wine gradually got a grip upon her. By custom her parents used to send her, a sober girl, to fetch wine from the cask. She would plunge the cup through the aperture at the top. Before she poured the wine into a jug, she used to take a tiny sip with the tip of her lips. She could not take more as she disliked the taste. What led her to do this was not an appetite for liquor but the surplus high spirits of a young person, which can overflow in playful impulses and which in children adults ordinarily try to suppress. Accordingly, to that sip of wine she added more sips every day—for 'he who despises small things gradually comes to a fall' (Ecclus. 19: 1)—until she had fallen into the habit of gulping down almost full cups of wine. Where then was the wise old woman and her vehement prohibition? She could have had no strength against the secret malady unless your healing care, Lord were watching over us. When father and mother and nurses are not there, you are present. You have created us, you call us, you use human authorities set over us to do something for the health of our souls. How did you cure her? How did you restore her health? You brought from another soul a harsh and sharp rebuke, like a surgeon's knife, from your secret stores, and with one blow you cut away the rottenness. The slavegirl who used to accompany her to the cask had a dispute

with her young mistress which happened when they were alone together. Bitterly she insulted her by bringing up the accusation that she was a boozer. The taunt hurt. She reflected upon her own foul addiction, at once condemned it, and stopped the habit. Just as flattering friends corrupt, so quarrelsome enemies often bring us correction. Yet you reward them not for what you use them to achieve, but according to their intention. The maidservant in her anger sought to wound her little mistress, not to cure her. That is why she spoke in private—either because the time and place of the quarrel happened to find them alone together, or perhaps because she was afraid of the fact that she had come out with it so belatedly.

But you, Lord, ruler of heaven and earth, turn to your own purposes the deep torrents. You order the turbulent flux of the centuries. Even from the fury of one soul you brought healing to another. Thereby you showed that no one should attribute it to his own power if by anything he says he sets on the right path someone whom he wishes to be corrected.

ix (19)   So she was brought up in modesty and sobriety. She was made by you obedient to her parents rather than by them to you. When she reached marriageable age, she was given to a man and served him as her lord. She tried to win him for you, speaking to him of you by her virtues through which you made her beautiful, so that her husband loved, respected and admired her. She bore with his infidelities and never had any quarrel with her husband on this account. For she looked forward to your mercy coming upon him, in hope that, as he came to believe in you, he might become chaste. Furthermore, he was exceptional both for his kindness and for his quick temper. She knew that an angry husband should not be opposed, not merely by anything she did, but even by a word. Once she saw that he had become calm and quiet, and that the occasion was opportune, she would explain the reason for her action, in case perhaps he had reacted without sufficient consideration. Indeed many wives married to gentler husbands bore the marks of blows and suffered disfigurement to their faces. In conversation together they used to complain about their husband's behaviour. Monica, speaking as if in jest but offering serious advice, used to blame their tongues. She would say that since the day when they heard the so-called matrimonial contract read out to them, they should reckon them to be legally binding documents by which they had become servants. She thought they should remember their condition and not proudly withstand their masters. The wives were astounded, knowing what a violent husband she had to put up with. Yet it was unheard of, nor was there ever a mark to show, that Patrick had beaten his wife or that a domestic quarrel had caused dissension between them for even a single day. In intimate talk the wives would ask her the reason. She told them of her plan which I have just mentioned. Those who followed her advice found by experience that they were grateful for it. Those who did not follow her way were treated as subordinate and maltreated.

(20) Monica's mother-in-law was at first stirred up to hostility towards her by the whisperings of malicious maidservants. Monica won even her over by her respectful manner and by persistence in patience and gentleness. The result was that her mother-in-law denounced to her son the interfering tongues of the slavegirls. By them domestic harmony between her and her daughter-in-law was disturbed, and she asked for them to be punished. So, after that, he bowed to his mother's request and, exercising his responsibility for discipline in the family and to foster peace in his household, he met his mother's wish by subjecting the girls of whom she complained to a whipping.[24] She declared that the same reward was to be expected by anyone who supposed it would give her pleasure if malicious gossip were passed on about her daughter-in-law. From then on, no one dared to utter a word, and they lived with a memorably gentle benevolence towards each other.

(21) Another great gift with which you endowed that good servant of yours, in whose womb you created me, my God my mercy (Ps. 58: 18), was that whenever she could, she reconciled dissident and quarrelling people. She showed herself so great a peacemaker that when she had heard from both sides many bitter things, such as the bilious and undigested vomit that discord brings up, the crude hatreds that come out in acid gossip in the presence of one woman

[24] The inferior status of the slave was enforced in antiquity by subjection to corporal punishment, the prime distinction between a slave and a free person being the fact that a slave 'has to answer for all offences with his body' (Demosthenes 22. 25; cf. 21. 72). John Chrysostom (on Ephesians, 15: 3) judged it a monstrous offence for a Christian wife to call in her husband to strip a slavegirl naked and whip her. Unlike Augustine who accepted corporal punishment, John thought it quite unfitting in a Christian household for a slave to be struck.

who is a friend and in the absence of another who is an enemy, Monica would never reveal to one anything about the other unless it might help to reconcile them. I would regard this good gift as a minor matter had I not had sad experience of uncountable numbers of people who, infected by a widely diffused sinful contagion, not only report the words angry enemies use about each other but even add words which were never spoken. On the contrary, it should be regarded as a matter of common humanity not to stir up enmities between people nor to increase them by malicious talk, if one lacks the resolve to try to extinguish them by speaking generously. That was the kind of person she was because she was taught by you as her inward teacher in the school of her heart.

(22)　At the end when her husband had reached the end of his life in time, she succeeded in gaining him for you. After he was a baptized believer, she had no cause to complain of behaviour which she had tolerated in one not yet a believer. She was also a servant of your servants: any of them who knew her found much to praise in her, held her in honour and loved her; for they felt your presence in her heart, witnessed by the fruits of her holy way of life. She had been 'the wife of one husband' (1 Tim. 5: 9). She repaid the mutual debt to her parents; she had governed her house in a spirit of devotion (1 Tim. 5: 4). She had 'testimony to her good works' (1 Tim. 5: 10). She had brought up her children, enduring travail as often as she saw them wandering away from you. Lastly, Lord—by your gift you allow me to speak for your servants, for before her falling asleep we were bound together in community in you after receiving the grace of baptism—she exercised care for everybody as if they were all her own children. She served us as if she was a daughter to all of us.

x (23)　The day was imminent when she was to depart this life (the day which you knew and we did not). It came about, as I believe by your providence through your hidden ways, that she and I were standing leaning out of a window overlooking a garden. It was at the house where we were staying at Ostia on the Tiber, where, far removed from the crowds, after the exhaustion of a long journey, we were recovering our strength for the voyage.

Alone with each other, we talked very intimately. 'Forgetting the past and reaching forward to what lies ahead' (Phil. 3: 13), we were searching together in the presence of the truth which is you yourself.

We asked what quality of life the eternal life of the saints will have, a life which 'neither eye has seen nor ear heard, nor has it entered into the heart of man' (1 Cor. 2: 9). But with the mouth of the heart wide open, we drank in the waters flowing from your spring on high, 'the spring of life' (Ps. 35: 10) which is with you. Sprinkled with this dew to the limit of our capacity, our minds attempted in some degree to reflect on so great a reality.

(24) The conversation led us towards the conclusion that the pleasure of the bodily senses, however delightful in the radiant light of this physical world, is seen by comparison with the life of eternity to be not even worth considering. Our minds were lifted up by an ardent affection towards eternal being itself. Step by step we climbed beyond all corporeal objects and the heaven itself, where sun, moon, and stars shed light on the earth. We ascended even further by internal reflection and dialogue and wonder at your works, and we entered into our own minds. We moved up beyond them so as to attain to the region of inexhaustible abundance where you feed Israel eternally with truth for food. There life is the wisdom by which all creatures come into being, both things which were and which will be. But wisdom itself is not brought into being but is as it was and always will be. Furthermore, in this wisdom there is no past and future, but only being, since it is eternal. For to exist in the past or in the future is no property of the eternal. And while we talked and panted after it, we touched it in some small degree by a moment of total concentration of the heart. And we sighed and left behind us 'the firstfruits of the Spirit' (Rom. 8: 23)[25] bound to that higher world, as we returned to the noise of our human speech where a sentence has both a beginning and an ending. But what is to be compared with your word, Lord of our lives? It dwells in you without growing old and gives renewal to all things.

(25) Therefore we said: If to anyone the tumult of the flesh has fallen silent, if the images of earth, water, and air are quiescent,[26] if the heavens themselves are shut out and the very soul itself is

---

[25] The force of this quotation is debated. Does Augustine imply that the ecstasy of Ostia was an anticipation of the beatific vision? Or does he mean the most divine part of the soul, most nearly akin to God, which analogy in Plotinus (5. 1. 3. 4–6) might suggest? Elsewhere Augustine interprets 'the firstfruits of the spirit' to mean the spirit of man, which would favour the latter view. The description of the vision at Ostia has affinities with Plotinus 5. 1. 2. 14 ff., a text also found congenial by St Basil.

[26] Similar language in Plotinus 5. 1. 2. 14 f.

making no sound and is surpassing itself by no longer thinking about itself, if all dreams and visions in the imagination are excluded, if all language and every sign and everything transitory is silent—for if anyone could hear them, this is what all of them would be saying, "We did not make ourselves, we were made by him who abides for eternity" (Ps. 79: 3, 5)—if after this declaration they were to keep silence, having directed our ears to him that made them, then he alone would speak not through them but through himself. We would hear his word, not through the tongue of the flesh, nor through the voice of an angel, nor through the sound of thunder, nor through the obscurity of a symbolic utterance. Him who in these things we love we would hear in person without their mediation. That is how it was when at that moment we extended our reach and in a flash of mental energy attained the eternal wisdom which abides beyond all things.[27] If only it could last, and other visions of a vastly inferior kind could be withdrawn! Then this alone could ravish and absorb and enfold in inward joys the person granted the vision. So too eternal life is of the quality of that moment of understanding after which we sighed. Is not this the meaning of 'Enter into the joy of your Lord' (Matt. 25: 21)? And when is that to be? Surely it is when 'we all rise again, but are not all changed' (1 Cor. 15: 51).

(26) I said something like this, even if not in just this way and with exactly these words. Yet, Lord, you know that on that day when we had this conversation, and this world with all its delights became worthless to us as we talked on, my mother said 'My son, as for myself, I now find no pleasure in this life. What I have still to do here and why I am here, I do not know. My hope in this world is already fulfilled. The one reason why I wanted to stay longer in this life was my desire to see you a Catholic Christian before I die. My God has granted this in a way more than I had hoped. For I see you despising this world's success to become his servant.[28] What have I to do here?'

xi (27) The reply I made to that I do not well recall, for within five days or not much more she fell sick of a fever. While she was ill, on one day she suffered loss of consciousness and gradually became unaware of things around her. We ran to be with her, but she

---

[27] Plotinus 1. 6. 7. 15 ff. speaks of the soul's shock in the experience of awe and delight in its ascent to the Good.

[28] i.e. an ascetic.

quickly recovered consciousness. She looked at me and my brother[29] standing beside her, and said to us in the manner of someone looking for something, 'Where was I?' Then seeing us struck dumb with grief, she said: 'Bury your mother here'. I kept silence and fought back my tears. But my brother, as if to cheer her up, said something to the effect that he hoped she would be buried not in a foreign land but in her home country. When she heard that, her face became worried and her eyes looked at him in reproach that he should think that. She looked in my direction and said 'See what he says', and soon said to both of us 'Bury my body anywhere you like. Let no anxiety about that disturb you. I have only one request to make of you, that you remember me at the altar of the Lord, wherever you may be.' She explained her thought in such words as she could speak, then fell silent as the pain of her sickness became worse.

(28)   But as I thought about your gifts, invisible God, which you send into the hearts of your faithful, and which in consequence produce wonderful fruits, I was filled with joy and gave thanks to you as I recalled what I knew of the great concern which had agitated her about the tomb which she had foreseen and prepared for herself next to the body of her husband. Because they had lived together in great concord, she had expressed the wish (so little is the human mind capable of grasping divine things) that a further addition might be made to her happiness and that posterity might remember it: she wished it to be granted to her that after her travels overseas the two partners in the marriage might be joined in the same covering of earth. But when, by your bountiful goodness, this vain thought began to disappear from her mind, I did not know. I was delighted and surprised that my mother had disclosed this to me. Yet even at the time of our conversation at the window, when she said 'What have I to do here now?', she made it evident that she did not want to die at home. Moreover, I later learnt that before, when we were at Ostia, she conversed one day with some of my friends with all a mother's confidence, and spoke of her contempt for this life and of the beneficence of death. I had not been present

[29] Navigius. The reference to Alypius as Augustine's 'brother in heart', above, IX. iv (7), may imply that Navigius did not share his brother's religious position or ascetic dedication. Augustine's biographer Possidius says that Augustine's nieces became nuns; and we hear of a son (perhaps a nephew) to Navigius who became subdeacon at Hippo.

on this occasion. But they were surprised at the courage of the woman (for you had given it to her), and asked whether she were not afraid to leave her body so far from her own town. 'Nothing,' she said 'is distant from God, and there is no ground for fear that he may not acknowledge me at the end of the world and raise me up.'

On the ninth day of her illness, when she was aged 56, and I was 33, this religious and devout soul was released from the body.[30]

xii (29)   I closed her eyes and an overwhelming grief welled into my heart and was about to flow forth in floods of tears. But at the same time under a powerful act of mental control my eyes held back the flood and dried it up. The inward struggle put me into great agony. Then when she breathed her last, the boy Adeodatus cried out in sorrow and was pressed by all of us to be silent. In this way too something of the child in me, which had slipped towards weeping, was checked and silenced by the youthful voice, the voice of my heart. We did not think it right to celebrate the funeral with tearful dirges and lamentations, since in most cases it is customary to use such mourning to imply sorrow for the miserable state of those who die, or even their complete extinction. But my mother's dying meant neither that her state was miserable nor that she was suffering extinction. We were confident of this because of the evidence of her virtuous life, her 'faith unfeigned' (1 Tim. 1: 15), and reasons of which we felt certain.

(30)   Why then did I suffer sharp pains of inward grief? It must have been the fresh wound caused by the break in the habit formed by our living together, a very affectionate and precious bond suddenly torn apart. I was glad indeed to have her testimony when in that last sickness she lovingly responded to my attentions by calling me a devoted son. With much feeling in her love, she recalled that she had never heard me speak a harsh or bitter word to her. And yet, my God our maker, what comparison can there be between the respect with which I deferred to her and the service she rendered to me? Now that I had lost the immense support she gave, my soul was

[30] Medieval pilgrims record the epitaph on Monica's tomb at Ostia placed early in the fifth century by Anicius Aucherius Bassus, consul in 431. In 1945 the tomb was accidentally discovered when boys were digging a hole for their basket-ball goal. The epitaph is evidence that the *Confessions* remained a best-seller.

wounded, and my life as it were torn to pieces, since my life and hers had become a single thing.

(31)   After the boy's tears had been checked, Evodius took up the psalter and began to chant a psalm. The entire household responded to him: 'I will sing of your mercy and judgement, Lord' (Ps. 100: 1).

When the news of what had happened got about, many brothers and religious women gathered and, according to custom, those whose duty it was made arrangements for the funeral. I myself went apart to a place where I could go without discourtesy and, with those who thought I ought not to be left alone, I discussed subjects fitting for the occasion. I was using truth as a fomentation to alleviate the pain of which you were aware, but of which they were not. They listened to me intently and supposed me to have no feeling of grief.

But in your ears where none of them heard me, I was reproaching the softness of my feelings and was holding back the torrent of sadness. It yielded a little to my efforts, but then again its attack swept over me—yet not so as to lead me to burst into tears or even to change the expression on my face. But I knew what pressure lay upon my heart. And because it caused me such sharp displeasure to see how much power these human frailties had over me, though they are a necessary part of the order we have to endure and are the lot of the human condition, there was another pain to put on top of my grief, and I was tortured by a twofold sadness.

(32)   When her body was carried out, we went and returned without a tear. Even during those prayers which we poured out to you when the sacrifice of our redemption was offered for her, when her corpse was placed beside the tomb prior to burial, as was the custom there,[30A] not even at those prayers did I weep. But throughout the day I was inwardly oppressed with sadness and with a troubled mind I asked you, to the utmost of my strength, to heal my pain. You did not do so. I believe that you gave me no relief so that by this single admonition I should be made aware of the truth that every habit is a fetter adverse even to the mind that is not fed upon deceit. I decided to go and take a bath, because I had heard that baths, for which the Greeks say *balaneion*, get their name from throwing anxiety out of the mind.[31] But I confess this to your mercy,

[30A] By African canon law burial preceded requiem.
[31] Etymology was deployed by Stoics and Alexandrian grammarians of the hellenistic age to explain the formation of language, and the results can be seen in part through a

father of orphans (Ps. 67: 6) that after I bathed I was exactly the same as before. The bitterness of sorrow had not sweated out of my heart. Finally, I fell asleep and on waking up found that in large part my suffering had been relieved. Alone upon my bed I remembered the very true verses of your Ambrose.[32] For you are

> Creator of all things.
> You rule the heavens.
> You clothe the day with light
> And night with the grace of sleep.
>
> So rest restores exhausted limbs
> to the usefulness of work.
> It lightens weary minds
> And dissolves the causes of grief.

(33)   From then on, little by little, I was brought back to my old feelings about your handmaid, recalling her devout attitude to you and her holy gentle and considerate treatment of us, of which I had suddenly been deprived. I was glad to weep before you about her and for her, about myself and for myself. Now I let flow the tears which I had held back so that they ran as freely as they wished. My heart rested upon them, and it reclined upon them because it was your ears that were there, not those of some human critic who would put a proud interpretation on my weeping.[33] And now, Lord, I make my confession to you in writing. Let anyone who wishes read and interpret as he pleases. If he finds fault that I wept for my mother for a fraction of an hour, the mother who had died before my eyes who had wept for me that I might live before your eyes, let him not mock me but rather, if a person of much charity, let him weep himself before you for my sins; for you are the Father of all the brothers of your Christ.

xiii (34)   My heart is healed of that wound; I could be reproached for yielding to that emotion of physical kinship. But now, on behalf of your maidservant, I pour out to you, our God, another kind of

---

work, well known to Augustine, Varro 'On the Latin language'. Augustine's derivation of the Greek for bath from the verb *ballo* (throw, eject) and *ania* (grief) is also found in Greek collections, e.g. the 12th century *Etymologicum Magnum*.

[32] Already quoted earlier, IV. x (15).

[33] Plotinus (1. 4. 4) says that the truly rational person does not grieve at the death of relatives and friends and will not allow himself to be moved; that part which is grieved is deficient in intelligence.

tears. They flow from a spirit struck hard by considering the perils threatening every soul that 'dies in Adam' (1 Cor. 15: 22). She, being 'made alive in Christ', though not yet delivered from the flesh, so lived that your name is praised in her faith and behaviour. But I do not dare to say that, since the day when you regenerated her through baptism, no word came from her mouth contrary to your precept. It was said by the truth, your Son: 'If anyone says to his brother, Fool, he will be liable to the gehenna of fire' (Matt. 5: 22). Woe even to those of praiseworthy life if you put their life under scrutiny and remove mercy. But because you do not search our faults with rigour, we confidently hope for some place with you. If anyone lists his true merits to you, what is he enumerating before you but your gifts? If only human beings would acknowledge themselves to be but human, and that 'he who glories would glory in the Lord' (2 Cor. 10: 17)!

(35) Therefore, God of my heart, my praise and my life, I set aside for a moment her good actions for which I rejoice and give you thanks. I now petition you for my mother's sins. 'Hear me' (Ps. 142: 1) through the remedy for our wounds who hung upon the wood and sits at your right hand to intercede for us (Rom. 8: 34). I know that she acted mercifully and from her heart forgave the debts of her debtors (Matt. 6: 12; 18: 35). Now please forgive her her debts if she contracted any during the many years that passed after she received the water of salvation. Forgive, Lord, forgive, I beseech you. 'Enter not into judgement' with her (Ps. 142: 2). Let mercy triumph over justice (Jas. 2: 13), for your words are true, and you have promised mercy to the merciful (Matt. 5: 7). That the merciful should be so was your gift to them: 'You have mercy on whom you will have mercy and show pity to whom you are compassionate' (Rom. 9: 15; Exod. 33: 19).

(36) I believe you have already done what I am asking of you; but 'approve the desires of my mouth, Lord' (Ps. 118: 108). As the day of her deliverance approached, she did not think of having her body sumptuously wrapped or embalmed with perfumes or given a choice monument. Nor did she care if she had a tomb in her homeland. On that she gave us no instruction; she desired only that she might be remembered at your altar which she had attended every day without fail, where she knew that what is distributed is the holy

victim who 'abolished the account of debts which was reckoned against us' (Col. 2: 14). He triumphed over the enemy who counts up our sins, and searches for grounds of accusation, but who found no fault in him in whom we are conquerors (John 14: 30; Rom. 8: 37).

Who will restore to him his innocent blood? Who will restore to him the price which he paid to buy us, so as to take us out of our adversary's hands? By the chain of faith your handmaid bound her soul to the sacrament of our redemption. Let no one tear her from your protection. Let not the lion and dragon (Ps. 90: 13) intrude themselves either by force or by subtle tricks. For she will not reply that she has no debts to pay, lest she be refuted and captured by the clever Accuser. Her answer will be that her debts have been forgiven by him to whom no one can repay the price which he, who owed nothing, paid on our behalf.

(37) With her husband may she rest in peace. She had no one as her husband before him and after him. She served him by offering you 'fruit with patience' (Luke 8: 15) so as to gain him for you also. My Lord, my God, inspire your servants, my brothers, your sons, my masters, to whose service I dedicate my heart, voice, and writings, that all who read this book may remember at your altar Monica your servant and Patrick her late husband, through whose physical bond you brought me into this life without my knowing how.[34] May they remember with devout affection my parents in this transient light, my kith and kin under you, our Father, in our mother the Catholic Church, and my fellow citizens in the eternal Jerusalem. For this city your pilgrim people yearn, from their leaving it to their return. So as a result of these confessions of mine may my mother's request receive a richer response through the prayers which many offer and not only those which come from me (2 Cor. 1: 11).

---

[34] Augustine deliberately refused to express a firm opinion on the question how the soul is united to the embryo, whether by heredity from the parents (as Manichees believed), or by special creative act by God, or because pre-existent. Cf. similar agnosticism in I. vi (7) above. Despite fierce criticism for his suspense of judgement, Augustine to the last refused to decide.

BOOK X

Memory

i (1)   May I know you, who know me. May I 'know as I also am known' (1 Cor. 13: 12). Power of my soul, enter into it and fit it for yourself, so that you may have and hold it 'without spot or blemish' (Eph. 5: 27). This is my hope, and that is why I speak. In this hope I am placing my delight when my delight is in what it ought to be. As to the other pleasures of life, regret at their loss should be in inverse proportion to the extent to which one weeps for losing them. The less we weep for them, the more we ought to be weeping. 'Behold, you have loved the truth' (Ps. 51: 8), for he who 'does the truth comes to the light' (John 3: 21). This I desire to do, in my heart before you in confession, but before many witnesses with my pen.

ii (2)   Indeed, Lord, to your eyes, the abyss of human consciousness is naked (Heb. 4: 13). What could be hidden within me, even if I were unwilling to confess it to you? I would be hiding you from myself, not myself from you. Now, however, my groaning is witness that I am displeased with myself. You are radiant and give delight and are so an object of love and longing that I am ashamed of myself and reject myself. You are my choice, and only by your gift can I please either you or myself. Before you, then, Lord, whatever I am is manifest, and I have already spoken of the benefit I derive from making confession to you. I am not doing this merely by physical words and sounds, but by words from my soul and a cry from my mind, which is known to your ear. When I am evil, making confession to you is simply to be displeased with myself. When I am good, making confession to you is simply to make no claim on my own behalf, for you, Lord, 'confer blessing on the righteous' (Ps. 5: 13) but only after you have first 'justified the ungodly' (Rom. 4: 5). Therefore, my God, my confession before you is made both in silence and not in silence. It is silent in that it is no audible sound; but in love it cries aloud. If anything I say to men is right, that is what you have first heard from me. Moreover, you hear nothing true from my lips which you have not first told me.

iii (3)   Why then should I be concerned for human readers to hear my confessions? It is not they who are going to 'heal my sicknesses' (Ps. 102: 3). The human race is inquisitive about other people's lives, but negligent to correct their own. Why do they demand to hear from me what I am when they refuse to hear from you what they are? And when they hear me talking about myself, how can they know if I am telling the truth, when no one 'knows what is going on in a person except the human spirit which is within' (I Cor. 2: 11)? But if they were to hear about themselves from you, they could not say 'The Lord is lying'. To hear you speaking about oneself is to know oneself.[1] Moreover, anyone who knows himself and says 'That is false' must be a liar. But 'love believes all things' (I Cor. 13: 7), at least among those love has bonded to itself and made one. I also, Lord, so make my confession to you that I may be heard by people to whom I cannot prove that my confession is true. But those whose ears are opened by love believe me.

(4)   Nevertheless, make it clear to me, physician of my most intimate self, that good results from my present undertaking. Stir up the heart when people read and hear the confessions of my past wickednesses, which you have forgiven and covered up to grant me happiness in yourself, transforming my soul by faith and your sacrament. Prevent their heart from sinking into the sleep of despair and saying 'It is beyond my power.' On the contrary, the heart is aroused in the love of your mercy and the sweetness of your grace, by which every weak person is given power, while dependence on grace produces awareness of one's own weakness. Good people are delighted to hear about the past sins of those who have now shed them. The pleasure is not in the evils as such, but that though they were so once, they are not like that now.[2]

My Lord, every day my conscience makes confession, relying on the hope of your mercy as more to be trusted than its own innocence. So what profit is there, I ask, when, to human readers, by this book I confess to you who I now am, not what I once was? The profit derived from confessing my past I have seen and spoken about. But

---

[1] Like Plotinus and Porphyry, Augustine understood the Delphic maxim 'Know yourself' as the path to knowing God; conversely, knowing God is the way to self-knowledge. Plotinus 5. 3. 7. 2 f.

[2] The paragraph shows Augustine sensitive to the possibility that some among his readers may have a prurient interest in the record of his sexual excesses in youth.

what I now am at this time when I am writing my confessions many wish to know, both those who know me and those who do not but have heard something from me or about me; their ear is not attuned to my heart at the point where I am whatever I am. So as I make my confession, they wish to learn about my inner self, where they cannot penetrate with eye or ear or mind. Yet although they wish to do that and are ready to believe me, they cannot really have certain knowledge. The love which makes them good people tells them that I am not lying in confessing about myself, and the love in them believes me.

iv (5)   But what edification do they hope to gain by this? Do they desire to join me in thanksgiving when they hear how, by your gift, I have come close to you, and do they pray for me when they hear how I am held back by my own weight? To such sympathetic readers I will indeed reveal myself. For it is no small gift, my Lord God, if 'many give you thanks on our account' (2 Cor. 1: 11), and if many petition you on our behalf. A brotherly mind will love in me what you teach to be lovable, and will regret in me what you teach to be regrettable. This is a mark of a Christian brother's mind, not an outsider's—not that of 'the sons of aliens whose mouth speaks vanity, and their right hand is a right hand of iniquity' (Ps. 143: 7 f.). A brotherly person rejoices on my account when he approves me, but when he disapproves, he grieves on my behalf. Whether he approves or disapproves, he is loving me. To such people I will reveal myself. They will take heart from my good traits, and sigh with sadness at my bad ones. My good points are instilled by you and are your gifts. My bad points are my faults and your judgements on them. Let them take heart from the one and regret the other. Let both praise and tears ascend in your sight from brotherly hearts, your censers. But you Lord, who take delight in the odour of your holy temple, 'have pity on me according to your mercy for your name's sake' (Ps. 50: 3). You never abandon what you have begun. Make perfect my imperfections.

(6)   When I am confessing not what I was but what I am now, the benefit lies in this: I am making this confession not only before you with a secret exaltation and fear and with a secret grief touched by hope, but also in the ears of believing sons of men, sharers in my joy, conjoined with me in mortality, my fellow citizens and pilgrims,

some who have gone before, some who follow after, and some who are my companions in this life. They are your servants, my brothers, who by your will are your sons and my masters. You have commanded me to serve them if I wish to live with you and in dependence on you. This your word would have meant little to me if it had been only a spoken precept and had not first been acted out.[3] For my part, I carry out your command by actions and words; but I discharge it under the protection of your wings (Ps. 16: 8; 35: 8). It would be a far too perilous responsibility unless under your wings my soul were submissive to you. My weakness is known to you. I am a child. But my Father ever lives and my protector is sufficient to guard me. He is one and the same who begat me and watches over me. You yourself are all my good qualities. You are the omnipotent one, who are with me even before I am with you. So, to those whom you command me to serve, I will reveal not who I was, but what I have now come to be and what I continue to be. 'But I do not sit in judgement on myself' (1 Cor. 4: 3). It is, therefore, in this spirit that I ask to be listened to.

v (7) You, Lord, are my judge. For even if 'no man knows the being of man except the spirit of man which is in him' (1 Cor. 2: 11), yet there is something of the human person which is unknown even to the 'spirit of man which is in him.' But you, Lord, know everything about the human person; for you made humanity. Although in your sight I despise myself and estimate myself to be dust and ashes (Gen. 18: 27), I nevertheless know something of you which I do not know about myself. Without question 'we see now through a mirror in an enigma', not yet 'face to face' (1 Cor. 13: 12). For this cause, as long as I am a traveller absent from you (2 Cor. 5: 6), I am more present to myself than to you. Yet I know that you cannot be in any way subjected to violence,[4] whereas I do not know which temptations I can resist and which I cannot. There is hope because 'you are faithful and do not allow us to be tempted beyond what we can bear, but with the temptation make also a way of escape so that we can bear it' (1 Cor. 10: 13). Accordingly, let me confess what I know of myself. Let me confess too what I do not know of myself. For what I know of myself I know because you grant me light, and

---

[3] By Jesus Christ.
[4] Manichees held the opposite opinion.

what I do not know of myself, I do not know until such time as my darkness becomes 'like noonday' before your face (Isa. 58: 10).

vi (8) My love for you, Lord, is not an uncertain feeling but a matter of conscious certainty. With your word you pierced my heart, and I loved you. But heaven and earth and everything in them on all sides tell me to love you. Nor do they cease to tell everyone that 'they are without excuse' (Rom. 1: 20). But at a profounder level you will have mercy on whom you will have mercy and will show pity on whom you will have pity (Rom. 9: 15). Otherwise heaven and earth would be uttering your praises to the deaf. But when I love you, what do I love? It is not physical beauty nor temporal glory nor the brightness of light dear to earthly eyes, nor the sweet melodies of all kinds of songs, nor the gentle odour of flowers and ointments and perfumes, nor manna or honey, nor limbs welcoming the embraces of the flesh; it is not these I love when I love my God. Yet there is a light I love, and a food, and a kind of embrace when I love my God—a light, voice, odour, food, embrace of my inner man, where my soul is floodlit by light which space cannot contain, where there is sound that time cannot seize, where there is a perfume which no breeze disperses, where there is a taste for food no amount of eating can lessen, and where there is a bond of union that no satiety can part. That is what I love when I love my God.[5]

(9) And what is the object of my love? I asked the earth and it said: 'It is not I.' I asked all that is in it; they made the same confession (Job 28: 12 f.). I asked the sea, the deeps, the living creatures that creep, and they responded: 'We are not your God, look beyond us.' I asked the breezes which blow and the entire air with its inhabitants said: 'Anaximenes was mistaken; I am not God.'[6] I asked heaven, sun, moon and stars; they said: 'Nor are we the God whom you seek.' And I said to all these things in my external environment: 'Tell me of my God who you are not, tell me something about him.' And with a great voice they cried out: 'He made us' (Ps. 99: 3). My question was the attention I gave to them, and their response was their beauty.

[5] Cf. above VIII. iv (9). The mystical idea of five spiritual senses (repeated in x. xxvii (38)) was developed already by Origen in the third century. For the ecstasy of Christ's arrow, like Cupid, see above IX. ii (3).

[6] Anaximenes of Miletus, in the sixth century BC, held air to be the origin of all else, and to be divine (cf. *City of God* 8. 5). The argument of Augustine here is strikingly like Plotinus 3. 2. 3. 20 ff.

Then I turned towards myself, and said to myself: 'Who are you?'
I replied: 'A man.' I see in myself a body and a soul, one external,
the other internal. Which of these should I have questioned about
my God, for whom I had already searched through the physical
order of things from earth to heaven, as far as I could send the rays
of my eyes[7] as messengers? What is inward is superior. All physical
evidence is reported to the mind which presides and judges of the
responses of heaven and earth and all things in them, as they say
'We are not God' and 'He made us'. The inner man knows this—I,
I the mind through the sense-perception of my body. I asked the
mass of the sun about my God, and it replied to me: 'It is not I, but
he made me.'

(10)   Surely this beauty should be self-evident to all who are of
sound mind. Then why does it not speak to everyone in the same
way? Animals both small and large see it, but they cannot put a
question about it. In them reason does not sit in judgement upon
the deliverances of the senses. But human beings can put a question
so that 'the invisible things of God are understood and seen through
the things which are made' (Rom. 1: 20). Yet by love of created
things they are subdued by them,[8] and being thus made subject
become incapable of exercising judgement. Moreover, created things
do not answer those who question them if power to judge is lost.
There is no alteration in the voice which is their beauty. If one
person sees while another sees and questions, it is not that they
appear one way to the first and another way to the second. It is
rather that the created order speaks to all, but is understood by
those who hear its outward voice and compare it with the truth
within themselves. Truth says to me: 'Your God is not earth or
heaven or any physical body.' The nature of that kind of being says
this. They see it: nature is a physical mass, less in the part than in
the whole.[9] In that respect, my soul, I tell you that you are already
superior. For you animate the mass of your body and provide it with
life, since no body is capable of doing that for another body.[10] But
your God is for you the life of your life.

---

[7] In ancient optics the eyes are not merely passive recipients of images transmitted
from the objects seen. A ray comes from the eyes: cf. Plotinus 4. 5. 7. 24; 5. 5. 7. 24 ff.

[8] Plotinus 5. 1. 1. 18: 'To be in admiring pursuit is to admit inferiority.' Plotinus goes
on (5. 1. 2) to argue the soul's superiority to all matter in earth or sky.

[9] Plotinus 5. 1. 2. 30 ff. has this argument.

[10] Plotinus 4. 3. 7. 14 f.; 4. 3. 10. 38.

vii (11)   What then do I love when I love my God? Who is he who is higher than the highest element in my soul? Through my soul I will ascend to him. I will rise above the force by which I am bonded to the body and fill its frame with vitality. It is not by that force that I find my God. For then he would be found by 'the horse and mule which have no understanding' (Ps. 31: 9), since it is the same force by which their bodies also have life. There exists another power, not only that by which I give life to my body but also that by which I enable its senses to perceive. The Lord made this for me, commanding the eye not to hear, the ear not to see, but providing the eye to see and the ear to hear, and each of the other senses in turn to be in its proper place and carry out its proper function.[11] I who act through these diverse functions am one mind. I will also rise above this power. For this also is possessed by the horse and the mule. They also perceive through the body.

viii (12)   I will therefore rise above that natural capacity in a step by step ascent to him who made me. I come to the fields and vast palaces of memory,[12] where are the treasuries of innumerable images of all kinds of objects brought in by sense-perception. Hidden there is whatever we think about, a process which may increase or diminish or in some way alter the deliverance of the senses and whatever else has been deposited and placed on reserve and has not been swallowed up and buried in oblivion. When I am in this storehouse, I ask that it produce what I want to recall, and immediately certain things come out; some things require a longer search, and have to be drawn out as it were from more recondite receptacles. Some memories pour out to crowd the mind and, when one is searching and asking for something quite different, leap forward into the centre as if saying 'Surely we are what you want?' With the hand of my heart I chase them away from the face of my memory until what I want is freed of mist and emerges from its hiding places. Other memories come before me on demand with ease and without any confusion in their order. Memories of earlier

---

[11] Echo of Plotinus 5. 5. 12. 1–6.

[12] *Memoria* for Augustine is a deeper and wider term than our 'memory'. In the background lies the Platonic doctrine of *anamnesis*, explaining the experience of learning as bringing to consciousness what, from an earlier existence, the soul already knows. But Augustine develops the notion of memory by associating it with the unconscious ('the mind knows things it does not know it knows'), with self-awareness, and so with the human yearning for true happiness found only in knowing God.

events give way to those which followed, and as they pass are stored away available for retrieval when I want them. All that is what happens when I recount a narrative from memory.

(13) Memory preserves in distinct particulars and general categories all the perceptions which have penetrated, each by its own route of entry. Thus light and all colours and bodily shapes enter by the eyes; by the ears all kinds of sounds; all odours by the entrance of the nostrils; all tastes by the door of the mouth. The power of sensation in the entire body distinguishes what is hard or soft, hot or cold, smooth or rough, heavy or light, whether external or internal to the body. Memory's huge cavern, with its mysterious, secret, and indescribable nooks and crannies, receives all these perceptions, to be recalled when needed and reconsidered. Every one of them enters into memory, each by its own gate, and is put on deposit there. The objects themselves do not enter, but the images of the perceived objects are available to the thought recalling them. But who can say how images are created, even though it may be clear by which senses they are grasped and stored within. For even when I am in darkness and silence, in my memory I can produce colours at will, and distinguish between white and black and between whatever other colours I wish. Sounds do not invade and disturb my consideration of what my eyes absorb, even though they are present and as it were hide in an independent storehouse. On demand, if I wish, they can be immediately present. With my tongue silent and my throat making no sound, I can sing what I wish. The images of colours, which are no less present, do not intrude themselves or interrupt, when I draw upon another treasury containing sounds which flowed in through the ears. So I recall at pleasure other memories which have been taken in and collected together by other senses. I distinguish the odour of lilies from that of violets without smelling anything at all. I prefer honey to a sweet wine, a smooth taste to a rough one, not actually tasting or touching at the moment, but by recollection.

(14) These actions are inward, in the vast hall of my memory. There sky, land, and sea are available to me together with all the sensations I have been able to experience in them, except for those which I have forgotten. There also I meet myself and recall what I am, what I have done, and when and where and how I was affected

when I did it. There is everything that I remember, whether I experienced it directly or believed the word of others. Out of the same abundance in store, I combine with past events images of various things, whether experienced directly or believed on the basis of what I have experienced; and on this basis I reason about future actions and events and hopes, and again think of all these things in the present. 'I shall do this and that', I say to myself within that vast recess of my mind which is full of many, rich images, and this act or that follows. 'O that this or that were so', 'May God avert this or that'. I say these words to myself and, as I speak, there are present images of everything I am speaking of, drawn out of the same treasure-house of memory. I would never say anything like that if these images were not present.

(15) This power of memory is great, very great, my God. It is a vast and infinite profundity. Who has plumbed its bottom? This power is that of my mind and is a natural endowment, but I myself cannot grasp the totality of what I am. Is the mind, then, too restricted to compass itself, so that we have to ask what is that element of itself which it fails to grasp? Surely that cannot be external to itself; it must be within the mind. How then can it fail to grasp it? This question moves me to great astonishment. Amazement grips me. People are moved to wonder by mountain peaks,[13] by vast waves of the sea, by broad waterfalls on rivers, by the all-embracing extent of the ocean, by the revolutions of the stars. But in themselves they are uninterested. They experience no surprise that when I was speaking of all these things, I was not seeing them with my eyes. On the other hand, I would not have spoken of them unless the mountains and waves and rivers and stars (which I have seen) and the ocean (which I believe on the reports of others) I could see inwardly with dimensions just as great as if I were actually looking at them outside my mind. Yet when I was seeing them, I was not absorbing them in the act of seeing with my eyes. Nor are the actual objects present to me, but only their images. And I know by which bodily sense a thing became imprinted on my mind.

ix (16) But these are not the only things carried by the vast capacity of my memory. Here also are all the skills acquired through the liberal arts which have not been forgotten. They are pushed

---

[13] This passage was found intensely moving by Petrarch.

into the background in some interior place—which is not a place. In their case I carry not the images but the very skills themselves. For what literature is, what the art of dialectical debate is, how many kinds of question there are—all that I know about these matters lies in my memory in this distinctive way. It is not that I retain the images and leave the object outside me. It is not a sound which has passed away, like a voice which makes its impression through the ears and leaves behind a trace allowing it to be recalled, as if it were sounding though in fact it is no longer sounding. Nor does it resemble an odour which, as it passes and evaporates in the winds, affects the sense of smell and so puts into the memory an image of itself, which we recover through an act of recollection. Nor is it like food which cannot actually be tasted once it is in the stomach, and yet leaves the memory of its taste. Nor is it analogous to something which the body touches and feels, which even after contact with us has ceased, can be imagined by the memory. These objects have no entry to the memory: only their images are grasped with astonishing rapidity, and then replaced as if in wonderful storerooms, so that in an amazing way the memory produces them.

x (17) When I hear that there are three kinds of question, viz. 'Does P exist? What is P? What kind of a thing is P?'[14] I retain images of the sounds which constitute these words. I know that they have passed through the air as a noise, and that they no longer exist. Moreover, the ideas signified by those sounds I have not touched by sense-perception, nor have I seen them independently of my mind. I hid in my memory not their images but the realities. How they came to me let them explain if they can. I run through all the entrance doors of my body but do not find one by which they have entered in. My eyes say: 'If they are coloured, we have informed you about them.' 'My ears say: 'If they made any sound, we were responsible for telling you.' My nostrils say: 'If they gave off any odour, they passed our way.' The sense of taste also says: 'If they are tasteless, do not ask me.' Touch says: 'If the object is not physical, I have no contact with it, and if I have no contact, I have no information to give on the subject.' Then how did these matters

---

[14] School questions (Cicero, *De partitione oratoria* 62), interestingly different from those of Aristotle's *Posterior Analytics* 2. 1. (Is it the case that P? Why it is the case that P; if X is; what X is. Aristotle does not ask if P exists, or what P is.) The Neoplatonic schools started from Plato (?), *Ep.* 7, 343b 8, as in Plotinus 5. 5. 2. 7.

enter my memory? I do not know how. For when I learnt them, I did not believe what someone else was telling me, but within myself I recognized them and assented to their truth. I entrusted them to my mind as if storing them up to be produced when required. So they were there even before I had learnt them, but were not in my memory. Accordingly, when they were formulated, how and why did I recognize them and say, 'Yes, that is true'? The answer must be that they were already in the memory, but so remote and pushed into the background, as if in most secret caverns, that unless they were dug out by someone drawing attention to them, perhaps I could not have thought of them.[15]

xi (18)   On this theme of notions where we do not draw images through our senses, but discern them inwardly not through images but as they really are and through the concepts themselves, we find that the process of learning is simply this: by thinking we, as it were, gather together ideas which the memory contains in a dispersed and disordered way, and by concentrating our attention we arrange them in order as if ready to hand, stored in the very memory where previously they lay hidden, scattered, and neglected. Now they easily come forward under the direction of the mind familiar with them. How many things in this category my memory carries which were once discovered and, as I have said, were ordered ready to hand—things we are said to have learnt and to know! Yet if for quite short periods of time I cease to recollect them, then again they sink below the surface and slip away into remote recesses, so that they have to be thought out as if they were quite new, drawn again from the same store (for there is nowhere else for them to go). Once again they have to be brought together (*cogenda*) so as to be capable of being known; that means they have to be gathered (*colligenda*) from their dispersed state. Hence is derived the word cogitate. To bring together (*cogo*) and to cogitate (*cogito*) are words related as *ago* (I do) to *agito* (agitate) or *facio* (I make) to *factito* (I make frequently).[16] Nevertheless the mind claims the verb cogitate for its own province. It is what is collected (that is, by force) in the mind, not elsewhere, which is strictly speaking the object of recollection.

[15] Augustine echoes Plato (*Meno*) that learning is remembering, bringing to the conscious mind something already present.

[16] Augustine follows Varro, 'On the Latin language' 6. 43. *Cogo*, derived from con + ago, means both 'collect' and 'compel'. *Cogito* is derived from con + agito.

xii (19) Moreover, the memory contains the innumerable principles and laws of numbers and dimensions. None of them has been impressed on memory through any bodily sense-perception. They are not coloured. They give out no sound or odour. They cannot be tasted or touched. I have heard the sounds of the words which signify these things when they are the subject of discussion. But the sounds are one thing, the principles another. The sounds vary according to whether the terms are Latin or Greek. But numerical principles are neither Greek nor Latin nor any other kind of language. I have seen the lines drawn by architects. They are extremely thin, like a spider's web. But in pure mathematics lines are quite different. They are not images of the lines about which my bodily eye informs me. A person knows them without any thought of a physical line of some kind; he knows them within himself. I am also made aware of numbers which we use for counting on the basis of all the senses of the body. But they are different from the numbers by which we are able to think mathematically.[17] Nor are they the images of numbers as mental concepts, which truly belong to the realm of being. A person who does not see that mental numbers exist may laugh at me for saying this, but I am sorry for the person who mocks me.

xiii (20) All these ideas I hold in my memory, and the way I hold them in the memory is the way that I learnt them. Many quite mistaken objections to these ideas I have heard and hold in my memory. Although they are false, yet it is not false that I remember them. I have seen the difference between the ideas which are true and the objections which are false, and this too I remember. Moreover, in one way in the present I see that I make this distinction, and in another way I remember how I often made this distinction whenever I used to give the matter thought. So I both remember that I often thought about these questions and also store up in the memory what in the present I discern and understand, so that afterwards I remember that at this time I understood them. Accordingly, I also remember that I remember, just as, in the future, if I recall the fact

[17] Aristotle, *Physics* 4. 11, observed 'Number has two senses: what is counted or countable, and that by which we count.' Ancient Pythagoreans and Platonists were fascinated by the problem of numbers, especially outside the world of the senses in the realm of mind. The impact of these debates on Aristotle is evident in the last two books of his *Metaphysics*. A wholly independent discussion of the nature of number (without influence on Augustine) is in Plotinus 6. 6.

that at this present time I could remember these things, I shall certainly be recalling this by the power of memory.

xiv (21)   The affections of my mind are also contained in the same memory. They are not there in the same way in which the mind itself holds them when it experiences them, but in another very different way such as that in which the memory's power holds memory itself. So I can be far from glad in remembering myself to have been glad, and far from sad when I recall my past sadness. Without fear I remember how at a particular time I was afraid, and without any cupidity now I am mindful of cupidity long ago. Sometimes also, on the contrary, I remember with joy a sadness that has passed and with sadness a lost joy. So far as the body is concerned, that is no cause for surprise. The mind is one thing, the body another. Therefore it is not surprising if I happily remember a physical pain that has passed away. But in the present case, the mind is the very memory itself. For when we give an order which has to be memorized, we say 'See that you hold that in your mind', and when we forget we say 'It was not in my mind' and 'It slipped my mind'. We call memory itself the mind. Since that is the case, what is going on when, in gladly remembering past sadness, my mind is glad and my memory sad? My mind is glad for the fact that gladness is in it, but memory is not saddened by the fact that regret is in it. Surely this does not mean that memory is independent of the mind. Who could say that? No doubt, then, memory is, as it were, the stomach of the mind, whereas gladness and sadness are like sweet and bitter food. When they are entrusted to the memory, they are as if transferred to the stomach and can there be stored; but they cannot be tasted. It is ridiculous to think this illustration offers a real parallel; nevertheless, it is not wholly inapposite.

(22)   Note also that I am drawing on my memory when I say there are four perturbations of the mind—cupidity, gladness, fear, sadness[18] and from memory I produce whatever I say in discussing them, when I am dividing particular cases according to their species and genus, and when I am offering a definition. I find in memory what I have to say and produce it from that source. Yet none of these perturbations disturbs me when by act of recollection I remember them. And even before I recalled and reconsidered them, they were

[18]   Cicero, *De finibus* 3. 10. 35; *Tusculan Disputations* 4. 6. 11.

there. That is why by reminding myself I was able to bring them out from memory's store. Perhaps then, just as food is brought from the stomach in the process of rumination, so also by recollection these things are brought up from the memory. But then why in the mind or 'mouth' of the person speaking, that is to say reminiscing, about past gladness or sadness is there no taste of sweetness or bitterness? Or is this a point where the incomplete resemblance between thought and rumination makes the analogy misleading? Who would willingly speak of such matters if, every time we mentioned sadness or fear, we were compelled to experience grief or terror? Yet we would not speak about them at all unless in our memory we could find not only the sounds of the names attaching to the images imprinted by the physical senses, but also the notions of the things themselves. These notions we do not receive through any bodily entrance. The mind itself perceives them through the experience of its passions and entrusts them to memory; or the memory itself retains them without any conscious act of commitment.

xv (23)   Whether this happens through the medium of images or otherwise, who could easily tell? For example, I mention a stone, or I mention the sun, when the objects themselves are not present to my senses. Of course images of them are available to me in memory. I may mention physical pain when it is not present to me and I feel no discomfort. Yet if its image were not present in my memory, I would not know what I was talking about, and in discussing it I could not distinguish it from pleasure. I mention physical health. When I am in good health, the thing itself is present to me. But unless the image of it were also present in my memory, I would in no way remember what the sound of this word signified, nor would sick people know what was meant when health was mentioned, unless by the power of memory they held the same image, even though the thing itself was absent from their body. I mention the numbers by which we count things. It is remarkable that in my memory are present not their images but the numbers themselves. I mention the image of the sun, and this is present in my memory. I recall not the image of its image, but the image itself. In my act of remembering this image is available to me. I mention memory and I recognize what I am speaking about. Where is my recognition located but in memory itself? Surely memory is present to itself through itself, and not through its own image.

xvi (24) What then? When I mention forgetfulness, I similarly recognize what I am speaking of. How could I recognize it except through memory? I refer not to the sound of the word but to the thing which it signifies. If I had forgotten what the force of the sound was, I would be incapable of recognizing it. So when I remember memory, memory is available to itself through itself. But when I remember forgetfulness, both memory and forgetfulness are present—memory by means of which I could remember, forgetfulness which I did remember. But what is forgetfulness except loss of memory? How then is it present for me to remember when, if it is present, I have no power of remembering? What we remember, we retain by memory. But unless we could recall forgetfulness, we could never hear the word and recognize the thing which the word signifies. Therefore memory retains forgetfulness. So it is there lest we forget what, when present, makes us forget. Should the deduction from this be that, when we are remembering forgetfulness, it is not through its actual presence in the memory but through its image? If forgetfulness were present through itself, it would cause us not to remember but to forget. Who can find a solution to this problem? Who can grasp what is going on?

(25) I at least, Lord, have difficulty at this point, and I find my own self hard to grasp. I have become for myself a soil which is a cause of difficulty and much sweat (Gen. 3: 17 f.). For our present inquiry is not to 'examine the zones of heaven',[19] nor are we measuring the distances between stars or the balancing of the earth. It is I who remember, I who am mind. It is hardly surprising if what I am not is distant from me. But what is nearer to me than myself? Indeed the power of my memory is something I do not understand when without it I cannot speak about myself. What shall I say when it is certain to me that I remember forgetfulness? Shall I say that what I recall is not in my memory? Or shall I say that forgetfulness is in my memory for this very purpose that I should not be forgetful? Both propositions are quite absurd. What of a third solution? Can I say that my memory holds the image of forgetfulness, not forgetfulness itself, when I am remembering it? How can I say this when, for the image of an object to be impressed upon the memory, it is first necessary for the object itself to be present, so that an impression of

[19] Ennius, *Iphigeneia*, quoted by Cicero, *On Divination* 2. 30; *Republic* 1. 30.

the image becomes possible? That is how I remember Carthage, and
all places where I have been, the faces of people I have seen, and
information derived from the other senses. That is also how I know of
the healthy or painful condition of my body. When these things
were present, memory took images of them, images which I could
contemplate when they were present and reconsider in mind when
I recollected them even though absent from me. If, then, memory
holds forgetfulness not through itself but through its image, forgetfulness must itself have been present for its image to be registered.
But when it was present, how did it inscribe its image upon the
memory, when, by its very presence, forgetfulness deletes whatever
it finds already there? Yet in some way, though incomprehensible
and inexplicable, I am certain that I remember forgetfulness itself,
and yet forgetfulness destroys what we remember.

xvii (26)   Great is the power of memory, an awe-inspiring mystery,
my God, a power of profound and infinite multiplicity. And this is
mind, this is I myself. What then am I, my God? What is my nature? It
is characterized by diversity, by life of many forms, utterly immeasurable. See the broad plains and caves and caverns of my memory. The
varieties there cannot be counted, and are, beyond any reckoning, full
of innumerable things. Some are there through images, as in the case
of all physical objects, some by immediate presence like intellectual
skills, some by indefinable notions or recorded impressions, as in
the case of the mind's emotions, which the memory retains even
when the mind is not experiencing them, although whatever is in
the memory is in the mind. I run through all these things, I fly here
and there, and penetrate their working as far as I can. But I never
reach the end. So great is the power of memory, so great is the
force of life in a human being whose life is mortal. What then ought
I to do, my God? You are my true life. I will transcend even this my
power which is called memory. I will rise beyond it to move towards
you, sweet light. What are you saying to me? Here I am climbing up
through my mind towards you who are constant above me. I will
pass beyond even that power of mind which is called memory,
desiring to reach you by the way through which you can be reached,
and to be bonded to you by the way in which it is possible to be bonded.

Beasts and birds also have a memory. Otherwise they could not
rediscover their dens and nests, and much else that they are habitually

accustomed to. Habit could have no influence on them in any respect except by memory. So I will also ascend beyond memory to touch him who 'set me apart from quadrupeds and made me wiser than the birds of heaven' (Job 35: 11). As I rise above memory, where am I to find you? My true good and gentle source of reassurance, where shall I find you? If I find you outside my memory, I am not mindful of you. And how shall I find you if I am not mindful of you?

xviii (27)   The woman who lost her drachma searched for it with a lamp (Luke 15: 8). She would not have found it unless she had remembered it. When she found it, how could she know that it was the one she lost, if she had failed to remember it? I recall myself to have searched for and found many lost items. From this experience I know that, when I was searching for one of them and someone said to me 'Perhaps this is it, perhaps that is', I would always say 'No' until I was offered the object which I sought. Unless I had it in my memory, whatever it was, even if an offer was being made to me, I would not have found it because I would not have recognized it. That is also what happens when we seek and find something lost. If anything such as a visible body disappears from sight but not from memory, its image is retained within, and the search continues until it is once more seen. When it is found, it is recognized from the image which is within. We do not say we have found the thing which was lost unless we recognize it, and we cannot recognize it if we do not remember it. The object was lost to the eyes, but held in the memory.

xix (28)   What when the memory itself loses something? This happens when we forget and attempt to recall. The only place to search is in the memory itself. If something other than what we want is offered us, we reject it until the thing we are looking for turns up. And when it comes, we say 'That is it.' We would not say this unless we recognized it, and we would not recognize it unless we remembered. It seems certain, then, that we had forgotten.

Or perhaps it had not totally gone: part was retained, and was used to help in the search for another part. That would presuppose that memory felt itself to be working with a whole to which it was accustomed; as if limping from being deprived of support to which it was accustomed, it would demand the return of the missing element. For instance, our eyes may happen on a person known to us or we may think of him, and we try to recall his name. Other names that occur will not fit the case, because we are not in the habit of associating them with him, and so we reject them until that one comes up which at once corresponds to the familiarly known and is accepted as correct. Where does the right name come from if not from memory itself? Even when we recognize it after being prompted by someone else, memory is its source. We do not believe it as something we are hearing for the first time but, because we remember it, agree that the name mentioned is correct. If, however, it were wholly effaced from the mind, we would not remember even when prompted. When at least we remember ourselves to have forgotten, we have not totally forgotten. But if we have completely forgotten, we cannot even search for what has been lost.

xx (29)   How then am I to seek for you, Lord? When I seek for you, my God, my quest is for the happy life. I will seek you that 'my soul may live' (Isa. 55: 3), for my body derives life from my soul, and my soul derives life from you. How then shall I seek for the happy life? It is not mine until I say: 'It is enough, it is there.' But then I ought to say how my quest proceeds; is it by remembering, as if I had forgotten it and still recall that I had forgotten? Or is it through an urge to learn something quite unknown, whether I never had known it or had so forgotten it that I do not even remember having forgotten it? Is not the happy life that which all desire, which indeed no one fails to desire? But how have they known about it so as to want it? Where did they see it to love it? Certainly we have the desire for it, but how I do not know. There is also another sense in which a person who has it is happy at a particular time, and there are some who are happy in hope of becoming so. The kind of happiness they have is inferior to that of those who have the real thing. But they are better than those who are happy neither in actuality nor in hope. Even they would not wish to be happy unless they had some idea of happiness. That this is what they want is quite certain, but how they came to know it I do not know. So also I do not know what kind of knowledge is theirs when they have it. My inquiry is whether this knowing is in the memory because, if it is there, we had happiness once. I do not now ask whether we were all happy individually or only corporately in that man who first sinned, in whom we all died [Adam, 1 Cor. 15: 22] and from whom we were all born into a condition of misery.[20] My question is whether the happy life is in the memory. For we would not love it if we did not know what it is. We have heard the term, and all of us acknowledge that we are looking for the thing. The sound is not the cause of our pleasure. When a Greek hears the Latin term, it gives him no pleasure when he does not understand what has been said. But we are given pleasure, as he would be too if he heard this expressed in Greek. The thing itself is neither Greek nor Latin. Greeks and Latins and people of other languages yearn to acquire it. Therefore it is known to everyone. If they could be asked if they want to be happy, without hesitation they would answer with one voice that they so wish. That would not be the case unless the thing itself, to which this term refers, was being held in the memory.

xxi (30)   That is surely not the way in which a person who has seen Carthage remembers it. For the happy life is not seen by the eyes, because it is no physical entity. It is surely not the way in which we remember numbers. A person who has a grasp of numbers does not still seek to acquire this knowledge. But the happy life we already have in our knowledge, and so we love it; and yet we still wish to acquire it so that we may be happy. Surely it is not the way in which we remember eloquence? No. When this word is heard, the thing itself is recalled by those who, though not yet eloquent, in many cases desire to be so. That shows that they already have a knowledge of it. It is through the bodily senses that they have seen other people who were eloquent, were given pleasure, and desired to possess it too. Yet without the basis of inward knowledge, they would not have been pleased nor wished to be eloquent unless they were given pleasure. But it is not by any bodily sense that we discern the happy life in others.

Surely this is not the way in which we recall joy? Well, perhaps it is. For even when sad, I remember my times of joy, like a wretched person thinking of the happy life. It is never by bodily sense that I have seen my joy or heard or smelt or tasted or touched it. I experienced it in my mind when I was glad, and the knowledge of it

---

[20] For Augustine Adam was not merely the start of the human race, but the representative of humanity, so that 'we are all Adam'.

stuck in my memory, so that I could remind myself of it, sometimes with scorn, sometimes with desire, according to the varied character of the things which I remember myself delighting in. For I derived a sprinkling of pleasure even from discreditable acts which I now recall with hatred and execration. But sometimes my delight was in good and honourable things, which I recall with longing even though they are no longer part of my life. In this sense I am sad as I remember joy of long ago.

(31)   Where and when, then, have I experienced the happy life for myself, so that I can remember and love and long for it? The desire for happiness is not in myself alone or in a few friends, but is found in everybody.[21] If we did not know this with certain knowledge, we would not want it with determination in our will. But what does this mean? If two people are asked if they want to serve in the army, it may turn out that one of them replies that he would like to do so, while the other would not. But if they are asked whether they would like to be happy, each would at once say without the least hesitation that he would choose to be so. And the reason why one would wish to be a soldier and the other would not is only that they want to be happy. Is it then the case that one person finds joy in one way, another in a different way? What all agree upon is that they want to be happy, just as they would concur, if asked, that they want to experience joy and would call that joy the happy life. Even if one person pursues it in one way, and another in a different way, yet there is one goal which all are striving to attain, namely to experience joy. Since no one can say that this is a matter outside experience, the happy life is found in the memory and is recognized when the words are uttered.

xxii (32)   Far be it from me, Lord, far from the heart of your servant who is making confession to you, far be it from me to think myself happy, whatever be the joy in which I take my delight. There is a delight which is given not to the wicked (Isa. 48: 22), but to those who worship you for no reward save the joy that you yourself are to them. That is the authentic happy life, to set one's joy on you, grounded in you and caused by you. That is the real thing, and there is no other. Those who think that the happy life is found

---

[21] From Cicero's *Hortensius*; cf. *Tusculan Disputations* 5. 28.

elsewhere, pursue another joy and not the true one. Nevertheless their will remains drawn towards some image of the true joy.[22]

xxiii (33) It is uncertain, then, that all want to be happy since there are those who do not want to find in you their source of joy. That is the sole happy life, but they do not really want it. But perhaps everyone does have a desire for it and yet, because 'the flesh lusts against the spirit and the spirit against the flesh so that they do not do what they wish' (Gal. 5: 17), they relapse into whatever they have the strength to do, and acquiesce in that, because in that for which they lack the strength their will is insufficient to give them the strength. For if I put the question to anyone whether he prefers to find joy in the truth or in falsehood, he does not hesitate to say that he prefers the truth, just as he does not hesitate to say he wants to be happy. The happy life is joy based on the truth. This is joy grounded in you, O God, who are the truth, 'my illumination, the salvation of my face, my God' (Ps. 26: 1; 41: 12). This happy life everyone desires; joy in the truth everyone wants. I have met with many people who wished to deceive, none who wished to be deceived. How then did they know about this happy life unless in the same way that they knew about the truth? They love the truth because they have no wish to be deceived, and when they love the happy life (which is none other than joy grounded in truth) they are unquestionably loving the truth. And they would have no love for it unless there were some knowledge of it in their memory. Why then do they not find their joy in this? Why are they not happy? It is because they are more occupied in other things which make them more wretched than their tenuous consciousness of the truth makes them happy. For among humanity there is 'still a little light'. May they walk, may they indeed walk, 'so that the darkness does not capture them' (John 12: 35).

(34) But why is it that 'truth engenders hatred'?[23] Why does your man who preaches what is true become to them an enemy (Gal. 4: 16) when they love the happy life which is simply joy grounded on truth? The answer must be this: their love for truth takes the form that they love something else and want this object of their love to be

---

[22] Plotinus 3. 5. 9. 47 writes of the sense of need, aspiration, and the memory of rational principles coming together in the soul to direct it towards the good.

[23] Terence, *Andria* 68.

the truth; and because they do not wish to be deceived, they do not wish to be persuaded that they are mistaken. And so they hate the truth for the sake of the object which they love instead of the truth. They love truth for the light it sheds, but hate it when it shows them up as being wrong (John 3: 20; 5: 35). Because they do not wish to be deceived but wish to deceive, they love truth when it shows itself to them but hate it when its evidence goes against them. Retribution will come to them on this principle: those who resist being refuted the truth will make manifest against their will, and yet to them it will not be manifest. Yes indeed: the human mind, so blind and languid, shamefully and dishonourably wishes to hide, and yet does not wish anything to be concealed from itself. But it is repaid on the principle that while the human mind lies open to the truth, truth remains hidden from it. Yet even thus, in its miserable condition, it prefers to find joy in true rather than in false things. It will be happy if it comes to find joy only in that truth by which all things are true—without any distraction interfering.

xxiv (35)   See how widely I have ranged, Lord, searching for you in my memory. I have not found you outside it. For I have found nothing coming from you which I have not stored in my memory since the time I first learnt of you. Since the day I learnt of you, I have never forgotten you. Where I discovered the truth there I found my God, truth itself, which from the time I learnt it, I have not forgotten. And so, since the time I learnt of you, you remain in my consciousness, and there I find you when I recall you and delight in you. These my holy delights you have given me, in your mercy looking upon my poverty.

xxv (36)   But where in my consciousness, Lord, do you dwell? Where in it do you make your home? What resting-place have you made for yourself? What kind of sanctuary have you built for yourself? You conferred this honour on my memory that you should dwell in it. But the question I have to consider is, In what part of it do you dwell? In recalling you I rose above those parts of the memory which animals also share, because I did not find you among the images of physical objects. I came to the parts of my memory where I stored the emotions of my mind, and I did not find you there. I entered into the very seat of my mind, which is located in my memory, since the mind also remembers itself. But you were not there because, just as you are not a bodily image nor the emotional feeling of a living person such as we experience when glad or sad, or when we desire, fear, remember, forget, and anything of that kind, so also you are not the mind itself. For you are the Lord God of the mind. All these things are liable to change. But you remain immutable above all things, and yet have deigned to dwell in my memory since the time I learnt about you.

Why do I ask in which area of my memory you dwell, as if there really are places there? Surely my memory is where you dwell, because I remember you since first I learnt of you, and I find you there when I think about you.

xxvi (37)   Where then did I find you to be able to learn of you? You were not already in my memory before I learnt of you. Where then did I find you so that I could learn of you if not in the fact that you transcend me? There is no place, whether we go backwards or forwards;[24] there can be no question of place. O truth, everywhere you preside over all who ask counsel of you. You respond at one and the same time to all, even though they are consulting you on different subjects. You reply clearly, but not all hear you clearly. All ask your counsel on what they desire, but do not always hear what they would wish. Your best servant is the person who does not attend so much to hearing what he himself wants as to willing what he has heard from you.

xxvii (38)   Late have I loved you, beauty so old and so new: late have I loved you. And see, you were within and I was in the external world and sought you there, and in my unlovely state I plunged into those lovely created things which you made. You were with me, and I was not with you. The lovely things kept me far from you, though if they did not have their existence in you, they had no existence at all. You called and cried out loud and shattered my deafness. You were radiant and resplendent, you put to flight my blindness. You were fragrant, and I drew in my breath and now pant after you. I tasted you, and I feel but hunger and thirst for you. You touched me, and I am set on fire to attain the peace which is yours.[25]

[24] Echo of Plotinus 4. 4. 10. 5 (of time).

[25] Augustine's Latin in this chapter is a work of high art, with rhymes and poetic rhythms not reproducible in translation. He is fusing imagery from the Song of Solomon with Neoplatonic reflection on Plato's *Phaedrus* and *Symposium*, and simultaneously summarizing the central themes of the *Confessions*. For the five spiritual senses see above x. vi (8).

xxviii (39)   When I shall have adhered (Ps. 72: 28) to you with the whole of myself, I shall never have 'pain and toil' (Ps. 89: 10), and my entire life will be full of you. You lift up the person whom you fill. But for the present, because I am not full of you, I am a burden to myself. There is a struggle between joys over which I should be weeping and regrets at matters over which I ought to be rejoicing, and which side has the victory I do not know. There is a struggle between my regrets at my evil past and my memories of good joys, and which side has the victory I do not know. Alas, 'Lord have mercy upon me' (Ps. 30: 10), wretch that I am. See, I do not hide my wounds. You are the physician, I am the patient. You are pitiful, I am the object of pity. Is not human life on earth a trial (Job 7: 1)? Who desires troubles and difficulties? You command that they should be endured, not loved. No one loves what he endures, even if he loves to be able to endure it. Although he is glad he can endure it, he would prefer that what he endures should not be there. In adversities I desire prosperity, in prosperous times I fear adversities. Between these two is there a middle ground where human life is not a trial? Cursed are the prosperities of the world, not once but twice over, because of the fear of adversity and the corruption of success. Cursed are the adversities of the world, not once or twice but thrice, because of the longing for prosperity, because adversity itself is hard, and because of the possibility that one's endurance may crack. Is not human life on earth a trial in which there is no respite?

xxix (40)   My entire hope is exclusively in your very great mercy. Grant what you command, and command what you will. You require continence. A certain writer has said (Wisd. 8: 21): 'As I knew that no one can be continent except God grants it, and this very thing is part of wisdom, to know whose gift this is.' By continence we are collected together and brought to the unity from which we disintegrated into multiplicity.[26] He loves you less who together with you loves something which he does not love for your sake. O love, you ever burn and are never extinguished. O charity, my God, set me on fire. You command continence; grant what you command, and command what you will.[27]

---

[26] Plotinus 4. 3. 32. 20: the higher soul gathers multiplicity into one. 1. 2. 5. 6: the soul collects itself apart from the body, aware of pleasure only when it has to be.

[27] This passage was quoted in the ears of Pelagius, the British monk, by a bishop who

xxx (41)   You command me without question to abstain 'from the lust of the flesh and the lust of the eyes and the ambition of the secular world' (1 John 2: 16). You commanded me to abstain from sleeping with a girl-friend and, in regard to marriage itself, you advised me to adopt a better way of life than you have allowed (1 Cor. 7: 38). And because you granted me strength, this was done even before I became a dispenser of your sacrament. But in my memory of which I have spoken at length, there still live images of acts which were fixed there by my sexual habit. These images attack me. While I am awake they have no force, but in sleep they not only arouse pleasure but even elicit consent, and are very like the actual act. The illusory image within the soul has such force upon my flesh that false dreams have an effect on me when asleep, which the reality could not have when I am awake. During this time of sleep surely it is not my true self, Lord my God? Yet how great a difference between myself at the time when I am asleep and myself when I return to the waking state. Where then is reason which, when wide-awake, resists such suggestive thoughts, and would remain unmoved if the actual reality were to be presented to it? Surely reason does not shut down as the eyes close.It can hardly fall asleep with the bodily senses. For if that were so, how could it come about that often in sleep we resist and, mindful of our avowed commitment and adhering to it with strict chastity, we give no assent to such seductions? Yet there is a difference so great that, when it happens otherwise than we would wish, when we wake up we return to peace in our conscience. From the wide gulf between the occurrences and our will, we discover that we did not actively do what, to our regret, has somehow been done in us.[28]

(42)   It cannot be the case, almighty God, that your hand is not strong enough to cure all the sicknesses of my soul and, by a more abundant outflow of your grace, to extinguish the lascivious impulses of my sleep. You will more and more increase your gifts in me, Lord, so that my soul, rid of the glue of lust, may follow me to you,

appeared to be condoning the number of Christians whose sexual life appeared unregenerate. The incident marked the start of the Pelagian controversy, Pelagius being the unqualified advocate of an ethical perfectionism as a requirement of the gospel and the opponent of the passivity in Augustine's understanding of grace.

[28] Porphyry also held that nocturnal emissions do not pollute the conscience. An epigram in the Greek Anthology (5. 2) turns on the greater vividness of an erotic dream in comparison with actuality.

so that it is not in rebellion against itself, and so that even in dreams it not only does not commit those disgraceful and corrupt acts in which sensual images provoke carnal emissions, but also does not even consent to them. You are omnipotent, 'able to do more than we ask or think' (Eph. 3: 20). It is no great matter for you to cause the impulse to give no pleasure at all or no more than can be checked at will in the chaste mind of a sleeping man, not merely in later life but at my present age. Nevertheless, I have now declared to my good Lord what is still my present condition in respect of this kind of evil. I 'exult with trembling' (Ps. 2: 11) in what you have granted me, and grieve at my imperfect state. I hope that you will perfect in me your mercies to achieve perfect peace (cf. Ps. 30: 7–8) which I shall have with you, inwardly and outwardly, when 'death is swallowed up in victory' (1 Cor. 15: 54).

xxxi (43)   There is another 'evil of the day', and I wish it sufficed for the day (Matt. 6: 34). We restore the daily decay of the body by eating and drinking, until in time you destroy both food and stomach (1 Cor. 6: 13), when you will kill need with a wonderful satiety and when you clothe this corruptible body with everlasting incorruption (1 Cor. 15: 53). But at the present time the necessity of food is sweet to me, and against that sweetness I fight lest I become a captive. I wage a daily battle in fastings, often 'bringing my body into captivity' (1 Cor. 9: 26–7). My pains are driven away by pleasure. For hunger and thirst are a kind of pain, which burns and can kill like a fever, unless the medicine of sustenance brings help. Because this cure is granted to us, thanks to the consolation of your gifts, by which earth and water and sky minister to our infirmity, a calamity can be called a delight.[29]

(44)   You have taught me that I should come to take food in the way I take medicines. But while I pass from the discomfort of need to the tranquillity of satisfaction, the very transition contains for me an insidious trap of uncontrolled desire.[30] The transition itself is a pleasure, and there is no other way of making that transition, which

[29] The discussion of the pull of the five bodily senses, here and in what follows, is akin to Porphyry, *On Abstinence from animal food* 1. 33 f. Plotinus 4. 4. 21 speaks of eating and drinking as to be controlled by reason, not desire. Augustine's biographer Possidius, who had lived with him, records the austerity of his table in food; but, no doubt as a sign of anti-Manichee convictions, there was always wine (*Vita* 22).

[30] Plotinus 1. 2. 5. 18–22: insofar as the soul is involved in hunger, thirst, or sexual desire, there is never involuntary and uncontrolled desire.

is forced upon us by necessity. Although health is the reason for eating and drinking, a dangerous pleasantness joins itself to the process like a companion. Many a time it tries to take first place, so that I am doing for pleasure what I profess or wish to do only for health's sake. They do not have the same measure: for what is enough for health is too little for pleasure. And often there is uncertainty whether the motive is necessary care of the body seeking sustenance or the deceptive desire for pleasure demanding service. In this uncertainty the unhappy soul finds a source of cheerfulness and by means of it has a ready-made defence and excuse. It is delighted not to be clear how much is sufficient to maintain health, so that the quest for pleasure is obscured by the pretext of health. Every day I try to resist these temptations. I invoke the help of your right hand (cf. Ps. 59: 7) and report to you my impulses, because in this matter my mind has not yet achieved a settled pattern.

(45)   I hear the voice of my God giving command: 'Your hearts shall not be weighed down in gluttony and drunkenness' (Luke 21: 34). Drunkenness is far from me; your mercy will ensure that it does not come close to me. But occasionally gluttony creeps up on your servant. May your mercy put that far from me. 'None can be continent unless you grant it' (Wisd. 8: 21). You give us many things when we pray, and whatever good we received before we prayed for it, we have received from you. We have also received from you the grace that later we came to realize this. I have never been a drunkard, but I have known drunkards made sober by you.[31] So it was your doing that those who never have been drunkards have been free of this vice, and that those who have been so have not been permanently addicted. It has also been your doing that both have come to realize that you brought this about. I heard another utterance of yours: 'Do not go after your lusts and forbid yourself from your pleasure' (Ecclus. 18: 30). By your gift I have also heard the saying which I have much loved: 'Neither if we eat are we the better, nor if we do not eat are we the worse' (1 Cor. 8: 8). That means that neither will eating make me prosperous nor will not eating bring me adversity. I have also heard another saying: 'I have learnt in whatever state I am that it is sufficient. I have learnt to be prosperous and I have learnt to suffer poverty. I can do all

[31] One of Augustine's letters (93. 48) records that drunkenness was a social problem in his time.

things in him who comforts me.' (Phil. 4: 11–12). See in this text the soldier of the heavenly host, not the dust which we are. But remember, Lord 'that we are but dust' (Ps. 102: 14). You have made man of the dust (Gen. 3: 19). 'He was lost and is found' (Luke 15: 24, 32). Paul had no power in himself because he was of the same dust as we, but he said these words under the breath of your inspiration and I loved him for it. 'I can do all things' (he said) 'in him who comforts me.' Strengthen me that I may have this power. Grant what you command, and command what you will. He confesses that he has received the power and that, when he glories, he glories in the Lord (1 Cor. 1: 31). I have heard another begging to receive help: 'Take from me', he asked, 'the lust of the belly' (Ecclus. 23: 6). That makes it clear, my holy God, that it is by your gift that your command is kept.

(46) Good Father, you have taught me 'All things are pure to the pure' (Titus 1: 15), but it is 'evil for the person who eats and is offended' (Rom. 14: 20). And 'all your creation is good, and nothing is to be rejected which is received with thanksgiving' (1 Tim. 4: 4). And 'meat does not commend us to God' (1 Cor. 8: 8). And 'Let no one judge us in the matter of food or drink' (Col. 2: 16). And 'one who eats is not to despise one who does not eat, and one who does not eat shall not judge one who does' (Rom. 14: 3).

I have learnt this, thanks to you, praise to you, my God, my teacher. Your words strike my ears (Rev. 3: 20), and illuminate my heart. Deliver me from all temptation (Ps. 17: 30). It is not the impurity of food I fear but that of uncontrolled desire. I know Noah was allowed to eat every kind of meat used for food (Gen. 9: 2); that Elijah was restored by eating meat (1 Kings 17: 6); that John, practising admirable abstinence, was undefiled by the animals, that is the locusts granted him for food (Matt. 3: 4); and I know how Esau was deceived by his greed for lentils (Gen. 25: 34), and David rebuked himself for wanting water (2 Sam. 23: 15 ff.). And our King was tempted to eat not meat but bread (Matt. 4: 3). That explains why the people in the wilderness deserved reproof, not because they wanted meat but because the desire for meat led them to murmur against the Lord (Num. 11: 1 ff.).[32]

---

[32] Augustine's texts significantly point to the conclusion that, while meat may be something of a luxury, total abstinence from it is not required; i.e. the argument reflects defence against Manichee criticism of Catholic failure to enforce vegetarianism.

(47)   Placed among these temptations, then, I struggle every day against uncontrolled desire in eating and drinking. It is not something I could give up once and for all and decide never to touch it again, as I was able to do with sexual intercourse. And so a rein has to be held upon my throat, moderated between laxity and austerity. Who is the person, Lord, who is never carried a little beyond the limits of necessity? Whoever this may be is great and will magnify your name (cf. Ps. 68: 31). I am not like that, for I am a sinful man. Yet I too magnify your name. And he who has overcome the world (John 16: 33) intercedes with you for my sins (Rom. 8: 34). He counts me among the weak members of his body, for 'your eyes have seen its imperfection and in your book everyone is inscribed' (Ps. 138: 16).

xxxii (48)   The allurement of perfumes is not a matter of great concern to me. When they are absent, I do not look for them. When they are present, I do not reject them. I am ready to go without them all the time. That is how I see myself, but perhaps I am deceived. For there are those deplorable blind spots where the capacity that lies in me is concealed from me. My mind on examining myself about its strengths does not regard its findings as easy to trust. What lies within is for the most part hidden unless experience reveals it. No one should be complacent in this life which is called a 'total temptation' (Job 7: 1). Anyone who could change from the worse to the better can also change from the better to the worse. There is one hope, one ground of confidence, one reliable promise—your mercy.

xxxiii (49)   The pleasures of the ear had a more tenacious hold on me, and had subjugated me; but you set me free and liberated me. As things now stand, I confess that I have some sense of restful contentment in sounds whose soul is your words, when they are sung by a pleasant and well-trained voice. Not that I am riveted by them, for I can rise up and go when I wish. Nevertheless, on being combined with the thoughts which give them life, they demand in my heart some position of honour, and I have difficulty in finding what is appropriate to offer them. Sometimes I seem to myself to give them more honour than is fitting. I feel that when the sacred words are chanted well, our souls are moved and are more religiously and with a warmer devotion kindled to piety than if they are not so sung. All the diverse emotions of our spirit have their various modes in voice and chant appropriate in each case, and are stirred by a mysterious inner kinship.[33] But my physical delight, which has to be checked from enervating the mind, often deceives me when the perception of the senses is unaccompanied by reason, and is not patiently content to be in a subordinate place. It tries to be first and to be in the leading role, though it deserves to be allowed only as secondary to reason. So in these matters I sin unawares, and only afterwards become aware of it.

(50)   Sometimes, however, by taking excessive safeguards against being led astray, I err on the side of too much severity. I have sometimes gone so far as to wish to banish all the melodies and sweet chants commonly used for David's psalter from my ears and from the Church as well. But I think a safer course one which I remember being often told of bishop Athanasius of Alexandria. He used to make the Reader of the psalm chant with so flexible a speech-rhythm that he was nearer to reciting than to singing. Nevertheless, when I remember the tears which I poured out at the time when I was first recovering my faith, and that now I am moved not by the chant but by the words being sung, when they are sung with a clear voice and entirely appropriate modulation, then again I recognize the great utility of music in worship.[34]

Thus I fluctuate between the danger of pleasure and the experience of the beneficent effect, and I am more led to put forward the opinion (not as an irrevocable view) that the custom of singing in Church is to be approved, so that through the delights of the ear the weaker mind may rise up towards the devotion of worship. Yet when it happens to me that the music moves me more than the subject of the song, I confess myself to commit a sin deserving punishment, and then I would prefer not to have heard the singer.

See my condition! Weep with me and weep for me, you who have within yourselves a concern for the good, the springs from which good actions proceed. Those who do not share this concern will not be moved by these considerations. But you 'Lord my God, hear, look and see' (Ps. 12: 4) and 'have mercy and heal me' (Ps. 79: 15). In your eyes I have become a problem to myself, and that is my sickness.

---

[33] Plato's *Timaeus* taught that the soul and music are akin.

[34] There was deep disagreement in the churches of North Africa at this time whether any music should be admitted to worship and, if so, of what kind.

xxxiv (51)   There remains the pleasure of the eyes of my flesh which I include in confessions which are heard by the ears of your temple—the devout ears of Christian brothers. So we may conclude the account of the temptations of the lust of the flesh which still assail me, despite my groans and my 'desire to be clothed with my habitation which is from heaven' (2 Cor. 5: 2). A delight to my eyes are beautiful and varied forms, glowing and pleasant colours. May these get no hold upon my soul; may God hold it! 'He has made these sights and they are very good' (Gen. 1: 31). But he is my good, not these. They touch me, wide awake, throughout the day, nor do they give me a moment's respite, in the way the voices of singers, sometimes the entire choir, keep silence. The very queen of colours, which bathes with light all that we see, wherever I may be during the day, comes down upon me with gentle subtlety through many media, while I am doing something else and not noticing it. But the light makes its way with such power that, if suddenly it is withdrawn, it is sought for with longing. And if it is long absent, that has a depressing effect on the mind.

(52)   Light which Tobit (4: 2 f.) saw when, with his eyes closed, he taught his son the way of life and walked before him with the step of charity, never erring!

Light which Isaac saw when, despite the state of his bodily eyes, weighed down and dimmed by old age, he was granted to bless his sons without recognizing them, yet in the act of blessing to distinguish one from the other (Gen. 27)!

Light which Jacob saw, though because of his great age he had lost his eyesight (Gen. 48–9)! With light in his heart, he shed radiance through his sons on the generations to come whom they prefigured. On his grandsons by Joseph he mystically laid crossed hands in blessing. This was not as their father wished, and he wanted to correct him; but he saw only the externals; Jacob himself discerned it by inward vision.

This light itself is one,[35] and all those are one who see it and love it.

The physical light of which I was speaking works by a seductive and dangerous sweetness to season the life of those who blindly

---

[35] Plotinus 6. 4. 8 sees the light of the sun as analogous to the light which is the One, and sharply distinguishes physical sunlight from the metaphysical Light of the transcendent realm (2. 1. 7. 28).

love the world. But those who know how to praise you for it, 'God creator of all things,'[36] include it in their hymn of praise to you, and are not led astray by it in a sleepy state. That is how I would wish myself to be. I resist the allurements of the eyes lest my feet are caught as I walk along your way. I lift up to you invisible eyes, that you may 'rescue my feet from the trap' (Ps. 24: 15). Repeatedly you are rescuing them, for they fall into the trap. You do not cease to rescue me, though I am frequently becoming stuck in the snares which surround me on every side, because 'you will not sleep nor slumber, you guardian of Israel' (Ps. 120: 4).

(53)   To entrap the eyes men have made innumerable additions to the various arts and crafts in clothing, shoes, vessels, and manufactures of this nature, pictures, images of various kinds, and things which go far beyond necessary and moderate requirements and pious symbols. Outwardly they follow what they make. Inwardly they abandon God by whom they were made, destroying what they were created to be. But, my God and my glory, for this reason I say a hymn of praise to you and offer praise to him who offered sacrifice for me. For the beautiful objects designed by artists' souls and realized by skilled hands come from that beauty which is higher than souls; after that beauty my soul sighs day and night (Ps. 1: 2). From this higher beauty the artists and connoisseurs of external beauty draw their criterion of judgement, but they do not draw from there a principle for the right use of beautiful things. The principle is there but they do not see it, namely that they should not go to excess, but 'should guard their strength for you' (Ps. 58: 10) and not dissipate it in delights that produce mental fatigue. But, although I am the person saying this and making the distinction, I also entangle my steps in beautiful externals. However, you rescue me, Lord, you rescue me. 'For your mercy is before my eyes' (Ps. 25: 3). I am pitifully captured by them, and in your pity you rescue me, sometimes without me realizing it because I had suffered only a light fall, and sometimes with a painful wrench because I became deeply involved.

xxxv (54)   To this I may add another form of temptation, manifold in its dangers. Beside the lust of the flesh which inheres in the delight given by all pleasures of the senses (those who are enslaved to it

---

[36] Ambrose's evening hymn praises God for light by day and spiritual illumination by night.

perish by putting themselves far from you), there exists in the soul, through the medium of the same bodily senses, a cupidity which does not take delight in carnal pleasure but in perceptions acquired through the flesh. It is a vain inquisitiveness dignified with the title of knowledge and science. As this is rooted in the appetite for knowing, and as among the senses the eyes play a leading role in acquiring knowledge, the divine word calls it 'the lust of the eyes' (1 John 2: 16). Seeing is the property of our eyes. But we also use this word in other senses, when we apply the power of vision to knowledge generally. We do not say 'Hear how that flashes', or 'Smell how bright that is', or 'Taste how that shines' or 'Touch how that gleams'. Of all these things we say 'see'. But we say not only 'See how that light shines', which only the eyes can perceive, but also 'See how that sounds, see what smells, see what tastes, see how hard that is'. So the general experience of the senses is the lust, as scripture says, of the eyes, because seeing is a function in which eyes hold the first place but other senses claim the word for themselves by analogy when they are exploring any department of knowledge.[37]

(55) From this observation it becomes easier to distinguish the activity of the senses in relation to pleasure from their activity in relation to curiosity. Pleasure pursues beautiful objects—what is agreeable to look at, to hear, to smell, to taste, to touch. But curiosity pursues the contraries of these delights with the motive of seeing what the experiences are like, not with a wish to undergo discomfort, but out of a lust for experimenting and knowing. What pleasure is to be found in looking at a mangled corpse, an experience which evokes revulsion?[38] Yet wherever one is lying, people crowd around to be made sad and to turn pale. They even dread seeing this in their dreams, as if someone had compelled them to look at it when awake or as if some report about the beauty of the sight had persuaded them to see it. The same is true of the other senses, but it would be too long to follow the theme through. To satisfy this diseased craving, outrageous sights are staged in public shows. The same motive is at work when people study the operations of nature which lie beyond our grasp, when there is no advantage in knowing

[37] 'Of all the senses, sight is the principal way in which we acquire knowledge': Aristotle, *Metaphysics* 1. 1.
[38] Plato, *Republic* 439e.

and the investigators simply desire knowledge for its own sake.[39]
This motive is again at work if, using a perverted science for the
same end, people try to achieve things by magical arts. Even in
religion itself the motive is seen when God is 'tempted' by demands
for 'signs and wonders' (John 4: 48) desired not for any salvific end
but only for the thrill.[40]

(56) In this immense jungle full of traps and dangers, see how
many I have cut out and expelled from my heart, as you have
granted me to do, 'God of my salvation' (Ps. 17: 47; 37: 23).
Nevertheless, when so many things of this kind surround our daily
life on every side with a buzz of distraction, when may I be so bold
as to say, when can I venture the claim, that nothing of the sort tugs
at my attention to go and look at it and that I am not caught by any
vain concern? True, theatres do not now capture my interest. I do
not study to understand the transit of the stars. My soul has never
sought for responses from ghosts. I detest all sacrilegious rites.
Lord my God, to whom I owe humble and simple service, how
many machinations are used by the Enemy to suggest to me that I
should seek from you some sign! But I beseech you by our King
and by Jerusalem our simple and pure home, that as consent to
these suggestions is far from me, so it may always remain distant
and even more remote. But when I pray to you for the good of
someone,[41] my intention is directed to a very different goal. Grant
me now and in the future to follow gladly as you do with me what
you will.

(57) Nevertheless, there are many respects, in tiny and contemptible
matters, where our curiosity is provoked every day. How often we
slip, who can count? How many times we initially act as if we put up
with people telling idle tales in order not to offend the weak, but
then gradually we find pleasure in listening. I now do not watch a
dog chasing a rabbit when this is happening at the circus. But if by
chance I am passing when coursing occurs in the countryside, it
distracts me perhaps indeed from thinking out some weighty matter.

---

[39] Augustine's attitude to 'curiosity' here, as in v. iii, contains an element of Academic
scepticism, mingled with Plotinus' doctrine that the clarity of the mind's vision depends
on whether it is contemplating purely intellectual things or muddy matter (4. 8. 4).

[40] That is to confuse means with ends, use with 'enjoyment', an error which is for
Augustine fundamental.

[41] Augustine contrasts his intercession for some sick or needy person with the
superstitious rites, magic, and astrology commonly employed by pagans for therapy.

The hunt turns me to an interest in the sport, not enough to lead me to alter the direction of the beast I am riding, but shifting the inclination of my heart. Unless you had proved to me my infirmity and quickly admonished me either to take the sight as the start for some reflection enabling me to rise up to you or wholly to scorn and pass the matter by, I would be watching like an empty-headed fool. When I am sitting at home, a lizard catching flies or a spider entrapping them as they rush into its web often fascinates me. The problem is not made any different by the fact that the animals are small. The sight leads me on to praise you, the marvellous Creator and orderer of all things; but that was not how my attention first began. It is one thing to rise rapidly, another thing not to fall. My life is full of such lapses, and my one hope is in your great mercy. When my heart becomes the receptacle of distractions of this nature and the container for a mass of empty thoughts, then too my prayers are often interrupted and distracted; and in your sight, while I am directing the voice of my heart to your ears, frivolous thoughts somehow rush in and cut short an aspiration of the deepest importance.

xxxvi (58) We can hardly regard this as a trivial matter. But nothing can restore hope to us except your mercy, known since you began to transform us. You know how great a transformation you have brought about. You cured me in the first place of my lust for self-justification to show yourself propitious to all my other iniquities; you heal all my diseases, you redeem my life from corruptions, crown me with compassion and mercy, and satisfy my longing with good things (Ps. 102: 3–5). By fear of you, you repressed my pride and by your yoke you made my neck submissive; now I carry that yoke, and it is gentle, exactly as you promised and as you made it (Matt. 11: 30). In truth it was gentle already, but I did not realize it at the time when I was afraid to submit to it.

(59) Lord you alone exercise rule without pride, since you alone are truly Lord (Isa. 37: 20), and you have no master. Surely the third kind of temptation (1 John 2: 16) has not ceased to trouble me, nor during the whole of this life can it cease. The temptation is to wish to be feared or loved by people for no reason other than the joy derived from such power, which is no joy at all. It is a wretched life, and vanity is repulsive. This is the main cause why I fail to love

and fear you in purity. Therefore 'you resist the proud but give grace to the humble' (1 Pet. 5: 5). You 'thunder' upon the ambitions of the world, and 'the foundations of the hills tremble' (Ps. 17: 4, 8). If we hold certain offices in human society it is necessary for us to be loved and feared by people, and the enemy of our true happiness is constant in attack, everywhere laying traps with 'Well done, well done' (Ps. 34: 21). When we are avid to amass such approval, we are caught off our guard. We cease to find our joy in your truth and place it in the deceitfulness of men. It becomes our pleasure to be loved and feared not for your sake, but instead of you. By this method the Enemy makes people resemble himself, united with him not in loving concord but in sharing a common punishment. The Enemy is he who 'decided to place his throne in the north' (Isa. 14: 13 f.) so that in the dark and the cold men should serve him who, by a perverted and twisted life, imitates you. But look, Lord, we are your little flock (Luke 12: 32), take possession of us (Isa. 26: 13). Stretch out your wings, and let us find refuge under them. Be our glory. Let it be for your sake that we are loved, and let it be your word in us which is feared. The person who wishes to be praised by men when you think him at fault will find no defence in any human support when you are the judge, nor will he escape if you condemn him. But when it is not a case of 'a sinner praised for the desires of his soul nor one being blessed for the wickedness of his actions' (Ps. 9B: 24), but rather of a person praised for some gift which you bestowed, who nevertheless finds more joy in being praised than in having the gift for which he is praised, then he also, though admired by human judgement, is blamed by you. In this case the person who gives the praise is superior to the recipient of the praise, for the former is pleased by God's gift to a man, whereas the latter is more pleased with what man gives than with what God has given.

xxxvii (60)   Every day, Lord, we are beset by these temptations. We are tempted without respite. The human tongue is our daily furnace (Prov. 27: 21). In this respect also you command us to be continent: grant what you command, and command what you will. In this matter you know the 'groaning' of my heart towards you (Ps. 37: 9), and the rivers which flow from my eyes (Ps. 118: 136). I cannot easily be sure how far I am cleansed from that plague (Ps. 18: 13). I have great fear of my subconscious impulses which your eyes know but mine do not (Ecclus. 15: 20).

In temptations of a different sort I have some capacity for self-exploration, but in this matter almost none. It is simple to see how far I have succeeded in restraining my mind from carnal pleasures and from curious quests for superfluous knowledge; for I do not indulge in these things, either by choice or because they are not available. I then ask myself whether it is more or less vexatious to me not to have them. Riches, moreover, are sought to provide means for one or two or all of the three lusts. If the mind cannot clearly perceive whether it despises the possession of them, that can be simply tested by giving them away.

But how can we live so as to be indifferent to praise, and to be sure of this in experience? Are we to live evil lives, so abandoned and depraved that no one who knows us does not detest us? Nothing more crazy can be suggested or imagined. If admiration is the usual and proper accompaniment of a good life and good actions, we ought not to renounce it any more than the good life which it accompanies. Yet I have no way of knowing whether my mind will be serene or upset to be lacking something unless it is actually absent.

(61) What then, Lord, have I to confess to you in this kind of temptation? I cannot pretend I am not pleased by praise; but I am more delighted to have declared the truth than to be praised for it. If I were given the choice of being universally admired, though mad or wholly wrong, or of being universally abused, though steadfast and utterly certain in possessing the truth, I see which I should choose. I would not wish the approving voice of another person to enhance my pleasure at the presence of something good in me. But I have to admit not only that admiration increases my pleasure, but that adverse criticism diminishes it. When this symptom of my wretched state disturbs me, self-justification worms its way into me, of a kind which you know, my God. But it makes me uncertain.

You have not only commanded us to be continent, that is to restrain our love for certain things, but also to maintain justice, that is, the object on which to direct our love. Your will is that we should love not only you but also our neighbour. Often when I am pleased to be praised by someone whose understanding is good, my pleasure

lies in my neighbour's progress or promise of it. On the other hand,
I am saddened by his failure when I hear him finding fault with
something which he does not understand or which is good. And
sometimes I am grieved at being admired when people approve
qualities in me which to myself are displeasing, or when they
estimate at more than their true value good things which are minor
and of slight importance. But once again how can I know whether
that is my reaction because I do not want my admirer to hold a view
of me different from my own, not because I am moved to consider
his benefit but because the same good qualities which please me
when I possess them are pleasanter to me when they also please
someone else?[42] In a certain sense it is to me no praise when my
opinion of myself is not approved, or when things which displease
me are commended, or when things which please me little are
admired more than they should be. So on this point I feel unsure of
myself.

(62)   Truth, in you I now see that, if I am praised, I should be
touched not on my own account, but for the benefit of my neighbour.
Whether that is my actual state of mind I do not know. In this
matter I know myself less well than I know you. I beseech you, my
God, show me myself so that to my brothers who will pray for me I
may confess what wound I am discovering in myself. Again I would
conscientiously put the question to myself: if what is good for my
neighbour should move me when I am being praised, why am I less
moved if someone else is unfairly blamed than if I am myself? Why
do I feel the sting of an insult directed against myself more acutely
than one flung against someone else in my presence, when in both
cases it is equally unfair? Or is this too beyond my knowledge? Is
the one remaining answer that I am deceiving myself (Gal. 6: 3) and
'do not the truth' (John 3: 21) before you in my heart and tongue?
Put this folly, Lord, far from me, lest the words of my mouth be 'the
oil of the sinner to make my head swell' (Ps. 140: 5).

xxxviii (63)   'I am poor and needy' (Ps. 108: 22), but am better if,
secretly groaning, I am vexed with myself and seek your mercy,
until my defect is repaired and I am perfectly restored to that peace
which is unknown to the arrogant observer. But the word proceeding

---

[42] Aristotle remarks that the pleasure given to a distinguished person by an honour is
to see other people agreeing with a conclusion long apparent to himself.

out of the mouth and the actions which become known to people contain a most hazardous temptation in the love of praise. This likes to gather and beg for support to bolster a kind of private superiority. This is a temptation to me even when I reject it, because of the very fact that I am rejecting it. Often the contempt of vainglory becomes a source of even more vainglory. For it is not being scorned when the contempt is something one is proud of.

xxxix (64) Within us lies another evil in the same category of temptation. This makes people who are pleased with themselves grow in vanity, though they either fail to please other people or actually annoy others whom they take no pains to please. But in pleasing themselves, they greatly displease you, not only because they think well of actions which are not good, but also because they claim good qualities as their own when you have bestowed them, or because they do not recognize them to be your gifts and think they have earned them by their merits. Or, if they know these gifts to be from your grace, they do not delight in sharing this grace with the community but grudge it to others. Amid all these temptations and in dangers and toils of this kind, you see my heart trembling. I have not ceased to experience such wounds, but continually they are being healed by you.

xl (65) Truth, when did you ever fail to walk with me, teaching me what to avoid and what to seek after when I reported to you what, in my inferior position, I could see and asked your counsel? To the best of my powers of sense-perception, I travelled through the external world. Starting from myself I gave attention to the life of my own body, and examined my own senses. From there I moved into the recesses of my memory, manifold vastnesses full of innumerable riches in wonderful ways, and 'I considered and was afraid' (Hab. 3: 2). Without you I could discern none of these things, and I found that none of these things was you. Nor was I you, though I had made these discoveries. I traversed everything, and tried to make distinctions and to evaluate each entity according to its proper rank. Some things I observed in interrogating the reports of my senses. Other things I felt to be mixed with my own self. I identified and numbered the senses reporting to me. Then in the wide riches of memory, I examined other things, hiding some away, drawing out others. But as I did this, the ego, that is the power by which I was

doing it, was not you. For you are the abiding light by which I
investigated all these matters to discover whether they existed,
what they were, and what value should be attached to them. I
listened to you teaching me and giving instructions. This I frequently
do. It gives me delight, and I take refuge in this pleasure from
necessary business, so far as I am able to take relief. But in all these
investigations which I pursue while consulting you, I can find no
safe place for my soul except in you. There my dispersed aspirations
are gathered together, and from you no part of me will depart.

And sometimes you cause me to enter into an extraordinary
depth of feeling marked by a strange sweetness. If it were brought
to perfection in me, it would be an experience quite beyond anything
in this life. But I fall back into my usual ways under my miserable
burdens. I am reabsorbed by my habitual practices. I am held in
their grip. I weep profusely, but still I am held. Such is the strength
of the burden of habit. Here I have the power to be, but do not wish
it. There I wish to be, but lack the power.[43] On both grounds I am
in misery.

xli (66)   So under the three forms of lust I have considered the
sicknesses of my sins, and I have invoked your right hand to save
me (Ps. 102: 3). For I have caught a glimpse of your splendour with
a wounded heart, and being rebuked I said 'Who can attain that?' 'I
am cast out from the sight of your eyes' (Ps. 30: 23). You are the
truth presiding over all things. But in my greed I was unwilling to
lose you, and wanted to have you at the same time as holding on to a
lie, in much the same way as no one wants to become such a liar as
to lose all awareness of what the truth is. This is why I lost you: you
do not condescend to be possessed together with falsehood.

xlii (67)   Who could be found to reconcile me to you? Was I to beg
the help of the angels? What prayer should I use? What sacred rites?
Many have tried to return to you, and have not had the strength in
themselves to achieve it, so I have been told. They have attempted
these methods and have lapsed into a desire for curious visions, and
have been rewarded with illusions.[44] For in their quest they have

---

[43] Plotinus 4. 8. 4. 33 has the same antithesis for the soul split between 'there' and
'here'. On the transience of the experience of mystical union see Plotinus 6. 9. 10; and
above VII. xvii (23).

[44] Pagan Neoplatonists made much of ritual practices ('theurgy') as means of attaining
mystical visions. This chapter anticipates the full-scale attack on Porphyry in City of God 9.

been lifted up by pride in their high culture, inflating their chest rather than beating their breast. Through an affinity in heart they attracted to themselves as associates and allies of their pride 'the powers of the air' (Eph. 2: 2) who deluded them with magical powers. They sought a mediator to purify them, and it was not the true one. For it was 'the devil transforming himself into an angel of light' (2 Cor. 11: 14). It was 'a potent enticement for proud flesh that he had no carnal body. They were mortal and sinful men. But you, Lord, to whom in pride they sought to be reconciled, are immortal and without sin. But a mediator between God and the human race ought to have something in common with God and something in common with humanity. If the Mediator were in both aspects like humanity, he would be far distant from God. If he were in both aspects like God, he would be far distant from humanity, and so would be no mediator. That is why the deceiving mediator, by whom through your secret judgements pride deserved to be deluded, has one thing in common with human beings, namely sin. He wishes to appear to have another feature in common with God: since he is not clothed with mortal flesh, he boasts that he is immortal. But because 'the wages of sin is death' (Rom. 6: 23), he in common with mankind is condemned to death.

xliii (68)   The true Mediator you showed to humanity in your secret mercy. You sent him so that from his example they should learn humility. He is 'the mediator between God and men, the man Christ Jesus' (1 Tim. 2: 5). He appeared among mortal sinners as the immortal righteous one, mortal like humanity, righteous like God. Because the wages of righteousness are life and peace (Rom. 6: 23), being united with God by his righteousness he made void the death of justified sinners, a death which it was his will to share in common with them. He was made known to the ancient saints so that they could be saved through faith by his future passion, just as we are saved through faith in his passion now that it is past. It is as man that he is mediator. He is not midway as Word; for the Word is equal to God and 'God with God' (John 1: 1), and at the same time there is but one God.

(69)   How you have loved us, good Father: you did not 'spare your only Son but delivered him up for us sinners' (Rom. 8: 32). How you have loved us, for whose sake 'he did not think it a usurpation

to be equal to you and was made subject to the death of the cross' (Phil. 2: 6, 8). He was the only one to be 'free among the dead' (Ps. 87: 5). He had power to lay down his soul and power to take it back again (John 10: 18). For us he was victorious before you and victor because he was victim. For us before you he is priest and sacrifice, and priest because he is sacrifice. Before you he makes us sons instead of servants by being born of you and being servant to us. With good reason my firm hope is in him. For you will cure all my diseases (Ps. 102: 3) through him who sits at your right hand and intercedes with you for us (Rom. 8: 34). Otherwise I would be in despair. Many and great are those diseases, many and great indeed. But your medicine is still more potent. We might have thought your Word was far removed from being united to mankind and have despaired of our lot unless he had become flesh and dwelt among us (John 1: 14).

(70)   Terrified by my sins and the pile of my misery, I had racked my heart and had meditated taking flight to live in solitude.[45] But you forbade me and comforted me saying: 'That is why Christ died for all, so that those who live should not live for themselves, but for him who died for them' (2 Cor. 5: 15). See, Lord, 'I cast my anxiety on you that I may live' (Ps. 54: 23), and 'I will consider the wonders from your law' (Ps. 118: 18). You know my inexperience and weakness (Ps. 68: 6). 'Teach me and heal me' (Ps. 6: 3; 142: 10). Your only Son 'in whom are hid all treasures of wisdom and knowledge' (Col. 2: 3) had 'redeemed me by his blood' (Rev. 5: 9). 'Let not the proud speak evil of me' (Ps. 118: 22), for I think upon the price of my redemption, and I eat and drink it, and distribute it.[46] In my poverty I desire to be satisfied from it together with those who 'eat and are satisfied' (Ps. 61: 5). 'And they shall praise the Lord who seek him' (Ps. 21: 27).

---

[45] Perhaps because of the influence of Athanasius' *Life of Antony*: above, VIII. vi (14). This text is unique evidence of Augustine's aspiration to be a hermit.
[46] In the Eucharist.

BOOK XI

Time and Eternity

i (1)   Lord, eternity is yours, so you cannot be ignorant of what I tell you. Your vision of occurrences in time is not temporally conditioned. Why then do I set before you an ordered account of so many things? It is certainly not through me that you know them. But I am stirring up love for you in myself and in those who read this, so that we may all say 'Great is the Lord and highly worthy to be praised' (Ps. 47: 1).[1] I have already affirmed this and will say it again: I tell my story for love of your love.[2] We pray, and yet the truth says 'Your Father knows what you need before you ask him' (Matt. 6: 8). Therefore I lay bare my feelings towards you, by confessing to you my miseries and your mercies to us (Ps. 32: 22), so that the deliverance you have begun may be complete. So I may cease to be wretched in myself and may find happiness in you. For you have called us to be 'poor in spirit', meek, mournful, hungering and thirsting for righteousness, merciful, pure in heart, and peace-makers (Matt. 5: 3–9).

See, the long story I have told to the best of my ability and will responds to your prior will that I should make confession to you, my Lord God. For 'you are good, for your mercy is for ever.' (Ps. 117: 1).

ii (2)   But when shall I be capable of proclaiming by 'the tongue of my pen' (Ps. 44: 2) all your exhortations and all your terrors and consolations and directives, by which you brought me to preach your word and dispense your sacrament to your people? And if I have the capacity to proclaim this in an ordered narrative, yet the drops of time[3] are too precious to me. For a long time past I have been burning to meditate in your law (Ps. 38: 4) and confess to you what I know of it and what lies beyond my powers—the first elements granted by your illumination and the remaining areas of darkness in my understanding—until weakness is swallowed up by

---

[1] Resuming the opening paragraph, above I. i (1).   [2] Above II. i (1).

[3] Metaphor from the water-clock. Augustine passes from autobiography (up to conversion and Monica's death) to an account of his theological concerns as bishop, especially anti-Manichee exegesis of Genesis and creation.

strength. I am reluctant to expend on any other subject those hours which I find free of the necessities for restoring the body, of intellectual work, and of the service which we owe to people or that which we render to them when under no obligation.[4]

(3) Lord my God, 'hear my prayer' (Ps. 60: 2), may your mercy attend to my longing which burns not for my personal advantage but desires to be of use in love to the brethren. You see in my heart that this is the case. Let me offer you in sacrifice the service of my thinking and my tongue, and grant that which I am to offer, 'for I am poor and needy' (Ps. 65: 15; 85: 1). You are 'rich to all who call upon you' (Rom. 10: 12). You have no cares but take care of us. Circumcise my lips (cf. Exod. 6: 12), inwardly and outwardly, from all rashness and falsehood. May your scriptures be my pure delight, so that I am not deceived in them and do not lead others astray in interpreting them. 'Lord, listen and have mercy' (Ps. 26: 7; 85: 3), Lord my God, light of the blind and strength of the weak—and constantly also light of those who can see and strength of the mighty: Listen to my soul and hear it crying from the depth. For if your ears are not present also in the depth, where shall we go? To whom shall we cry? 'The day is yours and the night is yours' (Ps. 73: 16). At your nod the moments fly by. From them grant us space for our meditations on the secret recesses of your law, and do not close the gate to us as we knock. It is not for nothing that by your will so many pages of scripture are opaque and obscure. These forests are not without deer which recover their strength in them and restore themselves by walking and feeding, by resting and ruminating (Ps. 28: 9). O Lord, bring me to perfection (Ps. 16: 5) and reveal to me the meaning of these pages. See, your voice is my joy, your voice is better than a wealth of pleasures (Ps. 118: 22). Grant what I love; for I love it, and that love was your gift. Do not desert your gifts, and do not despise your plant as it thirsts. Let me confess to you what I find in your books. 'Let me hear the voice of praise' (Ps. 25: 7) and drink you, and let me consider 'wonderful things out of your law' (Ps. 118: 18)—from the beginning in which you made heaven and earth until the perpetual reign with you in your heavenly city (Rev. 5: 10; 21: 2).[5]

[4] Echo of Cicero, *De officiis* 1. 4. 13.

[5] This would become the theme, 15 years later, of the *City of God*. Echoes of the Apocalypse of John pervade books XI–XIII.

(4) 'Lord have mercy upon me and listen to my desire' (Ps. 26: 7). For I do not think my longing is concerned with earthly things, with gold and silver and precious stones, or with fine clothes or honours and positions of power or fleshly pleasures or even with the body's necessities in this life of our pilgrimage. They are all things added to us as we seek your kingdom and your righteousness (Matt. 6: 33). My God, look upon the object of my desire (cf. Ps. 9: 14). 'The wicked have told me of delights, but they are not allowed by your law, Lord' (Ps. 118: 85). See Father: look and see and give your approval. May it please you that in the sight of your mercy (Ps. 18: 15) I may find grace before you, so that to me as I knock (Matt. 7: 7) may be opened the hidden meaning of your words. I make my prayer through our Lord Jesus Christ your Son, 'the man of your right hand, the Son of man whom you have strengthened' (Ps. 79: 18) to be mediator between yourself and us. By him you sought us when we were not seeking you (Rom. 10: 20). But you sought us that we should seek you, your Word by whom you made all things including myself, your only Son by whom you have called to adoption the people who believe (Gal. 4: 5), myself among them. I make my prayer to you through him 'who sits at your right hand and intercedes to you for us' (Rom. 8: 34). 'In him are hidden all the treasures of wisdom and knowledge' (Col. 2: 3). For those treasures I search in your books. Moses wrote of him (John 5: 46). He himself said this; this is the declaration of the Truth.

iii (5) May I hear and understand how in the beginning you made heaven and earth (Gen. 1, 1). Moses wrote this. He wrote this and went his way, passing out of this world from you to you.[6] He is not now before me, but if he were, I would clasp him and ask him and through you beg him to explain to me the creation. I would concentrate my bodily ears to hear the sounds breaking forth from his mouth. If he spoke Hebrew, he would in vain make an impact on my sense of hearing, for the sounds would not touch my mind at all. If he spoke Latin, I would know what he meant. Yet how would I know whether or not he was telling me the truth? If I did know this, I could not be sure of it from him. Within me, within the lodging of my thinking, there would speak a truth which is neither Hebrew nor Greek nor Latin nor any barbarian tongue and which uses

---

[6] Perhaps an echo of Plotinus's 'flight of the alone to the Alone' (6. 9. 11. 51).

neither mouth nor tongue as instruments and utters no audible
syllables. It would say: 'What he is saying is true'.[7] And I being
forthwith assured would say with confidence to the man possessed
by you: 'What you say is true.' But since I cannot question him, I
ask you who filled him when he declared what is true; you my God I
ask. 'Spare my sins' (Job 14: 16). You have granted to your servant
to utter these things; grant also to me the power to understand
them.

iv (6)   See, heaven and earth exist, they cry aloud that they are
made, for they suffer change and variation. But in anything which is
not made and yet is, there is nothing which previously was not
present. To be what once was not the case is to be subject to
change and variation. They also cry aloud that they have not made
themselves: 'The manner of our existence shows that we are made.
For before we came to be, we did not exist to be able to make
ourselves.' And the voice with which they speak is self-evidence.
You, Lord, who are beautiful, made them for they are beautiful.
You are good, for they are good. You are, for they are. Yet they are
not beautiful or good or possessed of being in the sense that you
their Maker are. In comparison with you they are deficient in
beauty and goodness and being. Thanks to you, we know this; and
yet our knowledge is ignorance in comparison with yours.[8]

v (7)   How did you make heaven and earth, and what machine did
you use for so vast an operation? You were not like a craftsman who
makes one physical object out of another by an act of personal
choice in his mind, which has the power to impose the form which
by an inner eye it can see within itself. This capacity it has only
because you have so made it. He imposes form on what already
exists and possesses being, such as earth or stone or wood or gold
or any material of that sort. And these materials exist only because
you had first made them. By your creation the craftsman has a
body, a mind by which he commands its members, material out of
which he makes something, a skill by which he masters his art and
sees inwardly what he is making outwardly. From your creation
come the bodily senses which he uses to translate his mental
concept into the material objects he is making, and to report back to

---

[7] Plotinus 4. 3. 18. 13 ff. In the intelligible world they use no words, but communicate
by intuition.

[8] The argument is close to Plotinus' vindication of providence: 3. 2. 3.

the mind what has been made, so that the mind within may deliberate with the truth presiding over it to consider whether the work has been well done.[9] All these praise you, the creator of everything. But how do you make them? The way, God, in which you made heaven and earth was not that you made them either in heaven or on earth. Nor was it in air or in water, for these belong to heaven and earth. Nor did you make the universe within the framework of the universe. There was nowhere for it to be made before it was brought into existence.[10] Nor did you have any tool in your hand to make heaven and earth. How could you obtain anything you had not made as a tool for making something? What is it for something to be unless it is because you are? Therefore you spoke and they were made, and by your word you made them (Ps. 32: 9, 6).

vi (8) But how did you speak? Surely not in the way a voice came out of the cloud saying, 'This is my beloved Son' (Matt. 17: 5). That voice is past and done with; it began and is ended. The syllables sounded and have passed away, the second after the first, the third after the second, and so on in order until, after all the others, the last one came, and after the last silence followed. Therefore it is clear and evident that the utterance came through the movement of some created thing, serving your eternal will but itself temporal. And these your words, made for temporal succession, were reported by the external ear to the judicious mind whose internal ear is disposed to hear your eternal word. But that mind would compare these words, sounding in time, with your eternal word in silence, and say: 'It is very different, the difference is enormous. The sounds are far inferior to me, and have no being, because they are fleeting and transient. But the word of my God is superior to me and abides for ever' (Isa. 40: 8). If therefore it was with words which sound and pass away that you said that heaven and earth should be made, and if this was how you made heaven and earth, then a created entity belonging to the physical realm existed prior to heaven and earth; and that utterance took time to deliver, and involved temporal changes.[11] However, no physical

[9] Cf. Plotinus 5. 8. 1 (beauty first in the designing artist's mind).

[10] Similarly Plotinus 5. 5. 9. 28 (no place existed before the world); 6. 8. 7. 26 (Nothing can bring itself into existence).

[11] Plotinus (5. 3. 17. 24) stresses the temporal successiveness of human words. See above IV. x (15); IX. x (24).

entity existed before heaven and earth; at least if any such existed,
you had made it without using a transient utterance, which could
then be used as a basis for another transient utterance, declaring
that heaven and earth be made. Whatever it might have been which
became the basis for such an utterance, unless it was created by
you, it could not exist. Therefore for the creation of a physical
entity to become the basis for those words, what kind of word
would you have used?

vii (9)   You call us, therefore, to understand the Word, God who is
with you God (John 1: 1). That word is spoken eternally, and by it
all things are uttered eternally. It is not the case that what was being
said comes to an end, and something else is then said, so that
everything is uttered in a succession with a conclusion, but everything
is said in the simultaneity of eternity. Otherwise time and change
would already exist, and there would not be a true eternity and true
immortality. This I know, my God, and give thanks. I know and
confess it to you, Lord, and everyone who is not ungrateful for
assured truth knows it with me and blesses you. We know this,
Lord, we know. A thing dies and comes into being inasmuch as it is
not what it was and becomes what it was not. No element of your
word yields place or succeeds to something else, since it is truly
immortal and eternal. And so by the Word coeternal with yourself,
you say all that you say in simultaneity and eternity, and whatever
you say will come about does come about. You do not cause it to
exist other than by speaking. Yet not all that you cause to exist by
speaking is made in simultaneity and eternity.

viii (10)   Why, I ask, Lord my God? In some degree I see it, but
how to express it I do not know,[12] unless to say that everything
which begins to be and ceases to be begins and ends its existence at
that moment when, in the eternal reason where nothing begins or
ends, it is known that it is right for it to begin and end. This reason
is your Word, which is also the Beginning in that it also speaks to
us. Thus in the gospel the Word speaks through the flesh, and this
sounded externally in human ears, so that it should be believed and
sought inwardly, found in the eternal truth where the Master who
alone is good (Matt. 19: 16) teaches all his disciples. There, Lord, I
hear your voice speaking to me, for one who teaches us speaks to

---

[12] Perhaps an echo of Plotinus 6. 8. 19. 1–3 who says the same.

us, but one who does not teach us, even though he may speak, does not speak to us. Who is our teacher except the reliable truth? Even when we are instructed through some mutable creature, we are led to reliable truth when we are learning truly by standing still and listening to him. We then 'rejoice with joy because of the voice of the bridegroom' (John 3: 29), and give ourselves to the source whence we have our being. And in this way he is the Beginning because, unless he were constant, there would be no fixed point to which we could return. But when we return from error, it is by knowing that we return. He teaches us so that we may know; for he is the Beginning, and he speaks to us.[13]

ix (11)   In this Beginning, God, you made heaven and earth, in your Word, in your Son, in your power, in your wisdom, in your truth speaking in a wonderful way and making in a wonderful way. Who can comprehend it? Who will give an account of it in words? What is the light which shines right through me and strikes my heart without hurting? It fills me with terror and burning love:[14] with terror inasmuch as I am utterly other than it, with burning love in that I am akin to it. Wisdom, wisdom it is which shines right through me, cutting a path through the cloudiness which returns to cover me as I fall away under the darkness and the load of my punishments. For 'my strength is weakened by poverty' (Ps. 30: 11), so that I cannot maintain my goodness until you, Lord, who 'have become merciful to all my iniquities, also heal all my sicknesses'. You will redeem my life from corruption and crown me with mercy and compassion, and satisfy my longing with good things, in that my youth will be renewed like an eagle's (Ps. 102: 3–5). For 'by hope we are saved', and we await your promises in patience (Rom. 8: 24–5). Let the person who can hear you speaking within listen. Confident on the ground of your inspired utterance, I will cry out: 'How magnificent are

[13] The argument here has analogies in Plotinus 5. 5. 9, and especially 6. 5. 7 on knowledge as the route of return to true being. But Augustine has inserted the incarnate Lord as the revealer.

[14] Similarly VII. x (16) above; Plotinus 1. 6. 7. Throughout this section Augustine wants to interpret the 'beginning' of Gen. 1: 1 to mean the Word or Son of God, to escape the temporal implications of 'beginning'. Books XI–XIII offer a diffidently exploratory exposition of Genesis 1, partly in refutation of Manicheism, but partly also against Catholic interpreters unconvinced by his Neoplatonic language about the transition from unformed to formed matter and about the spiritual (non-material) creation not mentioned in Genesis. He had more Catholic tradition behind him in discerning the Trinity working in the creation.

your works, Lord, you have made all things in wisdom' (Ps. 103: 24).
Wisdom is the beginning, and in that beginning you made heaven
and earth.

x (12)   See how full of old errors are those who say to us: 'What
was God doing before he made heaven and earth? If he was
unoccupied', they say, 'and doing nothing, why does he not always
remain the same for ever, just as before creation he abstained from
work? For if in God any new development took place and any new
intention, so as to make a creation which he had never made before,
how then can there be a true eternity in which a will, not there
previously, comes into existence? For God's will is not a creature,
but is prior to the created order, since nothing would be created
unless the Creator's will preceded it. Therefore God's will belongs
to his very substance.[15] If in the substance of God anything has
come into being which was not present before, that substance
cannot truthfully be called eternal. But if it was God's everlasting
will that the created order exist, why is not the creation also
everlasting?"[16]

xi (13)   People who say this do not yet understand you, O wisdom of
God, light of minds. They do not yet understand how things were
made which came to be through you and in you. They attempt to taste
eternity when their heart is still flitting about in the realm where
things change and have a past and future; it is still 'vain' (Ps. 5: 10).
Who can lay hold on the heart and give it fixity, so that for some
little moment it may be stable, and for a fraction of time may grasp
the splendour of a constant eternity? Then it may compare eternity
with temporal successiveness which never has any constancy, and
will see there is no comparison possible. It will see that a long time
is long only because constituted of many successive movements
which cannot be simultaneously extended. In the eternal, nothing is
transient, but the whole is present.[17] But no time is wholly present.
It will see that all past time is driven backwards by the future, and

---

[15] Below XII. xv (18); Plotinus 6. 8. 13. 7.

[16] Augustine's argument against Porphyry's Neoplatonic contention that the Incarnation is impossible because it implies change in God is here taken to be a principle equally affecting Creation. The argument is given a masterly statement at greater length in *City of God* 12.

[17] So also Plotinus 3. 7. 3.

all future time is the consequent of the past, and all past and future are created and set on their course by that which is always present. Who will lay hold on the human heart to make it still, so that it can see how eternity, in which there is neither future nor past, stands still and dictates future and past times? Can my hand have the strength for this? (Gen. 31: 29). Can the hand of my mouth by mere speech achieve so great a thing?

xii (14) This is my reply to anyone who asks: 'What was God doing before he made heaven and earth?' My reply is not that which someone is said to have given as a joke to evade the force of the question. He said: 'He was preparing hells for people who inquire into profundities.' It is one thing to laugh, another to see the point at issue, and this reply I reject. I would have preferred him to answer 'I am ignorant of what I do not know' rather than reply so as to ridicule someone who has asked a deep question and to win approval for an answer which is a mistake.

No, I say that you, our God, are the Creator of every created being, and assuming that by 'heaven and earth' is meant every created thing I boldly declare: Before God made heaven and earth, he was not making anything. If he was making anything, it could only be something created. I only wish that other useful matters which I long to be sure about I could know with an assurance equal to that with which I know that no created being was made before any creature came into being.

xiii (15) If, however, someone's mind is flitting and wandering over images of past times, and is astonished that you, all powerful, all creating, and all sustaining God, artificer of heaven and earth, abstained for unnumbered ages from this work before you actually made it, he should wake up and take note that his surprise rests on a mistake. How would innumerable ages pass, which you yourself had not made? You are the originator and creator of all ages. What times existed which were not brought into being by you? Or how could they pass if they never had existence? Since, therefore, you are the cause of all times, if any time existed before you made heaven and earth, how can anyone say that you abstained from working? You have made time itself. Time could not elapse before you made time. But if time did not exist before heaven and earth, why do people ask what you were then doing? There was no 'then' when there was no time.[18]

(16)   It is not in time that you precede times. Otherwise you would not precede all times. In the sublimity of an eternity which is always in the present, you are before all things past and transcend all things future, because they are still to come, and when they have come they are past. 'But you are the same and your years do not fail' (Ps. 101: 28). Your 'years' neither go nor come. Ours come and go so that all may come in succession. All your 'years' subsist in simultaneity, because they do not change; those going away are not thrust out by those coming in. But the years which are ours will not all be until all years have ceased to be. Your 'years' are 'one day' (Ps. 89: 4; 2 Pet. 3: 8), and your 'day' is not any and every day but Today, because your Today does not yield to a tomorrow, nor did it follow on a yesterday. Your Today is eternity. So you begat one coeternal with you, to whom you said: 'Today I have begotten you' (Ps. 2: 7; Heb. 5: 5). You created all times and you exist before all times. Nor was there any time when time did not exist.

xiv (17)   There was therefore no time when you had not made something, because you made time itself. No times are coeternal with you since you are permanent. If they were permanent, they would not be times.

What is time? Who can explain this easily and briefly? Who can comprehend this even in thought so as to articulate the answer in words? Yet what do we speak of, in our familiar everyday conversation, more than of time? We surely know what we mean when we speak of it. We also know what is meant when we hear someone else talking about it. What then is time? Provided that no one asks me, I know.[19] If I want to explain it to an inquirer, I do not know. But I

---

[18] Aristotle, *Metaphysics* 12. 6: 'Time cannot come into being or cease to be; if time did not exist, there could be no before and after.'

Philo, the Alexandrian Jew of St Paul's time, maintains that time was created with the cosmos (*De opificio mundi* 26). Several early Christians say the same, including Ambrose. Plotinus (3. 9. 8. 1 ff.) says that the question why the Creator creates is asked by people who are assuming that that which always is had a beginning in time. Like Augustine, Plotinus thinks time does not antedate the cosmos (3. 7. 12. 23; as Plato, *Timaeus* 38b6).

[19] Plotinus (3. 7. 1. 1–13) observes that we think we know what time is until we begin to think about it in depth. Augustine's discussion of time contains many echoes of philosophical debates among Platonists, Aristotelians, and Stoics, but is remarkable for its affinity with the Sceptical or 'Academic' position that for the human mind the question is unanswerable. At least Augustine does not answer it. His question is

confidently affirm myself to know that if nothing passes away, there is no past time, and if nothing arrives, there is no future time, and if nothing existed there would be no present time. Take the two tenses, past and future. How can they 'be' when the past is not now present and the future is not yet present? Yet if the present were always present, it would not pass into the past: it would not be time but eternity. If then, in order to be time at all, the present is so made that it passes into the past, how can we say that this present also 'is'? The cause of its being is that it will cease to be. So indeed we cannot truly say that time exists except in the sense that it tends towards non-existence.

xv (18)   Nevertheless we speak of 'a long time' and 'a short time', and it is only of the past or the future that we say this. Of the past we speak of 'a long time', when, for example, it is more than a hundred years ago. 'A long time' in the future may mean a hundred years ahead. By 'a short time ago' we would mean, say, ten days back, and 'a short time ahead' might mean 'in ten days' time'. But how can something be long or short which does not exist? For the past now has no existence and the future is not yet. So we ought not to say of the past 'It is long', but 'it was long', and of the future 'it will be long'. My Lord, my light, does not your truth mock humanity at this point? This time past which was long, was it long when it was past or when it was still present? It could be long only when it existed to be long. Once past, it no longer was. Therefore it could not be long if it had entirely ceased to exist.

Therefore let us not say 'The time past was long'. For we cannot discover anything to be long when, after it has become past, it has ceased to be. But let us say 'That time once present was long' because it was long at the time when it was present. For it had not yet passed away into non-existence. It existed so as to be able to be long. But after it had passed away, it simultaneously ceased to be long because it ceased to be.

(19)   Human soul, let us see whether present time can be long. To you the power is granted to be aware of intervals of time, and to

characteristically less philosophical than religious: what sense can we make of the chaos of history and the apparent meaninglessness of successive events? Between past and future humanity experiences what he will call a distending, a stretching out on a rack. Hence he picks up Aristotle's suggestion (*Physics* 4. 14) that time is an experience of the soul, but gives this idea a new development by seeing 'memory' as cardinal to the comprehension of time.

measure them. What answer will you give me? Are a hundred years in the present a long time? Consider first whether a hundred years can be present. For if the first year of the series is current, it is present, but ninety-nine are future, and so do not yet exist. If the second year is current, one is already past, the second is present, the remainder lie in the future. And so between the extremes, whatever year of this century we assume to be present, there will be some years before it which lie in the past, some in the future to come after it. It follows that a century could never be present.

Consider then whether if a single year is current, that can be present. If in this year the first month is current, the others lie in the future; if the second, then the first lies in the past and the rest do not yet exist. Therefore even a current year is not entirely present; and if it is not entirely present, it is not a year which is present. A year is twelve months, of which any month which is current is present; the others are either past or future. Moreover, not even a month which is current is present, but one day. If the first day, the others are future; if the last day, the others are past; any intermediary day falls between past and future.

(20) See—present time, which alone we find capable of being called long, is contracted to the space of hardly a single day. But let us examine that also; for not even one day is entirely present. All the hours of night and day add up to twenty-four. The first of them has the others in the future, the last has them in the past. Any hour between these has past hours before it, future hours after it. One hour is itself constituted of fugitive moments. Whatever part of it has flown away is past. What remains to it is future. If we can think of some bit of time which cannot be divided into even the smallest instantaneous moments, that alone is what we can call 'present'. And this time flies so quickly from future into past that it is an interval with no duration. If it has duration, it is divisible into past and future. But the present occupies no space.[20]

Where then is the time which we call long? Is it future? We do not really mean 'It is long', since it does not yet exist to be long, but

---

[20] The argument reflects older debates in the philosophical schools, e.g. that if time cannot properly be divided into past, present, and future, then only its indivisibility remains a live option. Sextus Empiricus (*Outlines of Pyrrhonism* 3. 143–5) preserves summaries of the Sceptical arguments that all discussions of time end in nonsense, so that nothing can be known for certain in this regard.

we mean it will be long. When will it be long? If it will then still lie in the future, it will not be long, since it will not yet exist to be long. But if it will be long at the time when, out of the future which does not yet exist, it begins to have being and will become present fact, so that it has the potentiality to be long, the present cries out in words already used that it cannot be long.

xvi (21) Nevertheless, Lord, we are conscious of intervals of time, and compare them with each other, and call some longer, others shorter. We also measure how much longer or shorter one period is than another, and answer that the one is twice or three times as much as the other, or that the two periods are equal. Moreover, we are measuring times which are past when our perception is the basis of measurement. But who can measure the past which does not now exist or the future which does not yet exist, unless perhaps someone dares to assert that he can measure what has no existence? At the moment when time is passing, it can be perceived and measured. But when it has passed and is not present, it cannot be.

xvii (22) I am investigating, Father, not making assertions. My God, protect me and rule me (Ps. 22: 1; 27: 9). Who will tell me that there are not three times, past, present, and future, as we learnt when children and as we have taught children, but only the present, because the other two have no existence? Or do they exist in the sense that, when the present emerges from the future, time comes out of some secret store, and then recedes into some secret place when the past comes out of the present? Where did those who sang prophecies see these events if they do not yet exist? To see what has no existence is impossible. And those who narrate past history would surely not be telling a true story if they did not discern events by their soul's insight. If the past were non-existent, it could not be discerned at all. Therefore both future and past events exist.

xviii (23) Allow me, Lord, to take my investigation further. My hope, let not my attention be distracted.[21] If future and past events exist, I want to know where they are. If I have not the strength to discover the answer, at least I know that wherever they are, they are not there as future or past, but as present. For if there also they are future, they will not yet be there. If there also they are past, they

[21] See below, XI. xxix (39) on the inherent 'distraction of multiplicity' in thinking about past, present, and future, when the reality of eternity is simultaneity in the present.

are no longer there. Therefore, wherever they are, whatever they are, they do not exist except in the present. When a true narrative of the past is related, the memory produces not the actual events which have passed away but words conceived from images of them, which they fixed in the mind like imprints as they passed through the senses. Thus my boyhood, which is no longer, lies in past time which is no longer. But when I am recollecting and telling my story, I am looking on its image in present time, since it is still in my memory. Whether a similar cause is operative in predictions of the future, in the sense that images of realities which do not yet exist are presented as already in existence, I confess, my God, I do not know. At least I know this much: we frequently think out in advance our future actions, and that premeditation is in the present; but the action which we premeditate is not yet in being because it lies in the future. But when we have embarked on the action and what we were premeditating begins to be put into effect, then that action will have existence, since then it will be not future but present.

(24) Whatever may be the way in which the hidden presentiment of the future is known, nothing can be seen if it does not exist. Now that which already exists is not future but present. When therefore people speak of knowing the future, what is seen is not events which do not yet exist (that is, they really are future), but perhaps their causes or signs which already exist.[22] In this way, to those who see them they are not future but present, and that is the basis on which the future can be conceived in the mind and made the subject of prediction.

Again, these concepts already exist, and those who predict the future see these concepts as if already present to their minds.

Among a great mass of examples, let me mention one instance. I look at the dawn. I forecast that the sun will rise. What I am looking at is present, what I am forecasting is future. It is not the sun which lies in the future (it already exists) but its rise, which has not yet arrived. Yet unless I were mentally imagining its rise, as now when I am speaking about it, I could not predict it. But the dawn glow which I see in the sky is not sunrise, which it precedes, nor is the

---

[22] Like Plotinus (4. 4. 12. 28–32), Augustine allows for the interpretation of fore-knowledge of the future as inspired insight into the meaning of events rather than a mantic ecstasy with suspension of reason.

imagining of sunrise in my mind the actuality. These are both discerned as present so that the coming sunrise may be foretold.

So future events do not yet exist, and if they are not yet present, they do not exist; and if they have no being, they cannot be seen at all. But they can be predicted from present events which are already present and can be seen.

xix (25)   Governor of your creation, what is the way by which you inform souls what lies in the future? For you instructed your prophets. By what method then do you give information about the future—you to whom nothing is future? Is it rather that you inform how to read the future in the light of the present? What does not exist, certainly cannot be the subject of information. This method is far beyond my power of vision. 'It is too mighty for me, I cannot attain it' (Ps. 138: 6). But it would be in my power with your help if you granted it, sweet light of my uncomprehending eyes.

xx (26)   What is by now evident and clear is that neither future nor past exists, and it is inexact language to speak of three times—past, present, and future.[23] Perhaps it would be exact to say: there are three times, a present of things past, a present of things present, a present of things to come. In the soul there are these three aspects of time, and I do not see them anywhere else. The present considering the past is the memory, the present considering the present is immediate awareness, the present considering the future is expectation. If we are allowed to use such language, I see three times, and I admit they are three. Moreover, we may say, There are three times, past, present, and future. This customary way of speaking is incorrect, but it is common usage. Let us accept the usage. I do not object and offer no opposition or criticism, as long as what is said is being understood, namely that neither the future nor the past is now present. There are few usages of everyday speech which are exact, and most of our language is inexact. Yet what we mean is communicated.

xxi (27)   A little earlier I observed that we measure past periods of time so that we can say that one period is twice as long as another or equal to it, and likewise of other periods of time which we are capable of measuring and reporting. Therefore, as I was saying, we measure periods of time as they are passing, and if anyone says to

[23] Augustine's view was anticipated by the Stoics.

me 'How do you know?' I reply: I know it because we do measure
time and cannot measure what has no being; and past and future
have none. But how do we measure present time when it has no
extension? It is measured when it passes, but not when it has
passed, because then there will be nothing there to measure.

When time is measured, where does it come from, by what route
does it pass, and where does it go? It must come out of the future,
pass by the present, and go into the past; so it comes from what as
yet does not exist, passes through that which lacks extension, and
goes into that which is now non-existent. Yet what do we measure
but time over some extension? When we speak of lengths of time as
single, duple, triple, and equal, or any other temporal relation of
this kind, we must be speaking of periods of time possessing
extension. In what extension then do we measure time as it is
passing? Is it in the future out of which it comes to pass by? No, for
we do not measure what does not yet exist. Is it in the present
through which it passes? No, for we cannot measure that which has
no extension. Is it in the past into which it is moving? No, for we
cannot measure what now does not exist.

xxii (28)   My mind is on fire to solve this very intricate enigma. Do
not shut the door, Lord my God. Good Father, through Christ I
beg you, do not shut the door on my longing to understand these
things which are both familiar and obscure. Do not prevent me,
Lord, from penetrating them and seeing them illuminated by the
light of your mercy. Whom shall I ask about them? And to whom
but you shall I more profitably confess my incompetence? You are
not irritated by the burning zeal with which I study your scriptures.
Grant what I love. For I love, and this love was your gift. Grant it,
Father. You truly know how to give good gifts to your children
(Matt. 7: 11). Grant it, since I have undertaken to acquire understanding and 'the labour is too much for me' (Ps. 72: 16) until you
open the way. Through Christ I beg you, in the name of him who is
the holy of holy ones, let no one obstruct my inquiry. 'I also have
believed, and therefore speak' (Ps. 115: 1; 2 Cor. 4: 13).[24] This is
my hope. For this I live 'that I may contemplate the delight of the
Lord' (Ps. 26: 4). 'Behold you have made my days subject to ageing'

---

[24] Augustine forestalls Christian critics who may think his abstruse inquiries remote
from his proper task of biblical exegesis, and invokes the mediation of Christ the high-
priest who gives access to the Father's mysteries.

(Ps. 38: 6). They pass away, and how I do not know. And we repeatedly speak of time and time, of times and times: 'How long ago did he say this?' 'How long ago did he do this?' 'For how long a time did I fail to see that?' And 'These syllables take twice the time of that single, short syllable.' We speak in this way, and hear people saying this, and we are understood and we understand. These usages are utterly commonplace and everyday. Yet they are deeply obscure and the discovery of the solution is new.

xxiii (29)   I have heard a learned person say that the movements of sun, moon, and stars in themselves constitute time.[25] But I could not agree. Why should not time consist rather of the movement of all physical objects? If the heavenly bodies were to cease and a potter's wheel were revolving, would there be no time by which we could measure its gyrations, and say that its revolutions were equal; or if at one time it moved more slowly and at another time faster, that some rotations took longer, others less? And when we utter these words do not we also speak in time? In our words some syllables are long, others short, in that the sounding of the former requires a longer time, whereas the latter are shorter.

God grant to human minds to discern in a small thing universal truths valid for both small and great matters. There are stars and heavenly luminaries to be 'for signs and for times, and for days and for years' (Gen. 1: 14). But I would not say that a revolution of that wooden wheel is a day; and that learned friend could not assert that its rotation was not a period of time.

(30)   I desire to understand the power and the nature of time, which enables us to measure the motions of bodies and to say that, for instance, this movement requires twice as long as that. I have this question to raise: the word 'day' is used not only of the interval of time when the sun is up over the earth, so that day is one thing, night another, but also of the sun's entire circuit from east to west, as when we say 'so many days have passed' where 'so many days' includes the nights, and the periods of night-time are not counted

---

[25] Plotinus (3. 7. 8. 8–19) likewise rejects this view. The opinion is to be found in St Basil. But Augustine may have in mind Plato's *Timaeus* (39 cd) which was available in Cicero's Latin version. Numerous ancient writers, from the author of Genesis 1: 14 onwards, observed that our years, months, and days are based on the cycle of heavenly bodies. But Augustine's argument is that no clue about the nature of time can be derived from this, or from the movement of any physical body. Time is not identical with the units by which we ordinarily measure it.

separately. So a complete day is marked by the movement and circuit of the sun from east to west. My question then is whether the sun's movement itself constitutes the day?[26] or the actual interval of time during which it is accomplished? or both?

In the first instance, it would still be a day even if the sun completed its course in the space of a single hour. In the second case, it would not be a day if from one sunrise to the next so short an interval as one hour passed, but only if the sun completed a day of twenty-four hours. In the third case—a day being both the circuit and the time taken—it could not be called a day if the sun completed its entire circuit in an hour, nor if the sun ceased to move and the length of time passed were the twenty-four hours normally taken by the sun in completing its entire course from sunrise to sunrise. I will not, therefore, now investigate what it is which we call a day, but the nature of time by which we can measure the sun's circuit and by which we might say that, if all was accomplished in twelve hours, the sun had completed its course in half the usual time. I ask what time is when we make a comparison and say that one interval is single and another double, even if the sun were to make its transit from east to west sometimes in single time, sometimes in twice the time.

Let no one tell me then that time is the movements of heavenly bodies. At a man's prayer the sun stood still, so that a battle could be carried through to victory (Josh. 10: 12 ff.): the sun stopped but time went on. That battle was fought and completed in its own space of time such as was sufficient for it. I therefore see that time is some kind of extension. But do I really see that? Or do I imagine that I see? You, light and truth, will show me.

xxiv (31)   Do you command me to concur if someone says time is the movement of a physical entity? You do not. For I learn that no body can be moved except in time. You tell me so, but I do not learn that the actual movement of a body constitutes time. That is not what you tell me. For when a body is moved, it is by time that I measure the duration of the movement, from the moment it begins until it ends. Unless I have observed the point when it begins, and if its movement is continuous so that I cannot observe when it ceases, I am unable to measure except for the period from the beginning to

[26] Plotinus (3. 7. 12. 34) has the same illustration.

the end of my observation. If my observing lasts for a considerable time, I can only report that a long time passed, but not precisely how much. When we say how much, we are making a comparison—as, for example, 'This period was of the same length as that', or 'This period was twice as long as that', or some such relationship.

If, however, we have been able to note the points in space from which and to which a moving body passes, or the parts of a body when it is spinning on its axis, then we can say how much time the movement of the body or its parts required to move from one point to another. It follows that a body's movement is one thing, the period by which we measure is another. It is self-evident which of these is to be described as time. Moreover, a body may sometimes be moving, sometimes be at rest. We measure by time and say 'It was standing still for the same time that it was in movement', or 'It was still for two or three times as long as it was in movement', or any other measurement we may make, either by precise observation or by a rough estimate (we customarily say 'more or less'). Therefore time is not the movement of a body.

xxv (32)   I confess to you, Lord, that I still do not know what time is, and I further confess to you, Lord, that as I say this I know myself to be conditioned by time. For a long period already I have been speaking about time, and that long period can only be an interval of time. So how do I know this, when I do not know what time is? Perhaps what I do not know is how to articulate what I do know. My condition is not good if I do not even know what it is I do not know. See, my God, 'before you I do not lie' (Gal. 1: 21). As I speak, so is my heart. You, Lord, 'will light my lamp'. Lord, my God, 'you will lighten my darknesses' (Ps. 17: 29).

xxvi (33)   My confession to you is surely truthful when my soul declares that times are measured by me. So my God, I measure, and do not know what I am measuring. I measure the motion of a body by time. Then am I not measuring time itself? I could not measure the movement of a body, its period of transit and how long it takes to go from A to B, unless I were measuring the time in which this movement occurs. How then do I measure time itself? Or do we use a shorter time to measure a longer time, as when, for example, we measure a transom by using a cubit length? So we can be seen to use the length of a short syllable as a measure when we say that a long syllable is twice its length. By this method we measure poems by the number of lines, lines by the number of feet, feet by the number of syllables, and long vowels by short, not by the number of pages (for that would give us a measure of space, not of time). The criterion is the time words occupy in recitation, so that we say 'That is a long poem, for it consists of so many lines. The lines are long, for they consist of so many feet. The feet are long for they extend over so many syllables. The syllable is long, for it is double the length of a short one.'

Nevertheless, even so we have not reached a reliable measure of time. It may happen that a short line, if pronounced slowly, takes longer to read aloud than a longer line taken faster. The same principle applies to a poem or a foot or a syllable. That is why I have come to think that time is simply a distension.[27] But of what is it a distension? I do not know, but it would be surprising if it is not that of the mind itself. What do I measure, I beg you, my God, when I say without precision 'This period is longer than that', or with precision 'This is twice as long as that'? That I am measuring time I know. But I am not measuring the future which does not yet exist, nor the present which has no extension, nor the past which is no longer in being. What then am I measuring? Time as it passes but not time past? That is what I affirmed earlier.

xxvii (34)   Stand firm, my mind, concentrate with resolution. 'God is our help, he has made us and not we ourselves' (Ps. 61: 9; 99: 3). Concentrate on the point where truth is beginning to dawn. For example, a physical voice begins to sound. It sounds. It continues to sound, and then ceases. Silence has now come, and the voice is past. There is now no sound. Before it sounded it lay in the future. It could not be measured because it did not exist; and now it cannot be measured because it has ceased to be. At the time when it was sounding, it was possible because at that time it existed to be

---

[27] Plotinus 3. 7. 11. 41 (tr. Armstrong) speaks of time as 'a spreading out (*diastasis*) of life . . . the life of the soul in a movement of passage from one way of life to another'. This text may have influenced Augustine's coining of the term *distentio*. But in Augustine this psychological experience of the spreading out of the soul in successiveness and in diverse directions is a painful and anxious experience, so that he can speak of salvation as deliverance from time (cf. above, IX. iv (10)). The theme is developed below, especially in XI. xxix (39) where St Paul's language about 'being stretched' (Phil. 3: 13) becomes linked with the thought of Plotinus (6. 6. 1. 5) that multiplicity is a falling from the One and is 'extended in a scattering'.

measured. Yet even then it had no permanence. It came and went. Did this make it more possible to measure? In process of passing away it was extended through a certain space of time by which it could be measured, since the present occupies no length of time. Therefore during that transient process it could be measured. But take, for example, another voice. It begins to sound and continues to do so unflaggingly without any interrruption. Let us measure it while it is sounding; when it has ceased to sound, it will be past and will not exist to be measurable. Evidently we may at that stage measure it by saying how long it lasted. But if it is still sounding, it cannot be measured except from the starting moment when it began to sound to the finish when it ceased. What we measure is the actual interval from the beginning to the end. That is why a sound which has not yet ended cannot be measured: one cannot say how long or how short it is, nor that it is equal to some other length of time or that in relation to another it is single or double or any such proportion. But when it has come to an end, then it will already have ceased to be. By what method then can it be measured?

Nevertheless we do measure periods of time. And yet the times we measure are not those which do not yet exist, nor those which already have no existence, nor those which extend over no interval of time, nor those which reach no conclusions. So the times we measure are not future nor past nor present nor those in process of passing away. Yet we measure periods of time.

(35) 'God, Creator of all things'—*Deus Creator omnium*[28]—the line consists of eight syllables, in which short and long syllables alternate. So the four which are short (the first, third, fifth, and seventh) are single in relation to the four long syllables (the second, fourth, sixth and eighth). Each of the long syllables has twice the time of the short. As I recite the words, I also observe that this is so, for it is evident to sense-perception. To the degree that the sense-perception is unambiguous, I measure the long syllable by the short one, and perceive it to be twice the length. But when one syllable sounds after another, the short first, the long after it, how shall I keep my hold on the short, and how use it to apply a measure to the long, so as to verify that the long is twice as much? The long does not begin to sound unless the short has ceased to sound. I can

[28] Ambrose's evening hymn.

hardly measure the long during the presence of its sound, as measuring becomes possible only after it has ended. When it is finished, it has gone into the past. What then is it which I measure? Where is the short syllable with which I am making my measurement? Where is the long which I am measuring? Both have sounded; they have flown away; they belong to the past. They now do not exist. And I offer my measurement and declare as confidently as a practised sense-perception will allow, that the short is single, the long double—I mean in the time they occupy. I can do this only because they are past and gone. Therefore it is not the syllables which I am measuring, but something in my memory which stays fixed there.

(36) So it is in you, my mind, that I measure periods of time.[29] Do not distract me; that is, do not allow yourself to be distracted by the hubbub of the impressions being made upon you. In you, I affirm, I measure periods of time. The impression which passing events make upon you abides when they are gone. That present consciousness is what I am measuring, not the stream of past events which have caused it. When I measure periods of time, that is what I am actually measuring. Therefore, either this is what time is, or time is not what I am measuring.

What happens when we measure silences and say that a given period of silence lasted as long as a given sound? Do we direct our attention to measuring it as if a sound occurred, so that we are enabled to judge the intervals of the silences within the space of time concerned? For without any sound or utterance we mentally recite poems and lines and speeches, and we assess the lengths of their movements and the relative amounts of time they occupy, no differently from the way we would speak if we were actually making sounds. Suppose someone wished to utter a sound lasting a long time, and decided in advance how long that was going to be. He would have planned that space of time in silence. Entrusting that to his memory he would begin to utter the sound which continues until it has reached the intended end. It would be more accurate to say the utterance has sounded and will sound. For the part of it which is complete has sounded, but what remains will sound, and

---

[29] Plotinus (3. 7. 11): Time is the soul's passing from one state of life to another, and is not outside the soul.

so the action is being accomplished as present attention transfers the future into the past. The future diminishes as the past grows, until the future has completely gone and everything is in the past.

xxviii (37)   But how does this future, which does not yet exist, diminish or become consumed? Or how does the past, which now has no being, grow, unless there are three processes in the mind which in this is the active agent? For the mind expects and attends and remembers, so that what it expects passes through what has its attention to what it remembers. Who therefore can deny that the future does not yet exist? Yet already in the mind there is an expectation of the future. Who can deny that the past does not now exist? Yet there is still in the mind a memory of the past. None can deny that present time lacks any extension because it passes in a flash. Yet attention is continuous, and it is through this that what will be present progresses towards being absent. So the future, which does not exist, is not a long period of time. A long future is a long expectation of the future. And the past, which has no existence, is not a long period of time. A long past is a long memory of the past.

(38)   Suppose I am about to recite a psalm which I know. Before I begin, my expectation is directed towards the whole. But when I have begun, the verses from it which I take into the past become the object of my memory. The life of this act of mine is stretched two ways, into my memory because of the words I have already said and into my expectation because of those which I am about to say. But my attention is on what is present: by that the future is transferred to become the past. As the action advances further and further, the shorter the expectation and the longer the memory, until all expectation is consumed, the entire action is finished, and it has passed into the memory. What occurs in the psalm as a whole occurs in its particular pieces and its individual syllables. The same is true of a longer action in which perhaps that psalm is a part. It is also valid of the entire life of an individual person, where all actions are parts of a whole, and of the total history of 'the sons of men' (Ps. 30: 20) where all human lives are but parts.

xxix (39)   'Because your mercy is more than lives' (Ps. 62: 4), see how my life is a distension[30] in several directions. 'Your right hand

[30] See above XI. xxvi (33).

upheld me' (Ps. 17: 36; 62: 9) in my Lord, the Son of man who is mediator between you the One and us the many, who live in a multiplicity of distractions by many things; so 'I might apprehend him in whom also I am apprehended' (Phil. 3: 12–14), and leaving behind the old days I might be gathered to follow the One, 'forgetting the past' and moving not towards those future things which are transitory but to 'the things which are before' me, not stretched out in distraction but extended in reach, not by being pulled apart but by concentration. So I 'pursue the prize of the high calling' where I 'may hear the voice of praise' and 'contemplate your delight' (Ps. 25: 7; 26: 4) which neither comes nor goes. But now 'my years pass in groans' (Ps. 30: 11) and you, Lord, are my consolation. You are my eternal Father, but I am scattered in times whose order I do not understand. The storms of incoherent events tear to pieces my thoughts, the inmost entrails of my soul, until that day when, purified and molten by the fire of your love, I flow together[31] to merge into you.

xxx (40)   Then shall I find stability and solidity in you, in your truth which imparts form to me. I shall not have to endure the questions of people who suffer from a disease which brings its own punishment and want to drink more than they have the capacity to hold. They say 'What was God doing before he made heaven and earth?', or 'Why did he ever conceive the thought of making something when he had never made anything before?'[32] Grant them, Lord, to consider carefully what they are saying and to make the discovery that where there is no time, one cannot use the word 'never'. To say that God has never done something is to say that there is no time when he did it. Let them therefore see that without the creation no time can exist, and let them cease to speak that vanity (Ps. 143: 8). Let them also be 'extended' towards 'those things which are before' (Phil. 3: 13), and understand that before all times you are eternal Creator of all time. Nor are any times or created thing coeternal with you, even if there is an order of creation which transcends time.[33]

---

[31] Augustine's image of the historical process is that of a flowing river or rivers, with many stormy cataracts. Underlying this passage is the language of Plotinus (6. 6. 1. 5) about the fall away from the One as a scattering and an extending. Temporal successiveness is an experience of disintegration; the ascent to divine eternity is a recovery of unity.

[32] See XI. xii (14), above.

[33] That is, the order of angels: *City of God* 12. 16. See below XII. ix (9).

xxxi (41)   Lord my God, how deep is your profound mystery, and how far away from it have I been thrust by the consequences of my sins. Heal my eyes and let me rejoice with your light. Certainly if there were a mind endowed with such great knowledge and prescience that all things past and future could be known in the way I know a very familiar psalm, this mind would be utterly miraculous and amazing to the point of inducing awe. From such a mind nothing of the past would be hidden, nor anything of what remaining ages have in store, just as I have full knowledge of that psalm I sing. I know by heart what and how much of it has passed since the beginning, and what and how much remains until the end. But far be it from you, Creator of the universe, creator of souls and bodies, far be it from you to know all future and past events in this kind of sense. You know them in a much more wonderful and much more mysterious way. A person singing or listening to a song he knows well suffers a distension or stretching in feeling and in sense-perception from the expectation of future sounds and the memory of past sound. With you it is otherwise. You are unchangeably eternal, that is the truly eternal Creator of minds. Just as you knew heaven and earth in the beginning without that bringing any variation into your knowing, so you made heaven and earth in the beginning without that meaning a tension between past and future in your activity. Let the person who understands this make confession to you. Let him who fails to understand it make confession to you. How exalted you are, and the humble in heart are your house (Ps. 137: 6; 145: 8). You lift up those who are cast down (Ps. 144: 14; 145: 8), and those whom you raise to that summit which is yourself do not fall.

BOOK XII

Platonic and Christian Creation

i (1)   In my needy life, Lord, my heart is much exercised under the impact made by the words of your holy scripture. All too frequently the poverty of human intelligence has plenty to say, for inquiry employs more words than the discovery of the solution; it takes longer to state a request than to have it granted, and the hand which knocks has more work to do than the hand which receives.[1] We hold on to the promise, which none can make null and void. 'If God is for us, who can be against us?' (Rom. 8: 31). 'Ask and you shall receive, seek and you shall find, knock and the door shall be opened to you. For everyone who asks receives and the door is opened to the one who knocks' (Matt. 7: 7–8). These are your promises, and when the promise is given by the Truth, who fears to be deceived?

ii (2)   My humble tongue makes confession to your transcendent majesty that you were maker of heaven and earth—this heaven which I see, the earth which I tread under foot and is the source of the earthly body which I carry. You were their maker. But where is the 'heaven of heaven', Lord, of which we have heard in the words of the psalm: 'The heaven of heaven belongs to the Lord, but the earth he has given to the sons of men' (Ps. 113: 16)? Where is the heaven which we do not see, compared with which everything we can see is earth? For this physical totality, which is not in its entirety present in every part of it,[2] has received a beautiful form in its very lowest things, and at the bottom is our earth. But in comparison with 'the heaven of heaven', even the heaven of our earth is earth. And it is not absurd to affirm that both of these vast physical systems are earth in relation to that heaven whose nature lies beyond knowledge, which belongs to the Lord, not to the sons of men.

---

[1] An echo of Cicero's *Hortensius*, cited in VIII. vii (17).

[2] The idea is in Plotinus 2. 3. 13. That even the lowest things have their proper beauty is in 3. 2. 7. 42–3.

The citation from the Psalter is one of very few to be marked as such.

iii (3)   Certainly this earth 'was invisible and unorganized' (Gen. 1: 2), a kind of deep abyss over which there was no light because it had no form. So at your command it was written that 'darkness was over the abyss'. This simply means the absence of light. For if light existed, it could only be above, shining down from on high. Where, then, light did not yet exist, the presence of darkness was the lack of light. That is why the darkness was 'above', because the light above it was not present, just as when there is no sound there is silence, and the place where there is silence, is the place where there is no sound. Is it not you, Lord, who instructed the soul which is making confession to you? Do I not owe to you the insight that before you gave form and particularity to that 'unformed matter' (Wisd. 11: 18), there was nothing—no colour, no shape, no body, no spirit? Yet it was not absolute nothingness. It was a kind of formlessness without any definition.

iv (4)   To give slower minds some notion of the meaning here no word is available except that of familiar usage. But among all the parts of the world what can be found to be closer to total formlessness than earth and abyss? For because of their lowly position they are less beautiful than all other things which are full of light and radiance. I have no reason to doubt that the formlessness of matter, which by your creation was made lacking in all definition and was that out of which you made so lovely a world, is conveniently described for human minds in the words 'the earth invisible and unorganized'.

v (5)   In this matter thought seeks to grasp what perception has touched, and says to itself: 'It is not an intellectual form like life or justice, because it is matter out of which bodies are made. Nor is it accessible to sense-perception, since in what is invisible and unorganized there is nothing of what we see and perceive.' Human thinking employs words in this way; but its attempts are either a knowing which is aware of what is not knowable or an ignorance based on knowledge.[3]

---

[3] The language and ideas here are in Plotinus 2. 4. 10 (the indefiniteness of matter cannot be the object of definite knowledge; yet the not knowing is capable of positive statement).

In a later letter (130) Augustine epigrammatically sums up his view of the inadequacy of human talk about God in the phrase 'learned ignorance'.

vi (6)   For myself, Lord, if I am to confess to you with my mouth
and my pen everything you have taught me about this question of
matter, the truth is that earlier in life I heard the word but did not
understand it, and those who spoke to me about it [the Manichees]
did not understand it either. I used to think of it as having countless
and varied shapes,[4] and therefore I was not thinking about matter at
all. My mind envisaged foul and horrible forms nevertheless. I used
to use the word formless not for that which lacked form but for that
which had a form such that, if it had appeared, my mind would have
experienced revulsion from its extraordinary and bizarre shape, and
my human weakness would have been plunged into confusion. But
the picture I had in my mind was not the privation of all form, but
that which is relatively formless by comparison with more beautiful
shapes. True reasoning convinced me that I should wholly subtract
all remnants of every kind of form if I wished to conceive the
absolutely formless.[5] I could not achieve this. I found it easier to
suppose something deprived of all form to be non-existent than to
think something could stand between form and nothingness, neither
endowed with form nor nothing, but formless and so almost nothing.

From this point onwards my mind ceased to question my spirit
which was full of images of bodies endowed with forms which
it could change and vary at will. I concentrated attention on the
bodies themselves and gave a more critical examination to the
mutability by which they cease to be what they were and begin to be
what they were not. I suspected that this passing from form to form
took place by means of something that had no form, yet was not
absolutely nothing. I wanted to know, not to suspect. If my voice
and pen were to confess to you all that you disentangled for me in
examining this question, no reader would have the patience to
follow the argument. Nevertheless my heart will never cease to give
you honour for this, and to sing your praises for this, which I have
not strength to express. For the mutability of changeable things is
itself capable of receiving all forms into which mutable things can
be changed. But what is this mutability? Surely not mind? Surely

[4] Simplicius *Commentary on Epictetus* 34 (27 p. 168 Salmasius) reports that Mani's
Prince of Darkness has 5 shapes: lion's head, eagle's shoulders, serpent's stomach, fish's
tail, demon's feet. The concept of matter in Manicheism is wholly different from that in
Neoplatonism. For Plotinus 3. 6. 10–13 matter is so distinct from form as to be as
immutable as God.

[5] The process of intellectual abstraction is described by Plotinus 1. 8. 9.

not body? Surely not the appearances of mind and body? If one could speak of 'a nothing something' or 'a being which is non-being', that is what I would say. Nevertheless it must have had some kind of prior existence to be able to receive the visible and ordered forms.[6]

vii (7)   Where could this capacity come from except from you, from whom everything has being insofar as it has being? But the further away from you things are, the more unlike you they become[7]— though this distance is not spatial. And so you, Lord, are not one thing here, another thing there, but the selfsame, very being itself, 'holy, holy, holy, Lord God almighty' (Isa. 6: 3; Rev. 4: 8). In the beginning, that is from yourself, in your wisdom which is begotten of your substance, you made something and made it out of nothing. For you made heaven and earth not out of your own self, or it would be equal to your only-begotten Son and therefore to yourself. It cannot possibly be right for anything which is not of you to be equal to you. Moreover, there was nothing apart from you out of which you could make them, God one in three and three in one.[8] That is why you made heaven and earth out of nothing, a great thing and a little thing, since you, both omnipotent and good, make all things good, a great heaven and a little earth. You were, the rest was nothing. Out of nothing you made heaven and earth, two entities, one close to you, the other close to being nothing; the one to which only you are superior, the other to which what is inferior is nothingness.

viii (8)   But the 'heaven of heaven' is yours, Lord. The earth which you gave to the sons of men to see and to touch was not such as we now see and touch. For it was 'invisible and unorganized', and an abyss above which there was no light. 'Darkness above the abyss' implies more darkness than 'in' the abyss. This abyss, now of visible waters, has even in its depths a light of its own, which is somehow visible to fish and to living creatures creeping along its bottom. But at that first stage the whole was almost nothing because

---

[6] Plotinus 3. 6 argues that only things with body are passible; not only are souls always active, never passive, but matter also is unaffected by form, incorporeal and ghostly, an underlying substrate which is non-being, apparently seeming to be either soul or body without being either (3. 6. 7).

[7] Plotinus 6. 9. 9. 12: we exist more as we turn to him, less as we turn away.

[8] 'Una trinitas et trina unitas'. Cf. below XIII. xxii (32).

it was still totally formless. However, it was already capable of receiving form. For you, Lord, 'made the world of formless matter' (Wisd. 11: 18). You made this next-to-nothing out of nothing, and from it you made great things at which the sons of men wonder. An extraordinary wonder is the physical heaven, the solid firmament or barrier put between water and water on the second day after the creating of light, when you said 'Let it be made' and so it was made. This firmament you called 'heaven', but a heaven to this earth and sea, which you made on the third day by giving visible shape to formless matter which you made before any day existed at all. Already you made heaven before any day, and that is the 'heaven of this heaven', because in the beginning you had made heaven and earth. But the earth itself which you had made was formless matter; for it was 'invisible and unorganized and darkness was above the abyss'. From the invisible and unorganized earth, from this formlessness, from this next-to-nothing, you made all these things of which this mutable world consists, yet in a state of flux. Its mutability is apparent in the fact that passing time can be perceived and measured. For the changes of things make time as their forms undergo variation and change. The matter underlying them is the 'invisible earth' of which I have been speaking.

ix (9)   That is why the Spirit, the teacher of your servant (Moses), in relating that in the beginning you made heaven and earth, says nothing about time and is silent about days. No doubt the 'heaven of heaven' which you made in the beginning is a kind of creation in the realm of the intellect.[9] Without being coeternal with you, O Trinity, it nevertheless participates in your eternity. From the sweet happiness of contemplating you, it finds power to check its mutability. Without any lapse to which its createdness makes it liable, by cleaving to you it escapes all the revolving vicissitudes of the temporal process. But even that formlessness, the 'invisible and unorganized earth', is not counted among the days of creation week. For where there is no form, no order, nothing comes or goes into the past, and where this does not happen, there are obviously no days and nothing of the coming and passing of temporal periods.

x (10)   May the truth, the light of my heart, not my darkness,

---

[9] Augustine interprets Genesis 1 not to describe any material creation, but the intelligible realm of mind. His 'heaven of heaven' is, like the world-soul in Porphyry (*Sententiae* 30), created but eternally contemplating the divine.

speak to me. I slipped down into the dark and was plunged into obscurity. Yet from there, even from there I loved you. 'I erred and I remembered you' (Ps. 118: 176). 'I heard your voice behind me' (Ezek. 3: 12) calling me to return. And I could hardly hear because of the hubbub of people who know no peace. Now, see, I am returning hot and panting to your spring. Let no one stand in my path. Let me drink this and live by it. May I not be my own life. On my own resources I lived evilly. To myself I was death. In you I am recovering life. Speak to me, instruct me, I have put faith in your books. And their words are mysteries indeed.

xi (11)   Already you have said to me, Lord, with a loud voice in my inner ear, that you are eternal. 'You alone have immortality' (1 Tim. 6: 16), for you are changed by no form or movement, nor does your will undergo any variation at different times. For that is not an immortal will which is first one thing and then another. 'In your sight' (Ps. 18: 15) this truth is clear to me. Let it become more and more evident, I pray you, and as it becomes manifest may I dwell calmly under your wings (cf. Ps. 35: 8).

Again you said to me, Lord, with a loud voice to my inner ear, that you created all natures and substances which are not what you are and nevertheless exist. The only thing that is not from you is what has no existence. The movement of the will away from you, who are, is movement towards that which has less being. A movement of this nature is a fault and a sin, and no one's sin harms you or disturbs the order of your rule, either on high or down below. 'In your presence' (Ps. 18: 15) this truth is clear to me. Let it become more and more evident, I pray you, and as it becomes manifest may I dwell calmly under your wings.

(12)   Again you said to me, in a loud voice to my inner ear, that not even that created realm, the 'heaven of heaven', is coeternal with you. Its delight is exclusively in you. In an unfailing purity it satiates its thirst in you. It never at any point betrays its mutability. You are always present to it, and it concentrates all its affection on you. It has no future to expect. It suffers no variation and experiences no distending in the successiveness of time.[10] O blessed creature, if there be such: happy in cleaving to your felicity, happy to have you as eternal inhabitant and its source of light! I do not find any better

[10] Above, XI. xxix (39).

name for the Lord's 'heaven of heaven' (Ps. 113: 16) than your
House. There your delight is contemplated without any failure or
wandering away to something else. The pure heart enjoys absolute
concord and unity in the unshakeable peace of holy spirits, the
citizens of your city in the heavens above the visible heavens.

(13)   From this may the soul, whose pilgrimage is far off, understand
if it has the experience of thirsting for you. Already its tears have
become its bread, while each day someone says to it: 'Where is your
God?' (Ps. 41: 3–4, 11). It now begs of you and makes this single
request, that it 'may dwell in your house all the days of its life'
(Ps. 26: 4)—and what is its life but you? and what are your 'days' but
your eternity, as are 'your years which do not fail, because you are
the same'? (Ps. 101: 28). From this, then, may the soul with power
to understand grasp how far above time you are in your eternity,
seeing that your House, which is not wandering in alien realms,
although not coeternal with you, nevertheless experiences none of
the vicissitudes of time because, ceaselessly and unfailingly, it
cleaves to you. In your sight this truth is clear to me. May it become
more and more evident, and as it becomes manifest may I dwell
calmly under your wings.

(14)   There is an inexpressible formlessness in the changes under-
gone by the lowest and most inferior creatures. Only a person
whose empty heart makes his mind roll and reel with private
fantasies would try to tell me that temporal successiveness can still
be manifested after all form has been subtracted and annihilated, so
that the only remaining element is formlessness, through the medium
of which a thing is changed and transformed from one species to
another. It is absolutely impossible for time to exist without changes
and movements. And where there is no form, there can be no
changes.[11]

xii (15)   In the light of these reflections, in the measure that you
grant me understanding, Lord, in that you stir me to knock and open
to my knocking, I find there are two things created by you which lie
outside time, though neither is coeternal with you. One of them is
so given form that, although mutable, yet without any cessation of

---

[11] In a section far from easy to follow Plotinus argued that matter, in the sense of the
ultimate formless sludge out of which particular things come to take shape and form, is
immune from change (3. 6. 10–13).

In XI. xxiv (31) above, Augustine has argued that no change can occur except in time.

its contemplation, without any interruption caused by change, it experiences unswerving enjoyment of your eternity and immutability. The other is so formless that it has no means, either in movement or in a state of rest, of moving from one form to another,[12] which is synonymous with being subject to time. But you did not leave it to its formless state since, before any day was created, in the beginning you made heaven and earth, and they are the two of which I have been speaking. 'Now the earth was invisible and unorganized, and darkness was above the abyss.' These words suggest the notion of formlessness to help people who cannot conceive of any kind of privation of form which falls short of utter nothingness. Out of this were made a second heaven and a visible ordered earth and beautiful waters and everything else mentioned in the creation narrative after days had come into existence. These things are such that they are subject to ordered changes of movement and form, and so are subject to the successiveness of time.

xiii (16)   This is my provisional understanding, my God, when I hear your scripture saying 'In the beginning God made heaven and earth. Now the earth was invisible and unorganized and darkness was above the abyss' (Gen. 1: 1–21). It does not mention a day as the time when you did this. My provisional interpretation of that is that 'heaven' means the 'heaven of heaven', the intellectual, non-physical heaven where the intelligence's knowing is a matter of simultaneity—not in part, not in an enigma, not through a mirror, but complete, in total openness, 'face to face' (1 Cor. 13: 12). This knowing is not of one thing at one moment and of another thing at another moment, but is concurrent without any temporal successiveness. 'Earth' I take to mean the invisible and unorganized earth which experiences no temporal succession in which first this happens, then that. Where there is no form, there can be no differentiation of this and that. So my interim judgement is that when scripture mentions no days in saying 'In the beginning God created heaven and earth', the reason for this is that it is referring to these two things. The one is endowed with form from the very first, the other is utterly formless; the one, 'heaven' being the 'heaven of heaven', the other, 'earth', being 'the earth invisible and unorganized'. For scripture immediately goes on to mention the 'earth' to which it was

---

[12] Plotinus (3. 6. 7. 19) speaks of the total impotence of 'matter'.

referring. The fact that scripture says the firmament was made on the second day and calls it heaven suggests what heaven is being referred to in the earlier text where no days are mentioned.

xiv (17)   What wonderful profundity there is in your utterances! The surface meaning lies open before us and charms beginners. Yet the depth is amazing, my God, the depth is amazing.[13] To concentrate on it is to experience awe—the awe of adoration before its transcendence and the trembling of love.[14] Scripture's enemies I vehemently hate (Ps. 138: 22). I wish that you would slay them with a two-edged sword (Ps. 149: 6); then they would no longer be its enemies. The sense in which I wish them 'dead' is this: I love them that they may die to themselves and live to you (Rom. 14: 7–8; 2 Cor. 5: 14–15).

But see, there are others who find no fault with the book of Genesis and indeed admire it. Yet they say: 'The Spirit of God who wrote this by Moses his servant did not intend this meaning by these words; he did not mean what you are saying, but another meaning which is our interpretation.'[15] Submitting to you as arbiter, God of all of us, this is my reply to them.

xv (18)   You will surely not assert to be false what the truth proclaims with a loud voice to my inner ear concerning the true eternity of the Creator, namely that his nature will never vary at different times, and his will is not external to his nature. It follows that he does not will one thing at one time, and another thing at another time. Once and for all and simultaneously, he wills everything that he wills. He does not need to renew his resolution. He does not want this now and that then, nor does he later come to will what formerly he did not will, or reject what previously he wished. For such a will is mutable, and nothing mutable is eternal. 'But our God is eternal' (Ps. 47: 15).

Again, surely you would not deny what he speaks to me in my inner ear, that the expectation of future events becomes direct apprehension when they are happening, and this same apprehension becomes memory when they have passed.

---

[13] Above, III. v (9).

[14] Above, VII. xvii (23); XI. ix (11).

[15] Augustine now turns his critique not on Manichees but on Catholic critics (unidentifiable), dissatisfied perhaps with his exposition of Genesis 1 in his book *De Genesi contra Manichaeos*, written in 388–9.

But every act of attention which undergoes change in this way is mutable, and anything mutable cannot be eternal. But 'our God is eternal'. I put together these propositions, make an inference, and find that my God, the eternal God, did not experience a new act of will when he made the creation, and his knowledge admits no transient element.

(19) What then will you who contradict me say? Are these propositions untrue? 'No', they say. What then? Surely it is not false that the only source of all nature endowed with form and matter capable of form is he who is supremely good because he supremely is. They say, 'We do not deny that.' What then? Do you deny that there is a sublime created realm cleaving with such pure love to the true and truly eternal God that, though not coeternal with him, it never detaches itself from him and slips away into the changes and successiveness of time, but rests in utterly authentic contemplation of him alone? For as it loves you to the extent you command, you, God, show yourself to it and are sufficient for it.[16] So it does not decline from you into self-concern. This House of God is not made of earth, nor is it corporeal made from any celestial mass, but is spiritual and participates in your eternity, because it is without stain for ever. For you have 'established it for ever and ever'; you have 'appointed a law and it will never pass away' (Ps. 148: 6). Yet it is not coeternal with you, because it had a beginning; for it belongs to the created order.

(20) We do not find that time existed before this created realm, for 'wisdom was created before everything' (Ecclus. 1: 4). Obviously that does not mean your wisdom, our God, father of the created wisdom. Your wisdom is manifestly coeternal and equal with you, by whom all things were created, and is the 'beginning' in which you made heaven and earth. Evidently 'wisdom' in this text is that which is created, an intellectual nature which is light from contemplation of the light.[17] For although created, it is itself called wisdom. But just as there is a difference between light which illuminates and that which is illuminated, so also there is an equivalent difference between the wisdom which creates and that which is created, as

---

[16] Analogous language in Plotinus 5. 3. 8. 31 f. on Soul's relation to Mind.

[17] Plotinus 4. 3. 17. 13 and 6. 4. 7. 27 has 'light from light', the derived light (unlike that of the Nicene creed) being inferior.

also between the justice which justifies and the justice created by justification.[18] For even we are said to be your justice. A certain servant of yours says 'That we may be the justice of God in him' (2 Cor. 5: 21). So there was a wisdom created before all things which is a created thing, the rational and intellectual mind of your pure city, our 'mother which is above and is free' (Gal. 4: 6) and is 'eternal in the heavens' (2 Cor. 5: 1). In this text 'heavens' can only be 'the heavens of heavens' which praise you (Ps. 148: 4); this is also the Lord's 'heaven of heaven' (Ps. 113: 16). We do not find there was time before it, because it precedes the creation of time; yet it is created first of all things. However, prior to it is the eternity of the Creator himself. On being created by him it took its beginning—not a beginning in time, since time did not yet exist, but one belonging to its own special condition.

(21)   Therefore it is derived from you, our God, but in such a way as to be wholly other than you and not Being itself. We do not find time either before it or even in it, because it is capable of continually seeing your face and of never being deflected from it. This has the consequence that it never undergoes variation or change. Nevertheless in principle mutability is inherent in it. That is why it would grow dark and cold if it were not lit and warmed by you as a perpetual noonday sun (Isa. 58: 10) because it cleaves to you with a great love. O House full of light and beauty! 'I have loved your beauty and the place of the habitation of the glory of my Lord' (Ps. 25: 7–9), who built you and owns you. During my wandering may my longing be for you! I ask him who made you that he will also make me his property in you, since he also made me. 'I have gone astray like a sheep that is lost' (Ps. 118: 176). But on the shoulders of my shepherd, who built you, I hope to be carried back to you (Luke 15: 4 f.).

(22)   What do you say to me, you opponents whom I was addressing? You contradict my interpretation, though you believe Moses to be God's devout servant and his books to be oracles of the Holy Spirit. Is not this House of God, though not coeternal with God, nevertheless in its own way 'eternal in the heavens' (2 Cor. 5: 1) where you look in vain for the successiveness of time because it is not to be found

---

[18] Augustine distinguishes here (and elsewhere) between the act of God in justification to which there is no human contribution, and the righteousness that grace imparts to transform the co-operating will.

there? For it transcends all distension between past and future, and all the fleeting transience of time. 'It is good for it always to cleave to God' (Ps. 72: 28). 'It is', they say. Which then of those things which 'my heart cried out to my God' (Ps. 17: 7) when it heard inwardly 'the voice of his praise' (Ps. 25: 7), do you now contend to be untrue? Is it that there was a formless matter and that because there was no form there was no order? But where no order existed, there could be no temporal successiveness. And yet this almost nothing, to the degree to which it was not absolutely nothing, was source of whatever exists, insofar as it is anything at all. 'This also', they say, 'we do not deny.'

xvi (23)   Those with whom I wish to argue in your presence, my God, are those who grant the correctness of all these things which your truth utters in my inner mind. Those who deny them may bark as much as they like and by their shouting discredit themselves. I will try to persuade them to be quiet and to allow your word to find a way to them. If they refuse and repel me, I beg you, my God, not to 'stay away from me in silence' (Ps. 27: 1). Speak truth in my heart; you alone speak so. I will leave my critics gasping in the dust, and blowing the soil up into their eyes. I will 'enter my chamber' (Matt. 6: 6) and will sing you songs of love,[19] groaning with inexpressible groanings (Rom. 8: 20) on my wanderer's path, and remembering Jerusalem with my heart lifted up towards it—Jerusalem my home land, Jerusalem my mother (Gal. 4: 26), and above it yourself, ruler, illuminator, father, tutor, husband, pure and strong delights and solid joy and all good things to an unexpressible degree, all being enjoyed in simultaneity because you are the one supreme and true Good. I shall not turn away until in that peace of this dearest mother, where are the firstfruits of my spirit (Rom. 8. 23) and the source of my certainties, you gather all that I am from my dispersed and distorted state to reshape and strengthen me for ever, 'my God my mercy' (Ps. 58: 18). But with those who do not criticize as false all those points which are true, who honour your holy scripture written by that holy man Moses and agree with us that we should follow its supreme authority, but who on some point contradict us, my position is this: You, our God, shall be arbiter between my confessions and their contradictions.

[19] Among Manichee hymns there was one called 'Love Song' to God.

xvii (24)   They say: 'Although this may be true, yet Moses did not
have these two things in mind when by the revelation of the Spirit
he said: "In the beginning God made heaven and earth" (Gen. 1: 1).
By the word "heaven" he did not mean the spiritual or intellectual
creation which continually looks on God's face, nor by the word
"earth" did he intend formless matter.' What then? They say:
'What that man had in mind was what we say he meant, and this is
what he expressed in those words.'

And what is that?

'By the phrase "heaven and earth"', they say, 'Moses meant to
signify in general and concise terms the entire visible world, so that
thereafter under the successive days he could arrange one by one
each category which it pleased the Holy Spirit to list in this way.
The character of the people addressed was rough and carnal, and
so he decided to present to them only the visible works of God.'

They agree, however, that if one understands formless matter to
be referred to as 'the earth invisible and unorganized' and a 'dark
abyss', there is no incongruity. For it was from this that in the
following verses all the visible things, known to everyone, are shown
to be created and ordered during those days.

(25)   What is to be said? Another interpretation may propose that
the phrase 'heaven and earth' is used by anticipation to mean this
formless and chaotic matter, because out of that the visible world
was created and perfected with all the natures which are clearly
evident to us; and this world is by common custom often called
'heaven and earth'. A yet further interpretation could be that 'heaven
and earth' is a proper way to describe invisible and visible nature,
and that by this phrase there is included in these two words the
entire created order which God made in wisdom, that is, in the
beginning. Nevertheless, all things were made not of the very
substance of God but out of nothing, because they are not being
itself, as God is, and a certain mutability is inherent in all things,
whether they are permanent like the eternal House of God or if
they suffer change, like the human soul and body. So the common
material of all things invisible and visible, when still formless but of
course receptive of form, is that from which heaven and earth
originate—that is the invisible and visible creation formed of both
elements. On this view this formless creation is intended by the

words 'the earth invisible and unorganized' and 'darkness above the abyss', but with the difference that 'the invisible and unorganized earth' means physical matter before it was given the quality of form, whereas 'darkness above the abyss' means the spiritual realm before its uncontrolled fluidity was checked[20] and before it was illuminated by wisdom.

(26)   There is a further interpretation that one can hold if one is so inclined, namely that in the text 'In the beginning God made heaven and earth', the words 'heaven and earth' do not mean already perfect and formed visible or invisible natures, but a still unformed beginning of things; what these words refer to is a matter capable of being formed and open to creativeness. In this inchoate state things were confused, not yet distinct in qualities and forms, which now are divided into their own orders and are called 'heaven and earth', the former meaning the spiritual creation, the latter the physical.

xviii (27)   After hearing and considering all these interpretations, I do not wish to 'quarrel about words, for that is good for nothing but the subversion of the hearers' (2 Tim. 2: 14). Moreover, 'the law is good' for edification 'if it is lawfully used, since its end is love out of a pure heart and a good conscience and unfeigned faith.' (1 Tim. 1: 8, 5). Our Master well knows on which two precepts he hung all the law and the prophets (Matt. 22: 40).[21] My God, light of my eyes in that which is obscure, I ardently affirm these things in my confession to you. So what difficulty is it for me when these words [of Genesis] can be interpreted in various ways, provided only that the interpretations are true? What difficulty is it for me, I say, if I understand the text in a way different from someone else, who understands the scriptural author in another sense? In Bible study all of us are trying to find and grasp the meaning of the author we are reading, and when we believe him to be revealing truth, we do not dare to think he said anything which we either know or think to be incorrect. As long as each interpreter is endeavouring to find in the holy scriptures the meaning of the author who wrote it, what evil is it if an exegesis he gives is one shown to be true by you, light of all sincere souls,

---

[20] Plotinus (5. 3. 8. 31) says the light of Intellect (Nous) does not allow the soul to disperse.

[21] Augustine regarded the two commandments to love God and to love one's neighbour as the central principle for the interpretation of all scripture. See below XII. xxv (35).

even if the author whom he is reading did not have that idea and, though he had grasped a truth, had not discerned that seen by the interpreter?

xix (28) It is true, Lord, that you made heaven and earth. It is true that the 'beginning' means your wisdom, in which you made all things (Ps. 103: 24). It is true that the visible world has its vast constituent parts, called heaven and earth in summary description of all natures made and created. It is also true that everything mutable implies for us the notion of a kind of formlessness, which allows it to receive form or to undergo change and modification. It is true that no experience of time can ever touch what has so close an adherence to immutable form that, although mutable, it undergoes no changes. It is true that formlessness, which is next to nothing, cannot suffer temporal successiveness. It is true that the source from which something is made can by a certain mode of speaking bear the name of the thing which is made from it. Hence the kind of formlessness from which heaven and earth are made can be called 'heaven and earth'. It is true that, of all things with form, nothing is closer to the formless than earth and the abyss. It is true that you made not only whatever is created and endowed with form but also whatever is capable of being created and receiving form. From you all things have their existence (1 Cor. 8: 6). It is true that everything which from being formless acquires form, is first formless and is then given form.

xx (29) All these true propositions are no matters of doubt to those to whom you have granted insight to see them with their inward eye, and who unmoveably believe that your servant Moses spoke 'in the spirit of truth' (John 14: 17). On the basis of all these axioms, a view may be urged to this effect: 'In the beginning God made heaven and earth' means that by his Word coeternal with himself God made the intelligible and sensible (or spiritual and corporeal) worlds. Another view could be that 'In the beginning God made heaven and earth' means that by his Word coeternal with himself, God made the universal mass of this physical world with all the natures it contains, manifest and well known to us. A third view might be that 'In the beginning God made heaven and earth' means that by his Word coeternal with himself he made the formless matter of the spiritual and physical creation. A fourth view might be that 'In the beginning God made heaven and earth' means that by his Word coeternal with himself God made the formless matter of the physical creation, when heaven and earth were still chaotic, though now we perceive them to be distinct and endowed with form in the physical mass of the world. A fifth view might say, 'In the beginning God made heaven and earth' means that at the very start of his making and working, God made formless matter containing in a confused condition heaven and earth, but now they are given form and are manifest to us, with all the things that are in them.

xxi (30)   In regard to the interpretation of the words which then follow, on the basis of all those true propositions, a view may be urged to this effect: 'Now the earth was invisible and unorganized and darkness was above the abyss' (Gen. 1: 2) means that the physical stuff which God made was still the formless matter of corporeal things without order or light. Another interpretation would say the text means that this totality called heaven and earth was still formless and dark matter, and out of it were made the physical heaven and physical earth with all the objects in it perceived by the bodily senses. Another interpretation would say that the text means that this totality called heaven and earth was still formless and dark matter, out of which was made the intelligible heaven, elsewhere called 'the heaven of heaven', and the earth, meaning the entire physical world of nature, including under that title the physical heaven also; that is, it was the source for the entire creation, invisible and visible. A yet further view would say the text does not mean that scripture called that formlessness by the name 'heaven and earth; for, it is urged, the formlessness was already in existence and was called 'the invisible and unorganized earth and the abyss', and the scripture had already said that God made heaven and earth, meaning the spiritual and physical creation. Another interpretation is that which says the text means there already existed a kind of formlessness, a matter out of which, scripture previously said, God made heaven and earth, that is the entire physical mass of the world divided into two very large parts, one above, the other below, with all the created beings in them familiar and known to us.

xxii (31)   One might be tempted to object to these last two opinions as follows: 'If you reject the view that this formlessness of matter is called heaven and earth, then something existed which God had not made, out of which he made heaven and earth. For scripture has not recorded that God made this formless matter unless we understand it to be referred to as heaven and earth or as earth alone in the words "In the beginning God made heaven and earth". In the words which come next "Now the earth was invisible and unorganized", though this is how scripture describes formless matter, we shall not understand this except as referring to that which God made, as in the previous text "he made heaven and earth".'

When these objections are heard by those who maintain these two opinions which we have put last in the list, or one or other of them, their reply will be along the following lines: 'We do not deny that the matter made by God was formless, though from God come all things and they are very good (Gen. 1: 31). Just as we say that what is created and given form has more of goodness, so we concede that there is less good in what is created and receptive of form. Nevertheless, it is good. Although scripture has not mentioned that God made this formlessness, it is also true that it has not mentioned the creation of Cherubim and Seraphim, and those powers separately enumerated by the apostle—"thrones, dominations, principalities, powers" (Col. 1: 16). Yet it is evident that God made them all. If in the sentence "he made heaven and earth", everything is included, what are we to say about the waters above which the Spirit was borne (Gen. 1: 2)? If the waters are understood to be included in the heading "earth", how can "earth" then be taken to mean formless matter, when we see how beautiful waters are? Or, if we do accept that exegesis, why does scripture say that out of this formlessness the firmament was made and called heaven, and why does it not say that the waters were made? For waters are not still formless and "invisible". We see them looking beautiful as they flow. If it is being suggested that they received their beauty at the time when God said "Let the water which is under the firmament be gathered together", understanding this gathering to be the bestowing of form, what reply can be made about "the waters which are above the firmament"? They would not have deserved to receive so honourable a position had they lacked form, and scripture does not record the utterance by which they received form. Genesis may be silent on God's making of something; yet sound faith and sure reasoning put it beyond any doubt that God made it. So also no sensible teaching will dare to say that the waters are coeternal with God on the ground that we hear about them in the narrative of the book of Genesis but find no record of when they were made. Why then with truth as our teacher may we not understand that the matter which this text of scripture calls "invisible and unorganized" and "a dark abyss", is formless, made by God out of nothing, and therefore not coeternal with him, even though the narrative omitted to record when it was made?'

xxiii (32)   After hearing and considering these views to the best of my weak capacity, which I confess to you, my God, who know it, I see that two areas of disagreement can arise, when something is recorded by truthful reporters using signs.[22] The first concerns the truth of the matter in question. The second concerns the intention of the writer. It is one thing to inquire into the truth about the origin of the creation. It is another to ask what understanding of the words on the part of a reader and hearer was intended by Moses, a distinguished servant of your faith. In the first category I will not be associated with all those who think they know things but are actually wrong. In the second category I will have nothing to do with all those who think Moses could have said anything untrue. But in you, Lord, those with whom I wish to be associated, and 'in you take my delight' (Ps. 103: 34), are those who feed on your truth in the breadth of charity (Eph. 3: 18–19). Together with them I would approach the words of your book to seek in them your will through the intention of your servant, by whose pen you imparted them to us.

xxiv (33)   Among many truths which are met by inquiring minds in those words which are variously interpreted, which of us can discover your will with such assurance that he can confidently say 'This is what Moses meant and this was his meaning in that narrative' as confidently as he can say, 'Whether Moses meant this or something else, this is true'? See, our God, 'I am your servant' (Ps. 115: 16). I have vowed a sacrifice of confession in this book, and I pray that, of

[22] Augustine was very aware that words mean different things to different people; the 'signs' which are words are ambivalent. His theory of signs enabled him to integrate principles of biblical interpretation with ideas about grammar, rhetoric, and logic; but biblical 'signs' convey sacred mysteries and therefore are particularly open to varied interpretation.

your mercy, I may render to you my vows (Ps. 115: 17–18). I say with utter confidence that in your immutable Word you made all things invisible and visible. I cannot say with equal assurance that this was exactly what Moses had in mind when he wrote 'In the beginning God made heaven and earth'. Though in your truth I see the proposition to be certain, yet I cannot see in Moses' mind that this is what he was thinking when he wrote this. When he wrote 'In the beginning', he could have been thinking of the initial start of the making process. In the words about heaven and earth in this text, he could also have meant not a nature endowed with form and perfection, whether spiritual or physical, but one both inchoate and still formless. I see of course that all the propositions stated above can be true statements. But which of them Moses had in mind in writing these words, I do not see so clearly. Nevertheless, whether it was one of these propositions or some other which I have failed to mention, which that great man had in mind when he uttered these words, I do not doubt that what he saw was true and that his articulation of it in words was appropriate.

xxv (34) 'Let no one trouble me' (Gal. 6: 17) by telling me: 'Moses did not have in mind what you say, but meant what I say'. If someone were to say to me 'How do you know Moses thought what you make his words mean?' I should have to take it in good part and reply perhaps as I have replied above, or at rather greater length if the critic were harder to convince. But when he says 'He did not have in mind what you say but what I say', yet does not deny that what each of us is saying is true, then my God, life of the poor, in whose bosom there is no contradiction, pour a softening rain into my heart that I may bear such critics with patience. They do not say this to me because they possess second sight and have seen in the heart of your servant the meaning which they assert, but because they are proud. They have no knowledge of Moses' opinion at all, but love their own opinion not because it is true, but because it is their own. Otherwise they would equally respect another true interpretation as valid, just as I respect what they say when their affirmation is true, not because it is theirs, but because it is true. And indeed if it is true, it cannot be merely their private property. If they respect an affirmation because it is true, then it is already both theirs and mine, shared by all lovers of the truth. But their contention that

Moses did not mean what I say but what they say, I reject. I do not respect that. Even if they were right, yet their position would be the temerity not of knowledge but of audacity. It would be the product not of insight but of conceit. Lord, 'your judgements are to be feared' (Ps. 118: 120); for your truth does not belong to me nor to anyone else, but to us all whom you call to share it as a public possession. With terrifying words you warn against regarding it as a private possession, or we may lose it (Matt. 25: 14–30). Anyone who claims for his own property what you offer for all to enjoy, and wishes to have exclusive rights to what belongs to everyone, is driven from the common truth to his own private ideas, that is from truth to a lie. For 'he who speaks a lie' speaks 'from his own' (John 8: 44).

(35) Listen, best of judges, God, truth itself, listen to what I say to this opponent, listen. Before you I speak and before my brothers who 'use the law lawfully for the end of charity' (1 Tim. 1: 8, 5). Listen to what I say to him and see (Lam. 1: 9–12) if it is pleasing to you. This is the brotherly and conciliatory reply which I make to him. 'If both of us see that what you say is true and that what I say is true, then where, I ask, do we see this? I do not see it in you, nor you in me, but both of us see it in the immutable truth which is higher than our minds. If then we do not quarrel about the light from the Lord our God, why should we quarrel about the ideas of our neighbour, which we cannot see as clearly as the immutable truth is seen. If Moses himself had appeared to us and said "This is my meaning", even so we would not see it but believe. Therefore "let no one be puffed up for one against another beyond what is written" (1 Cor. 4: 6). "Let us love the Lord our God with all our heart, with all our soul, with all our mind, and our neighbour as ourselves" (Matt. 22: 37–9). On the basis of those two command-ments of love, Moses meant whatever he meant in those books. If we do not believe, we make the Lord a liar (1 John 1: 10; 5: 10) because we attribute to the mind of a fellow servant a notion other than that which he taught. See now how stupid it is, among so large a mass of entirely correct interpretations which can be elicited from those words, rashly to assert that a particular one has the best claim to be Moses' view, and by destructive disputes to offend against charity itself, which is the principle of everything he said in the texts we are attempting to expound.'

xxvi (36) And yet, for my part, my God—you raise high my humble self and give rest to my toil, you hear my confessions and forgive my sins—since you bid me love my neighbour as myself, I cannot believe you gave a lesser gift to your most faithful servant Moses than I would wish and desire to be granted by you, if I had been born at the same time as he, and if you had appointed me to his position. I would wish that through the service of my heart and tongue those books should be published, which later were to be of such assistance to all nations and, throughout the entire world, would conquer by weight of authority the words of all false and proud doctrines. We all come 'from the same lump' (Rom. 9: 21) and 'what is man except that you are mindful of him?' (Ps. 8: 5). So had I been Moses—had I been what he was, and had been commissioned by you to write the book of Genesis, I would have wished to be granted such skill in eloquence and facility of style that those unable to understand how God creates would not set aside the language as beyond their power to grasp; that those who had this ability and by reflection had attained to some true opinions would find in some terse words used by your servant that their true perceptions were not left out of account; and that if, in the light of the truth, another exegete saw a different meaning, that also would not be found absent from the meaning of the same words.

xxvii (37) A spring confined in a small space rises with more power and distributes its flow through more channels over a wider expanse than a single stream rising from the same spring even if it flows down over many places.[23] So also the account given by your minister, which was to benefit many expositions, uses a small measure of words to pour out a spate of clear truth. From this each commentator, to the best of his ability in these things, may draw what is true, one this way, another that, using longer and more complex channels of discourse.

When they read or hear these texts, some people think of God as if he were a human being or a power immanent in a vast mass which, by some new and sudden decision external to itself, as if located in remote places, made heaven and earth, two huge bodies, one high, the other low, containing everything. When they hear 'God said, Let there be that, and that is made', they think of words

---

[23] Plotinus 3. 8. 10. 5 uses the illustration of a spring, but for a different point.

with beginnings and endings, making a sound in time and passing away. They suppose that after the words have ceased, at once there exists that which was commanded to exist, and have other similar notions which they hold because of their familiarity with the fleshly order of things. In such people who are still infants without higher insight, faith is built up in a healthy way, while in their state of weakness they are carried as if at their mother's breast by an utterly simple kind of language. By their faith they hold and maintain with assurance that God made all the natures which their senses perceive around them in all their wonderful variety. If any among them comes to scorn the humble style of biblical language and in proud weakness pushes himself outside the nest in which he was raised, he will fall, poor wretch.[24] 'Lord God, have mercy' (Ps. 55: 2), protect the chick without wings from being trodden on the path by passers-by. Send your angel (Matt. 18: 10) to replace it in the nest, so that it may live until it can fly.

xxviii (38)   There are others for whom these words are no nest but a dark thicket. They see fruit concealed in them, to which they fly in delight, chirping as they seek for it and pluck it. For when they read or hear these words of yours, eternal God, they see that by your stable permanence you transcend all past and future time, and yet there is nothing in the time-conditioned creation which you have not made. Your will, which is identical with your self,[25] has made all things by a choice which in no sense manifests change or the emergence of anything not present before. You did not make the creation out of yourself in your own likeness, the form of all things, but out of nothing, which is a formless dissimilarity[26] to you, though, nevertheless, given form through your likeness. So it returns to you, the One, according to the appointed capacity granted to each entity according to its genus. And all things are very good, whether they abide close to you or, in the graded hierarchy of being, stand further away from you in time and space, in beautiful modifications which they either actively cause or passively receive.

[24] Augustine has himself in mind.

[25] Plotinus 6. 8. 21. 13 says God's will is his substance.

[26] On 'the region of dissimilarity' see above, VII. x (16). The sentence here is remarkable for interpreting 'out of nothing' to mean out of next-to-nothing, relative but not absolute non-being.

To the limited extent that they can grasp the light of your truth in this life those who see these things rejoice.

(39)   One interpreter gives attention to the text 'In the beginning God made' and interprets wisdom to be the 'beginning' because this also 'speaks' to us (John 8: 25). Another interpreter of the same text understands 'beginning' to mean the starting-point of the creation and takes 'in the beginning he made' to mean 'first he made'. Moreover, among those who understand 'in the beginning' to mean 'in wisdom you made heaven and earth', one of them may believe 'heaven and earth' to mean the matter out of which heaven and earth is capable of being created, while another takes the phrase to refer to already formed and distinct natures. Yet another thinks one nature called 'heaven' is endowed with form and spiritual, while the other called 'earth' is formless physical matter. But those who understand 'heaven and earth' to be formless matter do not hold the same interpretation. On one view this is the source from which the intelligible and sensible creation are brought to perfection. On another view it is merely the source from which came the sensible physical mass containing within its vast womb the natures now evident and apparent to our eyes. Furthermore, those who believe that 'heaven and earth' in this passage means that the creatures were made already ordered and distinct, do not interpret this in only one sense. On one view this includes the invisible as well as the visible realm; on another view it refers only to the visible creation, in which we contemplate the heaven as source of light and the dark earth, together with everything they contain.

xxix (40)   However, the interpreter who takes 'in the beginning he made' simply to mean 'first he made' has no alternative but to understand 'heaven and earth' to refer to the matter of heaven and earth—that is, the entire intelligible and physical creation. If he tries to make it mean the entire creation already formed, the question will rightly be put to him what, if God made this first, he went on to make next. After the universe he will find nothing left to create, and will not be pleased to hear the question 'How did he make this first if later he did nothing?'

But if he says that first he made the formless creation, and then that with form, his position is not absurd—not at least if he is capable of distinguishing priority in eternity, priority in time, priority in preference, priority in origin.[27] An instance of priority in eternity would be that of God's priority to everything; of priority in time, that of the blossom to the fruit; of preference that of the fruit to the blossom; of origin, that of sound to song. In these four, the first and last which I have mentioned are the hardest to understand, the middle two very easy. For it is rare to see and very hard to sustain the insight, Lord, of your eternity immutably making a mutable world, and in this sense being anterior. And then who has a sufficiently acute mental discernment to be able to recognize, without intense toil, how sound is prior to song? The difficulty lies in the point that song is formed sound, and something not endowed with form can of course exist, but can what does not exist receive form? In this sense matter is prior to that which is made out of it. It is not prior in the sense that it actively makes; it is rather that it is made. Nor is priority one of temporal interval here. For it is not that first we emit unformed sound without it being song, and later adapt or shape it into the form of a song, in the way we make a box out of wood or a vase out of silver. In the latter instances the materials are in time anterior to the forms of the things made out of them, whereas in the case of a song, that is not so. When a song is sung, the sound is heard simultaneously. It is not that unformed sound comes first and is then shaped into song. Any sound that is made first passes away, and you will find no remnant of it which you can recover to impart coherence to it with artistic skill. That is why a song has its being in the sound it embodies, and its sound is its matter. The matter is given form to be a song. In this sense, as I was saying, the matter of making sound is prior to the form of singing. The priority does not consist in the potentiality to make song. The sound is not the maker causing the singing, but is provided by the body for the singer's soul to turn into song. It is not prior in time. It is emitted at the same time as the song. It is not prior in preference, for sound is not something preferred to song, seeing that song is not merely sound but also beautiful sound. But there is priority in

[27] Aristotle (*Categories* 12. 14a 26 ff.) distinguished five kinds of priority, including Augustine's second, third, and fourth, but not first which has a strongly Neoplatonic ring. The question, also discussed with a different list by Aristotle in the *Metaphysics* (4. 11. 1018b 9 ff.), was important in the debate whether universals are prior to particulars or vice versa. Plotinus alludes to the discussion in 1. 4. 3. 18; 6. 1. 25. 17; 6. 2. 17. 17. Porphyry's commentary on the *Categories* does not survive for this chapter, but is no doubt a likely source for Augustine here.

origin; for a song is not endowed with form to become sound, but sound receives form to become song.

This illustration may help any who can understand that the matter of things was made first and called 'heaven and earth' because heaven and earth were made out of this. But the matter was not made first in a temporal sense, because the forms of things provide the originating cause of the time process. This matter was formless, but now in time matter and form are perceived simultaneously. Nevertheless it is impossible to put into words any statement about formless matter without speaking as if it were prior in time.[28] In value it is on the lowest level, since obviously things with form are better than formless things. It is preceded by the Creator's eternity, so that the material out of which anything is made is itself out of nothing.

xxx (41)   In this diversity of true views, may truth itself engender concord, and may our God have mercy upon us that we may 'use the law lawfully', for the 'end of the precept, pure love' (1 Tim. 1: 8, 5). On this principle if anyone asks me which view was held by Moses your great servant, I would not be using the language of my confessions if I fail to confess to you that I do not know. Yet I know that those interpretations are true except for the carnal notions of which I have given my opinion as I thought right. But those immature in the faith, who are of good hope, are not alarmed by the language of your book, humbly profound and rich in meaning contained in few words. May all of us who, as I allow, perceive and affirm that these texts contain various truths, show love to one another, and equally may we love you, our God, fount of truth—if truth is what we are thirsting after and not vanity. And may we agree in so honouring your servant, the minister of this scripture, full of your Holy Spirit, that we believe him to have written this under your revelation and to have intended that meaning which supremely corresponds both to the light of truth and to the reader's spiritual profit.

xxxi (42)   So when one person has said 'Moses thought what I say', and another 'No, what I say', I think it more religious in spirit to say 'Why not rather say both, if both are true?' And if anyone sees a

[28] Likewise Plotinus 5. 9. 8. 20.

third or fourth and a further truth in these words, why not believe
that Moses discerned all these things? For through him the one
God has tempered the sacred books to the interpretations of many,
who could come to see a diversity of truths. Certainly, to make a
bold declaration from my heart, if I myself were to be writing
something at this supreme level of authority I would choose to write
so that my words would sound out with whatever diverse truth in
these matters each reader was able to grasp, rather than to give a
quite explicit statement of a single true view of this question in such
a way as to exclude other views—provided there was no false
doctrine to offend me. Therefore my God, I do not want to be so
rash as not to believe that Moses obtained this gift from you. When
he wrote this passage, he perfectly perceived and had in mind all
the truth we have been able to find here, and all the truth that could
be found in it which we have not been able, or have not as yet been
able, to discover.

xxxii (43)   Finally, Lord—who are God and not flesh and blood—
even if human insight perceived less than the truth, surely whatever
you were intending to reveal to later readers by those words could
not be hidden from 'your good Spirit who will lead me into the right
land' (Ps. 142: 10). This must be true, even if it were the case that
Moses, through whom this was said, had in mind perhaps only one
out of the many true interpretations. If this was so, we may allow
that the meaning which he had in his mind was superior to all
others. Lord, we beg you to show us either what that one meaning
is or some other true meaning of your choice. Make clear to us
either the understanding possessed by your servant or some other
meaning suggested by the same texts, that we may feed on you and
not be led astray by error.

My Lord God, I pray you, see how much we have written, how
much indeed on only a few words! How much energy and time
would at this rate be required to expound all your books! Grant me
therefore to make confession to you more briefly in commenting on
these words, and to select some one truth which you have inspired,
certain and good, even though many meanings have occurred to me
where several interpretations are possible. The understanding presupposed in my confessions is that if I have said what your minister
meant, that is correct and the best interpretation; and that is the

attempt I have to make. But if I have been unsuccessful in that endeavour, I pray that nevertheless I may say what, occasioned by his words, your truth wished me to say. For that Truth also spoke what it wished to him.

BOOK XIII

Finding the Church in Genesis 1

i (1)   I call upon you, my God, my mercy (Ps. 58: 18). You made
me and, when I forgot you, you did not forget me. I call you into my
soul which you are preparing to receive you through the longing
which you have inspired in it. Do not desert me now that I am
calling on you. Before I called to you, you were there before me.[1]
With mounting frequency by voices of many kinds you put pressure
on me, so that from far off I heard and was converted and called
upon you as you were calling to me. Moreover, Lord, you wiped out
all the evils which merited punishment, so as not to bring the due
reward upon my hands (Ps. 17: 21), by which I fell away from you.
In any good actions of mine you were there before me; in my merits
you were rewarding 'the work of your own hands by which you
made me' (Ps. 118: 73). Before I existed you were, and I had no
being to which you could grant existence. Nevertheless here I am as
a result of your goodness, which goes before all that you made me
to be and all out of which you made me. You had no need of me. I
do not possess such goodness as to give you help, my Lord and my
God. It is not as if I could so serve you as to prevent you becoming
weary in your work, or that your power is diminished if it lacks my
homage. Nor do I cultivate you like land, in the sense that you
would have no one to worship you if I were not doing so. But I serve
and worship you so that from you good may come to me. To you I
owe my being and the goodness of my being.

ii (2)   Your creation has its being from the fullness of your goodness.
In consequence a good which confers no benefit on you, and which
not being from you yourself is not on your level, can nevertheless
have its existence caused by you and so will not lack being. Before
you what merit have heaven and earth, which you made in the
beginning? Let the spiritual and physical creation, which you made
in your wisdom, tell us what merit they have before you. On your
wisdom depended even embryonic and formless things, all of which

---

[1] The theme of I. ii (2) is resumed.

in their own spiritual or physical category move towards the chaos
where there is no control, and to a far off dissimilarity to you.
Formless spiritual being is superior to formed body. Formless
physical entities are better than no existence at all. So formless
things are dependent on your Word. It is only by that same Word
that they are recalled to your Oneness and receive form. From you,
the One, the supreme Good, they have being and are all 'very good'
(Gen. 1: 31). What merit had these things before you even to
receive a formless existence when, but for you, they would not exist
at all?

(3)   What merit before you had physical matter even to be merely
'invisible and unorganized' (Gen. 1: 2)? It would not exist at all
unless you had made it. That it had no existence is the reason why
it had no claim on you to be given existence. What claim upon you
had the inchoate spiritual creation even to be merely in a dark fluid
state like the ocean abyss? It would have been dissimilar[2] to you
unless by your Word it had been converted to the same Word by
whom it was made, so that, illuminated by him, it became light and,
though not in an equal measure, became conformed to a form
equal to you (Rom. 8: 29; Phil. 2: 6). Just as in the case of a physical
body, to be is not the same as to be beautiful, since otherwise it
would be impossible for it to be ugly, so also for a created spirit to
live is not the same as to live wisely; otherwise it would be immutably
wise. But 'it is good for it always to cleave to you' (Ps. 72: 28) lest, by
turning away from you and by slipping back into a life like the dark
abyss, it lose the light it obtained by turning to you. For we also, we are
a spiritual creation in our souls, and have turned away from you our
light. In that life we were 'at one time darkness' (Eph. 5: 8). We toil
on in the remains of our obscurity[3] until, in your unique Son, we
are your 'righteousness' (2 Cor. 5: 21) like 'the mountains of God',
for we were 'your judgements like the deep abyss' (Ps. 35: 7).

iii (4)   Among the first acts of creation you said 'Let there be light,
and light was created' (Gen. 1: 3). I do not think it out of harmony
with the sense if we take this to mean the spiritual creation, since
there already was a kind of life for you to illuminate. But just as it

---

[2] Echo of Plato, *Statesman* 273d; Plotinus 1. 8. 13. 17. Above VII. x (16).

[3] Plotinus 2. 4. 10. 16: When all light has been taken from the soul, the remaining
darkness is indefinable.

had no claim on you to be the sort of life which could be illuminated, so also now that it existed, it had no claim to receive light. Its formlessness could not be pleasing to you unless it were made light not by merely existing but by contemplating the source of light and adhering to it. Both the fact of its life and the fact of its living in a blessed state it owed only to your grace. By a change for the better it has become converted to that which cannot change either for the better or for the worse. That is what you alone are. You alone are in absolute simplicity.[4] To you it is not one thing to live, another to live in blessed happiness, because you are your own blessedness.

iv (5) Even if the creation had either never come into existence or remained formless, nothing could be lacking to the good which you are to yourself. You made it not because you needed it, but from the fullness of your goodness,[5] imposing control and converting it to receive form—but not as if the result brought you fulfilment of delight. The corollary of your perfection is that the imperfection of created things is displeasing. So they seek perfection from you that they may please you, yet it is not that otherwise you would be imperfect and need to be perfected by their perfection. 'Your good Spirit' (Ps. 142: 10) 'was borne above the waters' (Gen. 1: 2), but not borne up by them as if resting weight on them. When scripture says your Spirit rests on people (Isa. 11: 2), it means that the Spirit makes them rest on himself. But your incorruptible and immutable will, sufficient to itself and in itself, was 'borne above' the life which you had made, a life for which to live is not the same as living in perfect happiness, because even while in a fluid state in darkness it had life. It remains for it to be converted to him by whom it was made, more and more to live by the fount of life, to see light in his light (Ps. 35: 10), and to become perfect, radiant with light,[6] and in complete happiness.

---

[4] Plotinus 5. 3. 16 says that the higher the grade in the continuum of the hierarchy of being, the greater the 'simplicity', and that at the summit utter simplicity is wholly self-sufficient. Similarly 5. 4. 1. The concept 'simplicity' for Augustine and the Neoplatonists means freedom from any element of distinction between substance and accidents or attributes, and has overtones of being without need. Goodness is therefore no attribute of Plotinus' One, but is inseparable from the One; cf. Plotinus 2. 9. 1.

[5] Plato, *Timaeus* 29d; Plotinus 5. 4. 1.

[6] Plotinus 5. 3. 17. 28 ff., on the mystical vision, is emphatic that the light by which the soul sees God is not other than the light of God: 'This is the soul's true end, to touch that light and see it by itself, not by another light, but by the light which is also its means of seeing.' (tr. Armstrong).

v (6)   Here in an enigmatic image (1 Cor. 13: 12) I discern the Trinity, which you are, my God. For in the beginning of our wisdom which is your wisdom, Father, begotten of your self, equal to you and coeternal, that is in your Son, you 'made heaven and earth' (Gen. 1: 1). We have said a lot about 'the heaven of heaven' (Ps. 113: 24), about 'the earth invisible and unorganized', and about the 'dark abyss'. It is dark because of the disordered flux of spiritual formlessness; but it became converted to him from whom it derived the humble quality of life it had, and from that illumination became a life of beauty. So it was the heaven of that heaven which was subsequently made to take its place between water and water (Gen. 1: 7). And now where the name of God occurs, I have come to see the Father who made these things; where the 'Beginning' is mentioned, I see the Son by whom he made these things. Believing that my God is Trinity, in accordance with my belief I searched in God's holy oracles and found your Spirit to be borne above the waters. There is the Trinity, my God—Father and Son and Holy Spirit, Creator of the entire creation.[7]

vi (7)   I bring my heart to you, Light that teaches truth. Let not my heart tell me vain fantasies. Disperse its darkness, and tell me—I beg you by love, our mother,[8] I beg you tell me: what was the reason why your scripture mentioned your Spirit only after it had mentioned heaven and earth 'invisible and unorganized' and 'darkness above the abyss'? Was it necessary for him to be brought in at this point so that he could be described as being 'borne above'? This could not be said unless first there was a reference to that above which your Spirit could be understood to be borne. For he was not borne above the Father and the Son, and he could not properly be said to be borne above anything if there was nothing above which he could be borne. First, therefore, it was necessary to say what it was that he was borne above, and then to speak of the Spirit, who could not have been described other than as being 'borne above'. Why, therefore, was it inappropriate to introduce the Spirit except with the words that he was 'borne above'?

vii (8)   Against this background the able reader can grasp your apostle's meaning when he is saying that 'love is diffused in our

---

[7] Ambrose (*Hexameron* 1. 8. 29) gives a similar exegesis of Genesis 1.
[8] 'Mother Charity' is a phrase liked by Augustine, also used by him elsewhere.

hearts by the Holy Spirit who is given to us' (Rom. 5: 5). Teaching us concerning the things of the Spirit he demonstrates that the way of charity is 'supereminent' (1 Cor. 12: 1). Moreover, he bows the knee for us to you that we may know 'the supereminent knowledge of the love of Christ' (Eph. 3. 14, 19). And so the Spirit, supereminent from the beginning, was 'borne above the waters.' To whom can I expound, and with what words can I express, the weight of cupidity pulling us downwards into the precipitous abyss and the lifting up of love given by your Spirit who was 'borne above the waters'? To whom can I communicate this? How can I speak about it? For it is not about literal places where we sink down and rise up. This symbolic language contains a resemblance, but also a difference. It means our feelings and our loves. The impurity of our spirit flows downwards because of our love of anxieties, and the holiness which is yours draws us upwards in a love of freedom from anxiety. So we may lift up our heart[9] and hold it to you, where your Spirit is 'borne above the waters', and we come to the supereminent resting-place when our soul has passed over 'the waters that are without substance' (Ps. 123: 5).[10]

viii (9) The angel fell, the human soul fell, and thereby showed that the abyss would have held the entire spiritual creation in deep darkness unless from the beginning you had said 'Let there be light, and light was created' (Gen. 1: 3). Every intellectual being in your heavenly city obediently adhered to you, and rested in your Spirit which is immutably borne above all that is mutable. Otherwise the very 'heaven of heaven' would have been a dark abyss in itself. But now it is 'light in the Lord (Eph. 5: 8). By the wretched restlessness of fallen spirits, manifesting their darkness as they are stripped naked of the garment of your light, you show how great a thing is the rational creature you have made. Whatever is less than you can never be sufficient to provide itself with the rest of contentment, and for this reason it is not even a source of contentment to itself. For you, our God 'will lighten our darkness' (Ps. 17: 29). From you comes our clothing (Isa. 61: 10), and our darkness will become as midday (Isa. 58: 10).

---

[9] The African eucharistic liturgy, echoed here, had 'Lift up your heart' (singular).

[10] Augustine's homily on this psalm explains that these waters are sins. His Old Latin version differs from the Vulgate.

My God, give me yourself, restore yourself to me. See, I love you, and if it is too little, let me love you more strongly. I can conceive no measure by which to know how far my love falls short of that which is enough to make my life run to your embraces, and not to turn away until it lies hidden 'in the secret place of your presence' (Ps. 30: 21). This alone I know: without you it is evil for me, not only in external things but within my being, and all my abundance which is other than my God is mere indigence.

ix (10)   Surely no one supposes that either the Father or the Son was borne above the waters. Indeed if one understands this of a body in space, neither was the Holy Spirit. But if it means the transcendence of immutable divinity above all that is mutable, then Father, Son, and Holy Spirit were borne above the waters. Why then is this said only of the Holy Spirit? Why is it said exclusively of him as if there were a place where he then was, though it is not a place? Of him alone is it said that he is your 'gift' (Acts 2: 38).

In your gift we find our rest. There are you our joy. Our rest is our peace.

Love lifts us there, and 'your good Spirit' (Ps. 142: 10) exalts 'our humble estate from the gates of death' (Ps. 9, 15). In a good will is our peace.[11] A body by its weight tends to move towards its proper place. The weight's movement is not necessarily downwards, but to its appropriate position: fire tends to move upwards, a stone downwards.[12] They are acted on by their respective weights; they seek their own place. Oil poured under water is drawn up to the surface on top of the water. Water poured on top of oil sinks below the oil. They are acted on by their respective densities, they seek their own place. Things which are not in their intended position are restless. Once they are in their ordered position, they are at rest.

My weight is my love. Wherever I am carried,[13] my love is carrying me. By your gift we are set on fire and carried upwards: we grow red hot and ascend. We climb 'the ascents in our heart' (Ps. 83: 6), and sing 'the song of steps' (Ps. 119: 1). Lit by your fire, your good fire, we grow red-hot and ascend, as we move upwards 'to the peace of Jerusalem' (Ps. 121: 6). 'For I was glad when they said to

---

[11] Echoed in Dante, *Paradiso* 3. 85.

[12] Similar analogy for the soul finding its proper habitat in Plotinus 2. 1. 3. On 'good will' cf. Plotinus 6. 8. 6. 32 ff.; 6. 8. 13. 12 ff.

[13] Plotinus (6. 8. 1. 26) also speaks of the will being 'carried away'.

me, let us go to the house of the Lord' (Ps. 121: 1). There we will be brought to our place by a good will, so that we want nothing but to stay there for ever.

x (11) Happy is that created realm which has known nothing other than bliss. Yet the story would have been different unless, by your gift which is 'borne above' all that is mutable, immediately upon its creation it was elevated with no interval of time by that call 'Let there be light,' and it became light. For in us there are distinct moments of time since at one stage we were darkness and then were made light (Eph. 5: 8). But concerning the higher creation, scripture only says what it would have been had it not received light; and the wording of the text speaks as if at an earlier stage it had been in flux and darkness, to emphasize the cause by which it was made to become different. That is, it became light by being turned towards the light that can never fail. Let him who can, understand this. Let him seek help from you and not 'trouble me' (Gal. 6: 17) as if it were in my power 'to light any man coming into this world' (John 1: 9).

xi (12) Who can understand the omnipotent Trinity? Yet everyone speaks about the subject, if indeed it can be the matter of discourse. It is a rare soul who knows what he is talking about when he is speaking of it. People debate and quarrel, and without peace no one sees that vision. I wish that human disputants would reflect upon the triad within their own selves. These three aspects of the self are very different from the Trinity, but I may make the observation that on this triad they could well exercise their minds and examine the problem, thereby becoming aware how far distant they are from it. The three aspects I mean are being, knowing, willing. For I am and I know and I will. Knowing and willing I am. I know that I am and I will. I will to be and to know.[14]

In these three, therefore, let him who is capable of so doing contemplate how inseparable in life they are: one life, one mind, and one essence, yet ultimately there is distinction, for they are inseparable, yet distinct. The fact is certain to anyone by introspection. Let him consider himself and reflect and tell me what is there. When, however, through his investigation of these three, he has

[14] Augustine announces the theme of his large work *On the Trinity*, begun a year or two after the completion of the *Confessions*, but requiring many years to complete. Some of the terminology has affinities with Plotinus (e.g. 6. 4. 14).

found something out and has made his report on that, he should
not suppose that he discovered the immutable that transcends
them—that which immutably is, immutably knows, and immutably
wills. It baffles thought to inquire whether these three functions are
the ground which constitutes the divine Trinity, or whether the
three components are present in each Person, so that each Person
has all three, or whether both these alternatives are true, in the
sense that, in ways beyond finite understanding, the ultimate Being
exists in both simplicity and multiplicity, the Persons being defined
by relation to each other, yet infinite in themselves. So the divine
being is and knows itself and is immutably sufficient to itself,
because of the overflowing greatness of the unity.[15] Who can find a
way to give expression to that? Who would venture in any way
whatever to make a rash pronouncement on the subject?

xii (13)   Proceed with your confession, my faith. Say to the Lord
your God: 'Holy, holy, holy', Lord my God (Isa. 6: 3; Rev. 4: 8). In
your name we are baptized, Father, Son, and Holy Spirit (Matt. 28:
19); in your name we baptize, Father, Son, and Holy Spirit. Among
us also in his Christ God has made a heaven and an earth, meaning
the spiritual and carnal members of his Church. Moreover, before our
earth received form, imparted by doctrine, it was 'invisible and unorganized' (Gen. 1: 2), and we were covered by the darkness (Ps. 54: 6)
of ignorance. For you 'corrected man for his iniquity', and 'your
judgements are like the great abyss' (Ps. 38: 12; 35: 7). But because
your 'Spirit was borne above the waters', your mercy did not abandon
our misery, and you said: 'Let there be light' (Gen. 1: 3). 'Do
penitence, for the kingdom of heaven has drawn near' (Matt. 3: 2;
4: 17). Because our soul was 'disturbed' within ourselves, we
'remembered you, Lord from the land of Jordan and from the
mountain', which is equal to you (Phil. 2, 6) but for our sakes
became 'little' (cf. Ps. 41: 7). Our darknesses displeased us. We
were converted to you (Ps. 50: 15), light was created, and suddenly
we 'who were once darkness are now light in the Lord' (Eph. 5. 8).

xiii (14)   Nevertheless we still act on faith, not yet on sight, 'For by
hope we have been saved' (2 Cor. 5: 7). 'Hope which is seen is not
hope' (Rom. 8: 24). 'Deep' still 'calls to deep', but now 'with the

---

[15] Plotinus 6. 8. 17. 25: The one is wholly self-related. 6. 5. 9. 35: It possesses
multiplicity 'by itself and from itself'.

voice of your cataracts' (Ps. 41: 8). In this life even he who says 'I could not speak to you as spiritual but as carnal' (1 Cor. 3: 1) does not think that he himself has comprehended. He 'forgets the things behind and stretches out to those things which lie ahead' (Phil. 3: 13). Weighed down he groans (2 Cor. 5: 4); 'his soul thirsts for the living God, like a hart for the springs of waters', and says 'when shall I come?' (Ps. 41: 2–3). He wishes to 'put on his habitation from heaven' (2 Cor. 5: 2). To the lower abyss he calls in the words 'Be not conformed to this world, but be reformed in the newness of your mind' (Rom. 12: 2), and 'Be not children in mind but be infants in malice that you may be fully adult in mind' (1 Cor. 14: 20), and 'O foolish Galatians, who has bewitched you?' (Gal. 3: 1). But now he is speaking not with his own voice but with yours. 'You sent your Spirit from on high' (Wisd. 9: 17) through him who 'ascended on high' (Ps. 67: 19), and opened the 'cataracts' of his gifts (Mal. 3: 10), so that 'the flood waters of the river made glad your city' (Ps. 45: 5). For that city the bridegroom's friend (John 3: 29) sighs, having already the firstfruits of the spirit within him; but he still groans within himself 'waiting for the adoption, the redemption of his body' (Rom. 8: 23). For that city he sighs, for he is a member of the bride. For her he is jealous, for he is the bridegroom's friend; for her he is jealous, not for himself. 'By the sound of your cataracts' (Ps. 41: 8), not by his own voice, he calls to the other deep. In his jealousy for it he fears lest 'as the serpent deceived Eve by his subtlety, so also their mind may be corrupted to lose chastity' (2 Cor. 11: 2) which is in our bridegroom, your unique Son. What a beautiful light that will be when 'we shall see him as he is' (1 John 3: 2), and there 'shall pass away the tears which have become my bread day and night, while it is daily said to me, Where is your God?' (Ps. 41: 4).

xiv (15)   I also say: My God, where are you? I see you are there, but I sigh for you a little (Job 32: 20) when I 'pour out my soul upon myself in the voice of exultation and confession, the sound of one celebrating a festival' (Ps. 41: 6). Yet still my soul is sad because it slips back and becomes a 'deep', or rather feels itself still to be a deep. My faith, which you have kindled to be a light before my feet (Ps. 118: 105) in the night, says to it: 'Why are you sad, soul, and why do you disturb me? Hope in the Lord' (Ps. 41: 6). 'His word is a light to your feet' (Ps. 118: 105). Hope and persevere until the night passes which is the mother of the wicked, until the Lord's wrath passes, whose sons we also once were (Eph. 2: 3). We were 'once darkness' (Eph. 5: 8), the remnants[16] of which we bear in the body which 'is dead because of sin' (Rom. 8: 10), 'until the day breathes and the shadows are removed' (Cant. 2: 17). 'Hope in the Lord. In the morning I will stand up and will contemplate you. I will ever confess to him. In the morning I will stand and I will see the salvation of my face' (Ps. 41: 6–12), my God 'who shall vivify even our mortal bodies through the Spirit who dwells in us' (Rom. 8: 11). For in mercy he was 'borne above' the dark and fluid state, which was our inward condition. From him during this wandering pilgrimage, we have received an assurance that we are already light (Eph. 5: 8). While still in this life, we are 'saved by hope' (Rom. 8: 24) and are 'sons of light' and sons of God, 'not sons of the night and of darkness' (1 Thess. 5: 5) which we once were. In this still uncertain state of human knowledge, you alone mark the difference between them and us. You test our hearts (Ps. 16: 3) and call light day and darkness night (Gen. 1: 5). Who can distinguish between us except you? But 'what do we possess which we have not received' from you? (1 Cor. 4: 7). From the same stuff some vessels are made for honourable functions and others are made for dishonourable uses (Rom. 9: 21).

xv (16)   Who but you, O God, has made for us a solid firmament of authority over us in your divine scripture? For 'the heaven will fold up like a book' (Isa. 34: 4), and now 'like a skin it is stretched out' above us (Ps. 103: 2). Your divine scripture has more sublime authority since the death of the mortal authors through whom you provided it for us. You know, Lord, you know how you clothed human beings with skins when by sin they became mortal (Gen. 3: 21). So you have stretched out the firmament of your book 'like a skin', that is your words which are not mutually discordant, and which you have placed over us by the ministry of mortal men. Indeed, by the very fact of their death the solid authority of your utterances published by them is in a sublime way 'stretched out' over everything inferior. While they were alive on earth, it was not stretched out to express this supreme authority. You had not 'stretched out the

---

[16] Above XIII. ii (3).

heaven like a skin', you had not diffused everywhere the renown of their death.[17]

(17) Lord, let us look at 'the heavens, the work of your fingers' (Ps. 8: 4). Dispel from our eyes the cloud with which you have covered them (Ps. 18: 8). There is a testimony to you, 'giving wisdom to infants'. My God, make perfect your 'praise out of the mouths of babes and sucklings' (Ps. 8: 3). We have not come across any other books so destructive of pride, so destructive of 'the enemy and the defender' who resists your reconciliation by defending his sins. I have not known, Lord, I have not met with other utterances so pure, which so persuasively move me to confession, make my neck bow to your yoke, and bring me to offer a free worship. May I understand them, good Father; as I submit to you, grant this to me, since for those who submit you have firmly established the scriptures' authority.

(18) There are, I believe, other waters above this firmament, immortal and kept from earthly corruption. Let them praise your name (Ps. 148: 2–5). Let the peoples above the heavens, your angels, praise you. They have no need to look up to this firmament and to read so as to know your word. They ever 'see your face' (Matt. 18: 10) and there, without syllables requiring time to pronounce, they read what your eternal will intends. They read, they choose, they love. They ever read, and what they read never passes away. By choosing and loving they read the immutability of your design. Their codex is never closed, nor is their book ever folded shut.[18] For you yourself are a book to them and you are 'for eternity' (Ps. 47: 15). You have set them in order above this firmament which you established to be above the weak who are on a lower level so that they could look up and know your mercy, announcing in time you who made time. For 'in heaven, Lord, is your mercy and your truth reaches the clouds' (Ps. 35: 6). 'The clouds pass' (Ps. 17: 13) but the heaven remains. Preachers of your word pass from this life to another life, but your scripture is 'stretched out' over the peoples to the end of the age. 'Heaven and earth will pass away, but your words will not pass away' (Matt. 24: 35).

[17] The 'coats of skins' adopted by Adam and Eve at the Fall symbolize human mortality. The inspired writings of the mortal biblical authors, being stretched above us like 'skin', bring a remedy for our mortality.

[18] This passage inspired one of John Donne's *Devotions*.

For 'the skin will be folded up', and the grass above which it was stretched out will pass away with its beauty; but your word abides for ever (Isa. 40: 6–8). Now your word appears to us in the 'enigmatic obscurity' of clouds and through the 'mirror' of heaven (1 Cor. 13: 12), not as it really is. For although we are beloved by your Son, 'it does not yet appear what we shall be' (1 John 3: 2). 'He looked through the lattice' of our flesh and caressed us and set us on fire; and we run after his perfume (Cant. 2: 9; 1: 3, 11). 'But when he appears, we shall be like him, for we shall see him as he is' (1 John 3: 2). 'As he is' Lord will be ours to see; but it is not yet given to us.

xvi (19) To know you as you are in an absolute sense is for you alone. You are immutably, you know immutably, you will immutably. Your essence knows and wills immutably. Your knowledge is and knows immutably. Your will is and knows immutably. In your sight it does not seem right that the kind of self-knowledge possessed by unchangeable light should also be possessed by changeable existence which receives light.[19] And so my soul is 'like waterless land before you' (Ps. 142: 6). Just as it has no power to illuminate itself, so it cannot satisfy itself. For 'with you is the fountain of life', and so also it is 'in your light' that 'we shall see light' (Ps. 35: 10).

xvii (20) Who has 'gathered the bitter' into one society? (Gen. 1: 9). For they pursue the same end of temporal and earthly felicity. This purpose dominates everything they do, even though the innumerable variety of their anxieties makes them fluctuate from one thing to another. Who, Lord, but you told the waters to gather into one assembly, and caused to appear the dry land, 'which thirsts after you' (Ps. 62: 2–3). For 'the sea is yours and you made it, and the dry land your hands have formed' (Ps. 94: 5). In this text 'sea' means not the bitterness of conflicting wills but the gathering together of waters. You restrain the evil desires of souls, and fix limits to prevent the waters advancing further (Job 38: 10 f.), so that their waves break upon themselves and thus, by the order of your ruling authority which is superior to all things, you make it a sea.

---

[19] In Plotinus 5. 3. 1–2 the self-knowledge possessed by Soul is inferior to that of Intellect (Nous).

(21) But souls which 'thirst after you and appear before you' (Ps. 62: 2–3), souls separated out from the society of 'the sea', you water with your hidden and sweet spring, 'so that the earth also may produce her fruit' (Gen. 1: 12). As the earth produces her fruit, so at your command, the command of its Lord God, our soul yields works of mercy 'according to its kind' (Gen. 1: 12), loving our neighbour in the relief of physical necessities, 'having in itself seed according to its likeness'. Aware of our own infirmity we are moved to compassion to help the indigent, assisting them in the same way as we would wish to be helped if we were in the same distress—and not only in easy ways, like 'the grass bearing seed', but with the protection and aid given with a resolute determination like 'the tree bearing fruit' (Gen. 1: 11). This means such kindness as rescuing a person suffering injustice from the hand of the powerful and providing the shelter of protection by the mighty force of just judgement.[20]

xviii (22) So, Lord, I pray you, as you are the maker, as you are the giver of cheerfulness and of power, let 'truth arise from the earth and justice look down from heaven' (Ps. 84: 12) and let there be 'lights in the firmament' (Gen. 1: 14). Let us 'break our bread to the hungry', and take into our house the homeless destitute; let us clothe the naked and not despise the domestic servants who share our human stock (Isa. 58: 7–8). As these fruits come up in the earth, see that it is good. Let our light which lasts but a short time 'break forth'. Passing from the lower good works of the active life to the delights of contemplation, may we 'hold the word of life' which is above and 'appear as lights in the world' (Phil. 2: 15) by adhering to the solid firmament of your scripture. For there you hold conversation with us to teach us to distinguish between intelligible and sensible things as between day and night, or between souls dedicated to the intelligible realm and souls dedicated to the material world of the senses. Then it is not only you in the secret place of your judgement who divide between light and darkness as you did before the making of the firmament; it is also your spiritual people established in the same solid firmament and distinguished by your grace manifested throughout the world. May they 'give light over the earth and divide day and night and be signs of the times' (Gen. 1: 14). For 'old

[20] Many of Augustine's letters and sermons concern help to destitute persons and protection to people suffering oppression; these activities were a substantial part of a bishop's duties.

things have passed away and new things are created' (2 Cor. 5: 17). 'Our salvation is nearer than when we believed: the night is advanced, the day is near' (Rom. 13: 11 f.). 'You bless the crown of your year' (Ps. 64: 12). 'You send out workmen into your harvest' (Matt. 9: 38) in sowing which 'others have laboured' (John 4: 38). You also send them into another sowing, whose harvest is at the end (Matt. 13: 39). So you answer the prayers of the person who petitions you (Ps. 55: 12), and you bless the years of the just (Ps. 64: 12). But 'you are the same' and in your 'years which never cease' (Ps. 101: 28) you prepare a granary for the passing years. By an eternal design at the appropriate times you give heavenly blessings to the earth.

(23) 'To one is given by the Spirit the word of wisdom', like 'a greater light' (Gen. 1: 16) for the sake of those who delight in the light of truth as for 'the rule of the day'. 'To another is given the word of knowledge by the same Spirit' like 'a lesser light'; 'to another faith, to another the gift of healings, to another miraculous powers, to another prophecy, to another the discernment of authentic spirits, to another a diversity of tongues'. All these are like the stars. For 'all these are the work of one and the same Spirit, dividing appropriate gifts to each person as he wills' (1 Cor. 12: 7–11). He causes stars to appear manifestly for the advantage of all. But the word of knowledge, containing all mysteries[21] (1 Cor. 13: 2) which vary at different times, is like the moon, and the other gifts recorded in the list which are mentioned last are like stars; in principle they belong to the night, inasmuch as they are inferior in brightness to the wisdom in which the 'day' previously mentioned rejoices. They are necessary for those to whom your most judicious servant could not speak as if to spiritual persons but as if to carnal. He speaks wisdom among the perfect. The natural man is as an 'infant in Christ' and a drinker of milk, until he is strengthened for 'solid food' (1 Cor. 3: 1–2; 2: 14; Heb. 5: 12–14), and acquires eyesight strong enough to face the sun. Let him not suppose his night to be destitute of all light, but be content with the light of the moon and stars. These matters you set out most wisely with us, my God, through your book, your solid firmament, so that we may discern

---

[21] Augustine's Latin word is *sacramenta*, which he defines as 'sacred signs'; he says they 'vary' because the Old Testament signs such as circumcision and passover have been succeeded for Christians by baptism and eucharist.

everything by a wonderful contemplation, even though for the present only by signs and times and days and years.

xix (24) But first, 'wash, be clean, remove malice from your souls and from the sight of my eyes' that the dry land may appear. 'Learn to do good; judge in favour of the orphan and vindicate the widow' that the land may produce pasture and fruitful trees. 'And come, says the Lord, let us reason together' (Isa. 1: 16–18), so that lights may be made in the firmament of heaven and give light over the earth. The rich man inquired of the good Master what he should do to obtain eternal life (Matt. 19: 16–22). The good Master (whom he thought to be man and nothing more, whereas he is good because he is God) would tell him that if he wished to enter into life, he should keep the commandments; he must separate himself from the bitterness of 'malice and wickedness' (1 Cor. 5: 8); he must not kill, commit adultery, steal, bear false witness. So the dry land may appear and be productive of honour to his mother and father and of love to his neighbour. 'I have done all these things', he replies. Then if the earth is fruitful, whence come so many thorns? Go, destroy the thorny jungle of avarice: 'Sell what you possess', and be filled with fruits by giving to the poor to win treasure in heaven. Follow the Lord 'if you wish to be perfect.' Join the society of those among whom he 'speaks wisdom (1 Cor. 2: 9), for he knows what belongs to the day and what to the night; then you too may know that. For you lights in the firmament are created. This will not happen unless your heart is in it, and that will not occur unless your treasure is there (Matt. 6: 21), as you have heard from the good Master. Sadly that earth was sterile, and thorns choked the word (Matt. 13: 7).

(25) But you, the 'elect race' (1 Pet. 2: 9), 'the weak of the world' (1 Cor. 1: 27), who have abandoned everything to follow the Lord (Matt. 19: 27), go after him and 'confound the mighty' (1 Cor. 1: 27). Go after him, 'beautiful feet' (Isa. 52: 7). Shine in the firmament so that the heavens may declare his glory (Ps. 18: 2 f.). Mark a division between the light of those who are perfect but not yet like angels, and the darkness of those who are infants but not without hope. Give light over all the earth. Let day brilliant with sunlight tell unto day the word of wisdom, and in the moonlight let night tell unto night the word of knowledge (Ps. 18: 3; 1 Cor. 12: 8). For the moon

and the stars give light to the night, and night does not obscure them. To the measure of their power, they are its source of illumination.

It is as if God says 'Let there be lights in the firmament of heaven', and 'suddenly there came a sound from heaven, as if a vehement wind blew, and tongues were seen split, like fire which sat on each of them' (Acts 2: 2–3). And the lights, made in the firmament of heaven, have the word of life (Phil. 2: 15–16). Run everywhere, holy fires, fires of beauty. Do not be under a bushel (Matt. 5: 14–15). He to whom you have adhered is exalted, and he has exalted you. Run and make it known to all nations (Ps. 78: 10).

xx (26)   Let the sea also conceive and bring forth your works. 'Let the waters produce reptiles of living souls' (Gen. 1: 20). As you separate the precious from the vile, you become the mouth of God (Jer. 15: 19) saying: 'Let the waters produce not the living soul which the earth will produce, but reptiles of living souls and flying creatures flying over the earth.' Through the works of your holy people, God, your mysteries have crept through the midst of the waters of the world's temptations to imbue the nations with your name through your baptism. And in the meanwhile great and wonderful things (Ps. 105: 21–2) have been made like vast sea monsters, and the voices of your messengers flying above the earth close to the firmament of your book; for this is the authority under which they have to fly, wherever they may go. For there are neither languages nor discourses in which their voices are not heard. Their sound is gone out into all the world, and their words to the ends of the earth because you, Lord, have blessed and multiplied these things (Ps. 18: 4 f.).

(27)   Surely I do not mislead my readers?[22] Surely I am not confusing things and failing to distinguish between the clear knowledge of these truths in the firmament of heaven and the bodily works done below in the waves of the sea and under the firmament of heaven? There are things of which the knowledge is fixed and

---

[22] The paragraph, among the most opaque in the *Confessions*, replies to criticism of his allegorical exegesis of Genesis 1. For Augustine the method is justified by its edifying results, and is in principle a working out of the correspondence or analogy between the physical and 'intelligible' worlds. The multiplicity of symbols answers to the restlessness of the human heart and mind, continually desiring change. But these symbols, in which scripture is so rich, point to eternal truths. Allegorical exegesis is the sacramental principle applied to scripture.

determined without evolving with the generations, such as the lights of wisdom and knowledge. But while the truths of these things remain the same, their embodiments in the physical realm are both many and varied. One thing grows out of another, and so, by your blessing, God, things are multiplied. You have relieved the tedium for mortal senses by the fact that what is one thing for our understanding can be symbolized and expressed in many ways by physical movements. 'The waters have produced' (Gen. 1: 20) these signs, but only through your word.[23] These physical things have been produced to meet the needs of peoples estranged from your eternal truth, but only in your gospel; for they were the product of the very waters whose morbid bitterness was the reason why, through your word, those signs emerged.[24]

(28) All things are beautiful because you made them, but you who made everything are inexpressibly more beautiful. If Adam had not fallen from you,[25] there would not have flowed from his loins that salty sea-water the human race—deeply inquisitive, like a sea in a stormy swell, restlessly unstable. Then there would have been no need for your ministers at work 'in many waters' (Cant. 8: 7) to resort to mystic actions and words in the realm of the bodily senses. That is the interpretation I now give to reptiles and birds; for human beings after instruction, initiation, and subjection to corporeal sacraments do not make further progress unless in the spiritual realm their soul comes to live on another level and, subsequent to the words of initiation, looks towards their perfection (Heb. 6: 1).

xxi (29) Moreover, it was not the deep sea but the land separated out from the bitter waters which produced, not the 'reptiles of living souls and birds', but 'a living soul' (Gen. 1: 24). This now has no need of baptism which the heathen need, in the way it did when it was covered by waters; for there is no entrance to the kingdom of heaven otherwise than by the way you appointed (John 3: 5). It does not ask for great miracles to bring faith into being. Nor does it

[23] The sentence is akin to Augustine's famous dictum about baptism: 'The word is added to the element (water) and it becomes a sacrament, itself a sort of visible word' (*Sermon on John*, 80. 3).

[24] Visible signs and sacraments are a necessity because of the fallen nature of humanity. Signs are required by sinful people, but truly spiritual Christians look higher, beyond material means.

[25] At the time of writing the *Confessions* Augustine had not yet come to hold that Adam and Eve had conjugal intercourse and offspring even before the Fall. Cf. above II. ii (3).

refuse to believe unless it sees signs and wonders (John 4: 48). For now the earth is believing and baptized, separated out from the sea-water bitter with faithlessness. Moreover 'tongues are a sign not to believers but to unbelievers' (1 Cor. 14: 2). The earth which you have established 'Above the waters' (Ps. 135: 6; 147: 15) has therefore no need for that kind of 'flying creature' which by your word 'the waters produced' (Gen. 1: 20). Send the earth your word by your messengers. We tell of their works, but it is you who work by them, so that they bring about 'a living soul'. The earth produces that, because it has this causative effect upon the soul, just as the sea was the cause of them producing 'reptiles of living souls and flying birds under the firmament of heaven' (Gen. 1: 20). These the earth does not need, though it eats the Fish raised from the deep at that table which you have 'prepared in the sight' of believers (Ps. 22: 5).[26]

He is raised from the deep to nourish the dry land. Birds also are a product of the sea, yet are multiplied on the earth. Human unbelief was the cause which made the first voices proclaim the gospel. But the faithful are encouraged and blessed frequently 'from day to day' (Ps. 60: 9). By contrast 'the living soul' takes its rise from the 'earth'. It is profitable only for already baptized believers to keep them from love of this world (Jas. 1: 27) that their soul may live to you (2 Cor. 5: 15). It was dead when it was living in pleasures (1 Tim. 5: 6), pleasures, Lord, which bring death. For you are the lifegiving pleasure of a pure heart.

(30)   May your ministers now do their work on 'earth', not as they did on the waters of unbelief when their preaching and proclamation used miracles and sacred rites and mystical prayers to attract the attention of ignorance, the mother of wonder, inducing the awe aroused by secret symbols.[27] That is the entrance to faith for the sons of Adam who forget you, who hide from your face (Gen. 3: 8) and become an 'abyss'. May they now do their work as on dry land

[26] That is in the Eucharist. The fish symbol for Christ was familiar to Ambrose and Augustine, as to all early Christians: *City of God* 18. 23.

[27] Augustine held that mathematical order and reason are primary marks of divine creation, but that it can be within the divine will for his world if special providences occur, that is miracles 'contrary not to nature but to what we know of nature'. The infant Church of the apostolic age was granted this special help, especially healings. In his own time Augustine stressed the sacraments as God's present means of special grace, and saw in conversion the greatest of miracles. Like miracles, however, the sacraments are a visible ladder to reach spiritual and invisible things.

separated from the whirlpools of the abyss. May they be an example to
the faithful by the life they live before them and by arousing them to
imitation (1 Thess. 1: 7). Thereby hearing them is no mere hearing but
leads to doing. 'Seek God and your soul shall live' (Ps. 68: 33), so
that the earth may 'produce a living soul'. 'Be not conformed to this
world' (Rom. 12: 2). Restrain yourselves from it. By avoiding this
world the soul lives; by seeking it the soul dies. Restrain yourselves
from the savage cruelty of arrogance, from the indolent pleasure of
self-indulgence, and from 'knowledge falsely so called' (1 Tim. 6: 20).
Then the wild animals are quiet and the beasts are tamed and the
serpents are rendered harmless: in allegory they signify the affections
of the soul.

The haughtiness of pride, the pleasure of lust, and the poison of
curiosity (1 John 2: 16) are the passions of a dead soul. The soul's
death does not end all movement. Its 'death' comes about as it
departs from the fount of life, so that it is absorbed by the transitory
world and conformed to it.

(31)   But the Word, O God, is fount of eternal life (John 4: 14) and
does not pass away. A departure from God is checked by your Word,
when it is said to us 'Be not conformed to this world' (Rom. 12: 2)
so that the 'earth may produce a living soul' through the fount of
life. By your word through your evangelists the soul achieves self-
control by modelling itself on the imitators of your Christ. That is
the meaning of 'after its kind'. For a man is aroused to rivalry
(Eccles. 4: 4) if a friend says 'Be as I am, since I also am as you are'
(Gal. 4: 12). So in the 'living soul' there will be beasts that have
become good by the gentleness of their behaviour. You have given
command, saying 'In gentleness do your works and you will be
loved by everyone' (Ecclus. 3: 19). There will be good 'cattle',
experiencing neither excess if they eat nor want if they do not eat.
There will be 'serpents' that are good, not harmful and dangerous but
astute in their caution (Matt. 10: 16) and exploring temporal nature
only to the extent sufficient to contemplate eternity 'understood
through the things which are made' (Rom. 1: 20). For these animals
serve reason when they are restrained from their deathly ways.
Then they live and are good.

xxii (32)   See, Lord our God, our Creator: when our affections
were restrained from loving the world by which we were dying

through living an evil life, then there began to come into being a 'living soul'. There was fulfilled the word which you spoke through your apostle: 'Be not conformed to this world'. Then followed that which you immediately went on to say 'But be renewed in the newness of your mind' (Rom. 12: 2). That is not a making 'according to kind', as if renewal were achieved by imitating a neighbour's example or by living under the authority of a human superior. For you did not say 'Let man be made according to his kind', but 'Let us make man according to our image and likeness' (Gen. 1: 26). So we may prove what your 'will is' (Rom. 12: 2).

With this intention your minister, who generates sons by the gospel (1 Cor. 4: 15) and does not wish to have permanently immature believers fed on milk (1 Cor. 3: 1–2) and cherished as if by a nurse (1 Thess. 2: 7), says 'Be renewed in the newness of your mind to prove what is God's will, which is a thing good and well-pleasing and perfect'. That is why you do not say 'Let man be made' but 'Let us make', and you do not say 'according to his kind' but 'after our image and likeness'. The person whose renewal is in the mind and who contemplates and understands your truth, needs no human to 'prove' it, imitating the example of humankind but, as you show, he 'proves what your will is, which is a thing good and well-pleasing and perfect'. Because such a person now has the capacity, you teach him to see the Trinity of the Unity and the Unity of the Trinity. Hence the plural is used 'Let us make man,' and then the singular follows 'and God made man'. The plural occurs for the first phrase 'in our image', but the singular is used for 'in the image of God'. So man 'is renewed in the knowledge of God after the image of him who created him' (Col. 3: 10). Being made spiritual, 'he judges all things' (that is, of course, things which need to be judged), 'but he himself is judged by no one' (1 Cor. 2: 15).

xxiii (33)   The saying 'he judges all things' is the meaning of the text that man has power over the fish of the sea and the birds of heaven and all cattle and wild beasts over all the earth, and all creeping things which creep upon the earth (Gen. 1: 26). He judges by an act of intelligence, by which he perceives 'what things are of the Spirit of God' (1 Cor. 2: 14; 3: 10). Contrariwise, 'a man in a position of honour has lacked understanding: he is compared to the mindless beasts, and has become like them' (Ps. 48: 13).

Therefore in your Church, our God, according to your grace which you have given to it, since we are your 'workmanship made in good works' (Eph. 2: 10), spiritual judgement is exercised not only by those who spiritually preside, but also by those subject to their presiding authority.[28] For 'you made man male and female' in your spiritual grace to be equal, so that physical gender makes no distinction of male and female, just as there is 'neither Jew nor Greek, neither slave nor free person' (Gal. 3: 28). So spiritual persons, whether they preside or are subject to authority, exercise spiritual judgement (1 Cor. 2: 15). They do not judge those spiritual intelligences which are 'lights in the firmament'; it would be inappropriate to judge such sublime authority. Nor do they sit in judgement on your book, even if there is obscurity there. We submit our intellect to it, and hold it for certain that even language closed to our comprehension is right and true. Even a person who is spiritual and is 'renewed in the knowledge of God according to the image of him who created him' (Col. 3: 10) has to be 'a doer of the law' (Jas. 4: 11), not its critic. Nor does he judge which persons are spiritual and which carnal. They are known to your eyes, our God. To us no works have as yet appeared so that we can know them by their fruits. Yet you, Lord, already know them and have made a division. You called them in secret before the firmament was made. The spiritual person does not judge the storm-tossed peoples of this world. How can he 'judge of those outside' (1 Cor. 5: 12) when he does not know who will come out of the world into the sweetness of your grace, and who will remain in the permanent bitterness of godlessness?[29]

(34) That is why man, though made by you in your image, has not received authority over the lights of heaven nor over the heaven beyond our sight nor over day and night, which you called into being before establishing the heaven, nor over the gathering of the waters which is the sea. But he received power over the fish of the

---

[28] Augustine holds that the perception of God's will for his Church does not belong only to the ordained, but is shared by all spiritual members, including of course women (recalling his own debt to Monica).

[29] Though the full development of Augustine's doctrine of predestination comes in the last decade of his life under the stress of the Pelagian controversy, the essentials were already established at the time of his writing the *Confessions*, 25 years earlier, with the crucial exception that he has not yet decided on his final distinction between divine foreknowledge, which is not causative, and predestination, which is.

sea and the birds of heaven and all cattle and all the earth and all creeping things which creep on the earth. He judges and approves what is right and disapproves what is wrong, whether in the solemn rite of the sacraments at the initiation of those whom your mercy searches out 'in many waters', or in that rite celebrated when there is offered the Fish, which was raised from the deep to be the food of the devout 'earth', or when considering the verbal signs and expressions which are subject to the authority of your book,[30] like birds flying beneath the firmament. He must assess interpretations, expositions, discourses, controversies, the forms of blessing and prayer to you. These signs come from the mouth and sound forth so that the people may respond Amen. The reason why all these utterances have to be physically spoken is the abyss of the world and the blindness of the flesh which cannot discern thoughts, so that it is necessary to make audible sounds. So, although birds are multiplied on the earth, they derive their origin from water. The spiritual person also judges by approving what is right and disapproving what he finds wrong in the works and behaviour of the faithful in their charitable giving—like the fruitful earth. He judges the 'living soul' in its affections made gentle by chastity, by fasting, by devout reflection on things perceived by the bodily senses. And lastly he is said to exercise judgement on questions where he possesses a power of correction.[31]

xxiv (35)   But what is this next text about, and what kind of a mystery is it? Lord you bless human beings so that they may increase and multiply and fill the earth. By this surely you are suggesting that we should perceive some further meaning here. Why did you not likewise bless the light which you called day, or the firmament of heaven or the heavenly lights or the stars or land or sea? I might say that you, our God, who created us in your image—I might say you intended to bestow this gift of blessing particularly on humanity, were it not that you have also in this way blessed fishes and whales to grow and multiply and fill the waters of the sea, and birds to multiply over the earth. I might further say that this blessing, had I found it bestowed on trees and plants and land

---

[30] i.e. baptism, eucharist (as in XIII. xxi (29)), and preaching.

[31] In counselling and absolution. 'The living soul' is the spiritually active members of the Church, the body in which the Holy Spirit is the soul. XIII. xxxiv (49), below, shows that they are characterized by strong ascetic discipline.

animals, belongs to those kinds which are propagated by reproduction; but for plants and trees and beasts and serpents, there is no mention of 'Increase and multiply', even though all these, like fish and birds and humankind, are increased and preserve their species by generation.

(36) What then shall I say, truth my light? That there is no special significance in this, and the text is empty of meaning? No indeed, Father of piety, be it far from a servant of your word to say this. And if I fail to understand what you intend by this utterance, let better interpreters, that is more intelligent than I, offer a better exegesis, according as you have given to each a gift of understanding. But let my confession also be pleasing before your eyes. I confess myself to believe, Lord, that you have not so spoken without a special intention, and I will not suppress what this passage happens to suggest to me. For it is true, and I do not see what objection there is to my thus interpreting the figurative words of your book. I know that at the bodily level one can give a plurality of expressions to something which in the mind is understood as a single thing, and that the mind can give a multiplicity of meanings to something which, at the physical level, is a single thing. How simple is the love of God and one's neighbour! At the bodily level it is expressed by numerous sacraments and in innumerable languages and in innumerable phrases of any particular language. An instance is that the offspring of the waters 'increase and multiply'. Again, consider what scripture offers and what its language expresses in a single phrase: 'In the beginning God made heaven and earth' (Gen. 1: 1). Cannot this bear many interpretations, not including misleading errors, but true interpretations of different kinds? In the same way the offspring of human beings 'increase and multiply'.

(37) If, therefore, we think of the natures of things not allegorically but literally, the word 'Increase and multiply' applies to all creatures generated by seeds. But if we treat the text as figurative (which I prefer to think scripture intended since it cannot be pointless that it confines this blessing to aquatic creatures and human beings), then we find multitudes in the spiritual and physical creations (to which 'heaven and earth' refer); in both just and unjust souls (called 'light and darkness'); in the holy authors through whom the law is ministered (called 'the firmament' established solidly between water and water);

in the association of people filled with bitterness ('the sea'); in the
zeal of devoted souls ('the dry land'); in works of mercy during 'this
present life' (1 Tim. 4: 8) ('the herbs bearing seed and the trees
bearing fruit'); in spiritual gifts which manifest themselves for
edification (the 'heavenly lights'); in affections disciplined through
self-control ('the living soul').

In all these things we find multitudes and abundances and
increases. But only in signs given corporeal expression and in
intellectual concepts do we find an increasing and a multiplying
which illustrate how one thing can be expressed in several ways and
how one formulation can bear many meanings. Signs given corporeal
expression are the creatures generated from the waters, necessary
because of our deep involvement in the flesh. But because of the
fertility of reason, I interpret the generation of humanity to mean
concepts in the intelligible realm. That is why we believe that you,
Lord addressed both categories in the words 'Increase and multiply'.
By this blessing I understand you to grant us the capacity and ability
to articulate in many ways what we hold to be a single concept, and
to give a plurality of meanings to a single obscure expression in a
text we have read. It is said 'the waters of the sea are filled', because
their movement means the variety of significations. Likewise the
earth is filled with human offspring: its dryness shows itself in
human energy and the mastery of it by reason.

xxv (38)   Lord, my God, I also want to declare what the following
text of your scripture suggests to me, and I will say it without fear.
With you inspiring me I shall be affirming true things, which by
your will I draw out of those words. For I do not believe I give a true
exposition if anyone other than you is inspiring me. You are the
truth but every man is a liar (Ps. 115: 11; Rom. 3: 4). That is why
'he who speaks a lie speaks from himself' (John 8: 44). Therefore I
depend on you to enable me to speak the truth. See, you have given
us for food 'every sown plant producing seed which is on the
surface of the earth, and every tree which has in itself the fruit of
sown seed' (Gen. 1: 29). You gave it not to us alone, but also to all
the birds of heaven and beasts of the earth and serpents. But you
did not give them to fish and whales. We were saying that these
fruits of the earth are to be allegorically interpreted as meaning
works of mercy, which are offered for the necessities of life from

the fruit-bearing earth. Such an earth was the devoted Onesiphorus
(2 Tim. 1: 16), to whose house 'you granted mercy because he often
refreshed' your Paul and 'was not ashamed of his chain'. This was
also done by the brethren, and they produced similar fruit when
'they supplied from Macedonia what he had lacked' (2 Cor. 11: 9).
But how Paul grieved over some trees which did not render the fruit
they owed him! He says 'At my first defence no one stood by me, but
all forsook me; may it not be imputed to their charge' (2 Tim. 4: 16).
These fruits are owed to those who minister spiritual teaching
through their interpretations of the divine mysteries, and the debt is
owed to them as men. But the debt is also owed to them as 'the
living soul'. For they offer themselves as a model for imitation in
ascetic restraint of all kinds. Moreover, it is owed to them as 'flying
birds' because of the blessings pronounced upon them which are
multiplied upon the earth; for 'their sound is gone out into every
land' (Ps. 18: 5).

xxvi (39)   Those who enjoy these foods are fed by them; but those
'whose god is their belly' (Phil. 3: 19) derive no pleasure from them.
But in those who provide the food, the fruit lies not in what they give
but the spirit with which they give it. So I readily see why Paul
rejoiced; he served God, not his belly, and I heartily join in his joy. He
received from the Philippians what they had sent by Epaphroditus.
Yet I see the ground for his joy: the source of his joy was the source
of his nourishment because he declares its true origin in the words
'I rejoiced greatly in the Lord that at last for a time you have revived
your sympathy for my welfare, for which you had been concerned,
but you had become weary' (Phil. 4: 10). The Philippians had
suffered a long period of weariness. They had as it were dried up in
producing the fruit of good work. He rejoiced for them that they
had revived, not for himself because they came to the help of his
wants. So he goes on 'I do not say that anything is lacking. I have
learnt in whatever state I am to be content. I know both how to
possess little, and I know also how to have abundance. In all things
and in every way I am instructed how to be thirsty and hungry and
to abound and to suffer penury. I can do all things in him who
strengthens me' (Phil. 4. 11–13).

(40)   What then is the reason for your rejoicing, great Paul? Why
your joy? Where do you find your nourishment? You are a man

'renewed in the knowledge of God after the image of him who
created you' (Col. 3: 10), a 'living soul' of great continence, a
tongue which flies like the birds as it proclaims mysteries. It is
indeed to such living souls that this food is due. What then is it
which gives you nourishment? Joy. Let me hear what follows:
'Nevertheless', he says, 'you did well in taking a share in my
tribulations' (Phil. 4: 14). The ground for his joy and for his
nourishment is that the Philippians had acted well, not that his
trouble was relieved. He says to you 'In tribulation you gave me a
large room' (Ps. 7: 21), for in you who strengthen him he 'knew
how to abound and how to suffer penury'. He says: 'You Philippians
know how at the first preaching of the gospel when I came from
Macedonia, no Church except you shared with me in the matter of
giving and receiving, for not once but twice you sent support for my
needs to Thessalonica' (Phil. 4. 14–16). He now rejoices at their
return to these good works and is glad at their revival, like a field
that is recovering its fertility.

(41) It was not Paul's own necessities which led him to say: 'You
sent support for my needs' (Phil. 4: 17). That was surely not his
reason for rejoicing. We can be sure of this, because he goes on to
say: 'Not that I seek a gift but I look for fruit'. From you, my God, I
have learnt to distinguish between gift and fruit. A gift is the object
given by the person who is sharing in these necessaries such as
money, food, drink, clothing, a roof, assistance generally. Fruit,
however, is the good and right will of the giver.[32] The good Master
has said not only 'he who receives a prophet' but also adds 'in the
name of a prophet'. He does not speak only of him who 'receives a
righteous person', but adds 'in the name of a righteous person'.
The former receives a prophet's reward, the latter a righteous
person's reward. Again, he does not merely say 'He who gives a cup
of cold water to drink to one of my least', but also adds 'only in the
name of a disciple', and then continues 'Amen, I say to you, he will
not lose his reward'. (Matt. 10: 41–2). So the gift is to receive a
prophet, to receive a righteous person, to offer a cup of cold water
to a disciple. But the fruit is the intention to do this 'in the name of
a prophet, in the name of a righteous person, in the name of a

---

[32] Augustine's ethic is marked by strong emphasis on intention as determining the
moral value of an act. Cf. Plotinus 1. 5. 9.

disciple'. It was fruit when Elijah was fed by a widow because she knew she was feeding a man of God, and fed him with that intention. But when he was fed by a raven that was only a gift. For the inward Elijah was not being fed but the outward man who, though a man of God, could starve for lack of food (1 Kgs. 17: 4–18).

xxvii (42)   On this ground Lord, I will make an affirmation which is true before you. We believe that 'fish and whales' symbolize the sacraments of initiation and miraculous wonders necessary to initiate and convert 'uninstructed and unbelieving people' (1 Cor. 14: 23). When such people receive your children to refresh them physically or to help them in some need of this present life, they do not know why they should do this, or what object they should have in mind. They are not really feeding your children, nor are your people actually being fed by them, because they are not doing it with a holy and correct intention; nor do your children find joy in their gifts where they do not yet see any fruit. Hence the mind is fed by the source of joy. That is why 'fish and whales' do not feed on food which the earth produces only after it becomes separate and distinct from the bitter waves of the sea.

xxviii (43)   And you, God, 'saw all that you had made, and it was very good' (Gen. 1: 31). To us also who see them, they are all very good indeed. In each category of your works, when you had said they should be made and they were made, you saw that every particular instance is good. Seven times I have counted scripture saying you saw that what you made is good. But on the eighth occasion when you saw all that you had made, it says they were not merely good but 'very good'—as if taking everything at once into account. For individual items were only 'good', but everything taken together was both 'good' and 'very good'. This truth is also declared by the beauty of bodies. A body composed of its constituent parts, all of which are beautiful, is far more beautiful as a whole than those parts taken separately; the whole is made of their well-ordered harmony, though individually the constituent parts are also beautiful.[33]

xxix (44)   I carefully set out to discover whether it is seven times or eight times that you saw your works were good and that they pleased you. In your seeing I found no occasions to help me

[33] Close parallel in Plotinus 1. 6. 1. 25 ff.

understand the meaning of the number of times that you saw what you had made. I said: Lord, surely your scripture is true, for you, being truthful and Truth itself, have produced it. Why then do you tell me that in your seeing there is no element of time, yet your scripture tells me that on each successive day you saw what you had made that it was good? I counted them, and ascertained how many times you did this. To this you replied to me, since you are my God and speak with a loud voice in the inner ear to your servant, and broke through my deafness with the cry: 'O man, what my scripture says, I say. Yet scripture speaks in time-conditioned language, and time does not touch my Word, existing with me in an equal eternity. So I see those things which through my Spirit you see, just as I also say the things which through my Spirit you say. Accordingly, while your vision of them is temporally determined, my seeing is not temporal, just as you speak of these things in temporal terms but I do not speak in the successiveness of time.'

xxx (45)   I listened, Lord, my God; I sucked a drop of sweetness from your truth, and I understood. There are people [Manichees] who are displeased at your works. They say you made many of them, such as the fabric of the heavens and the constellations of the stars, under the compulsion of necessity. They say you did not produce the creation from your own matter, but that its elements were already created elsewhere by another power, and that you gathered them together and assembled and organized them when, after defeating your enemies, you built the ramparts of the world so that they would be held in check by that construction and unable to fight against you again. Other things they deny you to have made or even to have assembled, such as all bodies and every tiny insect and all plants rooted in the earth. They claim that in the lower places of the world those things are generated and formed by a hostile mind and an alien nature, not created by you but opposed to you. This is the utterance of madmen. They do not see your works with the help of your Spirit and do not recognize you in them.

xxxi (46)   When people see these things with the help of your Spirit, it is you who are seeing in them. When, therefore, they see that things are good, you are seeing that they are good. Whatever pleases them for your sake is pleasing you in them. The things which by the help of your Spirit delight us are delighting you in us.

'For what man knows the being of man except the spirit of man which is in him? So also no one knows the things of God except the Spirit of God. But we (he says) have not received the spirit of this world, but the Spirit which is of God, so that we may know the gifts given us by God' (1 Cor. 2: 11–12). I am moved to declare: certainly no one knows the things of God except the Spirit of God. Then how do we ourselves know the gifts which God has given? The answer comes to me that the statement 'No one knows except the Spirit of God' also applies to the things we know by the help of his Spirit. Just as 'it is not you that speak' (Matt. 10: 20) is rightly said to those who are speaking by the Spirit of God, so also the words 'it is not you that know' may rightly be said to those whose knowing is by the Spirit of God. Therefore it is no less correct that 'it is not you that see' is spoken to those who see by the Spirit of God. Whatever, therefore, they see to be good by the Spirit of God, it is not they but God who is seeing that it is good.

It is one thing to think that what is good is evil, like those Manichees I mentioned above. It is another thing to say that what man sees to be good is good, just as your creation pleases many because it is good; nevertheless they are displeased with you in it. These latter people wish to find their enjoyment in the creation rather than in you.

It is a yet further matter to say that when a man sees something which is good, God in him sees that it is good. That is, God is loved in that which he has made, and he is not loved except through the Spirit which he has given. For 'the love of God is diffused in our hearts by the Holy Spirit which is given to us' (Rom. 5: 5). By the Spirit we see that everything which in some degree has existence is good;[34] for it derives from him who does not exist merely in some degree since he is Existence.

xxxii (47) Thanks be to you, Lord! We see heaven and earth, that is either the higher and lower material part or the spiritual and physical creation; and for the adornment of these parts, in which consists the entire mass of the world or the entire created order absolutely, we see light made and divided from the darkness. We see the firmament of heaven, either placed between the higher

[34] A Platonic axiom is here given the authority of the Holy Spirit. It is for Augustine a self-evident deduction from the doctrine of divine Creation. Cf. above, VII. xii. (18).

spiritual waters and the lower physical waters (the earliest physical entity in the world) or the space occupied by air, which is also called the sky.[35] Through this the birds of heaven wander between those waters, which are borne over it as vapour and on clear nights drop as dew, and the heavy waters flowing on earth. We see the beauty of the waters gathered in the expanses of the sea, and the dry land, whether bare of vegetation, or given form so as to be 'visible and ordered', the mother of plants and trees. We see the lights shining from above, the sun sufficing for the day, the moon and stars to cheer the night, and all of these to provide an indication and sign of passing time. We see wet nature on all sides, a rich source of food for fish and sea monsters and birds. For the flight of birds is supported by the density of the air, which is increased by the evaporation of water. We see the face of the earth adorned with earthly creatures and humanity, in your image and likeness, put in authority over all irrational animals by your image and likeness, that is by the power of reason and intelligence. And as in his soul there is one element which deliberates and aspires to domination, and another element which is submissive and obedient, so in the bodily realm woman is made for man. In mental power she has an equal capacity of rational intelligence, but by the sex of her body she is submissive to the masculine sex. This is analogous to the way in which the impulse for action is subordinate to the rational mind's prudent concern that the act is right. So we see that each particular point and the whole taken all together are very good.

xxxiii (48)   Your works praise you that we may love you, and we love you that your works may praise you. They have a beginning and an end in time, a rise and a fall, a start and a finish, beauty and the loss of it. They have in succession a morning and an evening, in part hidden, in part evident. They are made out of nothing by you, not from you, not from some matter not of your making or previously existing, but from matter created by you together with its form— that is simultaneously. For you gave form to its formlessness with no interval of time between. The matter of heaven and earth is one thing, the beauty of heaven and earth is another. You made the matter from absolutely nothing, but the beauty of the world from

---

[35] Augustine later in his *Revisions* censured this sentence as 'written without sufficient thought' (*Retr.* 2. 6. 2).

formless matter—and both simultaneously so that the form followed the matter without any pause or delay.[36]

xxxiv (49)   We have also considered the reasons for the symbolism in the fact that you willed created things to be made in a particular order or to be recorded in a particular order. And because particular things are good and all of them together very good, we have seen in your Word, in your unique Son, 'heaven and earth', the head and body of the Church (Col. 1: 18),[37] in a predestination which is before all time and has no morning and evening. But then you began to carry out your predestined plan in time so as to reveal hidden secrets and to bring order to our disordered chaos. For our sins were over us, and we had abandoned you to sink into a dark depth. Your good Spirit was 'borne over' it to help us 'in due season' (Ps. 142: 10). You justified the ungodly (Rom. 4: 5), you separated them from the wicked, and you established the authority of your book between those in higher authority who were submissive to you and those below who were subject to it. You gathered a society of unbelievers to share a single common aspiration, so that the zeal of the faithful should 'appear' and so bring forth for you works of mercy, distributing to the poor their earthly possessions so as to acquire celestial reward.

Hence you kindled lights in the firmament, your saints 'having the word of life' (Phil. 2: 16), shining with a sublime authority made manifest by spiritual gifts. And then to instruct the unbelieving peoples, you produced from physical matter sacraments and visible miracles and the sounds of the words of your book, symbolized by the 'firmament'. Believers also are blessed by them. Then you formed 'the living soul' of the faithful with their affections disciplined by a strong continence. Then you renewed the mind (Rom. 12: 2) after your image and likeness (Col. 3: 10) to be subject to you alone and in need of no human authority as a model to imitate. You made its rational action subject to the superiority of the intellect, as if symbolized by a woman's submissive role with her husband. To all the ministerial officers necessary to bring the faithful to perfection in this

[36] Plotinus (4. 3. 9. 16) holds that there was never a time when matter was not given form and order.

[37] The shortcomings of the empirical life of the churches are frequently deplored by Augustine. But the Church remained for him, on the ground of the Pauline doctrine of the body and head, the indispensable instrument of salvation in which Christ dwells by his Spirit. 'The whole Christ' is the Lord, head and members together.

life, you willed that the same faithful should provide for their temporal needs good works which could be fruitful for them hereafter. All these things we see, and they are very good, because you see them in us, having given us the Spirit by which we see them and love you in them.

xxxv (50)   'Lord God, grant us peace; for you have given us all things' (Isa. 26: 12), the peace of quietness, the peace of the sabbath, a peace with no evening (2 Thess. 3: 16). This entire most beautiful order of very good things will complete its course and then pass away; for in them by creation there is both morning and evening.

xxxvi (51)   The seventh day has no evening and has no ending. You sanctified it to abide everlastingly. After your 'very good' works, which you made while remaining yourself in repose, you 'rested the seventh day' (Gen. 2: 2–3). This utterance in your book foretells for us that after our works which, because they are your gift to us, are very good, we also may rest in you for the sabbath of eternal life.

xxxvii (52)   There also you will rest in us, just as now you work in us. Your rest will be through us, just as now your works are done through us. But you, Lord are always working and always at rest. Your seeing is not in time, your movement is not in time, and your rest is not in time. Yet your acting causes us to see things in time, time itself, and the repose which is outside time.

xxxviii (53)   As for ourselves, we see the things you have made because they are. But they are because you see them.[38] We see outwardly that they are, and inwardly that they are good. But you saw them made when you saw that it was right to make them. At one time we were moved to do what is good, after our heart conceived through your Spirit. But at an earlier time we were moved to do wrong and to forsake you. But you God, one and good, have never ceased to do good. Of your gift we have some good works, though not everlasting. After them we hope to rest in your great sanctification. But you, the Good, in need of no other good, are ever at rest since you yourself are your own rest.

What man can enable the human mind to understand this?

---

[38] This theme is developed in *City of God* 11. 10.

Which angel can interpret it to an angel? What angel can help a human being to grasp it? Only you can be asked, only you can be begged, only on your door can we knock (Matt. 7: 7–8). Yes indeed, that is how it is received, how it is found, how the door is opened.[39]

[39] The allusion to Matt: 7–8 picks up the theme of I. i (1) and XII. i (1).

Index

Abraham's bosom 158
academic sceptics xix, 84, 88–9, 104
actors 66, 122
Adam 11, 147, 149, 177, 197, 289 f.;
    apple 49
Adeodatus xvi, xviii, 163, 174
Aeneas 15 f.
Alexander of Lycopolis xix
almsgiving 303
Alypius of Thagaste xii, 99, 141 f., 146,
    160; asceticism 163; with Augustine at
    conversion 152–3; aversion to sex xvii,
    106 f.; baptized 163; character 98 ff.;
    Christology 129; Manichee 100
Ambrose xxiv, 3, 62–3, 87, 91–4, 104,
    129 n.,133 n., 134, 163, 176, 230 n.,
    241
Ammianus Marcellinus 28 n., 140 n.
anamnesis 189, 197
Anaximenes 183
angels 115, 218, 305
anger 31
animals: memory 194; sacrifice 43, 53
Antony, hermit xxv, 143, 153
Apollinarianism 129
arbitrations 92, 102
architect, Carthage 102; drawings 190
Arians 165
Aristotle 39, 69, 188, 211, 230–1
army 198
ascetic community 108 f.; eremitic life
    108; renunciation of kin 176 see also
    Antony
astrology 54 f., 117 f., 212
Athanasius 143, 208, 220
Augustine's consort xiii, xvi, 53, 109;
    son 163, 174
Aurelius Victor xv
Ausonius xii
authority 46, 95 f., 105
awe 227

Baptism 13, 57, 83, 107, 136 f., 177,
    180; sign of cross 135; soldier of
    Christ 140
bare feet 163
Basil 171, 237
bathing 175

beauty 10, 29–30, 61, 183–4, 201, 210,
    224, 246, 262, 274; On Beauty and the
    Fitting 64 ff.
beggar at Milan 97 f.
being and value 124, 126, 301
Bible xxii, xxv f., 40, 48, 86, 88, 94, 96,
    119, 129–31, 162, 222, 236, 254 ff.,
    265 f.; allegory 288; critics of
    Augustine's exegesis 256–65;
    different interpretations valid if true
    270–2; intention of writers 263;
    interpolated? 86
bird flight 302
bishops, arbitrators 92

Carthage 26, 35, 60, 80 f., 104, 194, 197
Cassiciacum 158–60
catechumen 13, 89, 104
catharsis 36 f.
Catiline 29 f.
celibacy 25, 92, 134, 203
certainty 94 f., 104, 121, 133, 145, 183,
    198
Christ: atonement 82, 178, 219; Cupid
    156, 183; fish 290, 294; head and body
    of the Church 303; holy of holy ones
    236; human mind and soul 129;
    humanity 3; incarnation 121 f.;
    mediator 128, 219, 223, 236; not
    named by Cicero 40, 89; between One
    and Many 244; priest and victim 220;
    virgin birth 64, 86, 128; Word of God
    and Beginning 227
Church: all equal in 139; authority 119;
    brothers of Christ 176; mother 13,
    178; nest 71, 267; penitential
    discipline 294; services 37, 83, 221;
    spiritual and carnal members 280; see
    also Baptism; Communion of Saints;
    Eucharist; Sacraments
Cicero xiii f., 18, 38–9, 44, 53, 59, 78,
    109; 'a certain Cicero' 38
circus 13, 98 f., 212; see also shows,
    public
colours 209
communion of saints 176, 181–2
concubinage xvi
confession, double meaning xi

American Literature

British and Irish Literature

Children's Literature

Classics and Ancient Literature

Colonial Literature

Eastern Literature

European Literature

Gothic Literature

History

Medieval Literature

Oxford English Drama

Poetry

Philosophy

Politics

Religion

The Oxford Shakespeare

A complete list of Oxford World's Classics, including Authors in Context, Oxford English Drama, and the Oxford Shakespeare, is available in the UK from the Marketing Services Department, Oxford University Press, Great Clarendon Street, Oxford OX2 6DP, or visit the website at www.oup.com/uk/worldsclassics.

In the USA, visit www.oup.com/us/owc for a complete title list.

Oxford World's Classics are available from all good bookshops. In case of difficulty, customers in the UK should contact Oxford University Press Bookshop, 116 High Street, Oxford OX1 4BR.